Midrash and Literature

Midrash and Literature

Edited by
Geoffrey H. Hartman and Sanford Budick

Yale University Press
New Haven and London

Designed by James J. Johnson
and set in Joanna Roman type by
Brevis Press, Bethany, Connecticut
Printed in the United States of America by
Vail-Ballou Press, Binghamton, New York

Library of Congress Cataloging-in-Publication Data
Main entry under title:

Midrash and literature.

  Bibliography: p.
  Includes index.
  1. Midrash—History and criticism—Addresses, essays, lectures.   I. Hartman, Geoffrey H.
II. Budick, Sanford, 1942–
BM514.M48   1986   296.1′406   85–17898
ISBNs 0–300–03453–9 (cloth)
      0–300–04198–5 (pbk.)

The paper in this book meets the guidelines for permanence and durability of the Committee on Production Guidelines for Book Longevity of the Council on Library Resources.

10 9 8 7 6 5 4 3 2

Contents

CONTEMPORARY MIDRASH

REFERENCE MATTER

Acknowledgments

This volume presents the fruits of a collective research project carried out by The Center for Literary Studies of The Hebrew University of Jerusalem from 1983 to 1985. During that time the editors and authors accumulated innumerable debts of gratitude to Dan Patinkin, President of The Hebrew University, Amnon Pazi, Rector, and Avraham Harman, Chancellor, as well as to Daniel Krauskopf of the United States-Israel Educational Foundation, Robert Petersen of the American Embassy in Tel Aviv, Kevin Allen of the British Council, and Jacques Teynier of the French Embassy, Tel Aviv. For unflagging interest, support and enthusiasm we wish to thank our many co-workers on Mt. Scopus, particularly Lawrence L. Besserman, Morton W. Bloomfield, Louisa Cuomo, H. M. Daleski, Kenneth Dauber, Jonas Fraenkel, Moshe Greenberg, Baruch Hochman, Edward Levenston, Stéphane Moses, Dov Noy, Dmitri Segal, Avigdor Shinan, and Shmaryahu Talmon.

Marc Bregman and David Stern deserve special thanks for continuous aid and counsel, as does Moshe David Herr for putting at our disposal, without stint, his astounding knowledge of rabbinic texts and sources. Beyond all calls of duty, Emily Budick contributed greatly with her eagle eye for knots, large and small, in the string of argument and with her uncanny ability to straighten and smooth. Ellen Graham, Editor of Yale University Press, guided our work at virtually every stage. Our manuscript editor, Elizabeth Jones, labored tirelessly over even the smallest details. Not least, we have been blessed with the dedicated help of the Center's excellent research assistants, Deborah Lifschitz, Lisa New, and especially Eva Vilarrubí.

Finally, we wish to record our deep appreciation to Mr. Max Zimmer of Los Angeles, California. His timely gift to The Center for Literary Studies greatly facilitated the completion and publication of this book.

Introduction

In rabbinic literature *midrash* designates both a genre of biblical exegesis and the compilations in which such exegesis, much of it initially delivered and later transmitted orally, was eventually preserved. The genre of midrash flourished most dramatically in the land of Israel during the periods of the Tannaitic and Amoraic Sages (70 C.E. to 220 and 220 to 400 C.E., respectively). Important collections of midrashim emerged continually, in diverse settings, from the fifth to the sixteenth centuries, though our knowledge of how or why midrashim were actually generated is extremely sparse.*

For contemporary literary studies, scrutiny of the nature and implications of midrash has become not only a matter of great interest but a pressing need. How this need developed is not an explicit concern of any of the following essays. Nonetheless it hovers in the background of almost all of them and demands, at the outset, a few words of historical observation.

From the time of Heine and Arnold, at least (Milton and others felt it much earlier), "Hebraism" has frequently been identified as one of the two counter-critiques by which western civilization has been kept vigorous and creative. Precisely what Hebraism is, however, has rarely been recognized. Arnold himself, for example, though sensitive to the special role of an Hebraic factor in western culture and keenly aware of powerful "alternations" between what he named Hebraism's "strictness of conscience" and Hellenism's "spontaneity of consciousness," did not or could not see that Hebraism had already achieved, through the presiding genius of midrash, an extensive and deep spon-

*Editors' note: See the second section of this volume for penetrating analyses of the available information and of the midrashic genre itself. See also the Glossary and Selected Bibliography.

taneity, as well as an extraordinary web of consciousness, not easily matched in the western tradition. Nor did he envisage the possibility of a partnership of conscience and consciousness—in one fully functional criticism—which did not forthwith collapse dialectically into a univocal resolution.

Insights about midrash on this order had, in fact, already begun to emerge, formally and critically, thirty-five years before Arnold wrote "Culture and Anarchy," in the writings of Heine's friend Leopold Zunz. Zunz had appealed to educated Europeans to allow the vitality of midrash its rightful place in modern culture. But despite the fact that midrash was not accorded this recognition as a literary-critical Weltanschauung (Zunz's appeal, ominously enough, was suppressed by the local authorities), the great poets who wrote out of the western tradition somehow evidenced its existence in our collective literary imagination. It was primarily the authorized interpreters—in church and university—who remained oblivious to its influence, ignoring midrash as a subject and misconceiving or misappropriating the Hebraic elements in our culture.

Little by little, however, institutional resistance to the implications of midrash has worn away. For some time now, it has been understood that many profoundly ingrained habits of western reading ("typology" in its many varieties and quite possibly expectations of "closure" itself) are historical derivatives of midrash—sometimes by way of emulation, sometimes as aggressive inversions. Even more recently, however, midrash has begun to emerge as the express object of academic discourse, and as it has come into its own, it has entered into competition among the many literary-critical approaches now vying for institutional approval.

What preoccupies the scholar, critic, theorist, and poet in this volume (these identities sometimes overlap) is, then, both the historical, cultural, Judaic phenomenon of midrash itself, and the resemblances between midrash and highly similar critical phenomena which, for whatever reasons, have acquired central importance in contemporary literature, criticism, and theory. Of course, resemblance is not identity. But the mapping of resemblance is often the closest we can get to knowing identity of any sort. And, from another point of view, the study of resemblance is perhaps the best chance we ever have for standing outside our present interpretive condition and locating or fixing it, even momentarily, with a leverage virtually external. The track

of the interpretive complex which for us represents, or is, reality—
whether it be midrash or literature or something else—may ultimately
be shifted in the process. But that is the uncertainty and the benefit
entailed by any significant interpretation.

The main features of resemblance between our two subjects can
be sketched here briefly and provisionally. As in midrash itself, we
need hardly specify which is the primary, which the secondary object
of our discussions. What we are concerned with throughout this volume is a variety of "open" modes of interpretation, a life in literature
or in scripture that is experienced in the shuttle space between the
interpreter and the text. Abiding in the same intermediary space is a
whole universe of allusive textuality (the history of writing itself, some
say) which lately goes by the name *intertextuality*. In this spacious scene
of writing the interpreter's associative knowledge is invested with remarkably broad powers, including even the hermeneutical privilege of
allowing questions to stand as parts of answers.

Both in midrashic and in post-formalist times, the drift of these
attitudes could have been, but did not turn out to be, linguistic and
literary nihilism. In fact these very attitudes have produced an immense
quantity and force of interpretive writing. By confronting the undecid-
ability of textual meaning, this species of interpretation does not par-
alyze itself. Instead its own activity is absorbed into the activity of the
text, producing a continuum of intertextual supplements, often in a
spirit of high-serious play. And even when we encounter play of a
seemingly outrageous kind we cannot dismiss it as mere self-indul-
gence, because the phenomena of intertextuality and supplementarity
systematically achieve, to a remarkable degree, the very effacement of
self. Here there are essentially no proprietary rights, nor, properly
speaking, are there any individuals to be proprietors. So it is, we might
say, with the midrashic exegeses of Rabbi Akiva, Reb Derrida, Reb
Kermode; as with Reb Milton, Reb Agnon, Reb Borges: pseudepigrapha
all.

There are, of course, ways in which midrash cannot possibly coincide with any secular poetics. Given the theological principles of divine
unicity and the inviolability of the sacred text there are—as Harold
Fisch, Judah Goldin, and James Kugel beautifully explain—significant
constraints and restraints upon the freedom of midrash. In midrash
the return to the prime text and what Fisch calls the "joy of recognition" are of central significance. Yet that significance is made deeper

and brought closer to recent poetic theories by what Moshe Idel describes as the infinities of the Torah, by a prime text which, as Betty Roitman shows, abolishes the category of the secondary.

In midrash we have tradition and the talent of individual interpreters, but without "the individual talent"; without, that is, myths of private genius. How this absorption of self into text is accomplished while a startling human coloration is still preserved; how a language of universal intimacy, such as David Stern indicates, is constructed—these are among the most important questions midrash raises.

Yet the literary study of midrash has barely begun. Our venture is therefore heuristic: an attempt to illuminate rather than delimit a mode of interpretation that has been lost to literary study, though the impulse behind it surfaced, historically, in many different ways. The important thing to recognize at this point is that, by and large, even students of Judaica had cut themselves off from this vast body of interpretive materials, centered on the Hebrew Bible, yet permeable to the epochs through which it passed, and displaying a high degree of imaginative consistency. Many texts that compose it are still in the process of being edited and translated. Its recovery seems crucial, not only because it contains so many strands of interest—topical, structural, folkloric, exegetic—but because its weaving together of prooftext and commentary quickens our understanding of textual production and suggests a symbiosis of interpretive and creative writing. Originality shifts its meaning or doubles its locus. The canon is transmitted and even extended by an intertextual reflection that has accepted the task of memory and preservation while adding a spacious supplement that derives from its primary source a strength and daring which is anything but secondary—which is, indeed, "literary" in the modern sense.

A word, finally, about the relationship between the main lines of the present inquiries and the modern history of midrash studies. It is worth noting that ever since the analytic study of midrash began (roughly 150 years ago), scholars have embraced the Zeitgeist of their times with all the enthusiasm that the adaptiveness of midrash itself counsels. Remarkably rich examples of this openness to a contemporary milieu are found in the generic classifications of Zunz, the Viconian-organicist models of Isaac Heinemann, the comparative methodology of Renée Bloch and Geza Vermes, and the folklore approaches of Dov Noy. (See the Bibliography for details.) The view of midrash frequently suggested in this book is undoubtedly also a child of its time. What now seems particularly interesting is the unclassifiability and waywardness of midrash, its ability to function without apparent boundaries. What especially fascinates at this moment is what Joseph Dan sees as the capacity of midrash to bring about the rebirth of tradition. Midrash somehow engages in ever-new revelations of an originary text, while the question of origins is displaced into the living tradition of writing. Indeed, the passwords into our era, still hard for our uncircumcised lips, may well be the "originary supplement" that Derrida and others began to trace out twenty years ago (see *Of Grammatology*, trans. Gayatri Chakravorty Spivak, Baltimore: Johns Hopkins University Press, 1974, p. 313) and which have lain inscribed in midrash for two millennia. In this emerging phase midrash is seen to affirm the integrity and authority of the text even while fragmenting it and sowing it endlessly. Seen in the terms of the latter-day midrashim which Derrida and Jabès offer, midrash is the open word, the open door, through which we are always just passing. No doubt this phase too will sooner or later be questioned. At least, however, it will have fallen into step with the reinterpretive roll that sounds all through the columns of midrash. And it will have acknowledged that the impact of midrash stems, in large measure, from the enduring power of the provisional which understands that it is provisional.

We could say much more about the insights of our fellow contributors and show also how they sometimes diverge from each other's views as well as from the intersecting assumptions sketched in this introduction. But we will let the essays speak for themselves.

June 1985

Note to the 1988 Printing

In this edition of *Midrash and Literature* we have corrected misprints and added a bibliographical supplement listing some omitted items and bringing the secondary literature more up-to-date. We wish to thank Steven Fraade for helping in this task.

Geoffrey Hartman and Sanford Budick
January 1988

Abbreviations

AJSLL	American Journal of Semitic Languages and Literatures
ANRW	Aufstieg und Niedergang der römischen Welt
AB	Anglia Beiblatt
BJRL	Bulletin of the John Rylands Library
BO	Bibliotheca Orientalis
CaSi	Cahiers Sioniens
CE	College English
ChauR	Chaucer Review
CIn	Critical Inquiry
CMHLB	Cahiers du Monde Hispanique et Luso-Brésilien (Caravelle)
FJB	Frankfurter judaistische Beiträge
HAR	Hebrew Annual Review
Heinemann	Research in Aggada, Targum and Jewish Liturgy in Memory of Joseph Heinemann
HibJ	Hibbert Journal
HR	History of Religions
HTR	Harvard Theological Review
HUCA	Hebrew Union College Annual
IOS	Israel Oriental Studies
Isl	Der Islam
JAAR	Journal of the American Academy of Religion
JAOS	Journal of the American Oriental Society
JBL	Journal of Biblical Literature
JEGP	Journal of English and Germanic Philology
JHI	Journal of the History of Ideas
JJewA	Journal of Jewish Art
JJS	Jewish Journal of Sociology
JQR	Jewish Quarterly Review
JSI	Journal for the Study of Judaism
JSS	Journal of Semitic Studies

JTS	The Jewish Theological Seminary of America
JWCI	Journal of the Warburg and Courtauld Institutes
LW	The Lutheran World
MeH	Medievalia & Humanistica
MelJ	Melton Journal
MGWJ	Monatschrift für Geschichte und Wissenschaft des Judentums
MiltonS	Milton Studies
MLN	Modern Language Notes
MP	Modern Philology
MW	The Muslim World
NLH	New Literary History
NT	Novum Testamentum
NTS	New Testament Studies
OS	Orientalia Suecana
PAAJR	Proceedings of the American Academy for Jewish Research
PAJHS	Publications of the American Jewish Historical Society
PMLA	Publications of the Modern Language Association of America
PQ	Philological Quarterly
RBibl	Revue Biblique
RB	Revue Bénédictine
REJ	Revue des Études Juives
RF	Romanische Forschungen
RFol	Research in Folklore
RHR	Revue de l'Histoire des Religions
RI	Revista Iberoamericana
RSCR	Recherches de Science Religieuse
RTAM	Recherches de Théologie Ancienne et Médiévale
SBF	Studii Biblici Franciscani
SBL	Society of Biblical Literature
SCenSt	Seventeenth-Century Studies
SEL	Studies in English Literature
SH	Scripta Hierosolymitana
SIDIC	Service International de Documentation Judéo-Chrétienne
SJF	Studies in Jewish Folklore
StPatrist	Studia Patristica
StudVoltaire	Studies on Voltaire and the Eighteenth Century
SUR	Revista Sur
TJHSE	Transactions of the Jewish Historical Society of England
UIsr	Univers Israélite

UTQ	University of Toronto Quarterly
VigC	Vigilae Christianae
YClS	Yale Classical Studies
YFS	Yale French Studies
ZAW	Zeitschrift für die alttestamentliche Wissenschaft
ZDMG	Zeitschrift der deutschen morgenländischen Gesellschaft
ZSm	Zeitschrift für Semitistik

A Note on Transliteration of Words in Hebrew and Aramaic

We have followed closely the "General" transliteration style suggested by the *Encyclopaedia Judaica* (1972 ed.), vol. 1, 90. However, in cases of commonly recognized usages or an author's strong preference, as well as, of course, quotations and printed titles, we have not imposed a mechanical consistency.

Bible and Midrash

GEOFFREY H. HARTMAN

The Struggle for the Text

"O which one? Is it each one?"

G. M. Hopkins

The question I have put to myself is: how is this text, the Hebrew Bible, different from all other texts? Is there a basis to the distinction between fiction and scripture? Can we discriminate the two kinds by rhetorical or textual qualities, rather than by external criteria that remain mysterious? To call the Bible a sacred text is to set it apart, to constitute it as such for the reader, but as Auerbach[1] and others have argued there is something in the text that prompts us toward this, not in order to keep the text's message hidden or enclosed, but on the contrary to make us enter its originative space: the unsaid as well as the said, the unmarked as well as the marked terrain, where the going is complex from both a scholarly and a spiritual point of view. What complicates the critic's situation is also, of course, that we cannot even begin to move into that territory without certain assumptions: for example, that despite the antiquity of the Bible or our removal in time from it, it has not become estranged beyond repair, or that it was not totally other to begin with (that, divinely inspired or not, it speaks, as the rabbis said, in the language of men), or that it was faithfully transmitted, or that, however accidented it may be, however diversified from book to book as well as within each book, there is something like a unitary perspective, if only as a horizon. Moreover, I cannot claim to possess enough global knowledge of texts that function as Scripture within other cultures to be sure that the qualities of the Hebrew Bible make it unique. My question as to its special character makes sense primarily within a tradition whose poetics have been Hellenic rather than Hebraic, so that the Bible, however influential, has never been entirely naturalized and even today remains a resident alien, at once familiar and unfamiliar.

3

Jacob's struggle with the angel, in Genesis 32, has become an inexhaustible source for parables and analogies in the Western tradition; in that sense it is not at all strange but rather a familiar guest in the literary and popular mind. The words are all known, and there are very few of them. One of the most uncanny stories in the Bible, it is also one of the sparest, even more so in Hebrew than in English. The core narrative consists of six verses and seventy words in all: to these are added an epilogue in which Jacob names the place of encounter, Peniel, and supplies the etymology "for I have seen God face to face," while the narrator appends what scholars call an etiological frame, which links this event to a dietary taboo.

The economy of presentation is closer to the Classical than to the Shakespearean stage: in the spotlight a man and another man, wrestling, then exchanging three sets of words. But the context remains unlit. Why does the fight begin? We are not told. Its outcome is as mysterious as its onset, though decisive for at least one of the protagonists. On the fringes, of course, are the people in the patriarchal narratives, reduced for this exceptional moment to extras: Esau and the Edomites, Laban and his retainers, the family and flock of Jacob. The Classical stage, after its stychomythia, often relieves and broadens its perspective by the great odes of the chorus. But here, where we might expect a breach in the narrative style, where a song-like elaboration might occur modeled on Genesis 27, Isaac's blessing of Jacob and then of Esau—episodes that anticipate the famous copia of blessings Jacob and Moses bequeath before their death on the B'nei Israel—here the style remains so laconic that one could suspect a decision to truncate, to allow the present moment a minimal telling. Wit, at this juncture, is not the wit of words: there is no rush of rhetoric, no verbal testing as so often in Shakespeare, where the characters parry and thrust and wound by overflowing puns. Wit is a matter of bearing up under, standing under, a directive called the Covenant or Promise or Blessing. It is no accident that the story turns on the manifestation of a name and a blessing: these charged vocatives have ominous as well as nominative value and are to be won rather than willfully seized or expended.

The words, then, stacked so close, with their roots still showing, are, as Auerbach says, *deutungsbedürftig*: demanding interpretation. Their meaning is a sediment that needs settling, almost like the wandering patriarchs themselves. I shall come back to this point; let me stress for the moment that the presence of a redactor, fusing cult legends centered on person and place, is more than an erudite hypothesis. The redactional process, provable or not, is descriptive of a style in which every sentence is a jealously guarded deposit, as if language had to have authority, whatever uncertainties encompassed the reported event or act of naming it. In that sense Jacob's struggle continues within the interpretive communities that receive this story as Scripture. In its determinate indeterminacy, in its authoritative and inscriptive spareness, one is reminded of Herman Melville's impression of Judea: "Stones of Judea. We read a good deal about stones in Scripture. Monuments and memorials are set up of stones; men are stoned to death; the figurative seed falls in stony places. . . . Judea is one accumulation of stones."[2]

Here is, in the King James version, what I call the core story, framed by Gen. 32:1–23 and 33:

And Jacob was left alone; and there wrestled a man with him until the breaking of the day. And when he saw that he prevailed not against him, he touched the hollow of his thigh; and the hollow of Jacob's thigh was strained, as he wrestled with him. And he said, Let me go, for the day breaketh. And he said, I will not let thee go, except thou bless me. And he said unto him, What is thy name? And he said, Jacob. And he said, Thy name shall be called no more Jacob, but Israel: for thou hast striven with God and with men, and hast prevailed. And Jacob asked him, and said, Tell me, I pray thee, thy name. And he said, Wherefore is it that thou dost ask after my name? And he blessed him there. And Jacob called the name of the place Peniel: for I have seen God face to face, and my life is preserved.

Nothing readies us for this event. Jacob is journeying to Canaan; he reaches Maḥanaim and makes preparations for meeting Esau. Suddenly, at night, this man (ish) appears. Was it a dream, perhaps? Maimonides thought so. Jacob, who had a vision at Beth-el, now has a vision at Peni-el. He is always, in his semitic state, in his wanderings, met by angels or divine messengers. Yet there is a difference. The meeting is not only sudden, like a vision or dream—this time what happens can be called a vision only by analogy, because the text is so terse, and says "man" not "angel," and no word about dreaming. Emily Dickinson expresses our feeling when she concludes a poem inspired by the episode,

> And the bewildered Gymnast
> Found he had worsted God.[3]

Such bewilderment is not lessened by the placement of the story, as chapter 32 becomes chapter 33. It is a combat not necessary to the sequence of events. We could omit it and still have a continuous narrative—indeed, a more continuous one. Remember the circumstances in which Jacob finds himself. He is afraid of Esau and wants to appease him. He settles down for the night in the camp (v. 14) and sends before him an avant-garde of propitiatory gifts: "two hundred she goats and twenty he goats, two hundred ewes and twenty rams, thirty milch camels," and so forth. A few lines further on we read again: "So these gifts passed over before him; and he himself lodged that night in the camp." Then, as if he were woken by a dream or unsure that enough gifts had been sent before, the text informs us, "he rose up that night, and took his two wives and two handmaidens, and eleven children, and passed over the ford of the Jabbok. He took them, and sent them over the stream, and sent over that which he had" (v. 23). From that somewhat tautological statement, which sounds to me like an attempted coda, we go to the laconic struggle with the "man." But in terms of the narrative we could cross easily to chapter 33, assuming the night has gone by. "Jacob lifted up his eyes, and looked, and behold, Esau came, and with him four hundred men."

Now everything is sequential, logical: this is how Jacob's camp meets that of Esau, and Jacob's cunning preparations work out. The brothers reconcile. Chapter 33, in fact, does not refer to Jacob as Israel but still as Jacob: the struggle by night is clearly an episode that has inserted itself into a funny-fearful story illustrating Jacob's resourcefulness.

So the struggle with the angel is not only a stark, mysterious event, but unnecessary in terms of the unfolding narrative. This narrative exhibits Jacob's character, or his conduct, which is prudent though not exactly courageous. In his wish to appease and flatter Esau, Jacob is almost blasphemous. In words that strangely echo "for I have seen God face to face and my life is preserved," Jacob says to his brother, "If I have found favor in your sight, receive my gift, for indeed I have seen your face as one sees the face of God."

Jacob is not an admirable person, patriarch though he may be. (Gunkel, in *The Legends of Genesis*, laconically entitles one section, "The Patriarchs not Saints."[4]) But it is not entirely Jacob's fault, for this is the story of two camps, Maḥanaim (Gen. 32:2–3), two nations, Edom and Israel, from the start—from the very womb of Rebeccah in which Jacob and Esau struggle. There too is a wrestling, and Jacob's name comes from that neonatal fight. "His hand had hold of Esau's heel (*akev*), and they called him Jacob (*Yaakov*)." You will also recall his tricking Esau out of his birthright and blessing; and his behavior with Laban. "*Vay-ignov Yaakov Lavan* . . . (31:20). Jacob is a *ganev*, though I won't claim Laban was much better; Jacob, I am sorry to say, is what he is called in the Bible: a heel.

Let me continue to put together what is well-known. The mysterious episode of Jacob's contest is actually what gives him his chance to prove himself. He has struggled with men and prevailed—but at some cost to his father, his brother, and our moral sense. No redactorial revision, no appeal to his fated role in a providential drama, can remove the suspicion that he is cunning rather than noble—in short, a trickster. It is true that Abraham and Isaac too can use deceit and subterfuge, but they are less called upon to do so. Did Abraham try to pass off a ram for his child? That is not what the Bible says. Yet about Jacob it is candid; and Jacob too, of course, will be deceived by his children when they break his heart by showing him Joseph's technicolor coat dipped in goat's blood.

How does Jacob prove himself during that night-contest? Think first of the irony of his situation: he prepares to meet the wrath of Esau; he puts his property and even his family in front of him, and whom does he meet, and when? "And Jacob was left alone." As Speiser says, "The carefully calculated never comes off."[5] There is nothing between Jacob and the wrestler, that antagonist from nowhere. Then it turns out the man is not a man, but God himself. Even if he is an angel and not God, no other patriarch, no other Biblical character except for Moses has so direct and dangerous an encounter with a divine agent.

Genesis Rabbah makes a startling suggestion when it quotes R. Berekiah. "There is none like God (Deut. 32:26); yet who is like God? Jeshurun, which means Israel the Patriarch. Just as it is written of God, And the Lord alone shall be exalted (Isaiah 2:11), so of Jacob too: And Jacob was left alone (Genesis 32:25)."[6] This is more than eulogy, for the allusion that identifies Jacob and Jeshurun is underwritten by the opening prooftext of the midrash: "There is none like unto God, O Jeshurun." The word *alone* acquires two senses: *only* Jacob, among all men, is noble or straight enough to be compared to God; but also, more radically, the *loneliness* of the human Jacob in this encounter can remind us of the *aloneness* of God. Jacob wrestles with God as God wrestles with Himself.

Through this unmediated encounter, everything shady in Jacob is removed: the blessing he stole he now receives by right; and his name, tainted by his birth and subsequent behavior, is cleared. No longer will he be called Jacob, that is, Heel or Usurper, but Israel, the God-fighter— quite a title, even if the redactor draws back and shows some cunning of his own, claiming it means "You have striven with God [Midrash: Angels] *and with men*." "As with men" would seem more exact, if it is an anaphoric reference to Jacob's trouble with Laban and Esau. Or should we take "You have striven with God [*elohim*] and with men" as a hendyadis, intending "you have striven with godlike men," or "with a godlike man"? The narrator's gloss tries to settle the meaning of *Yisrael*, but only complicates it. In the recent Torah Commentary issued by the Union of the American Hebrew Congregations, modern scholarship develops, without alluding to it, Rabbi Berekiah's midrash. "Jeshurun," another name for Israel the Patriarch, "means noblest and best": the rabbis suspect the name is rooted in the word for "upright" (*yashar*). So Yisrael, we learn from this newest Commentary, is probably derived from *yashar-el*, the one whom God makes straight, as opposed to *ya-akov-el*, the one whom God makes to limp.[7] Moreover, it has been suggested, the stems *akov* (heel) and *avek* (wrestle) may chime like anagrams. It hardly matters: the eponymic privilege passes to Jacob, whatever the title means. The name change denotes a character change, or the inner sense of Jacob's previous life breaking through. *Anokhi imkha*, God had said to him in the Beth-el or house of God vision (Gen. 28:15); there "I am with you" sounded comforting, but here the testing and dangerous side of it is disclosed, as a divinely inflicted bruise replaces a flaw of character.

"It is no sin to limp," Freud writes at the end of *Beyond the Pleasure Principle*.[8] He knows his démarche in this treatise has not been as straightforward, not as logical or scientific as he might wish; and I can only repeat Freud's genial self-defense. For you may wonder what is literary about my reflections so far. Am I not constructing a homily or midrash, and so competing with the Rabbinic sages instead of separating out a literary field with its own distinctive boundary?

While midrash must be viewed as a type of discourse with its own rules and historical development, and while we cannot assume that its only function was exegetical, little is more important today than to remind secular literary studies of the richness and subtlety of those strange rabbinic conversations which have been disdained for so long in favor of more objective and systematized modes of reading. Moreover, for any text to remain alive requires the attention and supplementation of commentary. But this sets up a paradox involving the relation of source-text to the concept *literature*. If we accept von Rad's view that the lateness and literariness of the Yahwist (the supposed author-redactor of the combat story) go hand in hand, and that "becoming literature meant in a sense an end for this [Biblical] material, which until then had already had a varied history behind it,"[9] then the proper task of midrashic or non-midrashic exegesis is to keep the Bible from becoming literature. Becoming literature might mean a material still capable of development turning into a closed corpus, a once-living but now fossilized deposit. The only virtue I can claim for the literary study of the Bible is, therefore, that while it can hardly be more imaginative than the masters of old, *it can dare to go wrong*. Let me try.

I return to our brief story. I have suggested its extraordinary summation of Jacob's character, its conversion of a cunning person, a sort of Jewish Odysseus, into a consecrated patriarch, touching and touched by God. Yet there are disturbing currents in the episode, which the Rabbis picked up but did not always pursue explicitly. Berekiah's remarks on "Jacob was left alone" show what the Rabbis could do. For the contemporary reader one perplexing feature is the sudden appearance of that "man." Another is the fact that he wishes to leave before sunrise. Finally, there is the unusual theme of wrestling with and overcoming divinity.

Maimonides, as I reported, thought it must have been a prophetic dream of Jacob's.[10] Rashi, abbreviating various commentators, suggests that the mysterious man was indeed an angel, but of a special sort—Esau's guardian angel. The encounter has a divine but also an unkosher aspect: this may be Esau's protector waylaying Jacob. In this case the surprise would be that Jacob encounters not the flesh-and-blood Esau, for whom he has so carefully prepared, but his demonic double. Being a ghost or demon, moreover, would explain why the man must get away before sunrise, although Rashi will not say more about this peculiarity than that the angel leaves to praise at break of day.

Gunkel too senses something strange in a story seemingly unable to make up its mind about the natural-supernatural character of this episode. "Jacob was really a Titan, and consequently we can scarcely avoid seeing a faded out myth."[11] Now Jacob himself, as well as his opponent, is more than human. In Genesis Rabbah we find, to our surprise, that the conversation turns mainly on the nature of angels: whether or not "The Holy One, blessed be He" creates a new company of angels every day, who utter a song before Him and then depart (i.e., cease to exist).[12] (This is a thought, by the way, which still haunted Walter Benjamin's imagination, as Scholem has shown.) Do we need this additional distraction, however beautiful, especially since it introduces yet another uncertainty? If, indeed, the angels are new each morning and do not last the rest of the day, what sort of being is this phantom of the night? Rabbi Helbo has an answer. "It was Michael or Gabriel, who are celestial princes; all others are exchanged, but they are not exchanged." In sum, the man may be divine and not divine; he may be a demon and not a demon; while Jacob may be a man or a transformed Titan, a usurper or a heroic challenger who wrests the blessing from God even as he had wrested it, by sleight of hand, from his father.

So far everything I have said merely emphasizes the betwixt-and-between status of Jacob: he is a wanderer; he dwells in the space of Maḥanaim, the double camp on this and the other side of the river; the outcome between him and his brother is not assured; and the combat itself, climaxing in the key phrase "you have striven with elohim and with men," keeps the nature of the opponent undecidable. On what side of the stream Jacob was, what the name of a person is or what it means, whether Peni'el or Penu'el is the right spelling, and whether Jabbok is or is not a metathesis of Ya'akov cannot be determined like a clearly marked border.

The same questionable border affects the filiation, in this episode, of folktale and Scripture. Gunkel sees in the combat a faded myth; we may also recall legends in which an evil spirit waylays, through jealousy or malice, a person chosen to be superior to the realm of such spirits. The rabbi's learned discussion about the praising, ephemerid angels may not be a digression after all, but rather a tacit acknowledgment that there is not always peace in the high heavens; that even up there beings exist who are jealous of man, who accuse him the more they praise God. For there is no praise without slander; and the angel who attacks Jacob may be the Satan who accuses Job. It is, fundamentally, Jacob's good name that is in question. What is man, that thou (God) shouldst magnify him? It is just as well the angels last only as long as sunrise, for this guarantees our safety: the dawn which means a return of life to us, of the soul to the body, means they cannot carry our night-thoughts before God's throne. They praise Him, then cease to exist.

Nothing said so far, I want to emphasize again, is strictly literary, except for the question of how much legend or folktale Scripture has displaced. But the type or structure of displacement, which will interest Roland Barthes, for example, has not been explored. What interests me are the fault lines of a text, the evidence of a narrative sedimentation that has not entirely settled, and the tension that results between producing one authoritative account and respecting traditions characterized by a certain heterogeneity. In Scripture, despite doubled stories and inconsistencies, there is a sometimes laconic, sometimes wordy, but always imperious unity. In Jacob's combat that unifying tension reaches a peculiar pitch. Listen once more to the following sentence:

And when he saw that he prevailed not against him, he touched the hollow of his thigh, and the hollow of Jacob's thigh was strained, as he wrestled with him. And he said, Let me go . . .

There is something twisted here, because while it is Jacob who is wounded, it is his antagonist who immediately pleads for release. This fact is sometimes explained by saying that Jacob triumphed despite the wound inflicted on him. But suppose that the text has passed over or modified a difficulty in the received versions. That difficulty would be, as I see it, that it was Jacob who touched the man's thigh and wounded him, but that it seemed impossible—to the narrator—for a divine being to be physically, literally hurt. One tradition or solution, therefore, might be to represent Jacob's antagonist as a "man." Yet the story has little point unless it bestows on Jacob the title *Yisrael*, and its connotation of a consecrating contact with divinity. It is possible, moreover, that the tradition was handed down in ambiguous form and made more believable or homogeneous by a redactorial process which, however, was careful to leave some traces. To understand the process, all we have to do is omit one word, the name *Ya'akov* from verse 26. The first "he" could then be Jacob rather than the angel: "And when he saw that he prevailed not against him, he touched the hollow of his thigh, and the hollow of his thigh was strained, as he wrestled with him." It could be Jacob who touched his opponent's thigh and by that blow—a low blow—assured victory for himself. This could be consistent with the Jacob we know, the trickster who gains the blessing by deceit.

It is the privilege of a literary interpreter to revive this uncomfort-
able perspective, though not in order to slander Jacob. Rather, once
again, to reveal the *maḥanaim* situation, the doubleness and duplicity
out of which Jacob must always emerge. Or simply to respect the
hendyadic, even polyphonic nature of all texts, as they strive for a
single, authoritative point of view. There are interesting asymmetries
and superfluities in so economical a story—the entire story itself, in
fact, introduces something baffling on the level of narrative that cannot
be smoothed over or harmonized without further redactional or interpretive moves. Without producing incoherence these baffles raise
questions that are at once textual and interpretive. A stronger way of
putting it is that the mode of existence of the text and the mode of
representation (mimesis) have fused beyond alteration—though not,
of course, beyond analysis.

Imagine a section of Genesis beginning, "Call me Israel." However
deep, struggling, or myriad-minded the ensuing narrative, we would
know ourselves in the presence of fiction, not Scripture. The same
holds, of course, for texts more scrabbled than the Bible, texts like
Joyce's *Finnegans Wake*. "Shem is as short for Shemus as Jem is joky for
Jacob." The problem we face, strangely enough, it not that we cannot
define Scripture but that having gradually redefined fiction in the light
of Scripture we now find it hard to distinguish between them. We see
both within a global definition of what textuality is; and the same merg-
ing occurs as we recover a knowledge of midrash, so that literary criticism and midrashic modes begin to blend into each other. It is no
accident that recent theories of intertextuality have devalued the principle of unity as it lodges with some organic or magical mastery attributed to the author of the work. The authority of the author, as that of
the Biblical redactor or redactors, comes from the way the intertextual
situation is handled; and in this authors are close to being redactors,
even if they do not acknowledge it. Any text, however seemingly autonomous, is also what Coleridge said truth is: a ventriloquist. Through
this text other texts speak. Eliot, when he characterized poetry as a
"medium" that digested the most disparate experiences, raised the
same issue of the unstable unity of art, or the tensions within it. The
New Criticism explored these tensions as the source of aesthetic value
and identified them with such formal properties as paradox, irony,
ambiguity and the use of complex or multiple plots. The newer criti-

cism, however, is less concerned with unity and more with the uniformity that comes through too anxious an emphasis on unity. It uses intertextuality as a "technique of suspicion" directed against both the romantic myth of originality and the classicist myth of normative language behavior.

The awareness that all writing is a fusion of heterogeneous stories or types of discourse—that it is layered or even macaronic while seeking the appearance of unity—has been fostered by some of the most important scholarship of recent times. Although there are anthropologists and historians of religion who still aim to find the dominant myth of a particular culture (that of the "High God," for example), many others dispute that there is a myth *an sich* rather than a corpus of stories interacting with a commentary-process that continually modifies, updates and syncretizes what is at hand. Levi-Strauss, while maintaining the concept of a "myth of reference" as the hypothetically stable, synoptic focus of stories called myths, and while trying to extract from them a logic common to all minds, savage or sophisticated, also describes the bricolage that repairs or revises the always faltering mythic narrative. Mikhail Bakhtin discloses a "heteroglossia" within novels that seem spoken or coordinated by a single authorial presence. Clifford Geertz and Jonathan Smith train our eyes like good literary exegetes to appreciate the thick tricky texture of native informants as well as distant fables. This more complex understanding came initially through the Higher Criticism of the Bible, which analyzed a unified, authorless narrative into its redacted and blended strands. With the Higher Criticism we are back, of course, to German scholarship of the nineteenth century, which introduced a sort of geologically structured sense of time into the development of Scripture.

I would like to assert that Scripture can be distinguished from fiction by its frictionality: not only its respect for friction, which exists also in literary texts, but its capacity to leave traces, which incite and even demand interpretation of what it has incorporated. Yet the contemporary theories I have described, which derive partly from Biblical scholarship, make such a distinction more difficult. There may be more cryptomnesia in fiction than in the Bible. But if there is a major difference, it bears on the fact that the respect which shapes variant stories into a narrative does not—in Scripture—reflect only the aesthetic problem of blending them into a unified whole. It recalls, or should recall, the authority of traditions handed down, each with its truth claim—a respect which makes every word, and not only the characters, "schwer von ihrem Gewordensein," to quote Auerbach: heavy with the fullness of having had to be formed.

Let me conclude by exemplifying this problem of definition in the work of Roland Barthes, whose essay "The Struggle with the Angel" on Genesis 32 is, except for Auerbach's chapter in *Mimesis*, the best modern commentary on a Biblical episode. Barthes is not interested in what makes this text Scripture rather than fiction. After Propp and Levi-Strauss he might dispute such a distinction. In his *Morphology of the Folktale* Propp established the structure of that form by analyzing out a finite number of "functions" or type-episodes which every folktale combines.[13] To describe Jacob's combat Barthes cites numbers 15 through 19, including the perilous *passage* from place to place; *combat* between villain and hero; *branding* or *marking* the hero or bestowing on him a special gift; *victory* of the hero; and so forth. Associated episodes such as the difficult crossing of a ford guarded by a hostile spirit also identify Jacob's struggle as having the same structure as a folktale. But this resemblance is not what holds Barthes's attention, and doubtless he could have analyzed a Homeric sequence in the same structuralist fashion. "What interests me most in this famous passage," he writes, "is not the 'folkloristic' model but the abrasive frictions, the breaks, the discontinuities of readability, the juxtaposition of narrative entities which to some extent run free from an explicit logical articulation. One is dealing here (this at least is for me the savour of reading) with a sort of *metonymic montage*: the themes (Crossing, Struggling, Naming, Alimentary Rite) are *combined*, not 'developed.' " Barthes ends by claiming that this "asyndetic character" or "metonymic logic" of the narrative expresses the unconscious and he asks for a reading that would lead to the text's "symbolic explosion," its "dissemination, not its truth," so that we would not reduce it to a signified, whether "historical, economic, folkloristic or kerygmatic," but would manage "to hold its *significance* fully open."[14]

Barthes's powerful application of Propp places the folkloric context beyond doubt. Yet one peculiarity of his account must be mentioned. How can he talk of the "asyndetic character of the narrative" when its most obvious syntactical feature is parataxis or syndeton: the linking of every verse segment by the conjunction *va* (and)? Only the last verse differs by substituting a coda-like *al ken* (therefore) and *ki* (because), which are simply heightened conjunctives.

Barthes cannot reply that he is referring to structural juxtapositions, for he has said specifically he is commenting on the "savour of the reading" not the "structural exploitation." In truth, this proclitic and ubiquitous *va* is like the rarer enclitic *yah* or *el*, signifying God. Barthes cannot value this initial sign tacked onto so much and pointing to a teleological direction, even if God remains hidden most of the time. Von Rad, a theologian, is nearer the mark when he observes that "the divine promise is like a sign before and over all these individual narratives, and within this bracket, so to speak, there is much good and evil."[15]

Barthes, then, is too obviously "deconstructing" a text normally identified as belonging to Scripture and teleological in its orientation. He does not see that the teleological impulse participates in the concatenative power of storyteller or redactor, in that motivating *va*, and in the will to shape by combining. The process of composition here is not exclusively unifying or agglomerative: divergencies are not always resolved. This produces a textual quality which is peculiar enough to be given a separate name, despite structural similarities with saga, folklore, or stories stuck together by what scholars call "contamination."

When Barthes, therefore, asks us to hold the significance of this Bible story "fully open," by stressing an asyndetic and metonymic logic that unsettles the signified and enables the story's "dissemination, not its truth," he leaves out, even structurally, what Auerbach in his *akedah* interpretation stresses so effectively. The truth claim of the Bible, Auerbach says, is so imperious that reality in its sensuous or charming aspect is not dwelt upon; and the spotlight effect, which isolates major persons or happenings, is due to the same anagogical demand that excludes all other places and concerns. Bible stories do not flatter or fascinate like Homer's; they do not give us something artfully rendered; they force readers to become interpreters and to find the presence of what is absent in the fraught background, the densely layered (Auerbach uses the marvelous word *geschichtet*) narrative.

By comparing two passages, the *akedah* from the Bible and a recognition scene from the nineteenth book of the *Odyssey*—passages that do not have the slightest thematic relation—and by refusing to disqualify one in the light of the other or to find the same basic structure in them, Auerbach maintains a gap between Scripture and fiction, if only in the form of Hebraic versus Hellenic. It is possible to object that this gap narrows because of the New Testament, or because of the

Hellenic phase Hebrew learning goes through. It is also possible to plead that the Hellenizing did not really change the Hebraic tradition in the long run. What remains important is that one mind brings together radically divergent modes of representation under the sign of difference. This would not have been possible if both stories did not belong, at some level, to the same culture. This culture is, or was, a reading culture: the curator not only of widely divergent types of literature but also of informed modes of interpretation that encourage a perspectival empathy. Yet by the time Auerbach wrote, a nationalism that had fostered the development of the vernaculars in the Renaissance, and made *Mimesis* possible by reflecting the depth and concreteness of historical life, was imposing a doctrinaire canon and tyrannical unity of expression. As an expatriate victim of German National Socialism, Auerbach was himself a *mahanaim* figure, though he did not seek a truer homeland, like Abraham, nor did he venture, like Odysseus, to return to his old place, in the hope it would still know him.

The question of the relation of place to destiny or spiritual strength is given extraordinary resonance by the story of the patriarchs and here by Jacob's combat. I am reminded of Booker T. Washington's remark about another people emerging from slavery. "They must change their names. They must leave the Old Plantation." In the Hebrew Bible this imperative is related to literature from the beginning: these narratives of exodus (starting with the command to Abraham, *lekh lekha*, or "get out"), these episodes fixing place names or proper names by paronomasia to a particular theophany, continue to demand an exegete despite various etiological frames intending to make those names less opaque. Each storied reasoning upon names recharges the name: semantic opaqueness is not removed, it is simply surrounded by the possibility that there was an original meaning or a specific and authoritative act of designation. Where did that authority, that performative strength come from? Does *nomen* become *numen*, except through the story inspired by it? Can spirit and place ever coincide except through the extended naming fiction enables?

The universality of Jacob's combat with the angel lies, finally, in that struggle for a text—for a supreme fiction or authoritative account stripped of inessentials, of all diversions, of everything we might describe as arbitrary, parochial, even aesthetic. It centers on a sparse and doubtful set of words, handed on by an editorial process which in its conflations or accommodations could seem to be the very antithesis of the unmediated encounter it describes. Nicknames like Yaakov or Yisrael, place names like Peni'el, and other agnominations accumulate as a sacred or a silly burden: they are, we sense, a stock of vocatives (ex-vocatives, perhaps) which the redactors cannot let go but count and recount, sorting gods and goats into something more than a list, a proprietary catalogue, a hoard of names. The accreted, promissory narrative we call Scripture is composed of tokens that demand the continuous and precarious intervention of successive generations of interpreters, who must keep the words as well as the faith.

NOTES

1. Erich Auerbach, *Mimesis: The Representation of Reality in Western Literature*, trans. Willard R. Trask (New York: Doubleday, 1957).

2. Herman Melville, *Journal of a Visit to Europe and the Levant, October 11, 1856—May 6, 1857*, ed. Howard C. Horsford (Princeton: Princeton University Press, 1955).

3. Emily Dickinson, "A little east of Jordan," in *Complete Poems*, ed. Thomas H. Johnson (Boston: Little Brown, 1960), no. 59.

4. Hermann Gunkel, *The Legends of Genesis: The Biblical Saga and History*, trans. William Herbert Carruth (New York: Schocken Books, 1970), pp. 113–16.

5. *The Anchor Bible: Genesis*, ed. and trans. Ephraim Avigdor Speiser (Garden City, N.Y.: Doubleday, 1964–83), p. 256.

6. *Genesis Rabbah*, vol. 1 of *Midrash Rabbah*, ed. Harry Freedman and Maurice Simon (London: Soncino Press, 1961), p. 710. Cf. the remarkable "we do not know who was victorious," p. 712. Berekiah's remarks do more than ennoble Jacob. They make Jacob and his story also reveal something about God: an attribute, or His "character." God, after all, is the ultimate author of Scripture and midrash holds up the mirror to that textual image in order to search out and catch what is knowable about Him.

7. *The Torah: A Modern Commentary*, ed. W. G. Plaut, B. J. Bamberger and W. Hallo, Union of American Hebrew Congregations (New York, 1981).

8. Sigmund Freud, *Beyond the Pleasure Principle*, in *The Standard Edition of the Complete Psychological Works of Sigmund Freud*, trans. James Strachey (London: Hogarth Press, 1955), vol. 18, p. 64.

9. Gerhard von Rad, *Genesis: A Commentary*, rev. ed. (Philadelphia, 1972), p. 18.

10. Moses ben Maimon (Maimonides), *The Guide of the Perplexed*, 2d ed., trans. Michael Friedlander (New York: Dover Publications, 1956), pt. 2, chap. 43 (in some editions chap. 42).

11. Gunkel, *Legends of Genesis*, p. 120.

12. *Genesis Rabbah*, p. 710.

13. Vladimir I. Propp, *Morphology of the Folktale*, rev. ed., trans. Laurence Scott, ed. Louis A. Wagner (Austin: University of Texas Press, 1968).

14. Roland Barthes, "The Struggle with the Angel," in *Image Music Text*, trans. Stephen Heath (London: Fontana Collins, 1977), pp. 125–41.

15. Von Rad, *Genesis: A Commentary*, p. 268. Von Rad also describes eloquently the stratified nature of this text. He writes: "In this narrative more than in any other of the ancient patriarchal traditions something of the long process of formation to which this material was subjected in history becomes clear. ... There are scarcely examples in

Western literature of this kind of narrative, which combines such spaciousness in content with such stability in form. Many generations have worked on them, as in the case of an old house; much of the content has been adjusted in the course of time, much has again been dropped, but most has remained. . . . Here is a passage where a much older form of our saga is revealed. . . . one might think at first, in view of the hopelessness of the fight, that Jacob has won the upper hand over his antagonist (by a trick of fighting?). This interpretation would best suit the continuation, in v. 26, where the antagonist asks Jacob to let him go and then also the later statement that Jacob had prevailed (v. 28b). This monstrous conception, however, that Jacob nearly defeated the heavenly being, is now concealed by the clear text of v. 25b and v. 32b" (pp. 320–21).

MICHAEL FISHBANE

Inner Biblical Exegesis: Types and Strategies of Interpretation in Ancient Israel

One of the great and most characteristic features of the history of religions is the ongoing reinterpretation of sacred utterances which are believed to be foundational for each culture. So deeply has this phenomenon become part of our modern literary inheritance that we may overlook the peculiar type of imagination which it has sponsored and continues to nurture: an imagination which responds to and is deeply dependent upon received traditions; an imagination whose creativity is never entirely a new creation, but one founded upon older and authoritative words and images. This paradoxical dynamic, whereby religious change is characterized more often by revisions and explications of a traditional content than by new visions or abrupt innovations, is strikingly demonstrated by the fate of the teachings of Gautama Buddha. For if this remarkable teacher devoted himself to the ideal of breaking free of tradition and the dependencies thereby engendered, his disciples quickly turned his own words into sutras for commentary. Among the great western religions, however, Judaism has sought to dignify the status of religious commentary, and in one popular mythic image transferred to it a metaphysical dimension. For the well-known Talmudic image of God studying and interpreting his own Torah is nothing if not that tradition's realization that there is no authoritative teaching which is not also the source of its own renewal, that revealed teachings are a dead letter unless revitalized in the mouth of those who study them.[1]

Pharisaic Judaism tried to minimize the gap between a divine Torah and ongoing human interpretation by projecting the origins of authoritative exegesis to Sinai itself.[2] But even this mythification of a chain of legitimate interpreters did not so much obscure the distinction between Revelation and Interpretation as underscore it. From this perspective, the interpretative traditions of ancient Judaism constitute a separate, non-biblical genre: a post-biblical corpus of texts which stand alongside the Sinaitic Revelation as *revelation* of new meanings *through exegesis*. Moreover, this dignification of interpretation in Pharisaic literature highlights another feature of ancient Judaism (and is a root cause of early Jewish polemics): the realization that there was no pure teaching of Revelation apart from its regeneration or clarification through an authoritative type of exegesis. The rabbinic guardians of Torah claimed to be its true teachers, their oral exegesis the only valid password to the written text.

Given these two issues—the distinction between Revelation and interpretative tradition, and their complex interdependence—we may ask: Do we in fact cross a great divide from the Hebrew Bible to its rabbinic interpreters, or is the foundation text *already* an interpreted document—despite all initial impressions to the contrary? Certainly any divide that may be perceived becomes a slippery slope when we look at the era around 150 B.C.E., which saw 1) the end to the production of texts which would be given authority in the canon of the Hebrew Bible and, 2) a proliferation of many and sophisticated modes of exegesis, in the legal and prophetic documents of the Qumran sectaries, in the rewritten biblical histories composed by proto- and para-Pharisaic circles (such as the *Book of Jubilees* or the *Testaments of the Twelve Patriarchs*), and in the Bible versions of the Greek-speaking Jews of Alexandria or the Samaritan community near Mt. Gerizim. To say, then, that rabbinic exegesis was fundamentally dependent upon trends in contemporary Greco-Roman rhetoric or among the Alexandrian grammarians is to mistake ecumenical currents of text-study and the occurrence of similar exegetical terms for the inner-Jewish cultivation of preexistent native traditions of interpretation.[3]

In what follows we shall explore some of the types of textual interpretation in ancient Israel—that is, within the Hebrew Bible itself—paying particular attention to how the texts that comprise it were revised and even reauthorized during the course of many centuries, and to how older traditions fostered new insights which, in turn, thickened the intertextual matrix of the culture and conditioned its imagination. Without any attempt to be comprehensive, we hope to suggest some of the ways by which the foundation document of Judaism, the

Hebrew Bible, not only sponsored a monumental culture of textual exegesis but was itself its own first product. We shall first consider the area of scribal exegesis and follow this with more extensive considerations of both legal exegesis and strategic revision in the Hebrew Bible.[4]

I

The process of the intercultural transmission of traditions may be considered one of the primary areas in which authoritative teachings or memories were received and revalued for new generations. Ancient Near Eastern myths were theologically adapted and historicized; nomadic recollections were revised in order to promote the prestige and claims of tribal ancestors; and narrative topoi were reworked with new moral or theological considerations in mind.[5] As the ancient oral culture was subsumed into a developing text culture by the first millennium B.C.E., these processes continued but were often more narrowly circumscribed. Then also, as before, the culture determined its values by what it chose to receive and transmit as authoritative. However, revision of these materials was increasingly more affected by the discriminating eye of the trained scribe, as he patiently copied out a text and reacted to its ambiguities and oddities, than by the ear of the wise cognoscenti of the tribe. Thus we find numerous instances in which old toponyms are retained but supplemented by their newer name ("Luz: it is Bethel"; Josh. 18:13), or foreign terms are translated on the spot ("pur: it is the lot"; Esther 3:7). As often as not these explanatory glosses are introduced by formulaic terms, thus underscoring the professional background of the scribal insertions. Moreover, even by such meager evidence, it is clear that the authoritative text being explicated was not considered inviolable but subject to the invasion of a tradition of interpretation which rendered it more comprehensible.

Such scribal intrusions should not be minimized, for they open a valuable window upon the regard ancient Israelite scribes had for authoritative texts, whose obliquities were retained alongside their explication. Indeed, it would certainly have been easier and more economical for these scribes to have removed or reformulated the disturbing words. For example, the scribes who noticed the jarring oddity in the historical narrative of Ezra 3:12 (which reports that when the cornerstone of the post-exilic second Temple was laid, "many priests, Levites, heads of patriarchal clans, and elders who had seen this first Temple *when it was founded* . . . cried loudly"), could have simply deleted the clause "when it was founded" or rephrased it so as to specify the ambiguous pronoun "it." For, as the text now stands, "it" may refer either to the founding of the contemporary second Temple or to the founding of the first one, four hundred years earlier—a historical howler. However, to resolve this ambiguity, the explicator chose neither of the aforenoted alternatives but inserted the syntactically disruptive phrase "*this is [refers to] the Temple*" after the words "when it was founded." Such a phrase manifestly directs the reader to the proper historical sense of the phrase; namely, a reference to the founding of the second Temple.[6] The point, then, is that "many priests," etc., who had seen the first Temple in its glory were dismayed and cried when they observed the foundation of the more modest second one. But since the explicatory comment pokes disruptingly out of the sentence, the latter-day reader is still constrained to pause and notice the original reading. Paradoxically then, by retaining the old together with the new, the scribes have insured that future readers would be forced to a realization not far removed from their own: that they are latecomers to the text, who must read it with the guidance of an oral—now written— exegetical tradition.

Such processes become all the more intriguing in texts which lay an even higher claim upon the culture: texts which claim to be divine revelations. Isa. 29:9–11 provides an instructive case.

9. Be astonished and dazed, revel and be blinded: you have drunk, but not from wine; totter, but not from drink;
10. For YHWH has poured over you a spirit of stupefaction: He has closed your eyes—*namely, the prophets*—and cloaked your heads—*the seers;*
11. All prophetic visions shall be sealed from you . . .

The object of the denunciation beginning in v.9 is unspecified. But inasmuch as the people of Judaea have been the object of scorn throughout the preceding oracles, and no new subject has been introduced, one may reasonably infer that the reference is to the people. It is they who are drunk and totter and who cannot fathom the prophetic visions given to them. From this perspective, the words "namely, the prophets" and "the seers" are problematic and reflect a shift in subject from the people to the prophets. Moreover, since these two phrases have a syntactically distinct, appositional relationship to their preceding clauses (the first is actually introduced by the particle 'et,[7] which normally introduces a direct object, after a clause ending with an object), and since the clauses without these disruptive words actually form a coherent chiasmus (literally, "He has closed your eyes" is inversely parallel to "your heads He has cloaked"), it is likely that Isa. 29:10 preserves scribal explications intruded into the old oracle.[8] A motivating concern of these interpretative comments may have been to elucidate the literary figure of "closed eyes." The result, however, is that an oracle condemning the people is transformed into a rebuke of false prophets. Tendentious motivations cannot, therefore, be entirely excluded. But whatever their origin or aim, the scribal comments in v.10 were made relatively early, for the Septuagint version presupposes the problematic syntax now found in the received Massoretic text and tries to normalize the prophetic condemnation—while extending its scope yet further.[9] The Lucianic reviser of this Greek text has further compounded the tissue of errors by seeking to improve on the Septuagint version which he had himself inherited without (apparently) ever consulting the Massoretic Hebrew version which we have cited.[10]

From the viewpoint of the exegetical processes involved, the textual strata represented by the Massoretic text and by the Septuagint and its Lucianic recension reflect continuous rereadings of the original oracle, though it is clear that the scribal hand which inserted "namely, the prophets" and "the seers" into Isa. 29:10 reflects the most invasive exegetical procedure, which transforms the meaning of the passage and disturbs its syntactic balance—a matter the later translators-commentators tried to rectify. Moreover, this striking transformation of an oracle against the people into one against the prophets shows the extent to which the interpretative tradition (we do not know if the scribe reflects his own reading or mediates that of a school) might introduce a new authority into a received tradition, so that these human comments compete with and ultimately transform the focus of the ancient, divine words. Accordingly, Isa. 29:9–11 succinctly underscores a paradoxical dimension of scribal exegesis; namely, that the tradition it receives (in this case, an oracle) is not necessarily the one it transmits. For the latter is now the bearer of multiple authorities for that generation of readers: the privileged voice of divine Revelation and the human voice of instruction have become one. That this paradox is not always perceived is a measure of the scribes' success in subordinating their voice to that of the tradition. Even more paradoxically: in the end it is *their* interpretations that have become the received tradition; their oral traditions are the written text given to the community.

II

We began our discussion of interpretation in ancient Israel by considering some aspects of scribal exegesis. These concisely demonstrate the dynamics which also characterize legal and theological exegesis. For if scribalism points to the fact that ordinary textual ambiguity or openness may serve to catalyze commentary and that these supplements, when incorporated into the received text, reflect the cultural dynamics of transmission, then law and theology, where the frequent incomprehensibility or noncomprehensiveness of divinely authorized rules requires human exegesis and expansion, offer an even richer sphere for study.[11]

At the outset, let us consider a case where the borders between scribal exegesis and legal instruction are somewhat blurred. Like the example in Isa. 29:9–11, here again we have a skein of successive explications, though now embedded entirely within the Hebrew text. Thus Lev. 19:19 provides a rule prohibiting different forms of mixtures: the mixed breeding of cattle, the mixture of sown seeds in a field, and the mixture of textiles in a garment. The injunction is formulaic and repeats the key-term *kilayim*, "mixtures." One may easily assume that the precise application of the general categories *cattle* and *field* were known to the audience or supplemented by oral tradition, so that the rule could be properly obeyed; and, indeed, when this teaching is repeated in Deut. 22:9–11 as Moses' own, one finds that the meaning of the legal topos of *field* in this rule is in fact unfolded in several directions (v.9).[12] It is, however, to the rule prohibiting textile mixtures that special notice may be given here: for the spare and rhythmic phraseology in the priestly rule is in this one instance disrupted by a pleonastic word, *sha'atnez*, which is in asyndetic opposition to *kilayim* and clearly intended to explain it. Whether this addition is a scribal comment or the written articulation of an oral tradition, it is certain that the intrusive *sha'atnez* constituted no lexical difficulty—which it clearly did in the later deuteronomic revision of the rule, where *kilayim* is deleted and the explicatory remark "wool and flax" is now in asyndetic opposition to *sha'atnez*.

Given the expository, often revisionary nature of many deuteronomic repetitions of earlier rules, one may conclude that in this particular instance the interpretative tradition has broken into the text and
established itself as the written, revealed teaching of God to Moses.
Conceivably, it was believed that the instructive elaboration only made
explicit what the traditional rule meant all along and that there was no
intent to displace the authoritative divine voice, even though this was
itself doubly mediated through Moses' revision of the original revelation. Nevertheless, the jostling of successive cultural voices in this skein
of pentateuchal texts, and the convergence of human instruction with
divine Revelation so that the former partakes of the prestige of the
latter but also makes it viable, demonstrates a root feature and the
paradoxical task of inner biblical (as well as later Jewish) exegesis: to
extend the divine voice into historical time while reasserting and re-
establishing its hierarchical preeminence over all other cultural voices.

Such a task for legal exegesis is the ideal, of course; and it is largely
achieved in the Hebrew Bible as we have it, though often as the result
of textual finesse. A valiant tour de force in this regard occurs in a series
of exegetical revisions of the sabbatical legislation in Exod. 23:10–11,
made in order to insure its comprehensiveness and interpretability. In
vv. 10–11a the old rule states, "You shall sow your land for six years
and reap its yield, but [during] the seventh you shall let it lie fallow and
abandon it; let the poor of your nation eat thereof, and let the beast
of the field eat what they leave over." This stipulation is clearly limited
to sown fields (agriculture). But as this would hardly have proved comprehensive in ancient Israel, the divine rule is supplemented in v. 11b
by an analogical extension that includes vineyards and olive groves
(viticulture), "*You shall do likewise* to your vineyard and your olive grove."
This addendum is introduced by a technical formula (*ken ta'aseh*) frequently used for such purposes in biblical regulations.[13] But even this
extension and absorption of a human supplement into a rule with
divine authority was hardly the end of the matter: for the manner of
application is left unstated. Could one prune in the seventh year,
though not reap? or eat from the vine if one did not prune it?

Undoubtedly these and similar ambiguities were resolved by oral
exegesis, and so it is quite notable when this appears in a written form,
as in the repetition of a rule in Lev. 25:3–7, which dutifully takes up
each of the operative phrases in Exod. 23:10–11a and clarifies every
point in vv. 4–7 in the light of questions that had emerged in lawyerly

and popular circles. For example, to the original lemma concerning the sabbatical release of sown fields and vineyards it adds: "you shall not sow your field or prune your vineyard; you shall not reap the aftergrowth of your harvest or gather the grapes of your untrimmed vines." But the most striking feature of this legal explication, which is not presented as a Mosaic repetition of an earlier dictum but as an original divine prescription, is the way it obscures innovation by its syntactical incorporation of the addendum of Exod. 23:11b into its citation of v. 10 ("You shall sow your fields for six years—*and you shall prune your vineyard for six years*—and reap its yield"). Quite clearly the emphasized clause is syntactically awkward and partially redundant, but the result is quite significant, for the original addendum has been normalized and with it the technical formula "you shall do likewise" dropped. In the process, the interpretative voice has been obscured, or redignified as a divine voice. Indeed, it is largely by means of such intrusions of living legal commentary into preexistent written rules that we can to some extent monitor the dependence of the divine teachings upon their human articulation in ancient Israel and the corresponding drive for pseudepigraphic anonymity in legal exegesis. But piety aside, what interpreter could ever hope for a better "hearing" for his words than by this self-effacement, by this covertly promethean act?

Rarely does the human teacher forget and starkly betray himself in his cultural task; though one may admit that he does so in Num. 15:22–29, when, prior to a phrase-by-phrase elaboration of Lev. 4:13–21, 27–31 (e.g., compare Lev. 4:20b with Num. 15:25–26), the comment is made that the ensuing teachings are those "which YHWH spoke to Moses" (v. 22; cf. v. 23)—even though the framework of the instructions is YHWH's active command to Moses to speak the divine words to the people. Thus the teacher has doubled (and, in a sense, subverted) the levels of authority in the text by revealing that his instruction quietly extends Moses' original recitation of the divine words. Jeremiah, on the other hand, in a later expansion of the Sabbath rule in the Decalogue (Deut. 5:12–13), more deftly obscures his handiwork. This Jeremiah maneuver deserves some comment.

The terse formulation prohibiting Sabbath labor found in the Decalogue, Exod. 20:18–21, is taken over virtually verbatim in the Mosaic citation of it in Deut. 5:12–14: "Heed the Sabbath day to sanctify it—as YHWH, your God, commanded you. Six days you may labor and do all your work, but the seventh is the Sabbath of YHWH, your God: do not do any work." But even Moses' recitation of the ancient rule ("as YHWH . . . commanded you") does little to explicate the details of prohibited work—a feature which was undoubtedly clarified by the oral and interpretative tradition, and which was part of the ongoing teaching of the priests whose mandate was "to instruct the Israelites" that they separate "the sacred from the profane" (Lev. 10:10–11; cf. Mal. 2:4–7). In this respect, it is significant to note that injunctions whose language is extremely similar to that of the Decalogue in Exodus are subsequently recited with such notable additions as that one who works "will be put to death" (see Exod. 31:12–18, esp. vv. 14–15), or that the definition of prohibited work included igniting fires (Exod. 35:1–3) or ignoring Sabbath rest during peak harvest seasons (Exod. 34:21). The ongoing process of legal clarification is also evident in narratives which report divine prohibitions of food-gathering (and baking or boiling foods) or wood-gathering on the Sabbath day (Exod. 16:4–27; Num. 15:32–36); and it seems that travels for mercenary purposes or even business negotiations were strongly discouraged in later periods (Isa. 58:13).

Jer. 17:21–22 falls within this larger compass of exegetical addenda to Sabbath rules. The notable difference from earlier types of revision of the Decalogue is that this one occurs within a prophetic oracle, not in a legal or priestly teaching. Its outward form is that of Jeremiah reporting God's command to address the people at one of the central gates of Jerusalem (vv. 19–20), and then his presentation of the oracle (vv. 21–27) in the divine voice (first person)—after an introit which disclaims his own authority: "Thus says YHWH: Be heedful *and do not bear any burden [for commerce]*[14] *on the Sabbath day and bring it to the gates of Jerusalem; and do not take any burden from your homes on the Sabbath day.* Do not do any work: you shall sanctify the Sabbath day, as I commanded *your forefathers*" (vv. 21–22). A close comparison of this citation with the passage from Deut. 5:12–14 cited earlier shows that such phrases as "be heedful," "the Sabbath day," "do not do any work," "you shall sanctify the Sabbath day," and "I commanded" are directly derived from that version of the Decalogue; whereas the emphasized clauses, which are embedded within this pentateuchal citation, explicate the rules of prohibited Sabbath labor by doubly restricting them: first, by prohibiting the bearing of burdens from one's house to the gates of Jerusalem for storage or sale;[15] and, second, by prohibiting the transfer of burdens from the private to the public domain. The fact that this second prohibition so circumscribes the first as virtually to obviate it, and that it is also not mentioned in vv. 24–27, whereas the first prohibition is, may suggest that this clause restricting bearable goods to one's home on the Sabbath is a secondary addition to the oracle— much as the Septuagint inserted the post-biblical prohibition of extended Sabbath travel into its own recension of v. 21 ("and do not go out of the gates of Jerusalem").

In any event, it is not solely the oracle-form, which uses the Decalogue as the framework for its exegetical expansions, that arrests one's attention. The more remarkable fact is that the divine voice adverts to the deuteronomic text ("as I commanded your forefathers") as if to emphasize the antiquity of the prohibition. For, by this means, the divine voice speaking through Jeremiah does not just reinforce the prohibition or merely cite Deut. 5:12 ("as YHWH ... commanded you") but *uses* this quotation-tag to authorize the legal innovation and imply that the Sabbath rule now articulated—with its additions—is the very same that was taught at Sinai! The new teachings are authorized by a pseudo-citation from the Pentateuch, spoken with divine authority.

This revision of the Mosaic recitation of an earlier divine command is thus an exemplary case of the exegetical extensions some legal teachings underwent in biblical literature. They preserve the hierarchical preeminence of the divine voice at all costs. But by the very activation of the earlier source via its citation, the hermeneutical imagination at work in Jer. 17:21–22 betrays itself: its desire to prolong the divine voice into a present which presupposes the entire Sinaitic revelation, and its willingness to subordinate the human exegetical voice, whose undisguised presence would then underscore a gap in the authority of the revealed law. The paradox of the interrelatedness and interdependence of revealed Torah and interpretative tradition is, it seems to me, no more firmly expressed and repressed than in this remarkable case of inner biblical exegesis found in the ancient Book of Jeremiah.

III

We may turn again to the oracles of Jeremiah in order to appreciate another aspect of the exegetical process found in the Hebrew Bible, one which expresses new teachings by means of strategic revisions of earlier traditions, often from different genres. Indeed, these reappropriations and transformations indicate the extent to which older authorities were in the mind of later teachers and part of their imagination—suggestively radicalizing their rhetorical stance through allusions to, and departures from, inherited *logia*. Many and varied are the forms of this achievement, whose range extends from discourses and oracles on the one hand to liturgies and historiography on the other.[16] In the process, many old revelations or traditions come alive.

Our appreciation of the oracle in Jeremiah 2:3 can be enhanced by a detour through another series of exegetical transformations: those which link and divide Exod. 19:5–6 from Deut. 7:6. In the deuteronomic revision of its source we find articulated a theological characterization of Israel which is presupposed by the divine oracle expressed by Jeremiah. Significantly, the first text from Exod. 19:5–6 is cast as a revelation through Moses—before the Sinaitic revelation—that informs the people "if you heed My voice and observe My covenant then you will be My special possession among the nations . . . and My . . . holy [kadosh] nation." Quite evidently the holy status of Israel is portrayed here as contingent on covenantal obedience. Given this, Moses' later independent recitation of this speech is remarkable for its transformation of Israel's status as unqualifiedly and unconditionally holy: "For you are a holy [kadosh] people to YHWH, your God . . . [His] special people among the nations." No longer is Israel's holiness a condition dependent upon covenantal obedience. It is now the preeminent condition for Israel's obedience to the divine regulations, such as those mentioned in vv. 1–5. With this in mind, as perhaps it was in the mind of the audience that once heard Jeremiah's oration, we may turn to the oracle itself:

"Israel is consecrated [kodesh] to YHWH, the first fruits of His produce; whoever destroys him [okhelav] will be judged guilty [ye'eshamu], and evil will befall them: oracle of YHWH.

One detects here a slight discrepancy between the reference to YHWH at the outset of the oracle and the closing formula which often denotes direct speech. Either Jeremiah or his disciples obscured the authority of the *prophetic* voice by the higher authority of the divine voice speaking directly. It is also conceivable that the final quotation mark serves to indicate that the prophet spoke about God under divine inspiration and was not of himself speaking divine words. At any rate, this initial mote that sticks in our eye, suggesting a tension between tradition and innovation, enlarges to a beam as the reference to Israel's special holiness recalls the tradition found in Moses' deuteronomic speech, and we observe the new setting and imagery which has renovated it. The more complicated intertextuality of the Jeremiah oracle stands revealed, and with it a remarkable instance of exegetical revision. To be sure, we cannot gauge exactly what was known by Jeremiah's audience, but we may safely say that the prophet is utilizing the following technical piece of priestly legislation:

And if a man eats a consecrated [kodesh] donation by accident, he must add one-fifth to its value and give the consecrated item to the priest. And they [the priests] shall not allow the consecrated donation of the Israelites to be desecrated, and thereby cause them [the Israelites] to bear [their] iniquity[17] of guilt [ashmah] when they [the Israelites] eat [okhelam] their [own] consecrated donations. . .

This regulation deals with the accidental desacralization by the laity of consecrated offerings donated to the Lord for the priests. The priests are to be vigilant in this: not for their own self-interest—since they nevertheless receive the perquisite plus a penalty surcharge in case of its desecration—but for the laity's sake, for through such inadvertence they cause the people to incur guilt. And because the regulation in Lev. 22:14–16 refers to concrete cultic behavior, the terms used have concrete force: the "consecrated" donations refer specifically to those animals and products (including first fruits) mentioned in Num. 18:11–19, 25–29, especially v. 12; the "eating" thereof means just that; and the "guilt" incurred involves a fixed reparation. Not so Jer. 2:3, which clearly uses all these technical terms but transforms them in an idiosyncratic, exegetical way. Indeed, in Jeremiah's rhetoric the various terms take on a figurative, even metaphorical, aspect. Israel, the covenant people, is not only "consecrated" to the Lord but His own "first fruits"; the "eating" thereof is semantically extended to connote destruction;[18] and the "guilt" involved is not a cultic fault requiring reparation but a matter of historical accountability.

The semantic transformations in this passage thus conceal a series of analogies with the older ritual rule. Israel is the consecrated donation of YHWH, just as the cultic offerings are the consecrated donations of the lay Israelites; and Israel's destruction by enemies involves retaliatory punishments, just as the accidental desecration of donations requires retributive reparation. But of course the analogies are not all symmetrical either—and this divergence gives hermeneutical power and tension to the new declaration. While the priestly rule is concerned with ritual accidents, Jeremiah's words imply aggressive intent; while the ritual accident in the priestly rule is committed by the donor, the destruction of Israel (the "ritual object") in the prophetic oracle is by a third party; while the reparation for the cultic fault is paid by the donor to the donee, in Jeremiah's reinterpretation of it the possessor (YHWH) of the holy produce (Israel) punishes those (the nations) who desecrate it.

These various asymmetries do not subvert the rhetorical force and analogical power of the exegetical application. Indeed, the evocation of an earlier textual authority through the diction and topos chosen for this new prophetic oracle so reactivates the older language as to provide a semantic foil for its revision. A simultaneity of voices is heard—the divine voice speaking the priestly rule through Moses, and the divine voice which uses its own words as it speaks through Jeremiah—and they do not cancel each other out.

But just what is it that generates Jeremiah's exegetical revival and reapplication of a relatively obscure priestly rule? We may return to the beginning of our discussion and suggest that the reason probably lies in, and may even draw upon, the same reinterpretation of the status of Israel as "holy," reflected in the deuteronomic revision of Exod. 19:4–6 noted earlier. The topos of Israel's sanctity and covenantal guilt may have activated old priestly associations and produced an oracle that gave cultic concreteness to the notion of Israel as a holy people. In a comparable way the deuteronomic draftsman has thoroughly transformed the conditional notion of Israel being a "priestly nation" found in Exod. 19:6 when he revised in Deut. 14:1–2 a rule from Lev. 21:5–6 which prohibited priests, consecrated to holiness, to cut their skin or pull out their hair when in mourning. In the deuteronomic text the *entire* people is categorically prohibited from doing this, precisely because it is, unconditionally, "a holy nation to YHWH."

The exegetical redeployment of Lev. 22:14–16 as a metonym for all the covenantal laws may serve as a concrete instance of the strategic reemployment of one delimited textual unit within another, equally delimited one. It is one type of the *textual-exegetical thinking* found in the Hebrew Bible. A related but distinct type is found where a later voice (real or fictive) speaks to a new situation by means of a variety of textual units, which are severally activated and in some instances transformed in their new setting.

As an example, we may consider 2 Chron. 15:2–7, a speech in which one Azzariah ben Oded delivers an oracle to King Asa of Judah:

2. YHWH will be with you when you are with Him: for if you seek Him [tidreshuhu], He will be present [yimaze] to you; but if you abandon Him, He will abandon you.

3. Now for a long time Israel was without a true God, without an instructing priest and without Torah.

4. But when in distress [bazar] Israel turned [vayashav] to YHWH, God of Israel, and sought Him [vayevakshuhu], He was present [vayimaze] to them.

5. On those times there was no peace for those who went out or came in [from battle], for tremendous disturbances [mehumot rabot] assailed the inhabitants of the lands.

6. And nations and cities smashed each other to bits, for God confounded them with every distress.

7. But now: be you strong and do not slacken: for there is recompense for your deeds.

This prophetic discourse (as also the prophet in whose name it is spoken) is unknown to earlier biblical sources, and appears to reflect the pseudepigraphic handiwork of the Chronicler who has woven together several strands of tradition in order to confront his contemporary readership (in the Persian period) with a matter of "prophetic" concern to him. The piece opens and closes (vv. 2,7) with echoes of exhortation known from earlier sources ("YHWH will be with you"; "be strong") where it introduces an attempt to press someone into military or even prophetic service. But the exhortation appears here with the assertion that YHWH will be present to those who seek Him and follow his ways, so that the old military language has been thoroughly subordinated, even transformed, by being juxtaposed to spiritual-covenantal concerns—much as the similar exhortation of strength in Deut. 31:7–8 is transfigured and reinterpreted as strength for spiritual endeavors in Josh. 1:7–8, which recites the earlier speech.

But the exegetical dimensions of this speech are more ramified. At first glance the resumption of v. 2 by vv. 3–6, which describes a time when YHWH abandoned Israel because of her sins but also anticipates a return of divine presence to sincere penitents, seems to be an indeterminate rhetorical conceit. But a closer inspection of the verses suggests that the Chronicler is actually alluding to the recent exile and reminding the people that repentance may reverse the terror of divine abandonment. A striking parallel occurs in Deut. 4:29–30, a passage

also of post-exilic origin, where the Israelites are told that if they be-
seech (*uvikashtem*) and seek (*tidreshenu*) YHWH and repent (*veshavta*,
"turn") in distress (*baẓar*), He will be present to them (*umeẓa'ukha*).

To portray the physical and spiritual horrors of exile, the Chronicler surrounds v. 4 with passages from earlier oracles of doom. Thus
the Chronicler's reference in v. 5b to "tremendous disturbances" (using the rare expression *mehumot rabot*) is based on Amos 3:17. And v. 3,
"for a long time Israel was without a true God, without an instructing
priest, and without Torah," is actually an exegetical revision of Hos.
3:4, which refers to the northern exile with the words "for many days
the Israelites dwelt without a king . . . or slaughter[19] . . . or image ['*ephod*]
or household gods [*terafim*]." Like this passage, the Chronicler has Azzariah refer to "many days" in exile "without a king" and without
means of divine instruction. But instead of referring to the older cultic-
mantic means of instruction known to Hosea, the later Chronicler is
concerned to emphasize instruction by priests—though he may also
allude to the loss of the priestly tradition of mantic practice in the exile
(cf. Ezra 2:63). In any event, the Chronicler's striking revision of the
Hosean text is underscored by his reference to "Torah"—a matter un-
noted in Hos. 3:4 but of recurrent concern to later biblical historiography.[20] In the light of the impact this old oracle had on the Chronicler,
it should not pass unnoticed that the prophet Hosea closes his list of
losses with the comment: "After that the Israelites will turn [*yashuvu*]
and seek [*uvikshu*] YHWH" (v. 5). The Chronicler does likewise.

Azzariah's speech not only reuses older phrases and recontex-
tualizes them, but the very allusions of his speech evoke these older
texts and draw lines of signification out from 2 Chron. 15:2–7 to the
richer textual-traditionary mass which stands behind the latter-day exhortation. Indeed, each of the allusions is very much like a metonym
for a different lemma in the tradition, so that the speaker in the Chronicler's text is a new-old voice: a voice of the present hour, but also a
voice which verbalizes older language for the sake of the reappropriation of the tradition. The substitutions or additions in the Chronicler's
text take on added force from this point of view. For the ear which
heard or the eye which read these words would presumably perceive
in their difference from the older literary models the gap of historical
time which had intervened between the one occasion and the other;
but it would also, perhaps, have recognized the earnest concerns which
generate the textual imagination here at play. In this exegetical anthol-

ogy, as in others from the period, older textual boundaries collapse before the pressure of an appropriating voice, and the complex inter-textuality of the culture is brought to view. Here, all significant speech is Scriptural or Scripturally-oriented speech. The voices of Israel's teach-ers will struggle to speak anew in traditions and words handed down from the past: Jacob and his exegetical imagination will always be a supplanter seeking the blessing of antiquity.

IV

This brief review of inner biblical exegesis is hardly a comprehensive display of its achievement in ancient Israelite literature. It may never-theless serve to isolate some strains of this important phenomenon, and it may even suggest some strategies used for retrieving older lem-mata centuries before the emergence of classical Judaism and its forms of biblical exegesis.

One of the features that emerges prominently is the fact that for inner biblical exegesis there is no merely literary or theological play-fulness. Exegesis arises out of a practical crisis of some sort—the in-comprehensibility of a word or a rule, or the failure of the covenantal tradition to engage its audience. There is, then, something of the dy-namic of "tradition and the individual talent" here—where the tradi-tion sets the agenda of problems which must be creatively resolved or determines the received language which may be imaginatively re-worked. The strategies vary from textual annotation, literary allusion, and types of analogical or synthetic reasoning. They include also the ethical, legal or even spiritual transformation of textual content.[21] In all cases the "tradition" maintains its generative and often determinative hierarchical preeminence, even as "individual talent" (of an individual in fact, or a school representative) clarifies or transforms tradition in the light of present-day ignorance or other exigencies.

Almost invariably, moreover, in the evidence preserved, individual talent has persistently exploited the received traditional context. Thus there are virtually no generalizations, abstractions, or context-free com-ments of the kind one finds in the developed rationality of Roman and Rabbinic Law. By the same token, abstract rules for rhetoric or pro-phetic discourse are not given, nor are there collocations of similar rhetorical types as in both early and late rabbinic Midrash. Tradition is the warp and woof of creative talent, the textual content whose lexical or theological knots are exegetically unraveled, separated, or recombined. In this sense tradition is also the retextured con-text.

But, further, tradition is often presented or represented as revelation. And so, from the viewpoint of how a new teaching is authorized, the intriguing issue is not just the interdependence of the two (i.e., how a new teaching uses the tradition) but the strategic subordination of the one to the other—what we may consider under the general category of "revelation and the individual talent." Our biblical sources display a complex variety of types along a spectrum that only in part reflects historical development. In some cases, new post-Sinaitic legal revelations given to Moses add exegetical content which had emerged over time; and in other instances, exegetical addenda are interpolated into the Mosaic mediation of the divine voice (in the laws found in Exodus or Leviticus) or the double mediation of that voice (in Deuteronomy). In still other cases legal innovations are mediated through a later prophetic voice (in Jer. 17:21–22, which uses Jeremiah; or Ezek. 44:9–31, which uses Ezekiel) or introduce exegetical developments under the authoritative citation of the Torah of Moses (in Ezra 9) or more obliquely (in the complex extension of Num. 9:9–14 in 2 Chron. 30:2–3). Only in the latter cases does the exegete's voice emerge to full view—an event of real cultural consequence.

The strategic subordination of the human exegetical voice to divine revelation in the Hebrew Bible should not, however, be regarded as a case of pious fraud or political manipulation of older sources—though here and there this perspective cannot be excluded. Rather we should recognize the inevitable preeminence of the divine voice in biblical culture and realize that many legal additions, for example, made the law livable; so that an interpreter may well have often believed that his interpretation was the explicit articulation of the received content of the tradition and that individual talent was marked by its very ability to perform this feat. It even seems likely that some circles believed the legal exegetes were inspired by God to perform their task through the very study of the divine word.[22] But this is not certain. In any case, the existence of revealed texts in the mind of later prophets was certainly a catalytic factor in their production of remarkably innovative discourses. The example from Jer. 17:21–22 is not the only case in point, for one could well point to Malachi's striking reuse and inversion of the Priestly Blessing in Mal. 1:6–2:9 as an additional instance, among others.[23] The case of Azzariah ben Oded, furthermore, shows how Revelation may activate older traditions in our historio-graphical sources—although as a rule the individual talent of the historian is disguised in the oblique, but no less authoritative, voice of the historical narrator.

Whether aggressive or naive, fully self-conscious or the product of divine inspiration, textual exegeses in the Hebrew Bible oscillate between the authoritatively given lemma and its renovation through syntactic, semantic, or generic maneuvers. One may say that the entire corpus of Scripture remains open to these invasive procedures and strategic reworkings up to the close of the canon in the early rabbinic period, and so the received text is complexly compacted of teachings and their subversion, of rules and their extension, of topoi and their revision. Within ancient Israel, as long as the textual corpus remained open, Revelation and Tradition were thickly interwoven and interdependent, and the received Hebrew Bible is itself, therefore, the product of an interpretative tradition.

With the closing of the corpus of Scripture, however, and the establishment of a fixed canon deemed prior in time and authority to rabbinic exegesis, there was a tendency to forget the exegetical dimensions of Scripture and to see Scripture solely as the source and foundation of later interpretation. Religious and political reasons among the ancient Pharisees aided this forgetting; and the pseudepigraphical techniques of inner biblical exegesis have served to obscure this matter yet further. It has therefore been one aim of this essay to reverse this forgetting for the sake of a historical anamnesis. The most characteristic feature of the Jewish imagination, the interpretation and rewriting of sacred texts, thus has its origin in the occasional, unsystematized instances of exegesis embedded in the Hebrew Bible, examples of which it has been my effort to recall.

NOTES

1. For the rabbinic image of God as a scholar of Torah, see b. Berakhot 8b, 63b, and b. Avodah Zarah 3b.

2. M. Avot I, 1 and parallels, on which now see M. Herr, "Continuum in the Chain of Transmission," Zion 44 (1979), 43–56 (in Hebrew).

3. The strongest argument for formal and terminological external influence has been made by D. Daube, "Rabbinic Methods of Interpretation and Hellenistic Rhetoric," HUCA 22 (1949), 239–65, and "Alexandrian Methods of Interpretations and the Rabbis," Festschrift H. Lewald (Basel: Helbing and Lichtenholm, 1953), pp. 27–44. S. Lieberman, Hellenism in Jewish Palestine (New York: Jewish Theological Seminary, 1962), pp. 56–68, has

denied a genetic influence and restricted the borrowing to terminology. We cannot pursue the matter here.

4. Much of the ensuing discussion draws upon my *Biblical Interpretation of Ancient Israel* (Oxford: Clarendon Press, 1985), hereinafter *BIAI*. The interested reader may find there a much fuller range of textual examples and conceptual analyses. I have not at all considered the reinterpretation of prophecies in this essay; for this see *BIAI*, pt. 4.

5. See, for example, G. Fohrer, "Tradition und Interpretation im Alten Testament," *ZAW* 73 (1961), 1–30.

6. This observation was already made by Ibn Ezra.

7. See also *BIAI*, pp. 48–49, and n. 15 there.

8. Already S. D. Luzzatto, *Il Propheta Isaia, volgarizzate e commentato* (Padua: A. Bianchi, 1855), pp. 337–38.

9. See H. W. Hertzberg, "Die Nachgeschichte alttestamentlicher Texte innerhalb des Alten Testament," in *Werden und Wesen des Alten Testaments*, ed. P. Volz, F. Stummer, and J. Hempel (BZAW 66; Berlin: Töpelman, 1936), p. 114.

10. See I. L. Seeligmann, *The Septuagint Version of Isaiah: A Discussion of Its Problems* (Mededeelingen en Verhandeelingen het VoorazIatisch-Egyplisch Genootschap "Ex Oriente Lux," g; Leiden: E. J. Brill, 1948), p. 19.

11. Cf. *BIAI*, pp. 89–95.

12. Ibid., pp. 60–62.

13. Ibid., pp. 187–97.

14. For the view that the Hebrew phrase *'al tis'u* means "do not barter," see C. Tchernowitz, *Toledot ha-Halakhah* (New York, 1945–53), 3:113–17; but see my criticism, *BIAI*, p. 132 n. 73.

15. Note the more explicit language in Neh. 13:15–16, which is based on this Jeremian text.

16. See *BIAI*, pt. 3.

17. Or "bear the responsibility/penalty"; cf. W. Zimmerli's analysis of the idiom *ns' 'wn* in "Die Eigenart der prophetischen Reden des Ezechiel: Ein Beitrag zum Problem an Hand von Ez. 14:1–11," *ZAW* 66 (1954), 8–12. The following *ashmah* is thus used in a consequential sense, in addition to the more general sense of legal "guilt" (as commonly in biblical Hebrew for this and related terms).

18. Cf. Jer. 30:16.

19. Possibly read *mizbe'ah*, "slaughter-site," for *zevah*, "slaughter." Cf. the parallelism in Hos. 10:1–2.

20. Cf., for example, the revision of 1 Kings 8:25 in 2 Chron. 6:16.

21. For an analysis with examples, see *BIAI*, pp. 247–54, 425–28.

22. Overall, see ibid., pp. 528–42.

23. See my discussion in "Form and Formulation of the Biblical Priestly Blessing," *JAOS* 103.1 (1983), 115–21.

Midrash and Aggadah

JOSEPH HEINEMANN

The Nature of the Aggadah

Aggadah is inextricably bound up with the idea of speech; indeed, *Hag-gadah*, the equivalent term used by Palestinian sources, is the noun-form of the verb *le-haggid*, which means "to say" or "to tell." Yet, it is not entirely clear just how this particular name became attached to the particular type of literature to which it refers. One possible approach to this question is suggested by the fact that *le-haggid* is synonymous with *le-sapper*, "to tell or relate a story." Many aggadot do, in fact, relate stories or at least add to or elaborate the biblical narrative—many but not all. For there is certainly no lack of aggadot which are strictly ex-egetical in nature, and many of these clarify the non-narrative portions of the biblical text. Nor is there a lack of aggadot which fall into the categories of wise sayings, moral dicta or maxims, philosophical spec-ulation, and the like. Another approach to this question, that suggested by Bacher,[1] is to see the name Aggadah-Haggadah as being derived from the technical term *maggid ha-katuv* ("Scripture says"), which is frequently used in midrashic literature to introduce a quotation from Scripture. But this suggestion, too, is not totally plausible, for this term occurs principally in halachic midrashim rather than in aggadic midrashim (I shall deal with the important distinction between Halakhah and Ag-gadah below). Whereas the first approach overemphasizes the narrative aspect of Aggadah, the second approach overemphasizes its exegetical aspect. For not all Aggadah is intended to clarify Scripture, but it may include anecdotes and folktales completely unrelated to the Bible. Fur-thermore, just as not all Aggadah is Midrash, not all Midrash—the ha-lakhic midrashim, for example—is Aggadah. Perhaps the most

Editors' note: This essay forms the first chapter of Joseph Heinemann's *Aggadah and Its Development* (Hebrew) (Jerusalem: Keter, 1974). This translation was prepared by Marc Bregman in consultation with Professor Heinemann and incorporates changes made by the author shortly before his death in 1978. A translation of the entire work is in prep-aration.

convincing explanation of the name Aggadah is one that relates the name not to the contents of the Aggadah but rather to its method of transmission. While Scripture was read aloud in the synagogue from a scroll, the aggadot were not read to the people in the context of the synagogue service. Rather, the aggadic tradition was transmitted chiefly by word of mouth, that is, by being related orally in the public sermon.[2]

Just as it is difficult to reconstruct the derivation of the name Aggadah, so too is it difficult to define precisely the nature of the Aggadah. In terms of content, it includes wise sayings, expressions of faith, expositions and elaborations of Scripture, stories, and so on. Its formal patterns include epigrams, anecdotes, examples of wit and humor, terse explanations of a single word in Scripture, and stories of almost epic length. Since the Middle Ages it has been customary to define the Aggadah by what it is not, as in this statement ascribed to R. Samuel ha-Nagid: "Haggadah is all commentary in the Talmud that deals with something other than *mizvah* [here in the sense of Jewish law]."[3] This definition is, of course, overly restrictive, for aggadot are found not only in the Talmud but first and foremost in the various works of midrashic literature. Second, as we have noted above, not all aggadot can be categorized as exegetical commentary. Nevertheless, to this day no more precise formulation has been found than to define Aggadah as that multifaceted type of material found in talmudic-midrashic literature which does not fall into the category of Jewish law (i.e., Halakhah).[4] The chief defect of this negative form of definition is, of course, that it conveys no positive information about the nature and character of what it seeks to define.

Aggadah, in all its rich variety of form and content, is, we may affirm, by and large the product of the Jewish community in Palestine. As far back as the middle of the Second Temple period, after the conquest of Palestine by Alexander the Great, the Aggadah began to take shape and continued to be a living literary form for more than a millennium, at least until the Arab conquest of Palestine.[5] To a certain extent, the Aggadah represents a creative reaction to the upheavals suffered by Israel in their land during this long period. It also represents an attempt to develop new methods of exegesis designed to yield new understandings of Scripture for a time of crisis and a period of conflict, with foreign cultural influence pressing from without and sectarian agitation from within. This period demanded a response to the crises brought about by historical events, foremost the destruction of Jerusalem and its Temple and the total loss of political independence. This complex of spiritual, political, and national challenges required constant grappling with problems and taking new stands suited to present needs. The Jewish people sought, successfully, to continue living according to the dictates of the Torah. To achieve this, it was necessary that the Torah remain dynamic and open to varying interpretation in order to meet the challenges of drastically varying circumstances. By developing a method of "creative exegesis" the aggadists were able to find in Scripture—which might otherwise have come to seem irrelevant to contemporary needs—the new answers and values which made it possible to grapple with the shifts and changes of reality.

The Aggadah, as we have noted, has many facets. In terms of content, we can categorize aggadot into three broad types: 1) aggadot that are inextricably related to the biblical narrative—the bulk of the aggadot in talmudic-midrashic literature falls into this category; 2) "historical" aggadot which tell of post-biblical personalities and events, and 3) "ethical-didactic" aggadot which offer guidance and outline principles in the area of religious and ethical thought. Such a categorization is unavoidable for there is certainly a qualitative difference between a legend about the life of Abraham and a story about Hillel or Rabbi Akiba, just as there is a fundamental difference between a tale about a woman who caused the death of her sons by rashly making a vow and aphorisms of the type found in Mishnah Avot (also known as "The Sayings of the Fathers"): "If I am not for myself who will be for me . . . and if not now when" (I 14), or "All is foreseen, but one is given freedom of choice" (III 15).

However neither the names nor the boundaries of these categories are entirely fixed. If we refer to a legend about the Emperor Titus or about the sage Hillel as a "historical aggadah," we must not forget that what we call "biblical aggadah" also tells of historical figures such as King David and the prophet Isaiah. On the other hand, we must not be deceived into thinking that what the sages relate about their own contemporaries is real history; the "tales of the sages" must also be considered aggadic legend and not reliable historical information. The story of the miracles that occurred during the debate between R. Eliezer and his colleagues and the Heavenly Voice that finally decided the issue is as much a part of aggadic legend as is the aggadah which determines that Nahshon was the first Israelite to plunge into the Red Sea. All of these legends arise out of the same motivations, and the same creative imagination is at work in all of them. It is preferable, therefore, when we refer to "the tales of the sages," that we speak of them not as "historical aggadot" but rather as "non-biblical" aggadot.

The term "ethical-didactic" aggadot is also somewhat misleading, for it seems to imply that biblical aggadot and tales of the sages have no moral intent. The opposite is true; aggadot of all types are generally intended to teach some lesson. This function is not limited to any particular category; rather, the uniqueness of the "ethical-didactic" aggadot lies in the fact that the didactic message is stated explicitly rather than conveyed implicitly through a story or attached to a biblical verse by way of proof.

Ultimately, this suggested categorization of aggadot into three types is insufficient. To which category do those parables belong which do not serve to clarify a difficult verse? What of anecdotes and folktales which are not about historical figures, such as the stories of riddles which show the wisdom of the "four Jerusalemites who came to Athens"? And even with the addition of these minor categories we have still not exhausted the great variety of material found in the Aggadah. It is of course possible to do without any categorization according to contents. We could categorize aggadot according to their form and literary-aesthetic means of expression or make our primary distinction between folk Aggadah and homiletic or scholarly Aggadah. This latter category would contain those aggadot created by the sages within the context of the study-houses and academies. These typologies are also legitimate, but none of them covers all the many manifestations of what we call the Aggadah.

Even the aggadot that are related to the Bible are not homogeneous, for they consist of both strict explication of the biblical text and expansive elaboration of biblical stories. Moreover, both these subcategories address themselves to their own time no less than to that of the Bible. Biblical Aggadah seeks to be contemporary or topical, to reveal the image of its own age in the ancient Scriptures. Already in the Septuagint, for example, "Aram before and Philistines behind" (Isa. 9:11) were identified with "the Syrians on the east and the Hellenes on the west." Similarly, we find an interpretation of "So I will stir them to jealousy with those who are no people" (Deut. 32:21) as referring to the Samaritans in Ben Sirah (50:25–26): "With two nations my soul is vexed and the third is no people, the dwellers in Seir and Philistia and the foolish nation that lives in Shechem." The prophecy "a star shall come forth out of Jacob and a specter shall rise out of Israel" (Num. 24:17) was generally given a messianic interpretation, as in Targum Pseudo-Jonathan. However, the Dead Sea Sect interpreted this verse as referring to their "Interpreter of the Law," and Christianity interpreted it as referring to Jesus, while R. Akiba interpreted as follows: "A star [kokhav] shall come forth out of Jacob—Kozba [Bar Kokhbah] has come forth out of Jacob . . . this is he, the king messiah!" (P. Ta'anit IV 8, 68d).[6] Moreover, there are many aggadot which in discussing events historically connected with the destruction of the First Temple, such as the legend about Zechariah's blood (see B. Sanhedrin 96b and parallels), are in fact implicitly commenting on the destruction of the Second Temple.

Biblical Aggadah, however, does not deal exclusively with exegesis. It also expands and elaborates the biblical narrative. The Aggadah tells of Satan's provocation of God that led to Isaac's almost being sacrificed, of Moses' wisdom and heroism as the commander of the army of Ethiopia, of the argument between Cain and Abel over the division of the world between them that led to Abel's murder, and of the altercation between Moses and the angels that took place when Moses ascended to heaven to receive the Torah. In fact there is almost no biblical story that did not undergo aggadic amplification and no biblical figure whose character is not portrayed more fully in the Aggadah. And we must speak not only of amplification but also of alteration. The biblical King David, the heroic fighter, bears little resemblance to the wise and pious David of the Aggadah, who day and night studies Torah. Esau is portrayed in the Aggadah as the utterly wicked enemy of Jacob from their mother's womb—indeed, he is made to symbolize Rome, "the wicked kingdom," and the strife between Israel and the oppressive Roman rulers. And, though the Bible makes it perfectly clear that Moses died just like any other human being, according to the Aggadah, "there are those who say" that Moses did not die but ascended to heaven where he now serves (Sifre to Deuteronomy, 357).

There were also many changes in matters of theology. The verse "Who is like Thee, O Lord, among the gods [ba'elim]" (Exod. 15:11) was interpreted by the sages as reading: " 'Who is like Thee among the mute [ba-'illemim]': for He sees His Temple in ruins and remains silent" (B. Gittin 56b and additional texts). This interpretation reflects a burning theological question: "His children are put in neck-irons—where is His might?" (ibid.). This could only be answered with the idea that divine silence and restraint was in itself a manifestation of God's might, for "Who is mighty? He who subdues his nature" (M. Avot IV 1). In the light of present suffering, it was impossible to hang on to the naive belief that no evil shall befall the righteous man and that he shall be rewarded for his good deeds in this life. The sages did not hesitate to reinterpret, in a spirit contrary to the simple, literal meaning, verses which gave expression to this belief. For example, "He has given sustenance [teref] to those who fear Him; He will ever be mindful of His Covenant" (Ps. 111:5) was reinterpreted by R. Joshua ben Levi: "He has given exile [teruf] to those who fear Him in this world; but in the world to come, 'He will be mindful of His covenant.' " (Genesis Rabbah XL 2). In the wake of the destruction of the Temple and the cessation of the sacrificial cult, which had been Israel's means of atonement, the masters of the Aggadah declared, "we have one means of atonement which is comparable. And what is it? It is deeds of loving-kindness" (Avot de-Rabbi Natan, ver. A, chap. 4). The Aggadah sees the central message of the biblical story of the sacrifice of Isaac not in Abraham's submissiveness to the will of God, but in Isaac's acceptance of martyrdom in allowing himself to be sacrificed. This new interpretation and emphasis of Isaac's role provided an example to Jews of the rabbinic period, many of whom were called upon to choose between martyrdom and apostasy during times of religious persecution.

Another sociohistorical change reflected in the Aggadah is in the concept of religious leadership. The Bible knows of two basic types: the priest, who represented the religious establishment, and the charismatic prophet. But by the talmudic period prophecy had long since ceased, and the power and importance of the priesthood decreased drastically, at least following the destruction of the Temple. Both these types of religious leader were replaced by the sage, the master of Torah. It is not surprising, then, that the aggadists should have sought within the Bible itself some authorization for this new type of leadership. R. Akiba, for example, employed his hermeneutic principle that every *et* (the sign of the direct object in Hebrew) in the biblical text implies or implicitly allows a midrashic amplification, to give a daring reinterpretation of the verse " 'Thou shalt fear [*et*] the Lord, thy God' (Deut. 10:20): *et*—to include the sages" (B. Pesaḥim 22b).

The Aggadah contains materials of a widely different nature which originated in highly distinct ways. On the one hand, there is no doubt that many aggadot are the creation of popular or folk imagination; this category includes particularly parables, anecdotes, and expanded stories of heroism of biblical figures, which ultimately found their way into apocryphal literature and rabbinic legend. Moreover, many aggadot were created by the authors and compilers of the apocrypha and other books written during the Second Temple period. These works include a literary genre that belongs entirely within the realm of the Aggadah, the rewritten biblical narrative. This type of Aggadah, which reworks the basic biblical stories adding many elaborations and alterations, is illustrated by the Book of Jubilees and the fragments of the Genesis Apocryphon discovered among the Dead Sea Scrolls.

My concern here, however, is dealing primarily with aggadot from talmudic and midrashic literature. Though this literature certainly absorbed much material which originated in the contemporaneous folk culture, rabbinic Aggadah itself is no longer the product of that culture but rather is the work of the sages themselves. The aggadot developed by them are not designed principally for entertainment but have a strong and self-conscious didactic function. Yet rabbinic aggadot were for the most part intended for the simple folk and were imparted to them in the public sermon. For this reason the sages utilized every sort of literary and rhetorical technique to make this material attractive and compelling to their audience.[7] Rabbinic Aggadah tends, therefore, not so much to relate stories as it intends to clarify Scripture and to draw from it some moral point. Indeed, it is for the most part inextricably tied to the biblical text, though this does not prevent it from reinterpreting Scripture, deriving new meanings from the ancient texts, and finding new morals to biblical stories. Thus, the bulk of talmudic-midrashic Aggadah does not stand by itself but rather serves the Bible, explicating and elaborating it, and also adapting it, as I have said, to present needs. For this reason rabbinic aggadot generally did not take the form of epic stories or extensive independent works. Since these rabbinic aggadot were most often told during the public homily which was linked to the reading of the scriptural lesson in the synagogue, they were automatically related to the relevant biblical stories. And thus the rabbinic aggadists saw no need to cast their expositions and comments in the form of complete, continuous stories, nor did they tend to retell the biblical stories themselves after the fashion of some of the apocryphal literature mentioned above. The sages were content to create a basically exegetical type of Aggadah and to allow the Bible itself to provide both narrative continuity and basic background. Their exegetical annotations, whether long or short, serve mostly to clarify, embellish, and enrich the biblical narrative. And so the Aggadah is, in its own words, "the delightful part of biblical interpretation" (Ecclesiastes Rabbah II 8).

The sages who created and developed the Aggadah took upon themselves a double task. On the one hand, since they assumed that the meaning of Scripture was manifold, they felt it was necessary to try to extract the full range of implications not only from the contents of the biblical text but from every apparently superfluous word as well. The assumption that "one biblical statement may carry many meanings" (B. Sanhedrin 34a) led to their interpretation of every locution in the biblical text, often in disregard of its meaning in context. The sages' commitment to discover all the ramified teaching concealed in Scripture[8] finds expression in their dictum: "Interpret and receive reward!"[9] They were of the opinion that the Bible intended to impart moral and religious instruction, to teach us how to live, rather than to supply dry factual information of a geographical or genealogical nature, for example. Indeed, they express surprise at verses which seem to supply merely historical information: " 'I also gathered for myself silver and gold' (Ecc. 2:8). Does the verse merely inform us of Solomon's wealth?! Rather, the scriptural passage refers to words of Torah! [i.e., to Solomon's vast learning]" (Ecclesiastes Rabbah II 8). And another example of this attitude: " 'Go up into this mountain of Avarim' (Num. 27:12), in another place you call it the mountain and the top of the peak, and so the same place is called by four names ... What need have men of this [information]?" (Sifre Zuta, p. 318). When one finds lists of geographical names such as "and Kinah and Dimonah and Adadah" (Josh. 15:22), it is not good enough to state that Scripture merely "lists the cities of the land of Israel." Rather, these names are to be creatively interpreted in order to derive from them a moral lesson: "everyone who has anger [kinah] against his fellowman and keeps silent [domem], the One who inhabits eternity [ade ad] brings him to justice" (B. Gittin 7a). Similarly, concerning the Book of Chronicles, which is largely taken up with lists of names and genealogical tables, the sages asserted: "the Book of Chronicles was given only to be [creatively] interpreted" (Leviticus Rabbah I 3).

On the other hand, while the rabbinic creators of the Aggadah

looked back into Scripture to uncover the full latent meaning of the
Bible and its wording, at the same time they looked forward into the
present and the future. They sought to give direction to their own
generation, to resolve their religious problems, to answer their theological questions, and to guide them out of their spiritual perplexities.
Yet the sages also based this second aspect of their task on scriptural
interpretation, for they believed that the Bible provided the answer—
if not explicitly, then implicitly—to every contemporary problem.[10]
Thus, most aggadot have two levels of meaning, one overt and the
other covert.[11] The first deals openly with the explication of the biblical
text and the clarification of the biblical narrative, while the second deals
much more subtly with contemporary problems that engaged the attention of the homilists and their audience. The aggadists who tell of
Koraḥ, the rebellious Levite, and his followers (see Num. 16, etc.), refer,
in reality, to the "scoffers of this generation" who despise the sages
and their teachings. The rabbis discuss Noah's coming out of the ark,
but the discussion implicitly presents differing attitudes toward the
liberation of Israel from foreign oppression: "Noah said, Just as I entered the ark only with permission [from God] so I will not come out
except with permission. R. Judah bar Illai said, If I had been there, I
would have broken it [the ark] and come out" (Genesis Rabbah XXXIV
4). Much of aggadic exegesis is, therefore, a kind of parable or allegory.
The aggadists do not mean so much to clarify difficult passages in the
biblical text as to take a stand on the burning questions of the day, to
guide the people and to strengthen their faith. But since they addressed
themselves to a wide audience—including simple folk and children—
they could not readily formulate the problems in an abstract way, nor
could they give involved, theoretical answers. In order to present their
ideas in a more comprehensible and engaging fashion, the sages cast
them in a narrative format and employed parables and other familiar
literary means which appeal to all.

Nevertheless, Aggadah can, in a way, be seen as the "philosophical
literature" of the rabbinic period, though the characteristics which
prompt such a view take the form of popular philosophy which avoids
theoretical, systematic discussions and austerely abstract formulations.
Such more purely philosophical characteristics are found indeed
among the "sayings of the sages," usually manifest in the form of principles set forth in an aphoristic, pithy style. These principles take a
different form in the two other types of Aggadah, that which expounds

the biblical narrative and that which tells of the lives of the sages themselves. Here, these philosophical principles and their actual meaning are generally not stated explicitly. Rather, they must be "read between the lines"; they may be inferred from the descriptive approach employed and from the general picture which emerges from these stories as told or retold by the sages of the Aggadah.

Aggadah ("lore") and Halakhah ("law") are two facets of the intellectual and spiritual work of the sages of the talmudic period. Though we must not ignore the qualitative difference between the Aggadah and the Halakhah, there is certainly a close link between these two patterns of rabbinic creativity. On the one hand the same sages who were most famous as creators and transmitters of Halakhah were also aggadists and homilists and there were very few Amoraim (at least in Palestine) who limited themselves exclusively to either Halakhah or Aggadah. Moreover, these two types of thinking are found together in intimate coexistence both in the two Talmudim and in the halakhic midrashim. Indeed, a talmudic discussion often inadvertently slips from rigorously analytical argumentation on some halakhic point into the lighter and more emotionally appealing aggadic mode of discourse. By the same token, Halakhah is not absent even from the most strictly aggadic midrashim. In some of them, the Tanḥuma-Yelammedenu Midrashim, for example, each section generally begins with an halakhic question, such as: "Let our master teach us [yelammedenu rabbenu]: If a court imposed a fast on the public in order to bring rain, and rain fell during that very day, must they carry on [with their fast until the end of the day]?" (Tanḥuma, ed. Buber, vol. 1, p. 94). Immediately following this question and a short answer concerning the halakhic point, the homilist develops an aggadic discussion which leads to the subject of the biblical pericope read on that day. It is not surprising that these aggadic midrashim, which derive their material principally from homilies which were preached before a general audience, deal with Halakhah only in passing. For the audience that rushed to hear the public sermon would not have been prepared to listen to involved, abstract halakhic discussions, which to them would have seemed dry and tiresome. This attitude on the part of the lay public is reflected in the comment of R. Isaac, who was also a famous homilist: "Formerly, when there was money about, a man would crave to hear a word of Mishnah and a word of Talmud, but now that there's no money about and, moreover, we suffer from [foreign] rule a man craves to hear a word of Scripture and a word of Aggadah" (Pesikta de-Rav Kahana Ba-Ḥodesh, ed. Mandelbaum, p. 205).

In terms of their essential subject matter as well, there is a reciprocal relationship between Halakhah and Aggadah—a relationship which was described and illustrated with penetrating insight by H. N. Bialik.[12] Aggadic thinking nourishes the Halakhah, and Halakhah, in turn, gives Aggadah a kind of permanency by evolving from it legal norms, that is, permanent patterns and life forms. Thus, several halakhic points were determined on the basis of the aggadic principle that "all the people of Israel are of royal birth" (B. Baba Meẓi'a 113b). Similarly, the Amora Rav grants to the Jewish day laborer the unilateral right to retract from his contract with the employer: "A worker may quit even in the middle of the day . . . [as may be shown from what is written in Scripture] 'For to Me the people of Israel are servants; they are My servants' (Lev. 25:55)—and they are not the servants of servants" (B. Baba Meẓi'a 10a). Moreover, in the Mishnah itself, which deals entirely with strict matters of Halakhah—apart from the tractate Avot—aggadic comments are occasionally woven into the fabric of the halakhic context. For example, in Mishnah Sanhedrin, which deals principally with capital crimes and the manner of executing the various death penalties, we find aggadic gems:

How does one make witnesses in capital cases aware of the seriousness of their testimony? . . . Know that civil cases are not like capital cases: In civil cases a man [who gives false testimony in order to condemn the innocent] makes monetary restitution and thereby atones for himself [i.e., for the damage which his false testimony has done]. In capital cases—his blood and the blood of his offspring [i.e., of the innocent man who was wrongly condemned to death] are on him [i.e., on the hands of the false witness] until the end of time . . . For this reason, man was first created in a single individual, to teach you that anyone who causes one person[13] to perish, Scripture considers him as if he had caused the whole world to perish. And in order to promote peace among men, so that no man shall say to his fellow: [my] father was greater than your father. And so that the sectarians shall not [have cause to] say: there are many powers in heaven . . . Therefore every one is obligated to say: The world was created for my sake. (M. Sanhedrin IV 5)

Nevertheless, there is also a great distance between the world of the Aggadah and that of the Halakhah. The latter is compared to bread and the former to wine: " 'They shall flourish like grain' (Hos. 14:8) this refers to Talmud, 'and blossom like the vine' (ibid.) this refers to Aggadah" (Leviticus Rabbah I 2). Talmud, that is, Halakhah, is characterized as man's chief nourishment without which existence is impossible; but, like wine, Aggadah "wears a smile" (Pesikta de-Rav Kahana, Ba-Ḥodesh, p. 223). Similarly, the sages interpreted "'the kidney fat of wheat' (Deut. 32:14)—these are halakhot, which are the substance of Torah; 'and of the blood of the grape' (ibid.)—these are haggadot, which captivate the heart of man like wine" (Sifre to Deuteronomy, 317). Man does not live by bread alone; wine has something that bread lacks—there is no joy without wine and one does not sing songs except over wine.[14] And indeed, Aggadah is "song"; it is poetic creation which has a vitality and a liveness which elevates and inspires the soul. Aggadic creativity partakes of the power of productive imagination; it embodies not only religious and moral values, but also artistic and aesthetic values of beauty and symmetry.

Not all the sages of the Halakhah were entirely at ease with the fertile imagination exhibited in the Aggadah. This reservation, which however was expressed by only a few of the greatest Amoraim particularly in Babylonia, is by and large a reaction to the large measure of freedom that the aggadist permitted himself. He is accused of saying "whatever occurs to him and whatever he perceives in his mind" (Mevo Ha-Talmud, ascribed to Samuel ha-Nagid). Similarly, "notions derived from scriptural passages that are called Midrash and Aggadah are largely conjecture; there are some which are so and some which are not" (Rav Sherira Gaon).[15] The aggadists are said to "invert and re-invert [the meaning of] the verses"; they interpret one way and then the exact opposite "and we learn nothing from it" (P. Ma'aserot III, end, 51a). "Halakhot and legal traditions, these are the fine flour [solet], and the words of the haggadot—refuse [pesolet]" (R. Samuel ben Ḥofni).[16] Unlike the teachers of the Halakhah, who transmit basic legal traditions which they personally received from their own teachers thus creating a reliable chain of tradition linking one generation to the next, the teachers of the Aggadah are not limited to transmitting what they heard from their own teachers. The aggadist adds, deviates from, changes, or permutes the traditions he has received according to his own devices and the dictates of his own will, and no one (for the most part) takes him to task. Moreover, whereas halakhic discussion and argument over opposing traditions are directed to one aim—clarifying the matter under discussion until it is possible to make a single legal ruling that is authoritative—in the Aggadah there is no ruling that decides among the various opinions. Furthermore, the pronouncements of earlier authorities do not necessarily carry more weight than those of later authorities; "for aggadic comments are unlike legal traditions; rather, each one interprets according to the dictates of his own heart, that is, what might be or could be said and it is not a conclusive statement. Therefore, one may not base [legal decisions] on them [i.e., on aggadic comments]" (R. Hai Gaon, in Oẓar Ha-Ge'onim, Ḥagigah, p. 59). And even concerning principles of faith—except for the most fundamental principles such as the belief that there is but one God and that the Torah represents His word—we find extreme differences of opinion; for example, whether or not there is recompense in this life for the observance of the commandments (B. Kiddushin 39b)[17] and whether the final redemption will occur at a predetermined date or whenever Israel will be truly and totally repentant (B. Sanhedrin 97b; P. Ta'anit I 1, 63d).[18] Indeed, the very belief in the coming of the messiah was open to question to such an extent that the Amora R. Hillel went so far as to claim: "Israel will have no messiah, for they have already enjoyed him [i.e., he already came] in the days of Hezekiah" (B. Sanhedrin 99a).[19]

Unlike the fixed and reliable Halakhah, which reaches unequivocal decisions as to both general rules and specific issues, Aggadah, as a way of thinking, is fluid and open; the wellsprings of its innovative vigor and its spirit of independent creativity were never blocked off. Moreover, alongside the Aggadah of the sages, folk Aggadah continued to develop and flourish. There was also a proliferation of aggadot originating in sectarian circles—sects which were rightly considered a threat to the very existence of Judaism. It is no wonder then that occasionally an extremely negative view was taken of this sort of Aggadah—particularly that found in some of the apocryphal literature. For example: "One who writes down Haggadah will have no share in the world to come, one who preaches it will be singed [in the fires of gehenna] and one who listens to it will receive no reward" (P. Shabbat XVI 1, 15c).[20]

This opposition is directed primarily against the writing down of aggadot, for by being recorded in graphic form they take on an authoritative character which by their true nature they do not possess. For the creation of Aggadah is fundamentally oral in character. It was related primarily within the context of the public homily, which was preached every sabbath, in every locality. The oral transmission of the Aggadah also preserved its vitality. For the homilist does not merely recite exactly what he heard. Rather, he adapts the material to the requirements of his homily and to the needs of his audience. In this way the Aggadah remains flexible, dynamic, and relevant to its own time. This aspect is reflected in the midrashic comment of R. Eleazar ben Azariah. Though he refers to "words of Torah" in general, his comment is an apt description of the multifaceted nature of the Aggadah:

"The words of the wise are like goads and like nails well planted" (Ecc. 12:11). Why are words of Torah compared to a goad? To tell you, just as the goad directs the heifer along its furrow in order to bring forth life to the world, so words of Torah direct the heart of those who study them from the paths of death and unto the path of life. But, you might think, that just as the goad is movable [and liable to change], so words of Torah are liable to change? So Scripture adds "like nails." But, you might think, that just as the nail [neither] decreases nor increases, so words of Torah [neither]²¹ decrease nor increase. So Scripture adds "well planted." Just as the plant grows and increases, so words of Torah grow and increase. (B. Ḥagigah 3b).

Translated by Marc Bregman

NOTES

1. Wilhelm Bacher, *Die exegetische Terminologie der jüdischen Traditionsliteratur* (Leipzig: J. C. Hinrichs, 1905), pp. 33–37.

2. See Yom-Tov L. Zunz and Chanoch Albeck, *Ha-Derashot be-Yisrael* (Jerusalem: Mossad Bialik, 1954), p. 250, no. 1; Elimelech Epstein (A. A.) Halevi, *Sha'arei ha-Aggadah* (Tel Aviv: Dvir, 1972), p. 2.

3. Mevo Ha-Talmud, ascribed to R. Samuel Ha-Nagid (printed in most editions of the Babylonian Talmud after Tractate Berakhot).

4. See S. Assaf and E. E. Urbach, "Aggadah," *Ha-Encyclopedia ha-Ivrit* vol. 1 (Jerusalem and Tel Aviv: Encyclopaedia Publishing, 1966), p. 353: "It is common practice to give a negative description of the Aggadah: that part of the Oral Torah which is not Halakhah."

5. Halevi, *Sha'arei ha-Aggadah*, pp. 4ff.

6. Cf. Lamentations Rabbah, ed. Buber, to Lam. 2:2 (p. 191) and see G. Vermes, "The Qumran Interpretation of Scripture in its Historical Setting," *The Annual of the Leeds University Oriental Society* 6 (1969), 91ff.; F. F. Bruce, *Biblical Exegesis in the Qumran Texts* (London: Tyndal Press, 1960), pp. 50ff.

7. Joseph Heinemann, *Derashot beẓibbur be-Tekufat ha-Talmud* (Jerusalem: Mossad Bialik, 1970), pp. 10ff.

8. See Isaak Heinemann, *Darkhei ha-Aggadah* (Givatayim: Magnes and Massada, 1970), pp. 9ff.

9. "Are then interpretations [*midrashot*] plain truth [*amanah*]?! Interpret and receive reward," P. Nazir VII 2, 56b according to the reading of R. Isaiah ha-Aharon (circa 1500 C.E.); see also Saul Lieberman, *Shki'in*, 2d ed. (Jersualem: Wahrmann, 1970), pp. 81–82.

10. Note the admonition of Ben Bagbag: "Turn it over [the Torah] and turn it over again, for everything is in it" (M. Avot V 22).

11. See Halevi, *Sha'arei ha-Aggadah*, p. 10.

12. Chaim Nachman Bialik, *Halachah and Aggadah*, trans. L. Simon (London: Education Department of the Zionist Federation of Great Britain and Ireland, 1944).

13. Concerning the variant reading, "causes one person *from Israel*," see E. E. Urbach, "Kol Ha-Mekayyem Nefesh Aḥat," *Tarbiẓ* 40 (1971), 268ff. and the literature cited there.

14. Cf. Abraham Joshua Heschel, *Theology of Ancient Judaism* (Hebrew), vol. 1 (London and New York: Soncino, 1962), pp. 11ff.

15. See Isaac Weiss, *Dor Dor ve-Dorshav* (Vilna: Romm, 1904), pt. 4, p. 152; Moshe David Herr, "Mahutah Shel ha-Aggadah," *Maḥanayyim* 100 (1966), 63ff.

16. See Simcha Assaf, *Tekufat ha-Ge'onim ve-Sifrutah* (Jerusalem: Mossad Bialik, 1955), p. 283.

17. See E. E. Urbach, *The Sages: Their Concepts and Beliefs*, trans. Israel Abrahams (Jerusalem: Magnes, 1975), pp. 441ff.

18. Ibid., p. 683.

19. Ibid., p. 681.

20. See Louis Ginzberg, *Al Halakhah ve-Aggadah* (Tel Aviv: Dvir, 1960), pp. 220, 295, n. 3.

21. The text of the Babylonian Talmud has been emended according to the reading of Tosefta Sotah VII 11, ed. Lieberman, p. 194.

JUDAH GOLDIN

The Freedom and Restraint
of Haggadah

Saul Lieberman in memoriam

Kamah Gedolim Divrei Ḥakhamim

Again and again when the principal components of the Oral Law are listed or described in midrashic-talmudic literature, three terms are employed: *midrash, halakhot, aggadot.* This then is the formal curriculum of the academy. For example:[1] "A man is duty bound to provide for himself [= to acquire] a master (*rav*) for his advanced learning (*le-ḥokh-mah*), so that he might learn from him midrash, [the] halakhot, and [the] aggadot." Although the following is apparently not unanimous,[2] it is nevertheless strongly urged that it is best to cover the whole curriculum with a single teacher, so that "the interpretation (*ta'am*) which the teacher neglected to tell him in the study of midrash, he will eventually tell him in the study of the halakhot; the interpretation which he neglected to tell him in study of the halakhot, he will eventually tell him in the study of aggadah. Thus that man remains in one place and is filled with good and blessing" (i.e., has profited).[3] Perhaps the passage is intended to emphasize how one becomes someone's disciple, not just an occasional or itinerant student.

At all events, midrash, the halakhot, and the aggadot are the three parts of the Oral Law, or Mishnah, its overall name.[4] Sometimes we read of only halakhot and haggadot;[5] sometimes—but not at all frequently—the word *haggadah* seems to stand simply for interpretation of a verse not necessarily haggadic;[6] sometimes the reference may be haggadic but is a simple interpretation of a text.[7] But the standard formula, inventory, stereotype (call it what you will) is midrash, halakhot, and aggadot—midrash being what is legitimately derivative from study

57

and interpretation of the Scriptures, and also analysis and exposition of teachings; halakhot, those handed-down halakhic rulings formulated and assembled independently, very likely apodictically, unaccompanied by the biblical interpretation to which they may be related, or even hanging by a hair for lack of almost any biblical association; and finally haggadot, which is still best defined as non-halakhic discourse and instruction.

The fact that in these formulations haggadah or haggadot is mentioned last, after midrash and halakhot, is not necessarily an indication that haggadah is least important. When you have a number of items to list, one item is inevitably first and the others are not first. But there is much to justify the view that haggadah was truly not the major course in the bet ha-midrash. Regardless of what variation we meet, haggadah is never mentioned first in the academic curriculum. And, interestingly, in the midrash,[8] a second-generation Palestinian amora, R. Isaac,[9] speaks of men whose ambition it is to be known as bar hilkhan (expert of halakhot like those in the Mishnah and baraitot), as bar mekh'ila (expert in the halakhic midrashim), as bar ulpan (as talmudic expert), but makes no mention of bar aggadeta, of anyone with ambitions for the reputation as haggadah master. And yet there are sages in amoraic times famous as haggadic experts: R. Simeon bar Yehozadak (third-generation amora) puts a question to R. Samuel bar Nahman, Because I've heard of you that you are a ba'al haggadah, a haggadic master;[10] R. Joshua ben Levi of the third century is known as baki be-aggadah, a know-it-all of haggadah,[11] although on his own he is unable to explain why, in the Exodus version of the Ten Commandments, in the commandment to honor father and mother it is not said "so that it will go well with thee," while in the Deuteronomy version it is said. And there are of course the rabbanan de-aggadeta!

The serious or, let us say, properly trained talmid hakhamim student-scholar, or full-fledged hakham teacher-authority, is one who is master of all three parts of the Oral Law. When you wish to compliment him (even allowing for bouquets of hyperbole, probably after his lifetime), you say (as was said of Yohanan ben Zakkai), "He did not neglect Scripture or Mishnah, Talmud (= Midrash), Halakhah, Aggadah" (and so on: "Toseftot, the subtleties of Scripture or the subtleties of the Scribes, or any of the Sages' rules of interpretation—not a single thing in the Torah did he neglect to study)."[12] Anyway, first and foremost talmud (i.e., midrash, as we have said), halakhot, and aggadot. The tribute in the Talmud[13] is even more florid, but the tripod on which the Oral Law stands is not affected.

And so too, when you undertake to console a man for the loss of his son (as it happens, once again involving Yoḥanan ben Zakkai), if you're gifted you say, "So too, my Master, you had a son who studied Scripture—Pentateuch, Prophets, and the Writings—and studied the Oral Law (mishnah), midrash [so read!], halakhot, and aggadot."[14]

More remains to be said of our theme, but it will not be intelligible unless we first jet (so to speak) over almost five to eight hundred years.[15] In the tenth century we hear from Saadia Gaon of Sura (882–942), *ein somekhin al divrei aggadah*, one may not invoke haggadic sayings as support for certain views. And in the latter half of that century Sherira Gaon of Pumbedita (968–998) in his personal notes, similarly, with a brief addition: "the derivations from verses of Scripture which are called midrash and aggadah, are mere guesses (*umdana*) . . . hence *ein somekhin al aggadah*, one may not invoke haggadic sayings as support, *amru ein lemedin*[16] *min ha-aggadah*, and it's been said [literally, "they said"; who?], One may not derive (*lemedin*, precedents or rules) from the aggadot. . . . Those of them that can be rationally (*min ha-sekhel*) or biblically confirmed we shall accept, for there is no end or limit to the aggadot." And in the eleventh century, his son Hai Gaon (998–1038), commenting on the treatise Ḥagigah (presumably on a passage on 14a) writes emphatically: "Know ye [or know thou] that aggadic sayings are not like a received tradition (*ha-shemu'ah*); they are simply what an individual expresses [teaches, *doresh*] of what occurs to him personally— [such as] 'it is like, it is possible, one may say'—it is not a clear-cut [decisive, *ḥatukh*] statement; and that is why they enjoy no authority [*ein somekhin aleihen*] . . . these midrashic views are neither a received tradition nor a halakhic ruling; they are no more than perhapses."

Note that the formula *ein somekhin al ha-aggadah* has already become a refrain, repeated virtually verbatim, and this will continue down to the twentieth century when a most exacting scholar, the late Saul Lieberman, will legitimately summon the same words (of course citing the Geonim) to establish that in a disputation the saintly Naḥmanides, *peh kadosh*, was not speaking tongue in cheek when he protested that a haggadic teaching need be no more binding than *sermones* of a bishop: if you like them, fine; if you don't, no offense to the Faith; therefore the rabbi is under no compulsion to believe a particular talmudic statement about the Messiah.[17] By now *ein somekhin al aggadah* is itself become a fixation, a kind of immovable tenet of about one third of the classic Oral Law curriculum. This can even filter down to creators of massive haggadic compendia, R. Isaac Aboab[18] and the martyr R. Israel Al-Na-kawa,[19] each of whom in his respective introduction apologizes—that is exactly the word I want—for his haggadic composition. It may not be halakhah but it can be useful!

Now, the geonic view of *ein somekhin* was not an arbitrary eruption of doctrinaire preference and idiosyncratic rejection, as we shall soon see. These scholars are living in an age and surroundings where Rationalism is the dominant intellectual persuasion. (There are already some mystics in the wings, but for the time being their voice is still not authoritative, at least in the higher echelons of the Babylonian yeshivot. Saadia's *Emunot ve-De'ot* has blazed the trail.) This Rationalism has certainly succeeded in removing the toxin from many dangerous, grossly anthropomorphic talmudic or para-talmudic sayings[20] on God's anatomy or laughter or tears or groaning and so on, or the specifics of Daniel's vision, or the experience of R. Ketina in the doorway of a necromancer,[21] or that the statement by R. Eleazar[22] that "when the Holy One, blessed be He, beheld the Flood generation" is not understood literally . . . but is meant . . . metaphorically.[23]

Obviously purging was called for. In the twelfth century Maimonides reports[24] that he "met a man who was a scholar, and as the Lord liveth, in his own opinion that man was expert since youth in the pugilism of Torah exercises (*milḥamtah shel Torah*); yet that man was still uncertain whether the Lord was or was not corporeal with eyes, hands and feet and intestines, as biblical verses put it." Others from other countries whom Maimonides has met are not in doubt about it at all: He is a physical being, and anyone denying this they regard as a heretic! And they cite many derashot (or derashot of the treatise Berakhot) as support of their views.

The demand to spiritualize and allegorize and to cultivate caution against unsophisticated literalism is not a prejudice of intellectual cranks who have been affected by some philosophical speculation. There is in addition a genuine need for defense against the charges of Karaite opponents (and sectarians and skeptics) who accuse talmudic teaching of blasphemy no less. As early as the tenth century, the Karaite Salmon ben Yeruḥim (and very likely others before him too) rhymes in outrage,[25] "[The talmudic rabbis] also say that the Holy One, blessed be He, binds tefillin [around His head] / / and the name Israel is inscribed on his turban // and the name Jacob is inscribed on His canopy // All such they say to infuriate Him. //// To the Garden of Eden [they say] the Holy One, blessed be He, will come and rejoice with His people // and will drink and dance with His company // and say, 'I and you are alike, where you go I go,' as it is said (Cant. 5:1), Eat, lovers, and drink: drink deep of love! // Woe to them that speak such words— they, they are the ones who reduce Him to brute matter." These are stock in trade charges,[26] "boisterous Objections," as Sir Thomas Browne would say.

When the Geonim reject aggadic literalism, they try nonetheless— or at least Rav Hai tries nonetheless[27]—to distinguish between aggadot incorporated in the Talmud and those preserved outside the talmudic canon. The latter are untrustworthy; and even those in the Talmud must be checked lest the text be corrupt or inexact. But whatever is included in the Talmud must be corrected if there is textual error, and if we don't know how to make the correction, the statement is to be treated like those sayings which are not halakhah. We don't have to go to such trouble with what is not included in the Talmud; but if the statement is proper and attractive we interpret and teach it; otherwise we pay no attention to it.

Whatever the distinction, it is still fundamental (ki kelal hu) that ein somekhin al aggadah.[28] Or again, on the talmudic[29] exchange regarding earthquakes (zeva'ot; the blessing to be recited[30] at such occurrences), Rav Hai:[31] "This discussion [subject, milta] is an aggadah, and of it and of everything like it our Sages (rabbanan) have said [where?] ein somekhin al divrei aggadah, haggadic statements are not to be employed as authoritative teaching"; he continues with a demonstration of a number of midrashic-talmudic expressions which must be interpreted metaphorically only and concludes, Although there are other views, the correct interpretation is as we have interpreted, and God forbid that there be a literal description [comparison, dimui] of our blessed and exalted Creator.

One thing is clear, namely, that there are obviously learned Jews, students of Talmud and Midrash, who are genuinely perplexed. To be sure, they pick up quite a number of notions from compositions and anthologies that circulate even among those who are Talmud devotees without reserve.[32] But these men are puzzled[33] not only by what they read in extra-talmudic haggadot; they are puzzled by what they find in the Talmud itself! That the gatherer of wood on the Sabbath (Num.

15:32ff.) was Zelophehad (see Num. 27:1ff.) was R. Akiva's view;[34] and it is touché when Judah ben Batyra rebukes him, "Akiva, one way or another you will in the future [Future] have to answer for this. If what you say is right, you're revealing what Scripture saw fit to cover up; if you're not right, you're slandering that saint!" But surely Judah ben Batyra hardly improves on Akiva: all Judah can be credited with is that he will not invent a *gezerah shavah* on his own!

To describe Jews who are tempted to take talmudic haggadot literally as gullible is no more than name-calling.[35] Of course there were also stupid ones in their midst, as in every midst. My literal-mindedness is gullibility; very well, yours is comparative anthropology or literary criticism. So it goes in scholarship as in interdepartmental feuds. After all, the two Talmuds themselves include substantial haggadic material in the midst of their preponderant halakhic *sugyot*, their halakhic proceedings. Did the redactors intend the preserved haggadot as intermissions, relaxations of mental strain? On one occasion when R. Jeremiah asked R. Zera[36] to teach him, R. Zera replied, *halish libbai ve-la yakhelna*, I don't feel well and am unable to teach halakhah (*litnei*). Whereupon R. Jeremiah said, Then tell me (*lema*), Master, something aggadic. "Said R. Zera to him, This is what R. Yoḥanan said: Why is it written (Deut. 20:19), 'For man is as a tree of the field?' Observe, immediately preceding (ibid.) it is written, 'For of it [masculine, him] you eat and it [him] you shall not cut down.' This is to tell you, If a scholar is a decent person (*hagun*), then eat from him and don't cut him down; otherwise destroy him utterly." What is this? *Aggadeta* is only for the weak-minded (*ḥalish libbai*)? Or an illustration of the extreme modesty of R. Zera? Or a left-handed rebuke of R. Jeremiah, that *he* may not measure up to the right kind of tree of the field? Poor R. Zera, his studies apparently used to wear him out.[37] But if we are going to build on such anecdotes, then we might as well subscribe to R. Ḥanina bar Iddi's myth that Torah has been compared to water to teach that even as water flows from top to bottom, "so the words of Torah leave him who is of haughty disposition and descend to him who is of humble disposition." Even as moralizing it lacks magnetism.

It is not in the least surprising that those loyal to talmudic authority should be tempted to accept all of it, its halakhah of course, but its haggadah too at first; since its haggadah is also the creation of the Tannaim and Amoraim, the initial impulse is to treat these "mighty hammers" seriously, reverently, whenever they speak up. These Jews can't forget how R. Yoḥanan reduced a skeptical student to a mound of bones[38]—doubtless a byword, but a potent repudiation. There is a difference betwen halakhah and haggadah which the men who turn for guidance to the Geonim are surely aware of—namely, that in halakhah you are essentially engaged with traditions that have come down from and been accepted by the ancients; *amar Rabbi Yoḥanan, mi-pi shemu'ah amarah, mi-pi Ḥaggai, Zekhariah u-Malakhi*,[39] [R. Yose's] view is not his own, but a tradition from as far back as the post-exilic prophets, hence incontestable. Of course disagreements (*maḥlokot*) can exist. What is the Talmud if not a storage of scholarly debates within the academy? The very controversies testify to the determination of the Rabbis and their constituencies to be faithful to the traditions they have inherited (Akavyah ben Mahalalel in M. Eduyot 5:6–7 is sufficient example) and to the exegesis which will demonstrate their continuing vitality; acceptance of reports of visions too. Controversy, however, is not the fabric of haggadah even though some of the preeminent Tannaim and Amoraim were masters of both halakhah *and* haggadah, and there may be disagreements in haggadah too. Yet, haggadah is literally free of all restraints, *ein sof ve-lo tikhlah le-aggadot*, and rejoices especially when the other side, be that other side what it may in your time and place, agrees,[40] even if reluctantly.[41] There may even be overlapping. The chief thing is that haggadah is not restricted by ancient legacy of practice, public or private, theoretical or applicable. In haggadah one is at liberty to draw cheerfully on his own intellect or imagination, on popular narratives and folk sayings, on anything congenial to his own spirit, to interpret a biblical verse or create a homily or amplify a scriptural anecdote or solicit parables or invoke a national or universal bon mot and so on. The key word here is *free*, be it explanation or musing. None of that *im halakhah nekabel, ve-im le-din yesh teshuvah*, if it's a tradition, very well; if your reasoning or logic, I can refute (Sifre Deut. 253, p. 279). Wit does not wait for precedent.

We must not misinterpret this sensation and phenomenon of freedom to create the impression that when the Sages indulge in haggadic speculation or teaching, all thought of tradition is expelled. "The old distinction between tradition and originality," writes T. G. Rosenmeyer in his *Art of Aeschylus*,[42] "crumbles before our increasing awareness of the subtle crosscurrents between the fluidity of the tradition, the autonomy of the creative forces latent in it, and the limitations upon authorial freedom." The Sages are not interested in escaping tradition, even as they give free rein to associating verses from one end of Scripture with the other end, in other words, even in their constantly surprising and original *petiḥot*, the proems or overtures to their immediate commentaries when the meaning of a verse in Genesis, let us say, can be produced by explanation of a verse in Job. The key word, we said, is *free*; the accompanying key word is *original*. In haggadah a man could display his originality.

Needless to say, approval may be hard to win. To return to early sources: when R. Akiva explains (Exod. 8:2) "And the frog [*ha-ẓefarde'a*, singular] came up and covered the land of Egypt," as "There was only one frog and it filled the whole land of Egypt,"[43] R. Eleazar ben Azariah protests vehemently: "Akiva, what business have you with haggadah. Cut out (*kaleh* or *kelakh*) such talk and go back to the subjects of plagues and tenting uncleannesses!" I appreciate the disapproval—though I must say, since we're talking of miracles, why not Akiva's emphasis on the singular *ha-ẓefarde'a* and the following *va-tekhas* [and it covered] of the verse? And that outrageous reprimand, go back to the laws of plagues and defilements—granted, not the lightest reading of the Talmud, and demanding profoundest expertise, hence an undeniable compliment—why should that unnerve a pious talmudist? Is Eleazar ben Azariah's explanation easier to digest? He says, "There was only one frog, but it croaked [lit., hissed] to all [the other frogs] and they came [and covered Egypt]." Then what of the singular *va-tekhas*? (Is it to be understood as the frog caused the other frogs to cover, *piel* as *hifil*?)

R. Eleazar ben Azariah seems to have relished his own style of rebuttal;[44] this may therefore be no more than a topos, and not too much is revealed by it, although it remains baffling that anyone would presume to minimize Akiva's haggadic prowess—for to Akiva we are indebted for some of the finest theological instruction.[45] Is Eleazar ben Azariah nursing a grudge of some sort?

Rejection of some haggadic views, in other words, exists, and anyone studying Talmud would be familiar with it, because it is not altogether rare. When R. Levi[46] interpreted the passive "was circumcised" (*nimol*) in connection with Abraham as, Abraham "inspected himself and found himself circumcised," R. Abba bar Kahana (who was really a good friend of Levi's[47]) let him have it, Liar, faker, Abraham was suffering pain so that the Holy One, blessed be He, might double his reward! Oriental rhetoric of course, but rejection no less (although Levi's interpretation is after all far from extreme as haggadah can go!).

For men who study Talmud or what they regard as talmudical there could certainly be nothing extraordinary about rejecting a haggadic statement. And when in the midst of a halakhic give-and-take[48] there is an exclamation, "Are midrashot a matter of faith?[49] *derosh ve-kabel sakhar*, Go ahead and interpret midrashically and be rewarded," in other words, don't take it too seriously, no one need be put off, for *derosh ve-kabel sakhar* is a cliché if ever there was one, especially in discussion[50] of halakhot now become theoretical. Note incidentally, not, Drop these subjects or pay them no mind or don't study them till you're forty years old, but, There's some reward even in study of these subjects albeit nothing practical will come of it.

Once upon a time, said R. Levi,[51] when money was abundant a man yearned to listen to mishnah and halakhah and talmud discussions; but now when money is scarce, and above all as a result of being worn out by subjection to the nations, people want to listen only to words of blessing and of comfort.[52] The most natural thing in the world! When you're in need of consolation, law reviews are not much help. And if people are listening to haggadah,[53] they are paying close attention to it, as they have been taught to do when studying the sources. And when they hear sensational things—like the varieties of the names of God[54] or the significance of dreams,[55]—or receive rumors and reports of mind-boggling stunts and experiences,[56] what more natural than to turn to the leading talmudic authorities and expect an explanation? Indeed, how *rational* is their inquiry, u-mah hefresh bein ma'aseh nevi'ut le-ma-'aseh khashfanut u-mah hi aḥizat einayim, By what criterion is one to distinguish between accounts of prophetic acts and acts of witchcraft; and what is this pulling the wool over one's eyes, this business of delusion?[57]

These are serious men (in another decade, who will believe the account of the Entebbe rescue?), neither strangers to the intellectual demands of Talmud study nor simpletons. The Geonim do not reply to them contemptuously. But what do they say? *ein somekhin ve-ein mevi'in re'ayah mi-kol divrei aggadah ve-ein makshin mi-divrei aggadah*, You base nothing on and bring no proof from any aggadic statements and you don't raise questions because of them.[58] An attempt will be made to distinguish between haggadot to be found in the Talmud and haggadot in other apparently popular compositions (as we said), but the pronouncement is summary, *ein somekhin, ein lemedin.*

I cannot find this rule in the Talmud itself.[59] How did it become an oft-repeated formula? The statement by R. Zeira in the name of Samuel in the Palestinian Talmud[60]—*ein lemedin min ha-halakhot ve-lo min ha-haggadot ve-lo min ha-tosafot ella min ha-Talmud* or, as P. Ḥagigah 1:8 reads, *ein morin,* that is, No decision is to be made from the compilations of the halakot (mishnah) or from the haggadot or from the tosafot (mishnaic supplements)[61] but only from the Talmud—is not talking about our subject. J. N. Epstein[62] has even put parentheses around the words "or from the haggadot," quite rightly, for what is being discussed in that passage is on what basis may you arrive at a practical, halakhic decision; and even if you adopt the reading of the regular printed editions, that is still the intent; and it is reminiscent of the baraita in the Babylonian Talmud,[63] *ein melamdin,* one is not to teach (= to decide) a halakhah either on the basis of academical study (*talmud*) or even on the basis of what was an actual case, but one must be taught the halakhah specifically on the basis of a halakhah now to be applicable (*halakhah le-ma'aseh*).[64] The nature of haggadah is not here the issue. For rendering decision it is useless, as are the halakhot or tosafot. True.

Ein somekhin al ha-aggadah is pretty strong, sweeping language. However, while nothing so categorical is known to me from the Talmud and Midrash themselves, no careful reading of the classical sources can obscure what I would like to call early traces of the idea, and by early I do mean tannaite. To begin with, there is the report of those legal scholars[65] (intellectual snobs? halakhah practitioners impatient with the stiff requirements of analysis and probing?) who say, I study halakhot, that's enough for me. Them the Midrash admonishes, "Study midrash, halakhot, and haggadot," and then proceeds to quote and interpret the biblical verse (Deut. 8:3) "man does not live on bread alone": "that refers to midrash; but [man lives] by everything which comes forth from the mouth of the Lord, 'that refers to the halakhot and the haggadot.' " So there are halakhic scholars who apparently feel superior to haggadah or feel that haggadah is superfluous, just as there are those who like to say, I will study the difficult sections (*parashah*) and pass up the easy ones. Both types (or are they one?) are to be rebuked (Deut. 32:47), "for this is no trifling thing for you"; what you call trifling "is your very own life." This association of "I will study only what's difficult, enough for me are the halakhot" registers clearly a disparagement of haggadah study though the normal curriculum calls for it too. And maybe it is in such scholars that the first signs of condescension toward haggadah rise to the surface. Did they feel that way towards haggadah because they thought it was easy, because it was infra dig?[66]

A superior attitude of this sort will not escape criticism, as the deuteronomic verses cited and interpreted above already testify. But there is even bolder rebuke, and that too in the Sifre. First a thoroughly innocent and we might say well-nigh literal comment.[67] "Take to heart these words with which I charge you this day" (Deut. 6:6), says the Sifre, "Take to heart these words, for thus you will come to recognize[68] Him Who Spake and the World Came to Be and cleave to His ways." However you wish to understand "these words," halakhically or haggadically, we are manifestly being exhorted to cleave to His ways. You can do that by taking His words to heart.

But then on Deut. 11:22, on the expression "cleave to Him,"[69] when astonishment is recorded—How can a human being ascend on high and cleave to the Fire?—first comes a rationalizing answer: This means "cleave to scholars and their disciples, and I shall account it to thee as though thou hast ascended on high" and taken the Torah captive—that seems to be the object of the concluding phrases, to overcome the angels who tried to prevent the giving of the Torah to Israel.[70]

Immediately after this we read:[71] "doreshei haggadot, the expositors of Haggadot say, If you wish to recognize (le-hakir, know, get a notion of, make known, acknowledge?) Him Who Spake and the World Came to Be, study Haggadah, for thus you will recognize Him Who Spake and the World Came to Be and cleave to His ways." Is this hyperbole triumphant? On the contrary! There is a finesse, a chastity of speech here it would be poor taste to bypass. First, it is to be noticed that there are obviously students or even masters known as doreshei haggadot, men who make haggadah study an important part of their intellectual pursuits. Second, since the biblical verse speaks of cleaving (u-le-davkah), these expositors adopt this very strong verb[72]—they do not paraphrase or modify or resort to synonym. Third, it is not the doreshei haggadot who speak of cleaving to the Fire; in their saying no reference is made to the Fire on high: only to "study haggadah." Fourth, note the refinement of observation: Scripture does not hesitate to say u-le-davkah vo, and cleave to Him: but the haggadists say, "and cleave to His ways!" Talk of avoiding possible offensive language about the Creator, in the Haggadah! And if you're curious about what God's ways are, the beginning of that very section of the Sifre[73] is ready to tell you in terms even stronger than those of Epictetus's *Discourses* as reported by Arrian:[74] no ifs, no maybes, no *if* faithful, *if* free, *if* beneficent, *if* high-minded, no *ei piston, ei elevtheron, ei energetikon, ei megalofron*. The Holy One, blessed be He, surely is, as Scripture teaches, *rahum ve-hanun, zaddik, hasid*; these are His ways, and so be yours if you seek intimate fellowship with Him.[75]

If you wish to cleave to His ways, study haggadah. On the importance of study of the halakhah, which is compared to the staff of life,[76] there is ready assent among the Rabbis. And as grandiose promise for such preoccupation there is, "He who studies (reviews, *shoneh*) the halakhot may be certain that he will be included in the World to Come."[77] But no one promises that if you study halakhot you will come to recognize the Holy One, blessed be He, and achieve *imitatio dei*, although it is affirmed by the Babylonian Rav Hisda[78] that "the Lord loves the gates of academe devoted to halakhic studies more than the synagogues and academies (*batei midrashot*): as the following was transmitted in the name of Ulla [second-third generation Palestinian amora?], 'Since the destruction of the Temple, with His whole world [to choose from] God confines Himself to the four ells of the Halakhah.' "[79] Or are these value judgments, as I now want to suggest, polemical remarks? These are not now, however, uppermost in my mind. I can get into the World to Come by taking a stroll of four ells in the Land of Israel:[80] which demonstrates how instructive such counsels are!

Now, these praises of halakhah are amoraic statements, but my contention is that they are a *continuation* of moods encouraged even in tannaite times in Palestine, as the midrash of the *doreshei haggadot* and as the self-satisfaction of "I've studied halakhot, enough" reveal. No anachronism is intended.

Those who study and teach haggadot are not talking to themselves or fantasizing or promising far-fetched, fairy-tale rewards. They are *engagé*, they are involved in argument with those who have a good word only for halakhah, who feel that the highest level of achievement is that of the *nomikos*, the man who will deal with midrash, with halakhot, and never mind the aggadot though they are the third required area of concentration of the bet ha-midrash. The *doreshei haggadot* declare, It is through the haggadot (does this mean only the haggadot?—I think it does) that you will come to cleave to His ways properly. The statement is a magisterial counterpolemic.

In short, already in the tannaite centuries there is a discernible tension between the two parts of the accepted curriculum, between midrash and halakhot on the one hand and haggadah on the other. And the Geonim, even if they hesitate to admit this explicitly (or maybe they do somewhere—Saadia does not hesitate to oppose a haggadic view),[81] are nevertheless sensitive to it. Not completely on their own do they invoke *ein somekhin*. And since they are principally students of the law, heads of academies where the law is constantly explored, their minds are inevitably upon it; and since they feel themselves above all responsible for the cohesiveness of the Jewish community, they opt for the most part in behalf of the Establishment, for what will stabilize it, and not for what is free association, the individual mind taking off on its own flight of fancy or the literalism dangerously close to a fundamentalism of vocabulary and understanding.

There are three parts of the Oral Law, midrash, halakhot, and aggadot, and I wish to submit that already in the early talmudic centuries there had developed a tension between the first two parts and the third. Keep to the four ells of the halakhah means bluntly, Haggadah is not important. Study haggadah if you wish to recognize the Creator and cleave to His ways means bluntly, It's not from halakhot that you'll learn this momentous lesson. We are in the presence of the permanent human agon between restraint and freedom. Generally we speak of halakhah and haggadah as though they were the literary remains of antiquity and a refraction also of the social history of their times, which indeed they are. Or they are presented as the highway to proper conduct and exhortation.[82] But they were always much more than that. They are an articulation of the fundamental, universal, interminable combat of obedience and individual conceit.

To resolve the tension or to transform the conflict into a creative collaboration takes genius. Yet even here the Talmud furnishes a charming anecdote, making good use at the same time of an Aesop fable.[83] Two scholars once visited R. Isaac Nappaha (second-third generation Palestinian amora). Said one to him, Sir, tell us something halakhic; the other said, Sir, tell us something aggadic. When R. Isaac began to speak of an aggadah, the one visitor would not let him go on; when he began to speak of a halakhah, the other visitor would not let him go on. R. Isaac said to them: You know what this is like? To a man who has two wives, one young and one old. The young one keeps pulling out his white hairs and the old one keeps pulling out his black hairs. As a result he ends up completely bald! So he said to them, I will tell you something that should appeal to both of you. It is said (in Exod. 22:5), "When a fire is started and spreads to thorns," that is, the fire started of its own, "he who started the fire must make restitution": The Holy One, blessed be He, said, I have to make restitution for the fire I started—it was I who set fire to Zion, as it is said (Lam. 4:11), "He kindled a fire in Zion which consumed its foundations"; therefore in the future I will rebuild it in fire, as it is said (Zach. 2:9), "And I Myself will be a wall of fire all around it, and I will be a glory inside it."

Now to the halakhic lesson. The Exodus verse began by speaking of damages caused by what a person owns (mamono, the reference is to that which is his property, not to him personally) and concluded by speaking of damages he personally was responsible for. This is to teach you that the fire one starts is like the arrow he shoots (in both cases the person is held responsible regardless of the distance travelled by the arrow or fire).

Maybe R. Isaac Nappaha was a genius. Anyway, I'm glad he began with the aggadic lesson.[84] It's not immaterial to the halakhah just taught. Or alternatively, possibly, the halakhah may have provoked the haggadah.

NOTES

1. Avot de Rabbi Natan A (ARNA), p. 39. Cf. statement on R. Akiva in Tractate Shekalim V, ed. A. Sofer (New York: Privately Published, 1954), p. 56, and critical apparatus there. The terms aggadah, aggadot, haggadah, haggadot are interchangeable. Cf. W. Bacher, Midrashic Terminology: Tannaim and Amoraim (Hebrew), trans. E. Z. Rabinowitz (Tel Aviv, 1922; rpt. Jerusalem: Carmiel, 1970), pp. 24–25.

2. Cf. ARNA, p. 16, and S. Lieberman, Siphre Zutta (New York: JTS, 1968), 89–90, n. 54 at bottom of page; and ARNB, p. 39. See also B. Avodah Zarah 19a–b; and Sefer Dikduke Soferim (Hebrew) (hereafter DS), ed. R. N. N. Rabinowitz (New York: M. P. Press, 1976), ad loc.

3. I have departed slightly from the reading adopted by S. Schechter (cf. his n. 3, p. 35), although Aknin, Sepher Mussar, ed. Bacher (Berlin: Mekitze Nirdamim, 1910), p. 11, seems to agree with ed. Schechter. Note L. Finkelstein's suggestion in Baer Jubilee Volume (n. 6, below), 30. On ta'am cf. Lev. R. XXXVI 1, p. 833.

4. On God's program of studies, see Seder Eliyahu Rabbah, ed. Friedmann (Jerusalem: Bamberger and Wahrman, 1960), p. 15. Cf. n. 79 below.

5. Cf., e.g., Canticles Rabbah (Vilna: Romm, 1938), II 5, 15b. Note also the combination of halakhot and haggadot (but midrash is referred to immediately preceding)

in Sifre ad Deuteronomium, ed. L. Finkelstein (New York: JTS, 1969), sec. 48, p. 113; and in Ginze Schechter, (Hebrew) ed. L. Ginzberg (New York: JTS, 1929), vol. 2, p. 567, "midrash and tosafot and aggadot" (cf. below, n. 61).

6. Cf. L. Finkelstein in Yitzhak F. Baer Jubilee Volume on the Occasion of His Seventieth Birthday (Hebrew with English summaries), ed. S. W. Baron et al. (Jerusalem: Historical Society of Israel, 1960), pp. 31–32; and Bacher, Midrashic Terminology, p. 24. The statement in Mekilta VaYassa, ed. and trans. J. Z. Lauterbach (Philadelphia: Jewish Publication Society, 1933), vol. 2, p. 95, on Exod. 15:26, that "doing what is upright in His sight" is a reference to "the praiseworthy haggadot that appeal to all men," is homiletical exhortation pure and simple, and has nothing to do with academic program or planning, as the context plainly reveals. For haggadah as homily, cf. B. Sotah 7b, and Avot de Rabbi Natan (ARN), ed. S. Schechter (New York: Feldheim, 1945), p. 67.

7. Cf. Genesis Rabbah, ed. J. Theodor and Ch. Albeck (Jerusalem: Wahrman, 1965), XLIV 8, p. 431: There are three to whom it was said, "Ask": Solomon, Aḥaz, and King Messiah. R. Berekhiah and R. Aḥi said in the name of R. Samuel bar Naḥman, "We can add two more from the aggadah, Abraham and Jacob," as can be proved from the idiom of Gen. 15:2 and 28:22b. On shoneh be-haggadot, see Midrash Psalms, ed. S. Buber (Vilna: Rom, 1892), LIX 3, p. 302 (but cf. Buber's n. 23): the "book" must refer to the expression "reading in the Torah."

8. Leviticus Rabbah, ed. M. Margulies (Jerusalem: Wahrmann Books, 1972), III 1, pp. 54–56 and Margulies' commentary. And observe how bar aggadah is referred to in anecdote, Genesis Rabbah LXXXI 2, p. 970! Note also, however, the praise of Israel, XL (XLI) 1, p. 388: "Some of them are masters of the Scripture, some of them masters of Mishnah, some of them masters of Talmud, some of them masters of Aggadah." With the idiom here, cf. that of Leviticus Rabbah IX 3, p. 177. See also XIII 5, p. 282; XV 2, p. 322.

9. Cf. R. Halperin, Atlas Etz Chayim (Hebrew) (Tel Aviv: Ruaḥ Yaakov, 1980), vol. 4: Tannaim and Amoraim, pt. 2, p. 238: R. Isaac bar Phineas.

10. Genesis Rabbah III 4, pp. 19–20.

11. B. Baba Kamma 55a. Said already of the tanna R. Ishmael by R. Tarfon, in B. Moed Katan 28b. On rabbanan de-aggadeta, cf. J. Heineman, Aggadah and Its Development (Hebrew) (Jerusalem: Keter, 1974), p. 212, n. 4. On baki cf. H. Yalon, Studies in Language (Hebrew) (Jerusalem: Mossad Bialik, 1971), p. 315.

12. ARNA, p. 57. Schechter's edition reads "gemara" instead of "talmud": the censor's substitution (talmud = midrash, as we said: cf. J. N. Epstein, Introductions to Tannaitic Literature [Hebrew], ed. E. Z. Melamed [Jerusalem: Magnes; and Tel Aviv: Dvir, 1957], p. 501). On such praise as stereotype, cf. ARNB, p. 29.

13. B. Sukkah 28a—but see also ARNB, p. 58, where "targum" = midrash; cf. S. Lieberman, Hellenism in Jewish Palestine: Studies in Literary Transmission, Beliefs and Manners of Palestine from the First Century BCE to the Fourth Century CE (New York: JTS, 1962), p. 48; but note Small Tractates: Tractate Soferim (Hebrew), ed. M. Higger (Jerusalem: Makor, 1970), p. 289. B. Baba Batra 134a. On toseftot see below, n. 61.

14. ARN, p. 59; note also the reading in Israel ben Joseph Al-Nakawa, Sefer Menorat ha-Maor (Hebrew), ed. H. G. Enelow (New York: Bloch, 1929–1932), pt. 3, pp. 522–23.

15. I have obviously drawn on the material in B. M. Lewin, Ozar ha-Geonim: The Responsa of the Babylonian Geonim and Their Commentaries According to the Order of the Talmud (Hebrew) (hereafter OhG), 13 vols. (vol. 1, Haifa: privately published, 1928; other vols. Jerusalem: various publishers, 1928–1943), especially the volumes on Berakhot and Ḥagigah. But no one familiar with that treasury will fail to recognize my indebtedness to S. Lieberman, his Shkiin and Yemenite Midrashim (Hebrew) (Jerusalem: Wahrman, 1970).

16. An adaptation of the idiom in B. Sanhedrin 17b?

17. Lieberman, *Shkiin*, pp. 81–83. (Note also Lieberman in Leviticus Rabbah, p. 881.) This is in no way to be interpreted as Naḥmanides' indifference to haggadah. Note, for example, how on Lev. 18:24–25 (*Explications on the Torah by R. Moshe ben Naḥman [Ramban]*, ed. D. Chavel [Hebrew] [Jerusalem: Mossad Harav Kook, 1960], pp. 107ff.), he keeps weaving haggadic views with his own (and earlier) interpretations. And note especially A. Funkenstein, "Naḥmanides' Typological Reading of History" (Hebrew), *Zion* 45 (1980), 35–59. See also Naḥmanides' poem at the head of his Torah commentary:

nafshi ḥashkah ba-torah

. . . .

laẓet be-ikvei ha-rishonim

. . . .

li-khtov ka-hem (ba-hem) peshatim bi-khtuvim u-midrashim be-miẓvot ve-aggadah arukhah va-kol u-shemurah
Va-asim li-meor panai . . .
perushei rabenu shelomo . . .
bi-devarav ehegeh . . .
ve-imahem yihyeh lanu masa u-matan, derishah ve-ḥakirah
u-feshatav u-midrashav ve-kol aggadah beẓurah, asher be-ferushav zekhura.

18. End of fourteenth century; see the introduction to Aboab's Menorat HaMaor (Stettin: Schrentzel, 1866), no pagination but equals 4a and following (with the delightful observation that Talmud is like bread, Haggadah is like water—and though one certainly needs bread to survive, water is all the more indispensable!).

19. Died Tammuz 1349 (cf. Enelow's introduction to Al-Nakawa Menorat ha-Maor, p. 15). How compare my work, writes Al-Nakawa (in *his* introduction, p. 12), to the works of the Sages? All [in my work] they knew on their own. But [the teachings here included] are scattered helter-skelter [Aboab also refers to this]. I'm not worthy to draw up such a work. Fortunately an angelic being (ish . . . *ayom ve-norah*) inspired the necessary trembling and resolution.

20. Cf. *OhG, Ḥagigah, Commentaries*, pp. 58, 59.

21. B. Berakhot 59a; *OhG, Berakhot, Commentaries*, pp. 91ff., and *Responsa*, pp. 131–32.

22. B. Ḥagigah 12a.

23. *OhG, Ḥagigah, Commentaries*, p. 54.

24. Maamar Teḥiyyat ha-Metim, ed. J. Finkel, *PAAJR* 9 (1939), 3, and J. M. Rabinowitz (Jerusalem, 1944), p. 345. As for Maimonides' views of Shiur Komah, see Lieberman apud Scholem, *Gnosticism* (New York: JTS, 1960), pp. 124–25.

25. Milḥamot ha-Shem, ed. I. Davidson (New York: JTS, 1934), pp. 110–11.

26. As can be seen also in Al-Qirqisani—trans. L. Nemoy, *HUCA* 7 (1930), 331, 350–51—who like Salmon ben Yeruḥim refers to works like Shiur Komah, Hekhalot, Alphabet de Rabbi Akiva. That one has to think hard about Shiur Komah: *OhG, Berakhot, Responsa*, p. 17; *Ḥagigah*, pp. 11–12.

27. *OhG, Ḥagigah, Commentaries*, p. 60.

28. Ibid., p. 29.

29. B. Berakhot 59a.

30. Mishnah Berakhot 9:1 "Blessed is He Whose might and power fill the universe."

31. *OhG, Responsa*, pp. 131–32.

32. See Lieberman, all of *Shkiin* and *Yemenite Midrashim*.

33. Cf. *OhG, Ḥagigah, Commentaries*, p. 60, n. 4.

34. B. Shabbat 96b–97a. See also 97a on Aaron. Cf. Sifre Numbers, ed. H. S. Horovitz

(Jerusalem: Wahrman, 1966), sec. 113, p. 122; sec. 133, p. 177, but note also interlocutors in Siphre Zutta, pp. 287, 317.

35. See the important remarks by G. Scholem, *Elements of the Kabbalah and Its Symbolism* (Hebrew) (Jerusalem: Mossad Bialik, 1976), pp. 153, 155–56.

36. B. Taanit 7a and also R. Ḥanina bar Iddi. And see Rashi on Prov. 9:9, beginning. On R. Jeremiah and R. Zera unwittingly misled by each other, cf. Genesis Rabbah LX 8, pp. 649–50. R. Jeremiah asks R. Zera a halakhic question in presence of a scholar's bier (but R. Zera replies): XCVI, p. 1238. See also Midrash Psalms XIX 14, p. 171 (R. Jeremiah?).

37. B. Berakhot 28a. On R. Zera turning sarcastically on R. Jeremiah cf. S. Spiegel in *Harry Austryn Wolfson Jubilee Volume on the Occasion of His Seventy-Fifth Birthday* (English and Hebrew) 3 vols. (Jerusalem: American Academy for Jewish Research, 1965) (Hebrew), vol. 3, p. 252.

38. B. Sanhedrin 100a and parallels. See also Isi ben Akiva in Midrash Psalms XXIII 5, p. 201.

39. B. Ḥullin 137b, top. (Note: *shemu'ah*, not *masoret*; cf. Bacher, *Midrashic Terminology*, pp. 74–75, 227. On *masoret haggadah*, cf. Leviticus Rabbah XVIII 2, p. 402, n. to l. 6.)

40. For example, see R. Judah in Genesis Rabbah XLIX 9, p. 511, and cf. H. de Lubac, "La Belle Captive," in *Exégèse médiévale: Les quatres sens de l'écriture* (Paris: Aubier, 1959), I, i, pp. 290–304.

41. Cf. St. Augustine, *City of God*, ed. T. E. Page et al., trans. Philip Levine (London: William Heinemann, Cambridge: Harvard University Press, 1966), 13:16, Loeb Classics, vol. 4, p. 191, ". . . who plume themselves on being called or being Platonists and whose pride in this name makes them ashamed to be Christians. They fear that, if they share one designation with the common mass (cum vulgo), it will detract for the wearers of the Greek cloak from the prestige of their fewness, for they are puffed up in inverse proportion to their numbers."

42. Berkeley: University of California Press, 1982, p. 315; and see also the frequently cited essay by T. S. Eliot, "Tradition and the Individual Talent," in his *Selected Essays*, new ed. (New York: Harcourt, Brace, 1950), pp. 3–11. On the latter, see S. E. Hyman, *The Armed Vision: A Study in the Methods of Modern Literary Criticism* (New York: A. A. Knopf, 1952), pp. 79–83.

43. B. Sanhedrin 67b; cf. Seder Eliyahu Rabbah, p. 41. See also Midrash Psalms I 8, p. 9. If for the benefit of the Age to Come one behemoth can squat over one thousand mountains (amoraic, Leviticus Rabbah XXII 10, pp. 524–25; see also tannaim, pp. 525–26), why not one frog teem at miracles in Egypt? One man's fantasy is the next man's ridiculousness. Haggadah is full of this.

44. B. Sanhedrin 38b; Midrash Psalms CIV 9, p. 442. See also B. Yoma 75b, Ishmael to Akiva.

45. Cf. J. Goldin, "Toward a Profile of . . . Aqiba ben Joseph," in *JAOS* 96 (1976), 38–56. See also L. Ginzberg in *Jewish Encyclopaedia*, vol. I (1901 ed.), pp. 304–10.

46. Genesis Rabbah XLVII 9, p. 476.

47. Cf. Theodor's note to line 5, ibid.

48. P. Nazir 7:2.

49. Cf. Lieberman, *Shkiin and Yemenite Midrashim*, p. 82.

50. To be revived in messianic times, B. Sanhedrin 51b; or regarding the rebellious son or the condemned town or the house leprously afflicted, 71a; or haggadic, Prov. 24:27, B. Sotah 44a.

51. Canticles Rabbah II 5, 15b.

52. Says the *Yefeh Kol*, "Therefore they do not listen even to words of aggadah!" But note also Agadath Shir Hashirim, ed. S. Schechter (Cambridge: Deighton Bell, 1896),

p. 30, lines 844–45. Pesikta de Rav Kahana, ed. Mandelbaum (New York: JTS, 1962), p. 205, and critical apparatus there.

53. Cf. also the touching story about R. Abbahu and R. Ḥiyya bar Abba in B. Sotah 40a. See also the quotation in n. 6, above.

54. OhG, Ḥagigah, Responsa, pp. 22–23. On Stoic speculation on varieties of deity's name, cf. Diogenes Laertius, trans. R. D. Hicks, ed. T. E. Page et al. (London: William Heinemann, 1959), VII, 147, Loeb Classics, vol. 2, pp. 251–52.

55. OhG, Ḥagigah, Responsa, p. 25. See also R. J. White, The Oneirocritica by Artemidorus (Park Ridge, N.J.: Noyes, 1975), pp. 7–10.

56. OhG, Ḥagigah, Responsa, pp. 16ff.

57. Ibid., p. 18. See, by the way, the exchange between Yoḥanan ben Zakkai, a heathen, and Yoḥanan's disciples in Pesikta de Rav Kahana, p. 74 and parallels (cf. Midrash Psalms L 1, pp. 278–79, in connection with R. Simlai; anti-Christian?). See also Maimonides, Introduction to Mishnah Avot (Hebrew), ed. J. Kafiḥ (Jerusalem: Mossad Harav Kook, 1964), VI, p. 259a. On aḥizat einayim cf. M. Kosovsky, Concordance to the Palestinian Talmud (Hebrew), 3 vols. (Jerusalem: Ministry of Education and Culture of the Israeli Government and the Jewish Theological Seminary of America), vol. 1 (1979), p. 190, col. b. G. H. Dalman, Aramaisch-Neuhebräisches Handwörterbuch zu Targum, Talmud, und Midrasch (Hildesheim: Olms, 1967), 13a, s.v. aḥiza.

58. OhG, Ḥagigah, Supplement, p. 65.

59. "In the Talmuds and midrashim, particular haggadic interpretations may be dismissed for one reason or another; but it is never said there in summary fashion that haggadah can't be invoked as authoritative doctrine ... Quite naturally, for that is still the creative and self-understood period. A principle like ein somekhin ... becomes articulate only after a traditional text has been sanctified in the course of time, and people come uncritically to treat every statement in it as the equivalent in value of every other statement in it. Rationalistic Geonim and subsequent rabbis thereupon attempt to restore balance or proper perspective. Their principle is not intended as disdain of lessons that may be learned from haggadah; it is a denial of the obligatory, doctrinaire character of the haggadah" (J. Goldin, "Midrash and Haggadah," in the forthcoming Cambridge History of Judaism, written 1974–75).

60. P. Peah 2:4

61. See J. N. Epstein, Introductions to Tannaitic Literature, pp. 241ff. (on the Tosefta).

62. Ibid., p. 241.

63. B. Baba Batra 130b; on the word talmud, cf. DS, ad loc. See also Genesis Rabbah LVI 6, pp. 601–02. See Ch. Albeck, Introduction to the Talmud (Hebrew) (Tel Aviv: Dvir, 1969), p. 548, n. 44.

64. Cf. B. Niddah 7b, bottom. Pirkoi ben Baboi will make much of it. Cf. Ginzberg, Ginze Schechter, vol. 2, pp. 556–59 (with reference to R. Yehudai Gaon), pp. 562, 571–72. And on Pirkoi, see the important study by S. Spiegel, Harry Wolfson Jubilee Volume, pp. 243ff. See also Genesis Rabbah C 7, p. 1291.

65. Sifre Deuteronomy, 48, p. 113.

66. There are also presumably easy halakhic discussions: Leviticus Rabbah XXXIV 4, p. 779.

67. Sifre Deuteronomy, 33, p. 59.

68. le-hakir; see also Mekhilta Shirta 3, vol. 2, p. 26, makirin atem oto.

69. Sifre Deuteronomy, 49, pp. 114–15. See also Pitron Torah (Hebrew) ed. Urbach (Jerusalem: Magnes, 1978), p. 251. Cf. Leviticus Rabbah XXV 3, pp. 572f. Note in addition B. Ketubot 111b.

The very question "How can a human being ascend on high and cleave to the Fire" may suggest a touch of mystical feeling. I'm not convinced that in the present instance it is so—despite what may lie behind the expression (on Fire, cf. H. Lewy, *Chaldaean Oracles and Theurgy: Mysticism, Magic and Platonism in the Later Roman Empire* [Paris: Michel Tardieu, 1978], pp. 25, 83f, 201, 241–45; and *alah* may well reflect *anagoge*, see ibid., pp. 487–89). But not every metaphor, even a bold one, is necessarily an expression of mysticism; and while our Sifre passage is echoing sounds of the Moses legend (see L. Ginzberg, *Legends of the Jews* [Philadelphia: Jewish Publication Society, 1910], vol. 3, pp. 109–14; vol. 6, pp. 47–48), it is speaking of "man" (*efshar lo le-adam*), not of Moses, and especially of "as though" (*ke-ilu alitah*), not of actual ascension. There is nothing in our Sifre passage of "ecstatic mysticism" or a mystical *exercise* or an elitist gnosis or secret password. See the excellent remarks of D. J. Halperin, *The Merkabah in Rabbinic Literature* (New Haven: American Oriental Society, 1980), p. 139, on *ma'aseh merkavah* mysticism.

70. Avot de Rabbi Natan, p. 10; B. Shabbat 88b–89a. On the angels opposed to the creation of Adam, see ARNB, p. 23 (but cf. also Ginzberg, *Legends*, vol. 5, p. 84, n. 33).

71. Note Finkelstein's critical apparatus. To this day, and despite Lauterbach, I'm still not sure I understand (*doreshei*) *reshumot*; but cf. Bacher, *Midrashic Terminology*, p. 125.

72. I have already commented on this verb in the *Harry Wolfson Jubilee Volume*, pp. 82–83 and nn. 44–47, 50.

73. Sifre Deuteronomy, 49, p. 114.

74. II, 14:13 (Loeb Classics, vol. I, pp. 308–09).

75. Cf. Mekhilta Shirta 3, vol. 2, p. 25, "Abba Saul."

76. Cf. B. Ḥagigah 14a, " 'Every prop of food' (Isa. 3:1, literally, bread) is a reference to the masters of talmud (cf. Rashi ad loc., s.v. *leḥem*), as it is said (Prov. 9:5), 'Come, eat my food (*laḥmi*)' . . ." Note by the way Isaiah da Trani on the Proverbs verse, III, p. 19, top. And see Aboab, Menorat HaMaor (4d; cf. n. 18 above) quoting B. Baba Batra 145b.

77. Twice in the Babylonian Talmud, Megillah 28b, bottom, and end of Niddah (where see also the last Tosafot), both quoting Tanna de-bei Eliyahu. See Seder Eliyahu Zuta, p. 173, and cf. Friedmann, Introduction, ibid., p. 45. D. Halivni, *Sources and Traditions* (Hebrew), *Seder Moed Shabbat* (New York: JTS, 1982), p. 23, n. 67.

78. B. Berakhot 8a. For identity of Ulla, cf. A. Hyman, *Histories of Tannaim and Amoraim* (Hebrew) (London: Express, 1910), III, 973a. And note DS ad loc. For haggadic praise of halakhah, see also Midrash Psalms XLIX 1, p. 278.

79. But note DS. Genesis Rabbah XLIX 2, p. 501: In the name of R. Judah (bar Ezekiel), "Not a day passes without the Holy One, blessed be He, offering fresh halakhot in the Court on high." See also n. 4 above.

80. B. Ketubot 11a. And on the passage at the end of Shekalim III, ed. Sofer, p. 37, see Y. Sussmann in *Researches in Talmudic Literature* (Hebrew), (Jerusalem: Israel Academy of Sciences and Humanities, 1983), pp. 50, 69. On this formula (promise) in mystical speculation, in *Merkavah Shelemah* (Hebrew) (Jerusalem: Mosaiev, 5681 [1921]), 39b, so! See S. Lieberman apud G. Scholem, *Gnosticism*, p. 123.

81. Cf. *Saadia's Polemic against Hivi Al-Balkhi*, ed. I. Davidson (New York: JTS, 1915), p. 58, n. 177. On the vigor of the Geonim to establish Babylonian, rather than Palestinian, teaching everywhere, cf. Spiegel, *Harry Wolfson Jubilee Volume*, pp. 246ff., 262ff.

82. On the inadequacy of the halakhah strictly applied, cf. Genesis Rabbah XXXIII 3, pp. 304ff. Note also the anecdote about R. Yose the Galilean, XVII 3, pp. 152–55. Cf. R. Joshua in B. Baba Kamma 55b (bottom). See also J. T. Noonan, Jr., on Cardozo, in *Persons and Masks of the Law* (New York: Farrar, Straus and Giroux, 1976), pp. 111ff. But either way, halakhah without haggadah or vice versa is reduction of a rich, complex construction to efficiency row housing.

83. B. Baba Kamma 60b, and see *Babrius and Phaedrus*, ed. and trans. B. Perry (London: W. Heinemann, 1965), pp. 33–34, Babrius, fable 22 and Phaedrus, pp. 235–36.

It takes a John M. Woolsey of the United States District Court of the Southern District of New York, attentive to "all questions of law and fact involved," to decide in 1933 on *legal grounds* that *Ulysses* "may . . . be admitted into the United States" for it must also "always be remembered that" the author's "locale was Celtic and his season Spring" (James Joyce, *Ulysses* [New York: Random House, 1934], ix–xiv).

84. Cf. Rabbah's pedagogic practice in B. Shabbat 30b.

JAMES L. KUGEL

Two Introductions to Midrash

I

There are a number of alphabetical psalms in the Bible, that is, psalms
in which each line or group of lines begins with a new letter of the
Hebrew alphabet. One such is Psalm 145—yet for some reason, at least
in the Masoretic text, the verse that should start with the Hebrew letter
"N" (nun) is missing. Did the verse somehow get lost in transmission?
Rabbinic tradition has a different answer: David, the author of the
Psalms, purposely omitted it.

Why is there no nun-verse in Psalm 145? Rabbi Yoḥanan explained that it is
because Israel's (as it were) downfall begins with that letter, as it is written,
"She-has-fallen [nafelah] and will no more rise, the virgin of Israel" (Amos 5:2).
But in the West (i.e. Palestine) the sages resolve [the problematic message of
that verse by dividing it up differently] thus: "She has fallen and will (fall) no
more; rise, O virgin of Israel!" Rabbi Naḥman bar Isaac said: [Though David
omitted the nun-verse because it would have invoked Israel's downfall,] nevertheless David reconsidered and, in divine inspiration, added the next verse,
"The Lord lifts up all who are fallen, and straightens up all who are bent."[1]

Those who are familiar with rabbinic exegesis certainly can follow the
drift of these remarks, but for the uninitiated a bit of explanation is
due. The fact that the "N" verse is missing has, in the mind of Rabbi
Yoḥanan, been imaginatively connected with another circumstance: it
so happens that one of the direst pieces of prophecy in the whole
Bible, Amos's blunt statement that Israel's fall will be irreparable and
eternal, also begins with the same letter. This, R. Yoḥanan argues, is no
mere coincidence. It is as if David, writing long before Amos but knowing what was to come, had purposely kept silent at "N" because of
Amos's dread words. To Yoḥanan's remark—which one might sup-

Note: This essay first appeared in *Prooftexts* 3 (1983), 131–55.

pose circulated widely, for everyone is troubled by an alphabetical psalm that is missing one verse—R. Naḥman bar Isaac is said to have appended another, still more striking, observation: the very next verse in the Psalm, which should follow the missing "N" verse and in effect now takes its place, also talks about falling, but, instead of saying that Israel has fallen and will rise no more, it says that God supports all those who fall. It is, Rabbi Naḥman says, as if David not only foresaw Israel's downfall, but then also perceived that it would indeed only be temporary and, peering into the far distant future, glimpsed Israel's eventual restoration; now he proclaimed: "The Lord lifts up all who are fallen."

This is wonderful midrash, not only in the apparent erudition and cleverness that inform these remarks, and not only in the way that, in solving one problem (the missing "N" verse), another (Amos's dire words) is also put to rest or at least defused, but still more generally in the way that this very act of exegesis celebrates the canon, the unity and univocality of all of Scripture, and allows it to speak directly to Judaism in its present situation. About all this we shall see more presently. But, to begin, it seems appropriate to touch on the one brief remark in our passage that has so far been neglected, the anonymous comment that in the West (i.e., in Palestine, as opposed to the Babylonian centers of Jewish learning) Amos's verse is in effect repunctuated to read: "She has fallen and will no more; rise, O virgin of Israel." This is also typically midrashic, though somewhat less subtly erudite, one might say, than the rest of our passage. In fact, it entails a grammatical difficulty, for the word "rise" (qûm), although it is fine in Amos's original meaning, here would probably best be modified slightly to fit the new sense, that is, turned into qûmî, the feminine imperative "rise!".[2] But, grammar notwithstanding, the change from

> She has fallen and will no more rise, the virgin of Israel

to

> She has fallen and will no more; rise, O virgin of Israel!

seems a most fitting pars pro toto for the whole midrashic enterprise. For, left alone, the first verse (and others like it) might have sounded the death knell of Israel's religion. Israel's God, the same God that controls her political destiny for all time, had sent prophets to inform the people of His will; their words were binding, for God's decree "shall not return to Me empty-handed, but will accomplish what I have wished" (Isa. 55:11). In other words, the sentence is final: Israel is to rise no more. Yet how might a Jew living in his homeland centuries after this decree was uttered and seeking to cling to the way of his fathers, a Jew whose whole sense of himself and his people was so much *defined* by Scripture and bound up in that "Israel," somehow square this verse with his own religiosity and his hopes for the future (indeed, with other prophecies, prophecies of redemption, which, it was his firm belief, were yet to be fulfilled)?[3] It is striking what he does *not* do. He does not argue that the words spoken by Amos are to be understood in the context of their times, hence that the phrase "will no more rise" might really mean "will not rise again for now," not right away (though this is a defensible reading); nor does he seek to limit its applicability on valid geographical grounds (for "Israel" here means the Northern kingdom and does not apply to Judah, to the Jews); nor yet does he invoke the divine prerogative of annulling evil decrees and sending further word, as in the messages of hope and comfort contained in Isaiah and Jeremiah. His solution is both less realistic and less relativistic: he goes at once to the text itself and— since the written text contained no punctuation or vowel-marks—simply repronounces the same words in such a way as to get them to say exactly the opposite of what Amos intended: a message of despair becomes that ungrammatical clarion call, "Arise (masculine imperative) O virgin of Israel!" Now here is a question which is crucial to our whole subject: what has our exegete accomplished thereby? Is it not obvious to him that he is doing an injustice to the text, twisting it around to say its opposite? Some students of midrash would argue— correctly, I think—that in the midrashic view divine words have an existence independent of circumstance and immediate intention, that, in short, a text is a text, and whatever hidden meaning one is able to reveal in it through "searching" simply *is there*, part of the divine plan. Yet such reasoning, while it is obviously a correct reading of rabbinic attitudes (and one that finds specific expression in the medieval period), seems on its own far too sober in the present circumstance. "Arise O virgin of Israel"?! It reminds one of that bygone favorite of high-school Latin teachers,

Mea mater sus est mala.

(A normal sixteen-year-old, asked to translate, blushes slightly: "My mother, uh, is a bad pig"—such is the obvious meaning of the words. But *mea, est,* and *mala* all have other, less common, meanings, and so "No, you dunce," the teacher roars, "it says *Mea, Mater,* 'Go, oh mother,' *sus est mala,* 'the pig is eating the apples.' Now let's not hear from you again until you learn to hold motherhood in greater respect!") Yet what is a joke in high school is the foundation stone of rabbinic exegesis, and here is the point which we hope eventually to approach: there is often something a bit joking about midrash too. The ultimate subject of that joke is the dissonance between the religion of the Rabbis and the Book from which it is supposed to be derived—and (at least a good part of the time) more precisely the dissonance between that book's supposedly unitary and harmonious message and its actually fragmentary and inconsistent components. Midrash, the perfect expression of rabbinic theology, is thus bound to be at the same time somewhat ironic and yet terribly in earnest. *Qum betulat yisra'el* is indeed amusing, the gallows humor of the prisoners of the Text; and it is the heartfelt hope of a people.

II

The midrashist's biography could safely begin at the end of the biblical period, in the last few centuries before the common era. But his true genealogy goes back much further, to the time of Israel's great prophets, and it is perhaps best to glance at these remoter origins before considering his personal existence proper. The beginnings of the Israelite institution of prophecy are themselves sufficiently diffuse, and disputed, as to defy summary. Recent research has focused on the fact that, on the one hand, those figures whom the text styles as "prophets" (though even here terminology is various) are sometimes strikingly different in function, and that, on the other hand, the office of prophet can be shown to overlap with other functions in Israel previously felt to be rather distinct from it: priest, judge, wisdom-teacher, royal counselor, and so forth. Prophecy in the north was different from prophecy in the south, and prophecy at its origins (if one can even speak in such terms) was different from prophecy in its heyday, the "classical" prophecy of Israel's great writing prophets. But what is perhaps most relevant to our subject is that even classical prophecy was no constant, and that during part of its very height, in the period before the Babylonian exile, it already bore some of the signs characteristic of the turn it was to take during and after that Exile. The prophet's speech had always been powerful, effective; it could be said of him what was said of the sooth-sayer Balaam ben Be'or, "those whom you bless are blessed, and those whom you curse are accursed" (Num. 22:6). In Israel this was repre-sentative of the prophet's special connection with God: his words were one with the divine will, and he could therefore be depended upon to announce God's plans and preferences in the affairs of his people. But once uttered, his words had an afterlife; for divine decrees or punishments sometimes required time before they were enacted, and he who wished to know what was God's will might not only harken to the words uttered by the prophet "from within thy midst" (an act, however, increasingly complicated by the retrospective contemplation of false prophecy),[4] but he might also scrutinize the words of prophets of old, those men now hallowed by tradition and known to have spo-ken God's word in truth. Prophets themselves echoed their predeces-sors or contemporaries and sometimes quite consciously structured their words around a well-known earlier message. One celebrated in-stance is the echoing of a verse of Jeremiah's, "Your words were found, and I ate them, and your words became to me a joy and the delight of my heart" (Jer. 15:16), in the book of Ezekiel (Ezek. 2:7–3:3). It is also a model, however grotesque, of what the word of God was be-coming:

"And you [Ezekiel] shall speak My words to them [the people of Israel] whether they hear or refuse to hear; for they are a rebellious house. But you, son of man, hear what I say to you: be not rebellious like that rebellious house; open your mouth, and eat what I give you." And when I looked, behold, a hand was stretched out to me, and lo, a written scroll was in it; and He spread it out before me; and it had writing on the front and the back, and there were written on it words of lamentation and mourning and woe. And He said to me, "Son of man, eat what is offered to you; eat this scroll, and go, speak to the house of Israel." So I opened my mouth, and He gave me the scroll to eat. And He said to me, "Son of man, eat this scroll that I give you and fill your stomach with it." Then I ate it; and it was in my mouth as sweet as honey.

Like a child at mealtime, Ezekiel is urged to "eat what is offered to you," and his compliance in the face of what looks to be a thoroughly undigestible meal makes him a model of obedience, the very opposite of the "rebellious" subjects he is to address. But what is so striking is the meal itself: the word of God! Already in Jeremiah's verse one could sense some of the diffuseness that the prophetic scenario had taken on: God's words just appear, "were found"—words spoken of old?

spoken directly to Jeremiah?—and Jeremiah does not simply pass them along, but "eats" them: they nourish him, equip him for his office ("for I am called by thy name"), and presumably they will be related to his mission only in the way our food is related to what we do and say: they give him the force to speak and act. But how significant it is that in Ezekiel God's speech has already become a *text*; and the very act of eating God's word now demands impossible obedience and self-control, swallowing up an actual scroll and then *not* (in both senses) "spitting it back," but digesting the twice uneatable thing, a scroll, and one of lamentation and mourning and woe, to find it—how obedience pays off!—not bitter, but sweeter than honey.

In exile, and all the more afterward, the divine word was increasingly a text, and it became the more hallowed the more the parchment yellowed and turned brown and cracked. For the word that had been lively in Israel's midst was now, in the restored province of Judea, disputed; self-appointed prophets and omen-seekers teemed, and some dreamed of a time when "every prophet will be ashamed of his vision when he prophesies; he will not put on the hairy mantle in order to deceive, but he will say, 'I am no prophet, I am a tiller of the soil' " (Zech. 13:4–5). Coupled with this was its apparent opposite, actually a corollary, the hope for true prophecy's restoration, when Elijah would return to earth (Mal. 4:5) or the divine spirit would be showered forth on the nation as a whole, "your sons and your daughters shall prophesy, your old men shall dream dreams, and your young men shall see visions" (Joel 3:1). For the true word was now remote, a thing of books.[5] Indeed, it is noteworthy that the scroll motif had undergone one final, still more telling, modification:

Again I lifted my eyes and saw, and behold a flying scroll! And He said to me, "What do you see?" I answered, "I see a flying scroll; its length is twenty cubits, and its breadth ten cubits." Then He said to me, "This is the curse that goes out over the face of the whole land; for every one who steals shall be cut off henceforth according to it, and everyone who swears falsely shall be cut off henceforth according to it. I will send it forth, says the Lord of hosts, and it shall enter the house of the thief, and the house of him who swears falsely by My name; and it shall abide in his house and consume it, timber and stones." (Zech. 5:1–4)

Here the prophet is not even given to touch the divine word, it does not enter his mouth even in the form of food, but he sees it passing by, a giant scroll—what greater literalization of "the word of God in action"?—to which he can only bear witness: its mission will be to destroy the house of thieves and perjurers, to avenge the transgression of that which is also (and most often) written, the Decalogue. But if this text represents in some form the disappearance, or mediation, of the prophet's own powerful speech, it also has a positive side: for here is Scripture as Actor, the written word which flies like an angel to carry out God's decrees and indeed, like the "angel of the Lord" in earlier writings, is even able to wreak physical destruction on those who have incurred the divine wrath.

In such a world of potent texts—sub specie divinitatis—God's human intermediaries become by necessity students of old scrolls, manipulators of documents, soferim, bookmen and copyists. And it would not be long before reading was no longer simply reading. For the words of God, whose simplicity and straightforwardness were once so obvious that one had to be blind and deaf not to perceive them (as per Isa. 6:10; or, as Amos expressed it, "When a lion roars, who is not fearful? And when the Lord God speaks, who can but prophesy?" Amos 3:8), now were felt to require careful study and inspection in order to be understood. The same alphabetical psalmist who exults in the world of Scripture (Ps. 119) also endlessly prays for "proper perception and knowledge" to understand it, aid in penetrating its "mysteries": "Give me understanding so that I may live," "Give me understanding according to your word." Nothing was obvious. God's deeds, that is, the accounts of them, had to be "scrutinized [derušim] by all who delight in them" (Ps. 111:2). Those who were to do the interpreting were very much the successors of the prophets—the new bearers of the divine word—and like prophets depended on something like divine inspiration in order to receive God's word.[6]

This is represented most clearly in the first part of the book of Daniel, whose principal theme is interpretation. Daniel is of course a "reader" of dreams (dreams are like texts)[7]—but how striking that, unlike Joseph, he is required not just to interpret the meaning of the dream, but to retell the dream to the dreamer in the first place (Dan. 2)! Later (Dan. 5), Daniel is called upon not only to interpret the message written on the wall of Belshazzar's palace, but first and foremost to decipher its undecipherable writing, and so be able to speak the mysterious prophecy.[8] Both features represent the same basic idea: interpretation begins by the interpreter reproducing the text itself, for the latter, whether dream or scribbling, is itself a gift from God granted *afresh to the interpreter*; proper understanding is inseparable from prophecy itself. To just such an interpreter ought to be revealed the "correct" sense of Jeremiah's plain speaking about the endurance of exile and domination (Jer. 25:11–12, 29:10); the "seventy years" meant seventy groups of seven years each (Dan. 9:24). Elsewhere, after interpretation is revealed, Daniel offers thanks to God—but it is a cryptographer's praising:

Blessed be the name of God forever and ever, to whom belong wisdom and might. He changes times and seasons; he removes kings and sets up kings; he gives wisdom to the wise, and knowledge to those who have understanding; he reveals deep secrets and mysterious things; he knows what is in the darkness, and the light dwells with him. (Dan. 2:20–22)

And when at last he is ordered to cease, we are not surprised at the form the order takes: "But you, Daniel, shut up the *words*, and *seal the book* until the time of the end."

The inspired interpreter, successor to the great prophets, already possesses Scripture, even though those acts of exclusion and pinning-down known as the canonization are not yet complete.[9] This is to say that he not only possesses sacred texts, but that holiness is attributed to them in their entirety: the "ancient words" have been received as Scripture. "Great are the deeds of the Lord, scrutinized by all who delight in them" tells us much about the early stages of Scriptural Authority, deeply instilled before the definition of the final canon. But the midrashist as such does not exist yet—or we might say more cautiously that the proto-midrashist coexists with others, who, while they share his reverence for the Text, will ultimately turn in a different direction.

III

It is something of a commonplace that Israel's God is a God of history. Of late the excesses in this line of thought have come under just attack—it is certainly true that "historical thinking" can be found in Israel's neighbors' speculations about the gods, as it is equally true that elements of "cyclical thought" are apparent in Israelite institutions and writings[10]—nevertheless it is striking to observe the extent to which, especially in relatively early biblical texts, God's power is seen to manifest itself uniquely in one-time events that, having happened, change things forever. "You were slaves in Egypt, I led you out; now you are free men." This is so much our own sense of time that it is difficult for us even to conceive of another, in which all that is real partakes of the returning and the repeating, and everything unique and *einmalig*, everything which cannot gain its reality from the great rounds, is therefore inconsequential.[11] But this other view of time (and truly it is not a single one but a spectrum of views), these understandings of time in which events of the world are not so strictly segregated in contemplation from the ever-returning, are indeed widespread in the world and in human history,[12] so much so that the sense of time characterized as "biblical"—on which is based not only the oft-cited conviction that history itself, "how things come out," is uniquely the product of the single, all-powerful Will, but along with it that peculiarly Israelite feeling of *consequentiality*, the unflagging consciousness of how events in the past *create* the present—such a sense of time appears in the broad perspective not only somewhat atypical but rather strange. So much is everyday reality the precise reflection of its Creator's whims that there is no inertia, nothing need necessarily keep going—the sun might stop in its tracks if such were desired (Josh. 10:12–13), or rivers or seas turn to dry land; at God's direction

The bow of the mighty falls slack, while weaklings are girded with strength;
Sleek men are hired out for bread, but the formerly hungry are well-stocked
   forever.
A childless woman ends up with seven, and she who had many is left alone.
The Lord kills or gives life back, sends down to the grave or brings up;
The Lord can make rich or make poor, can humble or lift up again.
(I Sam. 2:4–6)

In such a world, *causes* do indeed become an obsession. It is easy enough to accept gratefully that the sun shines or the rains come or Israel triumphs; but in darkness or drought or defeat, how can one simply be patient, wait for things to get better, when there is obviously a reason, a sin unatoned, a violator of ḥerem in one's midst? And so one does atone, and search in one's midst and in one's past; and if, in spite of all effort, conditions do not improve, what conclusion is available other than that atonement has not been sufficient, or that sinners continue even now, undetected, or that past infractions have so accumulated as to cause God's long-restrained wrath to run a lengthy course?

It is remarkable, and often remarked upon, that the book of Ecclesiastes, a relatively late biblical book, shows very little of this sense of consequentiality.[13] For its author, the sun rises because that is simply part of the ongoing round of things (Eccles. 1:5); it rises only to set and travel under the earth back to where it will rise again. Even the flow of a river's waters, which to other minds has presented itself as the model of an ever-changing, ever-unique universe, to Koheleth is only another instance of that which is beyond change; the rivers flow as they have always flowed and ever to the sea, for "what has been is what will be, and what has been done is what will be done again."[14] Here is not the place to rehearse the various possible influences on this book's author in his rather unique conception of things, other than perhaps to note the circumstance that his is, as stated, a *late* book, probably no earlier than the fifth or fourth century before the common era. And—here is the point—as such its sense of time is not nearly so unique as is sometimes claimed. For much "wisdom literature," especially that of later vintage, bears the same stamp.[15] Time itself seemed to be changing at the end of the biblical period, and there was growing stronger in Israel a type of writing still more striking in its sense of return: apocalyptic.

Apocalyptic books—and here are intended not so much the "apocalyptic elements" in such biblical books as Zechariah or Joel as that body of self-contained, often pseudonymous "apocalypses" (= "revelations"), testaments, and similar writings that sprang up at the end of the biblical period—such works as these conceive of God's activity in history as at once more pervasive and more remote than that portrayed in earlier biblical histories. "He who calls the generations in advance" (Isa. 41:4) has arranged all beforehand, and it is this order, and specifically the "last things" in history, that the apocalyptist discloses behind the veil of mysterious symbols and allusive numerology. He himself lives at the time of the "last things," and it is his intense appreciation of his own times as the unfolding of a previously planned sequence that often leads him to detailed descriptions of the present and the immediate future in the form of pseudonymous "predictions" uttered by this or that hoary character long before.[16] This might strike one as all too linear a sense of things, but it is the well-known characteristic of this literature that "Endzeit wird Urzeit," and that in coming to a close history will recapitulate or reenact the time of the beginning. Here is something not only circular,[17] but sometimes cyclical as well: for it is as if even God is not quite free to act as He will but must forever intervene only as He has in the past, adopting the same forms of cataclysm and release. Moreover, the typological interpretations of Scripture which characterize some of these works, in which events of biblical history become models or types of the great eschatological events which were either already occurring or just about to occur, are a still more vivid instance of this same way of thinking. Indeed, these three salient characteristics of this literature, i.e., eschatological concerns, pseudepigraphic forms, and the typological use of Scriptural history, all seem to embody a single, overall effort, that of projecting the biblical past onto the present, and so endowing the present with precisely the same divinely ordered quality that the past had, at least as witnessed in biblical texts.

There were, beside impending consummation, other ways for the present to achieve some biblical glow. Such an anodyne feature as the archaizing Hebrew of the book of Esther, or the "anthologizing" Hebrew style of the Qumran *hodayot*, or in general all the archaizing details and manners of so many post-biblical compositions, attest to this same desire to dress up present reality in biblical trappings; indeed, this is certainly an element in the halakhic reading of Scripture as well, and especially in the willingness of later Jews to assume upon themselves biblical strictures of purity and other details applying originally only to the priesthood.

The allegorized Bible of Alexandrian Judaism in its own way accomplished the same thing. For however much the allegorizing of Homer and Hesiod had served apologetic purposes, excusing offensive incidents and descriptions and helping to attribute to these ancient authors philosophical teachings of a later age,[18] the principal accomplishment of the allegorization of the Bible undertaken by Philo of Alexandria and his predecessors was the *de-particularization of the text*. Those little details of family and tribal history, geographical references, personal names, and so on that dot the Pentateuchal narrative were the prime target of Philo's activity precisely because their very existence in the Book of God called for some interpretation; taken literally, they seemed (however true) all too trivial, too *particular*, for the great divine utterance. And so, for Philo, the Bible in its highest form was a book of all times and places: the incidents of Israel's history become events of the soul, ever enacted anew in the spiritual life of man, and Near Eastern geography becomes a spiritual mappa mundi, allowing God's commandment to Abraham and company in Ur to become, in Philo's retelling:

Quit then your meddling with heavenly concerns, and take up your abode, as

I have said, in yourselves; leave behind your opinion, [which is represented by] the country of the Chaldeans, and migrate to Haran, the place of sense-perception, which is understanding's bodily tenement. For the translation of Haran is "hole," and holes are figures of the openings used by sense-perceptions.[19]

But rather than simply assimilate all such tendencies into one (for it will be, on the contrary, most important to distinguish them), one ought rather merely to see in their very existence symptoms of a common urge. That urge, to connect one's own world with the world of Scripture, to find some way of dwelling, as it were, in biblical reality, points to something basic about the late and post-biblical "sense of time": that the present world was somehow discontinuous with the Bible's, and that the Bible's simple, "consequential" view of God's workings could not be extended in linear fashion to cover recent history. For the divine manipulation of events, so manifest, it seemed, in days of yore, had since the return from Exile become increasingly attenuated. What pattern could be discerned in the ups and downs of Judah's recent fortunes? Cyrus's edict and the return itself were a definite upturn, but these were followed by years of struggle and disappointment; the incompleteness of Israel's restoration and the flagging attempts to rebuild the Temple were certainly a downturn, though the latter effort did finally meet with success; now the heyday of Ezra and Nehemiah, now the Greek conquest; the eventual replacement of Ptolemaic rule with Seleucid tyranny; successful revolt, independence, degeneration, reconquest—how was all this to correspond to some divine order? History no longer seemed to hold the simple message it had once contained,[20] and we may not be wrong in supposing that the (in various senses) cyclical views of time embodied in works as varied as Ecclesiastes and apocalyptic represent both a common reversion from biblical consequentiality to something less unilinear, and a desire nevertheless not to invalidate the truth of what had been, not to invalidate Scripture. (In some ways the perfect, indeed poetic, expression of this is Daniel's interpretation of the seventy years of Exile predicted by Jeremiah [mentioned above]; for the notion of "weeks of years" carries that peculiarly apocalyptic feeling for time being dealt out like a hand of cards, arrangeable into suits and subgroups—and yet Daniel's interpretation is manifestly aimed at bringing the present under the coverage of biblical prophecy, confirming Jeremiah's words as true-once-interpreted, and then pointing to the present as that predicted future.)

And so something paradoxical had happened to the Bible's unremitting sense of the *einmalig* progression of events, the ever-new unfolding of the Divine Plan: that whole space of time which was biblical history became, as it were, bracketed. The Bible's time was *other time*, discontinuous with later events and yet, because of its special character, one which was constantly about to impose its mark on the present. Bible-time was forever looming. The reading of the Torah's history itself became cyclical, indeed, eventually an annual event: Creation, Exodus, Sinai, and Moses' death were regular occurrences, and at the end the accumulated roll of scroll was unwound from one spindle and rolled back onto the other as it was in the beginning. The Bible's own historicization of the cyclical agricultural feasts was now recyclicalized: the Torah's treatment of the harvest festival booths as a historical allusion, a reminder that "I caused the Israelites to dwell in booths when I took them out of Egypt" (Lev. 23:43), was itself only an incident in the liturgical cycle of Scriptural readings, the ever-returning series of exoduses and desert wanderings that mark a man's days.

Here then is the crucial factor in the mentality of all early exegesis: for when what *happened* in Scripture happens again and again, unfolds over and over, it is because the Bible is not "the past" at all. For it to be the past, its sense of time would necessarily need to be continuous with our own, and we would have to live amid a series of similarly God-dominated events, so that the whole flow of time from Abraham to now could make for one simple, consequential, story. Once this is no longer the case, biblical time becomes "other," a world wholly apart from ours, and yet one which is constantly intersecting our own via the strategies just seen. The Bible's last authors and editors, however much they were convinced of God's Providence and absolute domination of history, had seen in the hallowed texts of the past far more than mere records of God's doings or transcriptions of His past pronouncements; they had seen Scripture, and it is this view that was transmitted to the Bible's first exegetes.

Having noticed these common features, it is nevertheless important to point out significant differences between the midrashic approach to Scripture and some of the other approaches mentioned, specifically with regard to their respective senses of time. Thus, for the allegorist, as we have seen, Scriptural time re-becomes continuous with the present in the sense that those events of the soul portrayed in

Scriptural history apply to each man in his own life. That is, God acts now as He has always acted: His ways with the soul of man have simply been portrayed by God in external form in the details of Israelite history and law, but their important time is truly eternal and non-specific, hence continuous with our spiritual present. For the apocalyptist, Scriptural time and present time also re-become continuous, though in a rather different way: the broad strokes of divine activity in the biblical past are actually reappearing in the present day, and they will be such as to overwhelm all the messy, inconsequential details of the intervening years. God has acted and is acting now, or is just about to act. Now later, rabbinic Judaism might seem similarly eschatological, for it awaits with each passing day the arrival of God's annointed and the setting aright of history—in this sense it appears to have much in common with the apocalyptists. But this has nothing to do with the stance of its exegesis (though a considerable bit of its content deals with messianic themes). For midrash, as opposed to Qumranic *pešer* and other "political" exegeses, generally views Scripture as a world unto itself, without direct connection to our own times; as one critic has phrased it, "God acted (in the past), will act (in the eschatological future), but is not acting in between."[21] Messianism, however important it may be, never becomes the bridge between the biblical past and the midrashist's present.[22] Such a bridge, if it exists at all, is the halakhic one: the Bible informs the present as the source of those practices which Jews undertake to adhere to. But there is no bridge between the Bible's *time* and our time: God has acted and will act, but for now His activity is suspended in a majestic state of kingship: He is responsible for everything, yet the ups and downs of political or daily life are conceded to His control without usually being held up to inspection. And if we are to designate the halakhic reading of Scripture as a bridge between the Bible and the present-day Jew, out of fairness one must add that the bridge has another (if anything, greater) lane going in the opposite direction. For in midrash the Bible becomes, as stated, a world unto itself. Midrashic exegesis is the way into that world; it does not seek to view present-day reality through biblical spectacles, neither to find referents of biblical prophecy in present-day happenings, nor to find referents to the daily life of the soul in biblical allegory. Instead it simply overwhelms the present; the Bible's time is important, while the present is not; and so it invites the reader to cross over into the enterable world of Scripture.

IV

Thus the midrashist has much in common with the other early exegetes mentioned, as well as a few things which distinguish him. Let not these common points be taken lightly, for together they point to important themes indeed: the idea of the Bible itself, that is, both the establishing of the special character of divine speech, and therefore the need for (inspired) interpretation, and the propounding—or rather the presuming—of the Scriptural Presumption, making the (still increasing) corpus of sacred books into a single, unified, revelatory pool. These traits may seem all too general, and so obvious as to bear no further insistence; but they are, as post-Renaissance exegesis was to learn, crucial to the Bible's very being; any exegesis which deviates from them undermines the Bible's unity and sacred character, until it in effect becomes a different book, or rather collection of books. This said, it will now be worthwhile to jump ahead several centuries and focus in on a more specialized and highly developed branch of this exegetical tendency, namely rabbinic midrash, biblical exegesis as it has come down to us in the literature of the tannaim and amoraim.

There are many recent works that seek to define midrash, and nothing would be gained here by attempting to reduce these efforts to a few sentences; though one might say more pointedly (and paraphrasing what a recent book had to say about definitions of irony) that, since these studies have already not defined midrash in ample detail, there is little purpose in our not defining it again here. Suffice it to say that the Hebrew word *midrash* might be best translated as "research," a translation that incorporates the word's root meaning of "search out, inquire" and perhaps as well suggests that the results of that research are almost by definition recherché, that is, not obvious, out-of-the-way, sometimes far-fetched. The word has been used to designate both the activity of interpretation and the fruits of that activity, and in Hebrew writings it was used extensively for the collective body of all such interpretations as well as in the name of certain collections of midrashic material (Midrash Rabbah, etc.). At bottom midrash is not a genre of interpretation but an interpretative stance, a way of reading the sacred text, and we shall use it in this broad sense. The genres in which this way of reading has found expression include interpretive translations of the Bible such as the early Aramaic targumim; retellings of biblical passages and books such as the "Genesis Apocryphon" (discovered amongst the Dead Sea Scrolls) or the medieval *Sefer hayashar*; sermons, homilies, exegetical prayers and poems, and other synagogue pieces; and of course the great standard corpora of Jewish exegesis, tannaitic midrashim, exegetical parts of the Mishnah and the Gemara, collections of *derashot* (as individual bits of exegesis are sometimes called) arranged in exegetical, historical, or other fashions, medieval commentaries on the Bible and other texts—in short, almost all of what constitutes classical (and much of medieval) Jewish writing. It is proper that this should seem an overwhelmingly broad field of inquiry, for at heart midrash is nothing less than the foundation stone of rabbinic Judaism, and it is as diverse as Jewish creativity itself.

Midrash, then, is a kind of recherché interpreting of Scripture which finds expression in all manner of contexts. Beyond such a broad (and, alas, not particularly helpful) general pronouncement, there are perhaps two other points about midrash which ought to find their way into any introductory overview. The first is that midrash's precise focus is most often what one might call surface irregularities in the text: a good deal of the time, it is concerned with (in the broadest sense) *problems*. The missing "N" verse in Psalm 145, a theologically troublesome pronouncement of the prophet Amos, or, indeed, simply a perceived contradiction between passages (for example, two slightly different versions of the same law), or a word that does not seem to fit properly in its context, or simply an unusual word, or an unusual spelling of a word—all of these are the sorts of irregularities which might cause the reader to trip and stumble as he walks along the biblical path; and so over such irregularities midrash builds a smoothing mound which both assures that the reader will not fall and, at the same time, embellishes the path with material taken from elsewhere and builds into it, as it were, an extra little lift. Or—to use a shopworn but more appropriate image—the text's irregularity is the grain of sand which so irritates the midrashic oyster that he constructs a pearl around it. Soon enough—pearls being prized—midrashists begin looking for irritations and irregularities, and in later midrash there is much material, especially list-making and text-connecting, whose connection with "problems" is remote indeed; in fact, like many a modern-day homilist, the midrashist sometimes betrays signs of having first thought of a solution and then having gone out in search of the problem to which it might be applied. This notwithstanding, the problem-solving approach is helpful in understanding the focus of much midrash, and it is worthwhile for the beginner to keep in mind.

The second fundamental point, still more basic, is that midrash is an exegesis of biblical verses, not of books. The basic unit of the Bible, for the midrashist, is the verse: this is what he seeks to expound, and it might be said that there simply is no boundary encountered beyond that of the verse until one comes to the borders of the canon itself—a situation analogous to certain political organizations in which there are no separate states, provinces, or the like but only the village and the Empire. One of the things this means is that each verse of the Bible is in principle as connected to its most distant fellow as to the one next door; in seeking to illuminate a verse from Genesis, the midrashist is as likely to have reference (if to anything) to a verse from the Psalter as to another verse in the immediate context—indeed, he sometimes delights in the remoter source.

Perhaps the clearest demonstration of this is to be found in the midrashic exegesis of the Song of Songs, embodied in such collections as *Midrash Ḥazita* ("Song of Songs Rabbah"). For here is a book whose place in the Bible must rest on the allegorical reading of it as a song of love between God and his people; here, even if nowhere else, one would expect a consistent interpretive line: God is the "Lover" and Israel the "Beloved." Yet, while it is true that this exegetical path is generally followed, other persons or figures in the song also are interpreted to be God or Israel: King Solomon, or the "daughters of Jerusalem," or even features of the landscape. At the same time, the figure of the Beloved in the song is not consistently read as Israel, but sometimes is interpreted as representing individual Israelites, Sarah or other biblical figures. Indeed, on one occasion it seems that the Beloved is understood to represent not Israel, or even individual Israelites, but God! For the four verses in which the Beloved addresses the daughters of Jerusalem with the phrase "I adjure you O daughters of Jerusalem" (Song of Songs 2:7, 3:5, 5:8, 8:4) are interpreted in one tradition as corresponding to four oaths which "He" (God) "caused Israel to swear to" during the Exile. Now how can anyone maintain that the Beloved is allegorically *both* Israel and God, or that Israel is represented by more than one character in the same song? The fact is that such inconsistencies were apparently not troubling, for what the midrashist addressed himself to was not first and foremost the book as a whole, that is, not

the allegory itself—"Granted, it is love song about God and Israel"—
but single verses, isolated in suspended animation. If the precise wording of a verse suggested an interpretive tack that would violate the
overall allegorical frame, the midrashist sometimes picked up the
suggestion nonetheless.[23] For the same reason, of course, midrashic
collections do not scruple at assembling different solutions to the same
problem in a verse, even though they may contradict one another: it
is not that one is right and the others wrong, but that all are adequate
"smoothings-over."

Thus, for example, Genesis Rabbah assembles a host of opinions
aimed at explaining away the apparent pleonasm of Gen. 21:1, "And
the Lord remembered Sarah as He had said, and the Lord did for Sarah
as He had spoken":

"And the Lord remembered Sarah as He had *said*" [refers to the promises of
God] introduced [in the text] by [the verb] "say" [as, e.g., God's promise in Gen.
17:19]; "and the Lord did for Sarah as He had *spoken*," [refers to] what was
introduced by "spoke" [as perhaps Gen. 15:18, introduced (15:1) by the root
d-b-r, "speak"]; R. Neḥemiah said, "as He had said" means what He had said
to her by means of an angel; "as He had spoken" means He Himself [i.e., Gen.
18:10 *vs.* 16:16]. R. Yehuda said "And the Lord *remembered* Sarah"—to give her
a son; "and the Lord *did* for Sarah"—to bless her with milk [to nurse that son,
as per Gen. 21:7]. R. Neḥemiah objected: Had anything been announced about
milk yet? But [if you wish to base the distinction on "remember" *vs.* "do"] let
this verse teach us that God returned her to her youthful condition. [That
would account for "remember"; then "do" would refer to granting her the
child itself.] R. Abbahu said: [first] He made her respected by all, so that none
should call her "barren woman" [as presumably Hagar did in 16:4, then he
gave her a son]. R. Yudan said: she lacked an ovary; the Lord [first] fashioned
an ovary for her [and then gave her a son].[24]

Such countenancing of contradictory interpretations reflects on the
essence of midrashic writings per se, which are not compositions but
compilations of comments that are usually focused on isolated, individual verses. Consistency within individual sections of a midrash or
even in larger units was apparently not an overriding consideration.[25]

The verse-centeredness of midrash is so fundamental that one hes-
itates even to ask why it should be so: it just is the way midrash proceeds. And yet it does seem to correspond well to the way in which
a text, familiar to the point of being largely known by heart, is carried
about in the memory. How easy it was, if someone cited the beginning
of a verse or some phrase within it, to produce the verse as a whole;
a gifted memory might also easily supply the succeeding verse or

verses. This capacity notwithstanding, it was sometimes difficult to re-call the larger context of the verse in question—"Is that what Abraham said to Abimelech, or what Isaac said?" "Is that in Psalm 145, or Psalm 34?" Midrash generally seems to be addressing its verse in the same relative isolation in which it is remembered: its focus is the word within that verse whose meaning one was never quite sure of, or that phrase which always did seem problematic—and it provides for the difficulty a pungent solution, often one that connects the verse to another, but also often without reference to the wider context. (Our midrashic com-pilations are in this sense potentially deceiving, since they seem to treat the whole text bit by bit; but, with the exception of certain patterns,[26] these "bits" are rather atomistic, and, as any student of rabbinic liter-ature knows, interchangeable, modifiable, combinable—in short, not part of an overall exegesis at all.) *Forever after*, one cannot think of the verse or hear it recited without also recalling the solution to its prob-lematic irritant—indeed, remembering it in the study-house or syn-agogue, one would certainly pass it along to others present, and together appreciate its cleverness and erudition. And so midrashic ex-plications of individual verses no doubt circulated on their own, in-dependent of any larger exegetical context. Perhaps in this sense it would not be inappropriate to compare their manner of circulating to that of jokes in modern society; indeed, they were a kind of joking, a learned and sophisticated play about the biblical text, and like jokes they were passed on, modified, and improved as they went, until a great many of them eventually entered into the common inheritance of every Jew, passed on in learning with the text of the Bible itself.

Much of this can be made more vivid in the presence of a concrete example. Let us consider the midrashic handling of a verse from Psalm 81, "Sing unto God our strength." The psalm begins easily enough: the first four lines urge listeners to join in God's praise, to "strike up song," "sound the timbrel," and so forth, connecting this with divine law, "Israel's statute it is, an ordinance from the God of Jacob." At the next line, however, the text becomes mysterious: "He"—presumably God—"set it as a testimony in Joseph when he"—perhaps Joseph, perhaps God—"went out over the land of Egypt, the tongue of one I did not know I hear." What all this might mean is still difficult for the modern exegete to sort out: the "speech of the unknown one" (or, alternately, the "unknown speech") seems actually to appear in the next line, "I have freed his shoulder from the burden, his hands are removed from hard toil," and we are probably right in supposing that these are God's words, spoken to the Israelites at the time He gave them the "testimony" (covenant). The general point of these verses thus seems to be that the God whose praise is being enjoined is He who made a covenant with the descendants of Joseph after the Exodus, He who said "I have freed his shoulder from the burden," and so on; that is why He ought to be praised. But the general point is most emphatically not what will interest the midrashist, but the troubling little details glossed over in this account; and it is the slightest of these, the fact that in verse five Joseph's name appears in an unusual spelling, *Yehosef* instead of the normal contracted form *Yosef*, that provides the midrashist with his point of attack. Now of course nothing would be easier than to explain this detail away as an insignificant variation—for does not the same contraction appear in other biblical names beginning *yeho* (thus Jonathan alternates with Jehonathan, Jonadab with Jehonadab, etc.)? But such is not the way of midrash. Instead, the circumstance of this unusual spelling suggests to the midrashist a whole scenario. He is reminded of how other Patriarchs' names were changed at key moments in their lives—Abram to Abraham, Jacob to Israel, and so forth—and it occurs to him that the spelling "Jehoseph" may in fact allude to a similar incident, previously unreported, in Joseph's life. The phrase "a testimony in Jehoseph" only seems to confirm this. For if the phrase were meant to indicate that God had set something as a testimony to or for Joseph, surely some other preposition would have been more appropriate! Then why in Jehoseph? Perhaps the point is precisely that extra *ho-* in Joseph's name; the testimony is "in Jehoseph" in the sense that it is in the name "Jehoseph." But if all this implies that God at some point changed Joseph's name to "Jehoseph" (establishing the extra *ho-* as some kind of "testimony"), what might the occasion for such a name change have been? The answer appears to be alluded to in the next (and also somewhat anomalous) phrase of our verse, "when he went out over the land of Egypt." For if the intention of this phrase were merely to indicate "during the time when Joseph was in Egypt," the verb "to go out" and the preposition "upon" or "over" would hardly have been used. Ah, but Joseph did *go out* of prison, was set free by Pharaoh so that he might become vizier *over* all the land—surely this must be the meaning of "went out over," being freed and indeed made ruler over Egypt.[27] And such therefore must have been the moment for Joseph's change of name, the time when he was let out of prison.

Moreover, it is striking to the midrashist that in Hebrew "Joseph" becomes "Jehoseph" through the addition of a single letter, the letter *heh* ("H"), for this is one of the letters found in the Divine Name, the tetragrammaton. What better proof that it was God, or one of His angels, that changed the name? In fact, the phrase "set it as a testimony in Jehoseph" can be read (because of the ambiguities of a vowelless, unpointed text) in another way: "he set it," Hebrew *śāmô*, might also be pronounced *šemô*, "His Name"—that is, God's name, or part of it— was inserted "in Joseph" as a kind of witness or testimony at the time he was let out of prison.

The last phrase of our verse, "a tongue I did not know I hear," provides the means for pulling all this together into a cohesive scenario. For it occurs to our midrashist that one of the attributes of a proper wise man in Pharaoh's court must certainly have been some linguistic knowledge; indeed, the complete sage ought to have been acquainted with all seventy languages of the world. And so, here comes our midrash: when Pharaoh suggested to his advisors that the man who had just emerged from prison and had interpreted his dream, Joseph, be made vizier over all of Egypt, they objected. "He is unworthy, a mere slave, and he certainly does not know the seventy languages of the world—in fact, he does not even know proper Egyptian!" Pharaoh said: "Tomorrow we will put him to the test." That night, an angel visited Joseph and changed his name to Jehoseph (presumably to make him a "changed man," grant him new powers) and taught him not only Egyptian, but all the languages of the world. The next morning, returning to Pharaoh's court, Joseph exclaims, "The tongue(s) [it might better be read as a plural, and can be without changing the consonantal text] I did not know I now understand."

What is by no means unusual about this piece of midrash, but is the point of our citing it nonetheless, is how strictly it observes the boundaries of the verse in question. That is, we have here a perfect integration of the previously mysterious words "He *set it as a testimony in Jehoseph, upon his going out over the land of Egypt, a tongue I did not know I understand*." Every problem in the verse has been explained via the foregoing imaginative scenario, and yet the verse itself is not integrated into its context any better than before: we still do not know what all this has to do with the rejoicing invoked in the first four lines, nor yet how all this is to be connected with the lines that follow, but *this is immaterial*, for the midrashist's aim was from the beginning only to take care of the verse in isolation. Now of course, as has already been stated, there are a great many midrashic interpretations which take on more than one line at a time, and even a whole type which seeks to interpret a series of consecutive references.[28] But the existence of such texts should not obscure the principle of insularity itself. A footnote sometimes appended to our midrash puts the point most graphically. Noting the unusual fact that the verse in question both begins and ends with the Hebrew letter *ayin*, it finds further support for the "seventy languages" interpretation, since *ayin* has the value of seventy in the Hebrew numerical system. But what more striking expression could there be of midrash's verse-centeredness? It is interested in what happens between the two *ayins*.

Having started with this concrete example, it may be worthwhile to examine some of the variant forms in which it appears in different midrashic collections, for the variants are instructive. The most important and striking of these is the attribution of the sentence "A tongue I did not know I now hear" not to Joseph but to Pharaoh. In some ways attributing it to Pharaoh would be preferable; for in Joseph's mouth, the verb "hear" must be taken in its (rarer) sense of "understand," and the sense of the whole clause remains somewhat fuzzy. In order to make the attribution to Pharaoh possible, these versions add this twist to the story: Joseph appears in Pharaoh's court, speaks the seventy languages and then adds some words in Hebrew, the holy tongue (and presumably, therefore, not to be numbered among the seventy); whereupon Pharaoh, or Pharaoh's advisors, can exclaim, "A tongue I did not know I hear." Not only is Joseph the master of the languages of the nations, but he knows the holy tongue as well, which even Pharaoh does not; surely he is qualified to become vizier![29] Moreover, it is interesting to note how some versions connect to this midrash Pharaoh's words when Joseph requests permission to return to Canaan to bury his father Jacob. In the Bible Pharaoh answers: "Go then and bury your father *as he caused you to swear*" (Gen. 50:6). These last words seem to imply that, were it not for the fact of Joseph's oath, Pharaoh would not have permitted him to go. But if so, why should Pharaoh be acting with such deference to oaths? It all goes back to the seventy languages incident:

The next day [after Gabriel had taught Joseph all the languages and had added the letter "H" to his name] in every language that Pharaoh conversed with him, he was able to answer him. But when he [Joseph] spoke to him in the holy tongue, he did not understand what he was saying. He [Pharaoh] said: "Teach me! He taught it to him but he could not learn. Said he [Pharaoh]: "Swear to me that you will not reveal [my ignorance]." He swore to him. [Later,] when he [Joseph] said to him, "My father caused me to swear . . ." (Gen. 50:5), he [Pharaoh] said: "Go out and be absolved of your oath [i.e., forget about it]!" Said he: "Then will I also forget about my [other] oath?" [Pharaoh] answered him: "Then go out, 'rise up and bury your father as he caused you to swear.' " (Gen. 50:6)   (B. Sota 36b)

It should be noted that not all midrashic interpretations of this verse rely on the "seventy languages" story; another interpretation has it simply that God added a letter of His Name to Joseph's in order to indicate that Joseph had not succumbed to the temptations of Potiphar's wife as was alleged (here the word "testimony" in Ps. 81:6 is being emphasized; the extra letter actually testifies to Joseph's innocence).[30]

Another point to be made about this example, and it is really our first point in a different guise, is the great versatility of this piece of midrash vis-à-vis larger compilations. Since it aims, first and foremost, at clearing up certain difficulties in a verse of Psalm 81, it would certainly be able to be incorporated into a collection of midrashic comments on that Psalm, as indeed it was.[31] But, precisely because it is so self-contained and not tied to an overall integrative exegesis of Psalm 81, our midrash can also be lifted bodily out of this context and inserted elsewhere, most obviously into the Genesis account of the story of Joseph, but also in other places where a connection, no matter how discursive, suggests itself: in a verse in Ecclesiastes touching on wisdom, in the account of the dedication of the tabernacle when commenting on the sacrifice offered by one of Joseph's descendants (here the phrase "seventy shekels" reminds the midrashist of the seventy languages), and so on and so forth. The very insularity of midrash's verse-centeredness meant that one interpretive story could be combined with another and/or incorporated into many different collections.

Lastly, one should take note of a process that might be called the "legendizing" of midrash. As we saw, the whole story of the seventy languages and the extra letter in Joseph's name was created for the purpose of explicating the difficulties in Ps. 81:6. So much is that verse the point that, in whatever context our midrash might appear, that verse will always be able to function as its "punch line," namely, "And that's why it says in Psalm 81, 'He set it for a testimony in Joseph, in his going out over the land of Egypt, a tongue I did not know I now hear.' " Yet it is a curious fact about such fanciful explications that they can become detached from their punch lines. However absurd (because tailor-made) the details of the explicative story may be, they eventually become part of the corpus of embellishments that accompany the written text and begin to take on a life of their own. Soon, someone retelling the events of Joseph's rise to power in Egypt might simply unfold the tale of the seventy languages, the angel's adding an extra letter to Joseph's name, and so forth, without ever mentioning (perhaps not even knowing) the verse that lies behind it all—in fact, this is precisely what happens in the case of our midrash[32] and with dozens, nay, hundreds, of others. Literalists of the imagination turn fanciful exegesis into would-be history.[33] And so "legendizing" is in some sense the last stage of the midrashic process, midrash come home to roost, for by it exegesis becomes part of the text itself.

NOTES

1. b. Ber 4b.
2. Either this fact did not bother the sages in question, for they surely knew of instances in the Bible where masculine verb forms are used for feminine nouns, and indeed of feminine nouns that have a masculine sense and are so treated—so that the form qûm would actually be acceptable—or else they mentally revocalized the qûm into qûmî, an act which can be performed under duress without changing the consonantal text.
3. For were not Jeremiah's words the divine antidote to Amos's prophecy when he said: "I shall yet rebuild you and you will be restored, O virgin of Israel" (Jer. 31:4)?
4. This in itself was a hermeneutic centered problem; see J. A. Saunders, "Hermeneutics in True and False Prophecy" in Canon and Authority, ed. G. W. Coats and B. O. Long (Philadelphia: Fortress Press, 1977), pp. 21–41.
5. See E. E. Urbach, "When did Prophecy Cease?" (Hebrew), Tarbiz 17 (1946), 1–11; also see D. L. Petersen, Late Israelite Prophecy (Missoula, Mont.: Scholars Press for the Society of Biblical Literature, 1977), pp. 25–26.
6. See Urbach, "When Did Prophecy Cease?" and Urbach, "Halakhah and Prophecy" (Hebrew), Tarbiz 18 (1947), 1–27; both these articles touch on the filiation of sage from prophet, a later rabbinic leitmotif. Thus, there was a single revelation at Sinai, from which stemmed not only the Mosaic teaching but the teachings of the prophets and the rabbis as well; see Exodus Rabbah XXVIII 6; also Tanḥuma Yitro, 11. "Dearer are the words of sages than the words of prophets" (P. Avodah Zarah II 8). For the historical setting of this transition and parallels to the inspired interpreter outside the rabbinic tradition see D. Patte, Early Jewish Hermeneutic in Palestine (Missoula, Mont.: Scholars Press for the Society of Biblical Literature, 1975).
7. Of course the dream or dream-vision which is interpreted as if it were a text is in itself a prophetic motif (thus Jer. 1:11–12), and the very means of interpreting the vision ("almond tree," šāqēd, means I will be šōqēd, "zealous") are precisely those found

in later Jewish exegesis. Indeed, the connection between Qumranic commentary (*pešer*), biblical dream-interpretation (*pitrôn*), and the midrashic topos "Rabbi X interpreted the verse" (*petar qerā'*) was explored by L. H. Silberman in "Unriddling the Riddle: A Study in the Structure and Language of 1 Q P Hab," *Revue de Qumran* 3 (1961), 323–64, and shortly thereafter by A. Finkel, "The Pesher of Dreams and Scriptures," *Revue de Qumran* 4 (1963), 357–70. Silberman argued that the same technique of dream interpretation found, for example, in the Talmud (P. Ma'aser Šeni IV, end; parallel passages with modifications in Lam. R. I 1, 16) characterize Qumranic exegesis of biblical texts, viz., atomization, metathesis of letters, substitution of roots, wordplay, etc. Similarly, such rabbinic exegetical tools as gematria and notarikon have their parallels in Greek dream-interpretation techniques. Apart from this important connection of interpretive devices and forms, the broader connection of dreams and texts, viz., the dream that gives rise to the text, may be traced in an unbroken line from biblical and classical instances through apocalyptic and pseudepigraphic dreams and such signal events as Macrobius's commentary on the *Somnium Scipionis* into the dream-visions of medieval Latin, and on to more recent examples.

    8. Here too Daniel's dream interpreting is reminiscent of rabbinic text interpreting, for the handwriting's message, apparently a list of different weights ("a mina, a shekel, half[-a-mina]") becomes significant through a repronunciation of the consonantal text: *mina'* becomes *mĕnē'* ("numbered"), *tĕqēl* ("shekel") becomes *tĕqīl* ("weighed"), and *pĕrās* ("half") becomes *pĕrīs* ("divided"), with the secondary association of *pārās*, "Persia." All that remained for the interpreter to do was to supply the intervening text. See Silberman, "Unriddling the Riddle," p. 332.

    9. See Patte, *Early Jewish Hermeneutic*, pp. 215–27.

    10. B. Albrektson, *History and the Gods* (Lund: Gleerup, 1967).

    11. This theme is approached in the writings of Mircea Eliade, especially *The Myth of the Eternal Return* (New York: Pantheon Books, 1954), a writer curiously not treated in James Barr's important study, *Biblical Words for Time* (London: SCM Press, 1962), which correctly criticizes the common opposition of the Greek "cyclical" sense of time to the Hebraic "non-cyclical." Barr urges, among other things, that the whole notion of the "cyclical view of time" be broken down into more specific categories, such as a) the circular movement of earthly existence, b) the circular movement of heavenly bodies which measure time, c) the application to time of circularity as the example of uniform motion, d) time as a cyclical cosmic process, occurring once but returning to where it began, e) time as a cyclical cosmic process repeating itself infinitely, and f) time as a temporal cycle in which all historical events recur as before. See p. 142.

    12. Again, Eliade, *Myth of the Eternal Return*.

    13. See H. W. Robinson's chapter "Time and Eternity," with an appendix on Koheleth's radically different sense of time from that evidenced in other biblical books, in his *Inspiration and Revelation in the Old Testament* (Oxford: Clarendon Press, 1946), pp. 121–22; see also G. A. F. Knight, *Christian Theology of the Old Testament*, 2d. rev. ed. (London: SCM Press, 1964), pp. 87–137; T. C. Vriezen, *An Outline of Old Testament Theology* (Oxford: Blackwell, 1958), p. 347.

    14. This view of time is manifest even in the form of the book itself, an "intellectual autobiography" of sorts (and one notably devoid of all historical allusion or concern with past causes), in which the man of wisdom is never permitted to rest, as it were, on his last *mashal*, but is constantly in motion, "I came back and saw," "Then I turned to consider," "Yet I saw furthermore," and so forth, sometimes contradicting what had just been concluded and, if not finally completing a perfect circle, then at least finding some contentment in the unresolved character of his aggregate wisdom, "All things having been heard . . ."

15. On the late biblical and post-biblical writings and their sense of time see briefly G. von Rad, "The Divine Determination of Times," in his *Wisdom in Israel* (London: SCM Press, 1972), pp. 263–83, and S. J. DeVries, "Observations on Quantitative and Qualitative Time," in J. G. Gammie, *Israelite Wisdom* (Missoula, Mont.: Scholars Press, 1978), pp. 263–76.

16. Much has been written of late in an attempt both to add greater precision to the characteristics of "apocalyptic," "apocalypticism," and "apocalyptic eschatology," and to explore the genesis of this genre/set-of-concerns and its attachment to earlier institutions such as prophecy and wisdom. Two recent surveys of scholarship are: E. W. Nicholson, "Apocalyptic," in G. W. Anderson, *Tradition and Interpretation* (Oxford, 1979), pp. 189–213; and M. A. Knibb, "Prophecy and the Emergence of the Jewish Apocalypses," in R. Coggins et al., *Israel's Prophetic Tradition* (Cambridge: Cambridge University Press, 1982), pp. 155–80.

17. In Barr's sense (d) cited above, n. 11.

18. See J. Tate, "On the History of Allegorism," *Classical Quarterly* (1934), 105–14.

19. "On the Migration of Abraham," 34:187–88, *Works of Philo*, trans. F. H. Colson (Cambridge: Harvard University Press, 1949), vol. 4, p. 241.

20. This is a statement about perception, for of course history's "message" in 1000 B.C.E. was no more simple or complex than it was in Second Temple times: it was the contrast between Scripture's perception of the former period and the later inability to "make sense of things" in a similar manner that was crucial.

21. Patte, *Early Jewish Hermeneutic*, p. 72 (re. targum). This formulation should evoke the liturgical formula "The Lord is king (*melekh*), the Lord has ruled (*malakh*), the Lord will rule (*yimlokh*) forever." Of course these biblical phrases (found, inter alia, in Ps. 10:16, 93:1, and Exod. 15:18) are certainly being invoked to create a paradigm; yet how fortuitous that to the post-biblical ear the "present tense" slot is filled with a mere assertion of divine supremacy: the Lord "is king" but not, in external political terms, "kinging."

22. These great generalizations will suffer the inevitable exceptions without real damage—rabbinic use of Scriptural prooftexts to support messianic predictions or even personalities (Bar Kokhba), or targumic reference to political figures and events of its own day or alteration of the text to reflect present-day realities (see, e.g., Pseudo-Jonathan on Gen. 21:21 [wife and daughter of Muhammad], Exod. 26:9 [six orders of Mishna], Num. 24:19 [Constantinople and Rome], and Deut. 33:11 [Yoḥanan], on which P. Kahle, *The Cairo Geniza*, 2d ed. [Oxford: Blackwell, 1959], p. 202; see also Dalman, *Grammatik des jüdisch-palästineschen Aramaisch*, 2d ed. [Leipzig: J. C. Hinrichs, 1905], p. 31.) While such occasional "referentializing" or "actualizing" is to be found, it hardly is the bridge between the biblical past and our present: that is the point.

23. Eventually, of course, these contradictions came to be troubling, and the history of the Song's Jewish exegesis is one of a tightening of the allegorical correspondences until they came to embody a fairly consistent set of historical allusions to events in Israel's past. There was no unanimity among Tannaim even as to where and when the Song was uttered (see S. Lieberman, "The Song of Songs" [Hebrew] appended to G. Scholem, *Jewish Gnosticism, Merkabah Mysticism, and Talmudic Tradition* [New York: Jewish Theological Seminary, 1960], pp. 118–26), and even the individual interpretive lines distinguished by Lieberman (in ibid.) were not consistently applied to each verse (how could they be?). The targum later tried to pin down verses to historical events presented more or less chronologically, but with "flashbacks" to account for recalcitrant verses or ones with well-entrenched interpretations that conflicted with the chronological scheme (cf. the remarks of R. Loewe, "Apologetic Motifs in the Targum to the Song of Songs" in *Biblical Motifs: Origins and Transformation*, ed. A. Altman [Cambridge: Harvard University Press, 1966],

pp. 159–96). The same problem was handled with great deftness by A. ibn Ezra through the stratagem of his multilevel exegesis, which allowed for a certain amount of judicious skipping over verses that would be problematic at the historical level and treating them in some other fashion; this preserved the impression of completeness. His historical retrospections at the end of each section (a feature also found in Sa'adya's commentary) were of similar effect. Somewhat later, the historical approach to the book's allegory was abandoned in favor of a Farabian dialogue between the individual soul and the Active Intellect, in ibn Aqnin's commentary, ed. A. Halkin (Jerusalem: Mekitze Nirdanim, 1964), or, in similar fashion, in Maimonides' view (see *Guide of the Perplexed* pt. 3, chaps. 51, 54; also *Mishneh Torah* "Repentance" 10:2).

24. See J. Theodor and Ch. Albeck, *Genesis Rabbah* (Hebrew), (Jerusalem: Wahrmann Books, 1965), pp. 559–60; above translation based on Ms. Vat.

25. Even in the Mishna one finds instances of different, sometimes conflicting interpretations of the same verse for halakhic purposes. See, e.g., M. Rosh Hashana 1:9 and 2:9.

26. As in the *petar qerā'* pattern mentioned above (n. 7). See I. Heinemann, *The Methods of Aggadah* (Hebrew) (Jerusalem: Magnes and Massada, 1970), pp. 57–58.

27. So Gen. 41:45 uses precisely this expression, "And Joseph *went out over* the land of Egypt," at this juncture in the Joseph story.

28. See above, n. 26. Moreover, even the insular midrash is capable of being reconnected to its immediate context: in our case, for example, the story of Joseph's being freed from prison is connected in several sources to the earlier reference in the same Psalm 81 to "sounding the shofar" in order to conclude that Joseph was set free from prison on the day of the New Year (when the shofar was sounded); the removal of Israel's collective shoulder from the toil of slavery was, by a similar logic, also said to have taken place on the same day. See b. Rosh Hashana 10b.

29. The trouble with attributing these words to Pharaoh is that he is nowhere mentioned or alluded to in our biblical verse (Ps. 81:6), whereas Joseph is. The midrashist must therefore mentally be supplying some parenthetical note to cover for the choppiness: "He [God] set it as a testimony in Jehoseph, upon [Joseph's] going out over the land of Egypt [which occurred thanks to the occasion on which Pharaoh exclaimed:] 'A tongue I did not know I now hear!' " It is perhaps this difficulty that is responsible for the version of the story in the form recounted above, which seems to underlie the treatment of the Joseph story in *Sefer ha-Yashar*, ed. L. Goldschmidt (Berlin: Benjamin Harz, 1923), pp. 174–75, 177–78. For here Joseph *begins* by speaking Hebrew to Pharaoh and his advisers. They then object to his being made ruler because he cannot speak the seventy languages, indeed, not even Egyptian: "Lo, this man speaks only the Hebrew tongue! How can there be over us a vizier who does not also know our language?" (For this reason Joseph had originally been allowed only to sit on the third step of the seventy steps in front of Pharaoh's throne, as was customary for a commoner unlearned in the languages of the world.) However, the version in which "A tongue I did not know . . ." is spoken by Pharaoh and/or his advisers is by far the more common in the sources, thus, B. Sota 36b and parallels.

30. Leviticus Rabbah 23:10.

31. Yalkut Shimoni, *ad* Psalm 81 (#831).

32. Sefer ha-Yashar (above, n. 29).

33. This is the effect created by L. Ginzberg's *Legends of the Jews* (Philadelphia: Jewish Publication Society, 1913), a masterful work of scholarship which, however, seems bent on submerging the exegetical function of midrash and turning it into mere tale-making, "legends." Yet one must in candor admit that long before Ginzberg this exegetical function was at times smothered as is evident from various retellings of biblical stories, piyyut, biblical commentaries, visual representations of biblical scenes, and so forth.

DAVID STERN

Midrash and the Language of Exegesis: A Study of Vayikra Rabbah, Chapter 1

For the student of literature, midrash most immediately suggests the exegetical features of fiction and poetry, the ways in which one text and its meaning are to be found in another. Midrash, however, touches upon literature not at the point where literature becomes exegesis but at what might be called its opposite conjunction, where exegesis turns into literature and comes to possess its own language and voice. As paradoxical as it may appear, the first duty of a literary approach to midrash, therefore, must be to suspend temporarily more immediate concerns with literature proper and to go over, as it were, to the other side in order to describe the specific language of midrash and the special conditions which created its literary forms and modes of expression. This is necessary whether those forms and modes are the recognizable techniques of narrative, or whether they constitute the more unusual exegetical vehicles which are far more typical of midrashic discourse and far more decisive for its formation.

The aim of this study is to discuss one literary vehicle of this sort, the homily, and to analyze in detail a specific example of this form whose very subject, as I hope to show, is the process through which midrashic exegesis creates a literary language of its own. The example is the first chapter in Vayikra Rabbah (henceforth to be referred to as VR), an aggadic midrash on the Book of Leviticus whose interpretations

Note: This study is part of a work-in-progress on language and meaning in Vayikra Rabbah. For the sake of brevity I have limited my remarks in this study to the first chapter of Vayikra Rabbah even though some of the arguments must be understood from the perspective of the midrash in its entirety; other assumptions, stated dogmatically in this paper, will be explained and proven at greater length in the completed work.

are mainly attributed to rabbis of the Amoraic period (third–fifth century C.E.). According to most scholars, the text of VR was redacted in the land of Israel in the late fifth or early sixth centuries in the common era, during or shortly after the classical period of rabbinic midrash.[1]

The midrashic works of this period can nearly all be classified under one of two categories, as either exegetical anthologies or collections of homilies. The exegetical anthology, like Bereshit (Genesis) Rabbah, presents a series of interpretive opinions on Scripture in the form of a running commentary, verse by verse, often phrase by phrase, without any other clearly discernible logic of organization.[2] The homiletical midrash, by contrast, does not offer a continuous exposition of a scriptural book or passage; instead, each chapter in the collection is devoted to the interpretation of the initial one or two verses in the Torah-reading and follows a conventional structure. Each chapter begins with several proems—a literary form I will discuss shortly—and then continues to comment upon its subject verse or verses, and sometimes upon topics raised in the course of earlier interpretations, and it concludes with a peroration that typically invokes the messianic hope or some other consolatory note through the citation of a final verse. Some homiletical collections, like VR, treat the weekly Torah-readings of a scriptural book (as the Torah was divided according to the Palestinian triennial cycle in one of its several versions);[3] others, like Pesikta de-Rav Kahana, are devoted to the Torah-readings on special Sabbaths and holidays in the Jewish year.

The distinction between the exegetical anthology and the homiletical collection has been a commonplace of rabbinic scholarship for at least a century.[4] More recently, however, the late Joseph Heinemann argued with remarkable perspecuity that the separate chapters in VR (and in similar homiletical collections) possess a coherence deeper than mere external form, a coherence which is, indeed, a product of literary art.[5] Heinemann himself characterized that deeper coherence in terms of the organic unity of theme: in his view, each chapter was a carefully chosen group of rabbinic traditions on a selected topic (for example, the greatness of Moses as a prophet, which Heinemann defined as the theme of the first chapter in VR). To describe these chapters, whose redaction he believed was a landmark in the history of midrash, Heinemann coined the term *literary homily* (to distinguish these redactional compositions from oral sermons).

While it is difficult to accept Heinemann's notion of organic unity,[6] I wish to build upon his basic insight that the chapters in the homiletical midrash possess literary coherence. Instead of viewing that coherence as deriving from unity of theme, however, I wish to suggest that each chapter consists of an extended exegesis of the scriptural verse that serves as its prooftext. This exegesis develops progressively, albeit discontinuously, through the homily, and though it is nowhere stated explicitly in the chapter, it becomes clear to the reader by the homily's conclusion. The coherence of the homily consequently results from the logic by which the redactor allows the exegesis to unfold before the reader. Furthermore, this logic is based, I wish to suggest, upon the structure of another midrashic literary form, the petiḥta or proem which, though not original to the literary homily, occupies a prominent position in it. By enlarging the rhetorical strategy of the petiḥta upon a grand scale, the redactor (or redactors) of VR (and of similar homiletical collections) invented the literary homily.

For our understanding of the petiḥta we stand in debt, once again, to Joseph Heinemann.[7] The petiḥta, as its name suggests, is an introduction to the lectionary-verse that begins the weekly reading from the Torah. According to Heinemann, the petiḥta originated as a kind of mini-sermon which the darshan delivered in the synagogue immediately before the Torah-reading. Just as the haftorah, the passage from the Prophets read after the Torah, serves as a kind of epilogue to the Torah-reading, so the petiḥta provided a kind of prologue to it. This putative Sitz im Leben for the petiḥta explains its strange "upside-down" shape. Instead of beginning with its proper subject, the lectionary-verse, the petiḥta opens with another verse—most frequently from the Writings, sometimes from the Prophets, on rare occasions from the Pentateuch—which, to all appearances, is unrelated to the lectionary-verse. From this verse, which I will call the petiḥta-verse, the darshan or preacher evolves a chain of interpretations, often involving the quotation and interpretation of still other verses, along with various other rhetorical devices of interpretation (like parables and enumeration-lists), stringing one bead of interpretation upon the next, until he arrives at a point where he makes the connection to the lectionary-verse with which the petiḥta then concludes. At the conclusion, the lectionary-verse is given a new interpretation, and some kind of connection between that verse and the opening prooftext can often be discerned—a word-tally, phonetic similarity, or semantic rhyme. Until this point, however, the precise way in which the darshan will connect the two verses is not clear; indeed, according to Heinemann, the opening pe-tiḥta-verse was chosen by the darshan specifically for its apparent re-moteness from the lectionary-verse. In this way, he aroused his audience's suspense and made them wonder how he would journey, as it were, from the one verse to the other, the petiḥta's destination, its telos—end but also ultimate determinant for the composition's shape and content.

Aside from clarifying its rhetorical function, the structure of the petiḥta exemplifies a fundamental tendency of midrash, the urge to unite the diverse parts of Scripture into a single and seamless whole reflecting the unity of God's will. This tendency derives directly from the rabbinic ideology of the canonical Torah—Pentateuch, Prophets, and Writings—as the inspired word of God, a timeless unity in which each and every verse is simultaneous with every other, temporally and semantically; as a result, every verse, no matter how remote, can be seen as a possible source for illuminating the meaning of any other verse. While this tendency is manifest throughout midrash—every place two otherwise unconnected verses are joined in order to reveal new nexuses of meaning—the petiḥta is undoubtedly its most sophis-ticated literary expression.

As illustration of this structure, consider the following example, the first petiḥta in chapter 1 of VR. I have labelled its sections for the purpose of the discussion that will follow:

R. Tanḥum b. R. Ḥanilai began his proem (pataḥ): "Bless the Lord, ye mes-sengers (malakhav) of His, ye mighty in strength that fulfill His word, hear-kening unto the voice of His word" [Ps. 103.20].

A. "Bless the Lord, ye messengers of His": Of what sort does Scripture speak?

1) If Scripture speaks of those who are above (ha'elyonim), does it not also say "Bless the Lord, all ye hosts of His" [Ps. 103.21]? And if Scripture speaks of those who are below (hataḥtonim), does it not say, "Bless the Lord, ye angels [literally, messengers] of His" [Ps. 103.20]?

2) It must therefore be that (ela) because those above are [all] able to execute the charges of the Holy One, blessed be He, Scripture says, "Bless the Lord, all ye hosts of His." Because those below cannot [all] execute the charges of the Holy One, blessed be He, Scripture says about them, "Bless the Lord, ye messengers of His," not "all ye messengers of His."

3) Another opinion: Prophets are called malakhim [e.g., angels]. This is what is written, "And He sent a malakh and brought us forth out of Egypt . . ." [Num. 20.16]. But was it a malakh, an angel? Was it not Moses? Why is he called a malakh? But from this source [we learn] that prophets are called malakhim.

Similarly, "And the malakh of the Lord came up from Gilgal to Bokhim" [Judg. 2.1]. But was it a malakh, an angel? Was it not Pinhas? So why is he called a malakh? R. Simon explained: The face of Pinhas, when the holy spirit rested upon him, flamed like a torch [thus appearing like an angel's face]. The Rabbis said: What did Manoah's wife say to her husband?—"A man of God came to me, and his countenance was like the countenance of a malakh of God" [Judg. 13.6]. She must have thought he was a prophet when he was really an angel!

R. Yohanan said: The prophets are called malakhim because of their source in Scripture [mi-bet av shelahen]. This is what is written: "Then spoke Haggai, the Lord's malakh, in the Lord's messengership [malakhut], to the nation, saying" [Hag. 1.13]. By necessity you must conclude that because of their origins prophets are called malakhim.

B. "The mighty in strength that fulfill His word": Of whom does the Scripture speak?

R. Isaac said: Scripture speaks of those who observe the Sabbatical year [shomrei shevi'it]. It is common in the world for a man to perform a precept for a day, or a week, or a month. But for a whole year? And yet this man sees his field untilled, he sees his vineyard untilled, he gives up his living, and still he says nothing! Is there a hero [gibor] greater than this man?

And if you should argue that this verse does not speak about the observers of the Sabbatical year, the proof that it does is that our verse says, "that fulfill His word [devaro]," and later it says, "And this is the matter [davar] of the Sabbatical year's release" [Deut. 15.2].

Just as in the latter verse Scripture uses the word davar to speak about the observers of the Sabbatical year, so in our verse Scripture uses the word davar to speak about the observers of the Sabbatical year.

C. "... ye ... that fulfill His word hearkening": R. Huna said in the name of R. Aha: Scripture speaks about the Israelites who stood before Mount Sinai and undertook to obey and hearken" [Ex. 24.7].

D. "Hearkening unto the voice of His word":

R. Tanhum B. Hanilai said: Normally a burden which is heavy for one is light for two. Or if it is heavy for two it is light for four. But is a burden that is too heavy for sixty myriads ever an easy load for a single person? Now all of the Israelites were standing before Mount Sinai, and they said, "If we hear the voice of the Lord our God any longer, then we shall die" [Deut. 5.22]. And yet Moses heard the voice of the Lord by himself and he lived! Know that this is so: For out of all of them, the Voice called to Moses alone. Therefore it is said, "He called unto Moses" [Lev. 1:1]. (VR 1:1)

The petihta begins with Ps. 103:20 and concludes with Lev. 1:1, the lectionary-verse for the weekly reading. The author of the petihta— perhaps R. Tanhum b. Hanilai, to whom the composition is attributed, but more probably the anonymous redactor of VR[8]—connects the two verses by dividing the petihta-verse, Ps. 103:20, into several smaller phrases each of which he then identifies with a different subject who is commanded to bless God (as the verse declares). One of the author's motives in doing this is undoubtedly to multiply the number of those who praise God[9]—from the celestial angels above to the peasants observing the Sabbatical year below—but the technique of "atomization" at work here is also the second major corollary of the rabbinic ideology of the Torah.[10] Since every verse, indeed, every word in the Torah is divine, it follows that nothing in it, not even a letter or enclitic, is without meaning or purely ornamental. Instead, every word and letter is susceptible to interpretation and, as with the separate phrases in Ps. 103:20, can be exploited as an occasion for interpretation.

In our petiḥta in VR, these interpretations and their identifications of subjects for the different scriptural phrases are accomplished mainly by means of word-tallies or puns. In addition, nearly all the subjects appear to exemplify a different type of obedience to God and His law. Thus, in the first section (A1–2), the word *malakhim*, which by usage designates angels, is interpreted as referring to earthlings because the verse stipulates that *all* these creatures cannot obey God's commands, a fact that is not true of angels (who, instead, are said to be the subjects of the following verse, Ps. 103:21, which speaks of the heavenly host who *all* obey God). The next phrase in the verse (B) the midrash identifies with the *shomrei shevi'it*, the observers of the Sabbatical year, paragons of selfless obedience to the law in a time of social and economic crisis.[11] The subsequent phrase, "ye . . . that fulfill His word hearkening" (C), is ingeniously interpreted as a reference to the children of Israel on the basis of the famous interpretation of Ex. 24:7, according to which they agreed to obey the law even before they heard it. Finally, the last phrase (D) is taken to refer to Moses who, against all natural logic, was able to endure the divine voice at Sinai and not perish. And so, the petiḥta concludes, proof of Moses's unique capacity to withstand the burden of God's revelation is confirmed by the fact that to Moses alone God called, as it is written, *va-yikra el moshe*. The midrash reads this verse as, in effect, "He called to Moses alone."

If this petiḥta has a single overarching message, it is that God addresses and reveals Himself only to those who have already proven themselves to be capable of sustaining and enforcing that revelation. This message is most explicit in the petiḥta's concluding exegesis of Lev. 1:1, and it informs the choice of Ps. 103:20 as the opening petiḥta-verse. This verse appears to have been chosen partly on the basis of a word-tally, never made explicit, between the second phrase in our lectionary-verse, *vayedaber . . . eilav*, "And He spoke to him," and the word *devaro* in the final phrase in Ps. 103:20, *lishmo'a kol devaro*, "hearkening unto the voice of His word" (which is identified with the Sinaitic revelation, thus forming a parallel to the revelation at the Tent of Meeting which Lev. 1:1 introduces). The two verses, Ps. 103:20 and Lev. 1:1, join together in a relationship that might almost be described as antiphonal: where Ps. 103:20 enjoins those messengers of God who have heard Him speak to bless Him, Lev. 1:1 describes God calling upon the exemplary messenger, Moses, in order to transmit the law through him to the children of Israel.

The relationship between these two verses, which form the skeleton of the petiḥta, can be described as the exegetical superstructure of the literary form. Yet there also exists within the petiḥta a second level of exegesis, an infrastructure of interpretation. This level consists of the more elementary exegetical operations that mark every step of the petiḥta's progress as it moves through its interpretations of Ps. 103:20 until it culminates in Lev. 1:1—the specific interpretations, for example, of the phrases "the mighty in strength that fulfill His word" or ". . . ye . . . that fulfill His word hearkening," as well as midrashic traditions, like the exegesis of Exod. 24:7 in C, that are merely alluded to in the petiḥta and never made explicit. While the superstructure is used to organize the local exegetical operations of the infrastructure in order to create the more complex literary form of the petiḥta, the individual exegeses in the infrastructure are never fully subordinated to the petiḥta's larger rhetorical strategy. Moreover, in contrast to the superstructure, which serves as the vehicle for the petiḥta's theme, the interpretations in the infrastructure have no necessary or direct connection to that theme.

To test the relationship between super- and infrastructure in the petiḥta, or between the statement of theme and the pure activity of exegesis, one might consider the place in our petiḥta of a lengthy digression whose mention I have deferred until now. I am referring to the "other opinion" (*davar aḥer*) in A3 that identifies the malakhim in Ps. 103:20 with prophets, a conventional use of the word in Scripture, for which the midrash offers two lines of explanation. According to the first, for which several examples are adduced, prophets are called angels because they look like them; according to the second, it is because of the chief passage, their locus classicus, as it were, Ḥag. 1:13, that describes the nature of their calling. Now, on strictly exegetical grounds, this "other opinion" is not necessary for the petiḥta's unfolding interpretation of Ps. 103:20. The part of the verse on which it is based, "ye messengers of His," has already been interpreted in the preceding section.

What, then, is the "other opinion" doing in the petiḥta? Several explanations are available. First, one might suggest that the "other opinion" is not a genuinely different opinion but simply a further specification of the identity of the earthlings (hataḥtonim) in the preceding section as prophets. It might also be suggested that the redactor of the homily included the "other opinion" in the petiḥta because of its relevance to what will later emerge as the homily's two central themes, prophecy (specifically the prophecy of Moses) and language (particularly the relation between name and thing).

Yet even without these explanations no reader familiar with midrash would ever be bothered by the presence of the "other opinion" in the petiḥta simply because there is nothing more common in midrash than another opinion. The "other opinion" represents the basic delight midrash always takes in offering still another interpretation, no matter what its relevance to the theme at hand may be. Which is only to say that in midrash the activity of exegesis is more powerful than the statement of theme. To be sure, the balance between the two is delicate. In the case of the petiḥta, too lengthy a thematic exposition would swell its shape beyond rhetorical effectiveness; on the other hand, if the exegetical structure is too schematic, the composition ceases to be interesting. But what finally gives the midrashic text its coherence, or semblance thereof, is not thematic unity but the pursuit of interpretation of the scriptural verse according to the rough linear sequence of that verse's words. So, too, what gives the petiḥta its coherence as a rhetorical form is the way it adheres, to all appearances, to the exegesis of the petiḥta-verse and nonetheless arrives at its destination in the culminating lectionary-verse.

The same sense of arriving at a destination, of coming to an end after a journey of some kind, is the key to the structure of the literary homily in VR. As I have already noted, the thirty-seven chapters in VR all share a similar shape. Each chapter begins with one or several petiḥta'ot, all of them culminating in the same lectionary-verse, as though the redactor wished to show that all roads, beginning anywhere in Scripture, lead to a single verse. Following the petiḥta'ot, the lectionary-verse itself and sometimes another verse or two (in our chapter Lev. 1:1 alone) became the subjects for additional interpretations that are presented in diverse literary forms. Finally, this series of opinions—called the *gufa* or body of the homily—culminates in the messianic peroration.[12]

Now this peroration is not simply a *simana denehemta*, a token of consolation the redactor proffers forth to the reader patiently making his way through the homily to its end to assure him that redemption, too, will arrive sooner or later. Nor is it simply tacked on mechanically to the homilectical interpretations that precede it. Rather, the peroration tends to follow closely upon the earlier interpretations, gathering up meanings that have accumulated in the course of the homily, often throwing them into sharper focus. Yet, aside from being a device of closure, the messianic peroration serves a rhetorical role in the homily that is directly analogous to the one the lectionary-verse serves in the petiḥta: it is the destination for the homily, and it retroactively imparts to all that has preceded it the shape of a journey, a kind of linearity that is almost plot-like in impression. Moreover—and this is what makes these homilies *midrashic* texts—the peroration-verse has exegetical significance. It relates to the homily's lectionary-verse by turning the entire homily into an exegesis of that verse.

One such exegesis is the reading, in the first petiḥta, of *va-yikra el moshe*, "He called unto Moses," a reading I have translated as "He called unto Moses alone." This reading is invoked elsewhere in the homily. Moses's unique capacity to endure the divine revelation is raised again in the third petiḥta, which also distinguishes between him, Abraham, and David, as well as in the fifth petiḥta (6). In a later pericope (9), Moses is differentiated from Adam, Noah, and Abraham, whom, as the midrash concedes, God addressed directly too. Finally, in the last two paragraphs in the homily (13–14), gentile prophets are distinguished from their superior Jewish counterparts and then the latter from Moses:

What was the difference between Moses and all other prophets. . . . The Rabbis say: All the other prophets beheld [God] in a blurred looking-glass . . . Moses beheld in a polished looking-glass. . . .
R. Pinhas said in the name of R. Hoshaia: It is like a king who revealed himself to his steward (*ben beito*) in his linen undergarments (*otanin*).[13] For in this world the Divine Presence (*ha-shekhinah*) reveals itself only to individuals. But in the world-to-come, what is written? "The glory of the Lord shall be revealed, and all the flesh shall see it together; for the mouth of the Lord hath spoken it" (Isa. 30.15).

Thus the peroration: Only in this world does God reveal Himself to individuals like Moses with such casual informality as when a king allows himself to be seen in his undershirt by his personal steward. In the world-to-come, however, God will reveal Himself to all men in this familiar way, and presumably everywhere, not just in the *ohel mo'ed*, the Tent of Meeting, from which in Lev. 1:1 God calls Moses.

This interpretation of *va-yikra el moshe* as specifying the uniqueness of the revelation vouchsafed to Moses reoccurs throughout the homily, but it is not the sole reading offered for the verse, and even in the passages just cited, the reading always has a nuance unique to the context in which it is presented. Elsewhere in the homily, the verse is read in such other senses as "God invited Moses into the Tent of Meeting" (7); "He impatiently summoned Moses" (5); "He called attention to Moses" (8); and "He consulted with Moses" (8). Finally, in the second petiḥta (2–3), the verse is given still another interpretation which is absolutely crucial to understanding the homily as a whole. The length of the petiḥta prevents quoting it in full; a summary will suffice.

The petiḥta's prooftext is Hos. 14:8: "They shall return, dwelling under his shadow: they shall make corn grow; they shall blossom as the vine as renowned as the wine of Lebanon." According to R. Abahu, to whom the petiḥta is attributed, this verse refers to converts to Judaism who come to dwell in the shadow of God. Interpreting the verse's conclusion, R. Abahu reports: "The Holy One, blessed be He, said (*amar ha-kadosh barukh hu*), 'Dear to Me (*ḥaviv'alai*) are the names of converts as the wine poured before Me upon the altar in the Temple.' " After giving several explanations for why the Temple is called by the name of Lebanon—in a discussion that recalls the passage in the preceding petiḥta as to why prophets are called malakhim—the midrash turns to a second prooftext, I Chron. 4:18, which occurs in the midst of the genealogies of the tribes of Israel. For this verse, "and his Judean wife bore Yered, the father of Gedor (*avi gedor*), Heber the father of Sokho (*avi sokho*), and Yekutiel the father of Zanoaḥ (*avi zanoaḥ*), and these are the sons of Bityah, the daughter of Pharaoh, whom Mered took," the midrash gives a lengthy interpretation whose gist is as follows: "Yokheved—the mother of Moses—gave birth to a man [e.g., Moses] among whose names are Yered, Avigdor, Ḥeber, Avisokho, Yekutiel, and Avizanoaḥ; and this man was the son of Bityah, the daughter of Pharaoh whom Caleb married." This Bityah is the same daughter of Pharaoh who rescued the infant Moses and named him; according to rabbinic aggadah, she forsook the idolatry of her fathers, converted to Judaism, and eventually married the famous scout Caleb.[14] Because she rescued Moses and adopted him, the verse calls him her son—a point the midrash then uses to return to the statement it had earlier reported in the name of God: "Dear to Me are the names of converts . . ." This statement is now, in effect, reinterpreted to refer not only to the names converts themselves bear but also to the names they give to others. And since Bityah, as Exod. 2:10 reports, "called him by the name of Moses," so, too, va-yikra el mosheh, "God called him by the name of Moses."

The difference between this reading of the lectionary-verse and the others we have seen is obvious. Yet even more significant than its exegetical content is the style of the petiḥta, its preoccupation with its own virtuosity and exegetical powers, and particularly with its powers of naming and renaming, as can be seen in the exegesis of I Chron. 4:18. This verse, like others in the Book of Chronicles, served the rabbis as a favorite ground upon which to let loose all their interpretive energies in free play; indeed, as several rabbis were said to have remarked, the Book of Chronicles was written in the first place only in order to be interpreted midrashically (le-dareish [3]).[15]

The object of this exercise in interpretation is not, however, the display of virtuosity for its own sake; rather, it points to a certain kind of language whose nature is suggested by a word repeatedly used in the petiḥta, the word ḥaviv, a very common adjective in rabbinic Hebrew that I have translated as "dear". The root of ḥaviv, h-b-b, occurs only once in the Bible, in Deut. 33:3, in the phrase af ḥoveiv amim where most commentators understand it to mean "one who loves" or "holds in affection."[16] Indeed, the word ḥaviv is cognate to ḥibah, love. The more exact connotation that the word ḥaviv has for the rabbis is suggested by the midrash on the phrase in Deut. 33:3 that is found in the tannaitic compilation, Sifre Deut. (ed. L. Finkelstein, 1939, repr. New York, 1969, para. 344, pp. 400–01): "This [verse] teaches that the Lord loved (ḥavav) Israel in a way He did not love any other nation or kingdom. . . . This teaches that the Holy One, blessed be He, did not allot His love (ḥibah) to the nations of the world as He alloted it to Israel." Israel's election is a direct consequence of God's ḥibah, and it is the latter that also bestows upon them their ḥavivut, literally preciousness as well as dearness. For the rabbis, in other words, the word ḥaviv connotes a kind of preciousness that derives its special value from the fact of being loved or held in a relationship of affection and intimacy. "R. Akiva used to say: Havivin are the people of Israel for they are called the children of God (banim la-makom)" (M. Avot 3:14). Now this assuredly does not mean that the Israelites are literally the children of God: what R. Akiva refers to is not biological filiation, but conversion-like affiliation; kinship that is established by intimacy and shared feeling, not by blood; havivut, in other words, that derives from familiarity, not from family.

In our petihta, the acknowledgment of precisely this kind of havivut produces the act of renaming which serves, in turn, as the key to the petihta's ultimate interpretation of the lectionary-verse. In answering the question of why I Chron. 4:18 calls Moses the son of Bityah, R. Joshua of Sikhnin in the name of R. Levi reports the following speech that God addressed to Bityah: "The Holy One, blessed be He, said to Bityah: Moses was not your son, and still you called him your son; so, too, you are not my daughter, yet I will call you my daughter"—not Bityah, in other words, but Batyah (a change in vowelization), literally "the daughter of God." And so, the reader will recall, God's earlier statement in the petihta, "Haviv to Me are the names of converts," is given a new meaning: because Bityah/Batyah called her adopted son by the name of Moses—that name being, in fact, a perpetual reminder of the act of havivut that established Bityah's special adoptive relationship with Moses when she pulled him out of the river—so, too, God called him by the name of Moses. The language of converts, of those Jews who are called the children of God not by virtue of biological or familial descent but on account of an act of havivut on their own parts—this language of havivut, of familiarity and intimacy, God Himself adopts as His own to speak to His chosen people.

Now in a homily so dominated by a verse that relates how God speaks to a man, the invocation of this language of havivut has a special significance. Though it is never explicitly named,[17] this language, the type of speech it represents, makes its presence felt throughout the homily, indeed, whenever the midrash reports God speaking to Moses, as in the fourth petihta with its almost tongue-in-cheek portrayal of God's impatience with Moses' legendary (and somewhat wearisome) modesty. Most of all it is felt in the parable that forms the transition to the peroration: in that parable we are told of the time when God will reveal Himself to all men, everywhere, with precisely the kind of familiarity and intimacy associated with the word ḥaviv. In the parable's own imagery, this is the way a king casually reveals himself to his steward, his ben beito, literally the son of his house.

Before arriving at that peroration, however, the darshan presents a series of interpretations in the final part of the gufa. These opinions nearly all deal with the second half of the lectionary-verse, vayedaber . . . eilav mei-ohel mo'ed leimor, "He spoke to him from the Tent of Meeting, saying," and are especially significant for their literary form. If the first half of the homily is dominated by the petiḥta, its second half is defined by the parable; in the final eight paragraphs of the chapter, there are seven complete parables and several quasi-parabolic images. Now the function of these parables is for the most part praise, their object of praise being either Moses or Jewish prophets in general. Such praise is a common rhetorical function of the parable in midrash.[18] In our homily, however, the parable serves not only as a rhetorical device but also as a model of representation. Through parabolic narratives about a human king and his treatment of the members of his court, the darshan is able to represent those situations of intimacy and familiarity between God and Moses (or other Jewish prophets) which characterize the language of ḥavivut. The sudden proliferation of parables in the homily suggests the paradoxical fact that God's ḥavivut with Israel can be dramatized only through human representation.

Such is their form. In content, the opinions in the latter half of the gufa nearly all deal with language and writing or with matters of sequence and relation. Thus, the very first of these opinions raises the question of semikhut, of the significance residing in the sequential order between the last verse in the book of Exodus and our lectionary-verse, the first in the Book of Leviticus (para. 7). The explanation given for this sequence of verses rests upon an analogy between the honor Moses paid to God in building the Tabernacle—an act of honor described explicitly in terms of inscription and writing—and the honor God repaid Moses by inviting him into the Tent of Meeting, that is to say, by speaking to him alone. Following a parable, a series of analogies are drawn between the Tabernacle and the institution of prayer (para. 8). The relevance of the latter to the theme of intimate speech is obvious: prayer is the human analogue to the language of ḥavivut in which God addresses mankind. In the next passage (9), the difference between Moses and his predecessors—Adam, Noah, and Abraham (to whom God also spoke)—is explained and confirmed by the citation of Is. 48:15,[19] a verse in which God announces through the prophet the election of Cyrus as His instrument for Israel's redemption and whose invocation at this point in the homily directly looks forward to the peroration and its evocation of the messianic fulfillment.

In the final section of the gufa, the matter of temporal sequence first raised in the semikhut-interpretation reappears in the exegesis offered for the phrase mei-ohel mo'ed, "from the Tent of Meeting." Instead of taking the preposition mei- in a locative sense, as designating the place from which God addressed Moses, the midrash interprets it temporally, as from the time when the Tent of Meeting was established. As the midrash proceeds to adumbrate it (paras. 10–12), the significance of this time was charged with ambivalence. This was the time when the Law was first publicly promulgated to the children of Israel, thereby making them accountable for its observance. Yet this was also the time when the Divine Voice was first contained within the precincts of the Tent of Meeting. Earlier, when God's voice sounded through the world, it so terrified the earth's inhabitants—that is, the gentiles— that they could not contain themselves or control their bodily functions. Indeed, the midrash remarks, if the gentiles had only understood the great benefits the Tent of Meeting conferred upon them, they would have fortified and protected it—and not, as we are surely meant to understand, destroyed the Temple. Finally, this was the time when prophecy ceased among the gentiles—when, in other words, the very nature of divine revelation underwent a radical change—and God chose to address Jews alone. In fact, from this time, God directly addressed Moses alone—a fact that distinguishes him from all other Jewish prophets (para. 14)—and solely from within the Tent of Meeting— an unhappy situation, but one that will be overturned and corrected in the world-to-come, as the homily's peroration tells us, when God will address all mankind in every place.

The importance of this final section, viewed from the perspective of its culmination in the peroration, is that it decisively alters our sense of the homily's direction. Until the very last pericope, Moses hardly figures in the majority of the interpretations; indeed, their real subject is not Moses but the kind of intimate and familiar discourse, the language of ḥavivut, that was first given expression in the petiḥta about Bityah, and which is, as now becomes clear, a kind of revelatory language in which God addresses man. This language of revelation is not a form of prophecy in the classical sense; its significance does not lie so much in the content of discourse as in its style, its mode of familiarity. But this language is nonetheless an authentic form of revelation inasmuch as it is the medium through which God reveals His presence to His messengers. As the prophet par excellence, Moses exemplifies the man with whom God holds such discourse, but he was not the first man in history to whom God spoke with such familiarity, though he may have been the last, until, in any case, human history itself will end in the world-to-come.

If the exposition of this language of ḥavivut is the homily's theme, what was its meaning for the redactor and his audience? The answer to this question is to be found in the exegetical function the homily serves in connection with Lev. 1:1. As the reader will have noted, there is no mention in the homily of the laws of sacrifice and of the burnt offering which form the basis for the greater part of the Torah-reading that begins with Lev. 1:1. The reason for this absence, however, is not the intrinsic insusceptibility of this halakhic material to midrash. To the contrary: the tannaitic midrash on Leviticus, Sifra, deals mainly with these laws. Rather, the reason that these laws are not mentioned in VR is simply because in the fifth century in the common era, nearly four hundred years after the Temple had been destroyed and the sacrifices had ceased to be offered, after the aborted attempt to rebuild the Temple under Julian (and when the redactor and his audience probably suspected that the Temple was not likely to be rebuilt in the imminent future), the laws of the Temple cult had little practical import.

Confronted by this situation, the redactor of VR faced a considerable problem in expounding the Torah-reading: what significance to make of it? The solution he found was to shift the entire burden of meaning for the reading away from its content, away from the substance of the revelation God addressed to Moses at the Tent of Meeting—the sacrificial laws in all their details—and to place it instead upon the event of revelation and, in particular, the style of its language, the kind of speech that I have attempted to characterize by the term ḥavivut. Furthermore, the redactor was able to find a key to this meaning in the lectionary-verse, Lev. 1:1. Though most readers might discount the importance of the verse—after all, it seems to tell us only the identities of the participants in the revelation and its location—the verse does, in fact, call attention to God calling upon Moses. The word *va-*

yikra may also have called to the redactor's mind the phonetically similar word, *yakar*, which like *haviv* means both precious and dear.[20] Finally, the specific meaning the redactor located in the lectionary-verse—the language of *havivut*—is, I would propose, suggested in the Torah's own account. If one compares the thunder-and-lightning of the circumstances surrounding the Sinaitic revelation with the description of the revelation at the Tent of Meeting, the latter is indeed far more prosaic. And yet, to borrow an analogy offered in a parable in our homily (para. 8), just this prosaic quality might have suggested to the rabbis the kind of tête-à-tête, the familiar and confidential interview, a concerned Roman emperor might have held with a trusted provincial administrator over the economic and political situation in a remote Eastern province of the Empire.

Part of the motive for our homily's exegesis may also lie beyond the scriptural text. E. E. Urbach has persuasively argued that many rabbinic references to the prophets of the nations, and especially Balaam (like those in our homily [13]), are to be interpreted as references to Christian-Gnostics who claimed to have received ecstatic divine communications.[21] Although the rabbis vehemently denied the authenticity of these claims, they may, according to Urbach, have based their own conceptions of prophecy upon the reports of the Christian-Gnostics. Along the lines suggested by Urbach's argument, the exegesis for Lev. 1:1 in our homily would therefore read: No prophecy God has revealed to anyone, Jew or Gentile, before or after the Tabernacle, has been as intimate or as direct as the prophecy He communicated to Moses (who, it is to be understood, transmitted that prophecy to Israel in the laws of the Torah). On the other hand, the kind of discourse God held with Moses is not inherently vouchsafed to Jews. At the end of days, God will address all mankind in its voice. In the meantime—since Moses and until the world-to-come—the repository of that voice is to be found in midrash, particularly in the way midrash represents God speaking to mankind—in homiletical exegeses like those in our chapter in VR, but also every time midrash makes use of that all-so-common yet bold formula *amar ha-kadosh barukh hu*, "The Holy One, blessed be He, said," following which God speaks, not in the words of Scripture but in the language of midrash's own invention, as if through the mouth of the darshan.[22] To be sure, neither this formula, *amar ha-kadosh barukh hu*, in particular nor midrash in general lays claim to the authority of classical prophecy. And yet, in a time when classical prophecy had ceased among the Jews, the activity of midrash served a comparable religious need: it helped to restore the sense of God's presence through discourse. By joining ḥavivut with midrash, a new religious language was created whose very purpose was to reinvoke God as a familiar and intimate presence.

The emergence of this kind of language was not a uniquely Jewish phenomenon in this period. In the Christian sermon, as it was perfected by such early Church Fathers as Augustine (fifth century), a similar kind of language is found in the form of the *sermo humilis*. Like the language of ḥavivut, the sermo humilis consists in what Erich Auerbach once described as "a new eloquence" capable of encompassing "sublime matters in a lowly or humble style," an eloquence that eschews rhetorical virtuosity for the use of language as an instrument of ethical persuasion, as the means for the preacher to communicate directly with his audience, for teaching them, admonishing, consoling, giving hope—in short, for directly affecting his audiences' religious lives.[23] Like the language of ḥavivut, sermo humilis is a didactic, homiletical language; its singular power comes from the fact that it never loses sight of the urgency of the lesson it has to teach or of the task it must perform.

To be sure, sermo humilis and the language of ḥavivut are very different as well. As Auerbach has described its history, sermo humilis was born out of the confrontation between the rigid stylistic hierarchies of classical rhetoric and the newly egalitarian religious beliefs of early Christianity; according to Auerbach, the conflict between those two systems was epitomized in the word *humilis* with its classical connotations of stylistic lowliness set against the new meaning of spiritual humility it assumed in Christian thought, a humility, lowly yet sublime, that was thought to be exemplified in the person of Jesus Christ himself. In rabbinic Judaism, humility as a value or ideal of this sort does not really exist; the value that takes its place is that of modesty, as embodied in those exemplars of modesty, Moses and Hillel, for the latter of whom, our own homily tells us (para. 5), an act of humbling could also be a form of exultation. Unlike sermo humilis, the language of ḥavivut is not a language epitomizing humility but the kind of speech God addresses to a modest man like Moses. This language owes its birth not to the breaking of stylistic decorum, but to a simpler religious urge, the desire to recreate a sense of God as a familiar and as an intimate, as a God who still addresses His people between the lines of

Scripture—through midrash, in other words—in the absence of a more direct form of revelation.

To describe ḥavivut as the language of exegesis (for its origins, as we have seen, are to be found in Scripture, in the second petiḥta's interpretation of Lev. 1:1) returns us to the question with which we began this essay: how can the language of midrash be described in its own terms? The answer lies, in part, in the speech with which the darshan/redactor represents God addressing Israel and in the form of the literary homily which serves as the medium for conveying that language of midrash. Ḥavivut and the homily might both be described as the literary inventions of midrash. Just as ḥavivut represents an attempt through literary discourse to recover God as a speaking presence, so the literary homily must be seen as an attempt on the part of the redactor to capture in writing those qualities of intimacy and familiarity that would have been associated by a reader with the oral sermon: hence the conscious preservation and imitation of the rhetorical forms of the oral sermon, like the petiḥta and the parable, in the literary homily. Moreover, just as the language of ḥavivut attempts to restore the fullness of divine presence by attributing to God a special way of speaking rather than a particular message with a specific content, so the literary homily presents the interpretation of Torah as process and activity rather than as a fully grasped understanding of the world.[24] To be sure, this activity is not fully open-ended, but, then, neither is the homily (which by convention culminates in the messianic peroration).

Finally, as we have seen, the homily is not an entirely new invention of the redactor; rather, it is an elaboration of a previously existing literary form in midrash, and its defining characteristic is still as a medium of exegesis, of that special kind of exegesis that midrash represents. In the same way, the language of ḥavivut is not presented by the rabbis as a new religious revelation but as a result of exegesis, a product of midrash. This is not surprising. For the rabbis who occupied themselves with midrash, there was hardly another form of imaginative expression conceivable to them apart from midrash, at least not until that time when, as Scripture tells us, "the glory of God shall be revealed, and all mankind shall see it."

NOTES

1. All references are to Mordecai Margulies, Midrash Leviticus Rabbah, 3 vols. (Jerusalem, Wahrmann, 1972), 1: 1–32. An English translation of the chapter, along with

the entire midrash, is in the Soncino series, in Midrash Rabbah: Leviticus, trans. J. Israelstam (London, Soncino, 1939), pp. 1–17. Note that para. 15 on pp. 17–18 is not an authentic part of the text according to Margulies' text; the Soncino translation is based on an uncritical text. All translations in this paper are my own.

2. This is, admittedly, something of an exaggeration since redactional organization can be discerned in sections of Mekhilta (Shirta especially), Genesis Rabbah, and Eikha Rabbah. The distinction between the two genres of midrash is partly heuristic; still, there is no consistent or systematic or recurring plan to the exegetical anthology.

3. On the triennial cycle and its relation to the homiletical midrash, see Jacob Mann, *The Bible as Read and Preached in the Old Synagogue*, ed. I. Sonne (Cincinnati: by author, vol. 1, 1940, vol. 2, 1966); J. Heinemann, "The Triennial Lectionary Cycle," *JJS* 19 (1968), 41–48; M. Bregman, "The Triennial Haftarot and the Perorations of the Midrashic Homilies," *JJS* 32 (1981), 74–84.

4. For example, see J. Theodor, "Zur Composition der aggadischen Homilien," *MGWJ* 29 (1879), 108; Chanoch Albeck, "Midrash Leviticus Rabbah," in *Louis Ginzberg Jubilee Volume*, ed. Alexander Marx (New York: American Academy for Jewish Research, 1946), Hebrew section, pp. 25ff.; Margulies, intro. to Midrash Leviticus Rabbah, vol. 3, pt. 5, pp. ix–x.

5. J. Heinemann, "The Art of Composition in Midrash Leviticus Rabbah" (Hebrew), *Hasifrut* 2 (1971), 808–834, which was published in a shortened English version as "Profile of a Midrash," *JAAR* 39 (1971), 141–50; cf. also *Public Sermons in the Talmudic Period* (Hebrew) (Jerusalem: Mossad Bialik, 1970) and "Sections of Leviticus Rabbah Whose Originality Is Questionable" (Hebrew), *Tarbiz* 37 (1967–68), 339–54. Heinemann's influence upon other scholars who have recently written about the homily has been considerable. See, for example, L. H. Silberman, "Toward a Rhetoric of Midrash: A Preliminary Account," *The Biblical Mosaic*, ed. R. Polzin and E. Rothman (Philadelphia: Fortress, 1982), pp. 15–26; and "A Theological Treatise on Forgiveness: Chapter Twenty Three of Pesiqta Derab Kahana," in *Studies in Aggadah, Targum, and Jewish Liturgy in Memory of Joseph Heinemann*, ed. J. Petuchowski and E. Fleischer (Jerusalem: Magnes, 1981), pp. 95–107; L. M. Barth, "Literary Imagination and the Rabbinic Sermon," *Proceedings of the Seventh World Congress of Jewish Studies [Studies in the Talmud, Halacha, and Midrash]* (Jerusalem: World Union for Jewish Studies, 1981), pp. 29–36.

6. The notion of organic unity poses both literary-theoretical problems and practical-midrashic ones. On the former, see R. Scholes and R. Kellogg, *The Nature of Narrative* (New York: Oxford University Press, 1976), pp. 106–07; on the latter, see N. J. Cohen, "Structure and Editing in the Homiletic Midrashim," *AJS Review* 6 (1981), 1–20.

7. J. Heinemann, "The Proem in Aggadic Midrashim: A Form-Critical Study," in *SH* 22 (1971), 100–22; Heinemann, "The Petihtaot of the Aggadic Midrash—Their Origin and Function" (Hebrew), in *Papers of the Fourth World Congress of Jewish Studies* (Jerusalem: World Union for Jewish Studies, 1965), pp. 43–47; earlier bibliography is cited in the notes in both articles. In addition, see Heinemann's interpretive articles, "The Amoraim of Israel as Artists of the Sermon" (Hebrew), *Hasifrut* 25 (1977), and "On Life and Death: Anatomy of a Rabbinic Sermon," *SH* 27 (1978), 52–65. Cf. as well A. M. Goldberg, "Petihta und Hariza," *JSJ* 10 (1980), 213–18; Avigdor Shinan, "On the Petihta" (Hebrew), in *Jerusalem Studies in Hebrew Literature* 1 (1981), 135–42; M. Bregman, "Circular Proems and Proems Beginning with the Formula Zo hi shene'emra beruah hakodesh" (Hebrew), in Petuchowski and Fleischer, *Studies* . . . ; R. S. Sarason, "The Petihtaot in Leviticus Rabbah: 'Oral Homilies' or Redactional Constructions?" *JJS* 33 (1982), 557–67; and most recently M. S. Jaffee, "The 'Midrashic' Proem: Towards the Description of Rabbinic Exegesis," in *Approaches to Ancient Judaism*, vol. 4, ed. W. S. Green (Chico, Calif.: Scholars Press, 1983), pp. 95–112.

8. On the attribution, see Margulies' note, p. 1, where he explicitly describes the petiḥta as a redactional construction.

9. This is proven by the fact that the proof-phrase for section C, "... ye ... that fulfill His word hearkening," overlaps with the preceding and subsequent proof-phrase (B and D).

10. On atomization, see I. Heinemann, *The Methods of Aggadah* (Hebrew) (Jerusalem, 1970), pp. 96ff.

11. Cf. S. Safrai, "The Observance of the Sabbatical Year Following the Destruction of the Second Temple" (Hebrew), *Tarbiẓ* 35 (1966), 304–28; 36 (1967), pp. 1–21, esp. p. 15. Note that Margulies (VR, p. 4) rejects Safrai's reading of *arnona*, the special tax the Romans levied upon the Jews, in favor of *annona*; but see S. Lieberman's correction in VR, vol. 2, p. 869.

12. On the peroration, see E. Stein, "Die homiletische Peroratio im Midrash," *HUCA* 8–9 (1931–32), 353–71, and Bregman, "The Triennial Haftarot."

13. On the reading *otanin*, not *ikonin*, see Margulies' note, p. 32; but for the correct interpretation of the Greek loanword, *othanion*, see S. Lieberman's note in Margulies' ed. of VR, vol. 2, p. 870.

14. On the conversion of Bityah and her rejection of idolatry, see Exodus Rabbah I 23; cf. also Targum Yerushalmi *ad* Ex. 2:5.

15. Cf. B. Megillah 13a, and Margulies' note, pp. 7–8.

16. Cf. G. A. Buttrick, ed., *The Interpreter's Bible* (New York: Abingdon Press, 1953), vol. 2, pp. 528–29; *Mikra'ot Gedolot* and commentaries *ad loc.*; for a different interpretation of the word, cf. Naḥmanides *ad loc.*

17. Cf. however, para. 13 (p. 28), where God's speech to Jewish prophets is contrasted with His speech to gentiles. To the latter, he speaks in the language of impurity, to the former, "in the language of holiness, the language of purity, a clear language, the language in which the angelic host praise Him." In his apparatus, Margulies quotes variants that correspond to the versions of the lemma in Genesis Rabbah 52:5 (ed. Theodor-Albeck, p. 544) and 74:7 (p. 864), which read, respectively, *leshon ḥibah* (the language of love) and *leshon kedushah ve-ḥibah* (the language of holiness and love). Here, again, one notes the antiphonal character of language which we saw in the first petiḥta.

18. On the use of the parable, see my article, "The Function of the Parable in Rabbinic Literature" (Hebrew), in *Jerusalem Studies in Hebrew Literature* 7 (1985), 90–102.

19. The use of this verse in our homily remains somewhat problematic; cf. Ma-HaRZU *ad loc.*

20. I wish to thank Professor Dov Noy for pointing out this wordplay; cf. the use of Prov. 20.15 (*u-kli yakar siftei da'at*) as the petiḥta-verse in para. 6.

21. E. E. Urbach, "Rabbinic Homilies on Gentile Prophets and on the Biblical Portions Concerning Balaam" (Hebrew), *Tarbiẓ* 25 (1956), 272–89.

22. On the formula, see M. Hirshman, "The Prophecy of King Solomon and Ruaḥ ha-kodesh in Midrash Ecclesiastes Rabbah" (Hebrew), in *Jerusalem Studies in Jewish Thought* 3 (1982), 7–14, esp. 12–13.

23. On the origin of the phrase and the application to Augustine and other early Christian writers, see Erich Auerbach, "Sermo Humilis," in *Literary Language and Its Public in Late Latin Antiquity and in the Middle Ages* (1958), trans. R. Manheim (New York: Pantheon, 1965), pp. 25–81, esp. 45ff. Cf. also Peter Brown, *Augustine of Hippo* (London: Faber and Faber, 1967), pp. 257–58, esp. p. 259.

24. This notion of exegesis resembles the definition put forward by Paul Ricoeur in his *Interpretation Theory: Discourse and the Surplus of Meaning* (Fort Worth: Texas Christian University Press, 1976), when he speaks of the meaning of the text as "the direction of thought opened up by the text" (p. 92) and interpretation as "nothing less than an attempt to make estrangement and distanciation productive" (p. 44). See also Jaffee, "The 'Midrashic' Proem," p. 105.

From Midrash to Kabbalah

JOSEPH DAN

Midrash and the Dawn of Kabbalah

The combining of kabbalah and midrash today should create a very potent formula. In the last quarter-century, when scholars in the various disciplines of the humanities have become aware of the scholarly works of Gershom Scholem, kabbalah has emerged as a dignified topic in academic discussion, and terms like *Lurianism* and *Zoharic mythology* are to be found in the most surprising places in scholarly essays. Recently, midrash has followed kabbalah in the same path, acquiring status as a puzzling, intriguing, literary genre. Few doubt that midrash, like kabbalah, is a meaningful term, though even fewer can explain exactly why. When these two fashionable terms are joined in the phrase *kabbalistic midrash*, they may be expected to communicate a profound message to our fin de siecle academic culture.

Yet, the object of this essay is nothing more than a description of a clear, unambiguous historical phenomenon; namely, the initial emergence of the kabbalah in Europe in the form of a midrash, in the pseudepigraphic work Sefer ha-Bahir, "The Book of Light."[1] It is my aim in this paper to analyze a section of this work, in order to try to understand the midrashic technique used by the anonymous twelfth-century writer and thus to convey something of his mystical insights.

While a definition of a midrash is a difficult task, its function can be explained quite clearly, especially in the context of mystical literature. The midrash (from a functional point of view) is the result of the inherent paradox which haunts a religion based upon a body of sacred scriptures: the conflict between the wish and the need to innovate, and the religious maxim which states that all truth is to be found in the scriptures. This means that, in order to be true, every new statement should be old. The midrashic technique is the traditional Jewish answer to this paradox. A midrashic statement is innovative, but it proves at the same time that, because Moses received the written with

127

the oral torah in the Mount Sinai theophany, the statement itself was hidden deep in the heart of Jewish sacred texts.

The Hebrew midrash is alien to western literary, exegetical, and homiletical tradition because of the vast differences between the Jewish and Christian scriptures. Christian preachers had to rely, when interpreting scriptures and revealing their hidden meaning, mainly on the ideonic side, the implications of the content of the verse. Jewish preachers could use a total text, hermeneutically discussing not only the meaning of terms and words, but also their sound, the shape of the letters, the vocalization points and their shapes and sounds, the te'amim (the musical signs added to the Hebrew words), the tagin (the small decorative additions to the letters), the frequency with which words and letters appear in a verse or a chapter, the absence of one of the letters from a biblical portion, the variety and number of divine names included in the text, the numerical value of letters, words, and whole verses, the possible changes of letters (etbash, temurah), the new words formed from the initial or final letters of a biblical section (notarikon), and the countless ways other than ideonic content and meaning by which the scriptures transmit a semiotic message. It should be emphasized that these methods are in themselves not mystical, and any message, even the mundane or humorous, can be and was reached in these ways. This kind of midrashic treatment is completely neutral on possible meaning and was used in the Middle Ages and modern times (relying on sources originating from the ancient period) by every Jewish preacher and exegete, each according to his own preferences and tastes. Pietists, philosophers, traditionalists, and mystics shared the same midrashic tradition.

The possibility of using the totality of the text is created by the nature of the original Hebrew language of the Jewish scriptures. This is in marked contrast to the fact that Christians in the Middle Ages and modern times have usually had to use a translated text. Some of the Christian scriptures were written originally in Greek, but in most Christian Bibles all of the Old Testament and most of the New are translations. In reading the Vulgata, most Christian preachers in the western church had a text which in many cases had undergone two translations. Such a text cannot preserve the sanctity of the shape of letters; at best, it can convey the ideonic meaning of the original.

Even in regard to the simple meaning of the text, there is a vast difference between reading a text in what is believed to be the language of revelation and reading a translation. Many, probably most, of the verses in the Old Testament, for example, can be translated in more than one way, because there are at least several shades of meaning, and sometimes even complete obscurities, in the text. A translator has to choose between all possible interpretations and present one of them, losing in this way the richness, as well as (from a religious point of view) the profundity of the original. The translated text thus conveys a sense of clarity which is completely missing from the original. The translator does not transmit the text, but one possible meaning of it, creating a new text which is much more flat and unequivocal than the original (especially so if it is a translation from a translation, as is the case with the Gospels). This is one of the reasons why the Roman Catholic Church could develop a set of dogma. Dogmatic thinking must rely on an unambiguous text. The Hebrew Bible does not lend itself easily to the formulation of dogma, because of the obscurities which haunt almost every biblical verse.

These two differences—the ability to use the total semiotic message of the text, and the use of an obscure, and therefore polysemous, Hebrew original—create a most significant gap between Jewish and Christian exegetes and preachers. In Rabbinic Judaism it is almost impossible to use a biblical verse as a final proof in a religious controversy; every verse can be and was interpreted in fully legitimate ways to support conflicting arguments. An opponent's way of interpreting a scriptural verse would rarely, if ever, be considered as falsifying the text. A biblical verse is brought to support an argument in a decorative manner, but it cannot be the decisive element in an argument. Even the halakhah does not derive its authority from an alleged literal meaning of the scriptures; its legal power is based upon the tradition that Moses received detailed instructions concerning ritual and ethical behavior and transmitted these orally to Joshua, from whom they were passed from generation to generation. Roman Catholics developed a somewhat similar, though less emphatic, notion of a tradition preserved by the Church. This included the contents of that tradition, as well as its authority, but it did not derive directly from the Scriptures. Protestants, however, who rely on the literal meaning of the twice or thrice translated text (and Protestantism to a great extent began with the third translation to European languages), are thus removed as far as one can imagine from the atmosphere of the Jewish ancient and medieval midrash. Paradoxically enough, Protestants, despite this distance, were among the first and leading scholars both in biblical studies and in literary criticism.

Let me give an illustration of the spirit of midrash, derived from a period contemporary with the compilation of the Bahir. In 1217, Rabbi Eleazar ben Judah of Worms, distressed by the death of his great teacher, Rabbi Judah ben Samuel the Pious, the great leader and teacher of Ashkenazi Hasidism, decided to write down the teachings of his deceased master. He wrote a short book called Sefer ha-Ḥokhmah (The Book of Wisdom),[2] most of which was dedicated to the systematic interpretation of the first verses of the first chapter of Genesis. These verses were interpreted in dozens of ways, and in the introduction to the Sefer ha-Ḥokhmah Rabbi Eleazar gave the list of the seventy-three sha'arei ḥokhmah, "gates of wisdom," which are in fact seventy-three methods of midrashic interpretation.[3] The body of the work consists of examples of how to use these methods (the number 73 was derived from the numerical value of the word ḥokhmah, wisdom, in the sincere belief that if the number of these methods was anything but 73, a different term or spelling would have been used by the Bible to denote "wisdom").[4]

Rabbi Eleazar was not bothered by the contradictions, apparent or real, involved in interpreting the same verse many times according to different midrashic methods. The truth hidden within these verses was regarded as rich enough to be revealed in countless ways. If so, the larger midrashic method is on the one hand superfluous, because if everything is true (even contradictory statements) why bother with a midrash? But on the other hand it is the only way to point out a traditional source for a new idea or attitude. The midrash thus becomes a necessary tool for a religion based on divine revelation, once actual revelation no longer takes place. The texts of previous revelations are used to supply new answers to new questions, even though direct contact with the source of revelation is lost.

The Jewish mystics of the Middle Ages could choose between two ways of substantiating their revolutionary ideas. They could rely either on mystical revelation or on the midrashic method. Many of them indeed described divine powers that were revealed to them while asleep or awake, or told of the appearance of Elijah the prophet, or the hearing of voices, and so on. But most of them, including the author of the earliest kabbalistic work which has reached us, the book Bahir, preferred the midrash. I now turn to the Bahir.[5]

Section 123 of the Bahir initiates a detailed discussion of the "priests' benediction," a group of three verses in Numbers 6:24–26 which are interwoven into the daily prayer. The blessing of the people by the first priest, Aaron (Lev. 9:22), and its connection with the sacrifices are both analyzed. On this occasion the author explains the Hebrew term for sacrifice, korban, as being derived from the verb k-r-v, to bring close, so that the sacrifice is intended to bring together the people of Israel and the celestial powers (ha-elyonim). The homily proceeds in section 124:

What is the reason for the raising of hands and the blessing given to them? This is because there are ten fingers in the hands, which is a hint for the ten sefirot in which the [creation] of heaven and earth was signed. Those ten correspond to the ten commandments, and in these ten all 613 commandments are included; if you count the number of letters in the ten commandments you will find 613 letters, which include all 22 letters except the tet. And why is that, this is to teach you that the tet is the abdomen, and is not counted among the sefirot.

The homilist creates here a connection between the number three and the number ten. The priests' benediction contains three verses, while the hands which are raised in this prayer include ten fingers. He then proceeds to discuss the number ten, and gives two further examples of its centrality—the ten sefirot and the ten commandments.

Concerning the sefirot, there is no reason to believe that the author means anything corresponding to the kabbalistic meaning of the term, that is, the ten divine hypostases which are central to kabbalistic theosophy. He refers to the origin of the term in Sefer Yeẓirah, an ancient cosmological work of the talmudic period,[6] in which the sefirot have several meanings but the main one is the ten cosmic directions of five dimensions: North, South, East, West, Up, Down, Beginning, End (corresponding to contemporary notions of the four dimensions, three spatial ones and the temporal one); Good and Evil conclude the list of ten. In Sefer Yeẓirah these are the ten directions of the divine infinity, and the Bahir uses here mainly the totality expressed by the number ten. There need not be any hint of anthropomorphic interpretation in the association of fingers with sefirot; all the homilist does is to note the classical examples of the occurrence of this number.

The same totality is represented by the ten commandments, which include, by the number of letters in them, all the 613 commandments of Judaism, as the ten sefirot include the whole cosmos. As an aside, the author refers to the absence of the ninth letter of the alphabet from the ten commandments (which harms the comprehensiveness of this biblical section). He explains that this letter represents the abdomen (because of its form; another interpretation, found also in the Bahir section 84, connects this letter with the final *mem*). The concluding statement of this section is enigmatic: there are only ten sefirot but twenty-two letters of the alphabet, so there should not be any surprise that every letter does not refer to a sefirah; and if the sefirot are represented by the ten first letters (and *tet* is the ninth), which letter takes its place? and why does the similarity in form between the *tet* and the abdomen prohibit it from representing a sefirah? No answer is suggested to these questions.

The homiletical methods used here obviously employ not only numerical structure, but also the shape of the letters and Rabbi Eleazar of Worms's method of *ne'elam*, wherein the absence of a given letter from a verse or a biblical section becomes a source of midrashic interpretation.

Section 125 proceeds with a brief question and a succinct answer: "And why are they called *sefirot*? Because it is written: 'The heavens declare the glory (*kavod*) of God (Ps. 19:2).' " This is a traditional midrash, moving from the suggested connection between sefirot and numbers (*misparim*) to another use of the same verb in Hebrew, one connected with a continuous divine revelation—the sky reveals (*mesaprim*) the glory of God. Again, this interpretation of the term (which is etymologically enigmatic; and indeed no agreed etymology is to be found in modern scholarship) does not denote any meaning of the term which is not found in the Sefer Yeẓirah.

Section 126 opens with another question on the same subject:

And what are they [the sefirot]? They are three, and they include three armies and three forces [*memshalot*]. The first force is Light, and the Light of Life of Water. The second force is the sacred beasts and the wheels [*ofanim*] and the wheels of the chariot, and all God's battalions, they bless and adore and beautify and praise and sanctify the King, great in holiness and adored in the great secret of saints, a King terrible and frightful, and they crown Him with three *kedushot*.

In a most surprising manner the homilist returns from the number ten to the number three. He himself stated that the sefirot are ten in number, and his source, Sefer Yeẓirah, states most emphatically "ten and not nine, ten and not eleven," a fundamental axiom which was revered by all kabbalists who, in all their different theosophies, never departed from the sanctity of the number ten for the sefirot. Yet here the author claims that the sefirot are three forces or armies, of which he describes only two. There is little doubt, however, that this transition is motivated by the term *kavod*, in the verse cited in the previous section, as the unfolding homily later proves.

The second force is quite clear. It is the world of Ezekiel's chariot, as described in talmudic exegesis and the Hekhalot and Merkavah literature, the ancient mysticism of the talmudic period.[7] The hosts of angels and celestial forces (some of them undoubtedly divine in nature) sanctify and adore God in the form of a great king sitting on the throne of glory. The style the author uses here is that of Hekhalot and Merkavah literature. The first force, however, is more obscure, and the author does not support the statement with a biblical or talmudic source. It still seems that he is referring to the sefirot of Sefer Yeẓirah. In that work, after the discussion of the ten cosmic directions or dimensions, four sefirot are given different characteristics. They represent the evolution or emergence of the three elements from the divine spirit. The first is the Spirit of the Living God (*ru'aḥ Elohim Ḥayim*); the second is the evolution of the element air, or wind, from that source; the third is the evolution of water from the air; and the fourth is fire from water (the ancient cosmologist did not perceive earth as an element). It seems that the obscure reference to water and to the Light of Life—especially if we substitute Spirit for Light—brings it very close to the Sefer Yeẓirah presentation. But why change from Spirit to Light? This can be perceived as the author's declaration of independence from the Sefer Yeẓirah terminology. He uses the ancient source, but he does so in a creative manner, introducing, without homiletical support, his preference for the term *Light*.

This section concludes with the homiletical element which connects it to the continuation of the sermon. The celestial hosts crown God with the three *kedushot*, a reference to the third benediction in the prayer, based on the "holy, holy, holy" of Isaiah 6. Section 127 continues thus:

And what are the three *kedushot*? Why not four? Because divine holiness is three,

three, as it is written: "God is King, God has reigned, God will reign forever." And it is written: "The Lord bless thee," "The Lord make his face shine upon thee," "The Lord lift up His countenance upon thee" (Numbers 6:24–26), and it is written "God God" and the rest of the *midot*. And where is the third "God"? God is a merciful God, etc., the thirteen *midot*.

Like section 124, this section is devoted to giving examples of the sanctity of a number, in this case the number three. The first example is not biblical, even though it is presented as such. This is the classical explanation of the traditional vocalization of the sacred name, YHWH, as a combination of the past, present, and future of the Hebrew verb "to be," h-y-h. The Bahir's mistake in believing this explanation to be found in the Bible was a common one. The frequency of the appearance of the explanatory phrase in the prayers and in Hebrew literature made it seem like a biblical verse. The Bahir states, therefore, that the most sacred divine name is a combination of three elements, God's kingdom in the past, present, and future.

The second example of a sacred triad is the original subject of this homily—the priests' benediction, comprised of three verses. In this way the homilist creates a numerical identification between this benediction and the phrases of the kedushah. The third example is the three times in which God's name is mentioned in the verse (Exod. 34:6) which, according to talmudic tradition, includes the thirteen attributes of mercy.[8] It should be noted that the introduction of this verse enables the author to combine the two main numbers of this homily—ten and three, united in God's thirteen midot. In the later kabbalah, the term *midot* is often found as an appellation of the sefirot, the Zohar actually preferring it over the Sefer Yezirah terminology. The tension between ten and thirteen is to be found throughout kabbalistic midrash.

Only in section 128, the sixth section of this homily, does the Bahir present for the first time its mystical terminology:

And what are "Holy, Holy, Holy" and then "God of Hosts the whole earth is full of his glory" (*kavod*) (Isa. 6:3), but holy is the supreme *crown*, holy is the *root of the tree*, holy is united and special in all of them, God of hosts whose glory fills the whole earth.

This is clearly a homiletical interpretation of a verse which is repeated both at the beginning of the brief section and its end. It should be noted—and this is characteristic of Bahir homiletics—that the key mystical terms are not presented as a result of homiletical exegesis. The midrash actually concerns only the number three. The different nature of each of these three "holies" is described by terminology not directly derived from these verses or any other ancient source.

The system thus presented may correspond to the previous three forces of section 126, at least from a structural point of view—the divine world is divided into three parts. The parts, however, denote in this section the highest and most supreme Godhead. The "supreme crown" is presented in section 141 as the first and highest of the divine manifestations.The term itself is peculiar to the Bahir, though it undoubtedly evolved from Heikhalot mysticism and Ashkenazi Ḥasidic sources which recognized the existence of a supreme crown at the top of the divine world.[9] The second term—the "root of the tree"—is, as Scholem proved, one of the basic elements that the Bahir accepted from ancient gnostic speculations. Several sections of the Bahir describe the Godhead as a cosmic tree growing upside down, its branches being the divine manifestations active in the created world, while its root (resembling the letter *shin*) is the highest part.[10] The third term, "united and special" (*davek u-meyuḥad*), is a combination of two terms which describe the divine glory, the kavod in the neo-Platonic philosophy of Abraham ibn Ezra (middle of the twelfth century), and Ashkenazi Ḥasidic terminology referring to the "special cherub" sitting on the throne of glory and being revealed to the prophets.[11]

The sefirot, as cosmic dimensions, are ten; but the divine world is described by the number three, the third being the kavod, the divine glory which fills the whole earth. To this third and lowest power the author devotes the next sections of his homily:

[Section 129] And what is the Holy which is united and special? This is similar to a king who had sons, and the sons—sons. When their sons [i.e., the grandsons] perform His wishes He enters among them and makes everything exist and satisfies them and His goodness flows into them, so that the fathers and their sons will be satisfied. When the sons [grandsons] do not perform his wishes He satisifes the father as much as they need.

The homily and the parable are based on the contradiction between the two terms *davek* and *meyuḥad*, "united" and "special," the first denoting proximity and the other distance and separation. The Bahir states that these are two alternatives, the first existing when God's wishes are performed, and the second when they are not. Obviously, the sons are the divine powers, which are satisfied in every case, while the grandsons are the people of Israel, whose actions decide the amount of divine sustenance flowing from the Godhead towards earth.

The Bahir does not base his homily in this section on a verse, a letter, or a talmudic saying, but on his own medieval terminology. Here theology is the most important element, and elementary word-exegesis assists it.

The third "Holy," the kavod, as a central part of the kedushah, is the subject of the next four sections, each interpreting one of its characteristics:

[Section 130] And what is "The whole earth is full of his glory?" But it is the whole of that earth which was created on the first day, which is above and corresponding to Eretz Israel, and it is full of God's glory. And what is it, Wisdom, as it is written: "The wise shall inherit honor [kavod]" (Proverbs 3:35), and it is said "Blessed be the glory [kavod] of God from His place" (Ezek. 3:12).

The systematic exposition of the verse in Isaiah continues with the discussion of the term *earth*, which is full of the divine glory. The homilist explains that this is not the earth we know, but a celestial country, which corresponds to the earthly Eretz Israel and was created in the first day (probably relying on Gen. 1:1). The nature of this "fullness" of divine glory is described by the term *wisdom*, which is derived in a traditional midrashic manner from the verses in Proverbs and Ezekiel, and from the idea originating from the rabbinic attribution of wisdom to the air of Eretz Israel (here, of course, referring to the celestial country).[12] However, the most important part of this section from the point of view of the structure of the homily is the introduction of the verse from Ezekiel, which is part of the kedushah and was the subject of discussion in talmudic and Hekhalotic texts. The next section, 131, opens with a reference to this verse and an explanation of its meaning:

And what is this *kavod*? This is similar to a king who had a great lady [matronita] in his room, and all his servants [ḥayalotav] were fascinated by her [mishta'ashe'in bah]. And she had sons, who came every day to see the face of the king and bless him. They said to him: Where is our mother? He told them: You cannot see her now. They said: Blessed is she wherever she is.

The parable explicates a well-known midrash in b. Ḥagigah 14b, which interprets Ezekiel's verse as meaning that the angels themselves do not know where the kavod is, and therefore they use the term *mimkomo*, understood as "wherever He may be." The Bahir adds nothing to this understanding, except the possible hint that the kavod is a female figure, the mother of the people of Israel who pray to her and bless her and the king every day. But this repetition by parable of an old midrash is only the beginning. The essence of the Bahiric mystical approach is revealed in the next section.

[Section 132] And what is the meaning of the verse from "His place"? This is because nobody knows its place. This is similar to a princess who came from afar, and nobody knew where she came from, until they saw that she was capable, beautiful, and just in all her doings. They said: This one certainly was taken from the side of light [mizad ha-or; a different version reads here: mizurat ha-or, 'from the form of light'], because her deeds bring light to the world. They asked her: Where are you from? She answered: From my place [mimkomi]. They said: If so, great are the people of your place, blessed are you and blessed her place.

This is a second parable, explaining the same verse in Ezekiel, emphasizing the same word in the verse ("From His place") in a sense diametrically opposite to the first one. While in the previous parable the female figure was hidden and was blessed without her place being known, here the female figure is present. Only her place of origin is unknown and is blessed together with her, she being the representative of the place and the proof of its worthiness. The homilist does not hesitate to negate the meaning of the verse as presented by the talmudic midrash, and he insists that the kavod is actually revealed and resides among the praying people. Only its divine sources are hidden. This kind of radical modification is not restricted to kabbalistic midrash, but it is most pronounced in such texts. The atmosphere of freedom that mystical speculation creates enables the homilist to negate previous notions drastically, even while presenting those previous notions without argument. The text clearly insists that even though the two interpretations are in conflict, both are true and should be accepted equally. This is the most important and unique characteristic of the Hebrew midrash: the verses contain an infinite number of true interpretations, and there is no need and no possibility of choosing one true version.

While explaining this verse from the kedushah, the author introduces, without any biblical or rabbinic basis, a new term and a new concept: "from the side of light." Scholem clearly identified in this section the influence of gnostic mythological descriptions of the female divine power in exile, wandering around the world, away from her dwelling-place in the divine world of light and goodness. The gnostic element is clearer in this section than in many others in the Bahir. The author does not feel pressed, when introducing new, revolutionary symbols to the traditional Jewish prayer, to support these new terms with a midrashic connection to scriptures. Like his introduction of the supreme crown, the root of the tree, and the "united and separated" divine glory in section 128, there is no direct homiletical connection with previously known Jewish concepts.

It seems that the source of authority for the homilist in such cases is the general midrashic form of the book. The whole work is presented as the teachings of the ancient sages, so that it is unnecessary to give midrashic substantiation to every single detail. If the new symbol is interwoven into the general framework of the traditional midrash, traditional authorization is achieved.

The homily continues in section 133 by bringing a parable which explains the "outsideness" of the divine glory, and section 134 which describes the glory as the heart of the world, connecting it with Sefer Yeẓirah once more by hinting at the number 32 (the numerical value of heart, lev), which is the number of "secret paths" of the creation in the opening paragraph of the ancient cosmological work. In section 135 the subject of the priests' benediction returns, through a discussion of the raising of Moses' hands during the war against Amalek.

The early kabbalists followed faithfully all the methods of the traditional midrash. Like other medieval homilists, they tended to emphasize midrashic methods of interpretation, including the shape of the letters, their vocalization, their numerical value and structure, and the absence of letters from certain biblical portions. This was not a revolutionary attitude. It merely represented a different emphasis. Similarly, the introduction of new symbols, ideas, and terms did not present any difficulty to the kabbalistic homilist. Some of these were presented and interpreted as were more traditional ideas, and others were included in the general framework of the midrash. The midrashic structure offered them the requisite open literary form, which could welcome contradictory and new ideas without changing the basic literary and ideological rules of the genre.

It may be said in conclusion that the nature of the midrashic form facilitated the acceptance and integration of the kabbalah in Jewish culture. It enabled the European mystics of the Middle Ages to present their new symbols as if they were an integral part of ancient tradition.

NOTES

1. The title's meaning is practically identical with that of the Zohar, which was written a hundred years after the Bahir, also in the form of a traditional midrash.

2. This work is found in three manuscripts at the Bodleian Library, Oxford. Portions were printed in my *Studies in Ashkenazi Ḥasidic Literature* (Hebrew) (Tel Aviv: Massada, 1975), pp. 44–57.

3. I have described the main text which used the system of the *Gates of Wisdom* in "The Ashkenazi Hasidic *Gates of Wisdom*," in *Homage à Georges Vajda*, ed. G. Nahon and C. Touati (Louvain: Peeters, 1980), pp. 183–89.

4. Concerning the use of the numerical value of letters, words, and verses, it should again be emphasized that there is nothing mystical in this usage. Unlike European languages and Arabic, Hebrew does not have an authentic system of writing numbers that is separate from the letters in which words are written (in this respect it is similar to Greek). When an *aleph* is written down, it can mean one of three things: the number one, the number one thousand, or the sound of the aleph. There is no other way to write the number one but to draw the letter *aleph*. When reading the letters comprising the word *ḥokhmah* the reader has a choice: either to read the word meaning wisdom, or to read the number 73. When opening a page in the Bible, one can, with equal legitimacy, read it as a series of words or as a series of numbers; there were quite a few Jews throughout history who tended to see in letters first the numbers and only later the words—many of them were mystics, but the method itself is a direct result of the simplest characteristics of the Hebrew language. When Arabic numerals were adopted by Hebrew writers to denote numbers, a gap was created between the reading of words and the reading of numbers, but this is a recent phenomenon, undreamed of by ancient, medieval, and traditional modern Jewish writers. *Gematria*, therefore, is neither mystical nor bizarre, but a simple use of the inherent double meaning, as a word or a number, of every group of Hebrew letters.

5. It is not certain that the sections to be discussed here were indeed written by one author in a homiletical sequence: the Bahir probably contains many strata and additions. The section under discussion, 123–134, however, seems to me to be a continuous homily. A brief description of the Book Bahir can be found in G. Scholem's first monograph, *Das Buch Bahir* (Leipzig, 1923; rpt. Darmstadt: W. Drugulin, 1970). His most detailed discussion is included in his history of the early kabbalah: *Ursprung und Anfänge der Kabbala* (Berlin: W. de Gruyter, 1962).

6. Concerning Sefer Yeẓirah see I. Gruenwald, "A Preliminary Critical Edition of the Sefer Yeẓirah," IOS 1, 132–77; and REJ 132 (1973), 475–512.

7. G. Scholem devoted the second chapter in his book, *Major Trends in Jewish Mysticism*, 2d ed. (New York: Schocken, 1954), pp. 40–78, to the ancient Jewish mystical school known as Hekhalot Mysticism. His study concerned wholly with this subject is *Jewish Gnosticism, Merkabah Mysticism and Talmudic Tradition* (New York: JTS, 1960; revised edition, 1965). A survey of the texts and the main problems of this field is presented in I. Gruenwald's *Apocalyptic and Merkabah Literature* (Leiden: E. J. Brill, 1980).

8. B. Rosh ha-Shanah 17b.

9. Concerning the early references to this term see my *Esoteric Theology of Ashkenazi Ḥasidism* (Hebrew) (Jerusalem: Mossad Bialik, 1968), pp. 119–25.

10. About this symbol see Scholem, *Ursprung und Anfänge der Kabbala*, esp. pp. 110–11.

11. I have studied the term and its history in a monograph included in my *Studies in Ashkenazi Ḥasidic Literature*, pp. 89–111.

12. B. Baba Batra 158b.

MOSHE IDEL

Infinities of Torah in Kabbalah

The purpose of this paper is to describe different kinds of infinities which were attributed to the Torah by early kabbalists. The emergence of these conceptions was the result of a crystallization of earlier mystical motifs, which are presented here as mainly non-rabbinic tendencies. In the kabbalistic writings we discover that the midrashic view—in which the distances between God, the interpreter, and the Torah are scrupulously preserved—has been exchanged for a view in which the infinities of the Torah are seen as coexisting with a virtual closure of the gaps between God, interpreter, and Torah.

I

The nature of midrashic interpretation is determined by two main components of the interpretative experience: the text and the interpreter. The text is the canonized Hebrew Bible whose precise borders are delimited and whose sacrosanct status is sealed.[1] The situation of the interpreter is altogether different. As the text became fixed, the terms of his task altered. The Divine Spirit which was instrumental in the formation of the canon was excluded from the interpretative process.[2] The rabbinic interpreter, no more than a simple human being before divine revelation, had now to function without the divine help so necessary to fathoming the messages inherent in the text. In penetrating the intricacies of the Bible, he had only two tools: the first was the tradition and the second his own intellectual abilities and capacity to apply the authorized rules of interpretation. The Godhead now expected that man, on his own, would articulate His intentions as instilled for eternity in the revealed book.

Man faced, then, a silent Godhead and a text which was for centuries the single source of divine guidance. No wonder that close scrutiny of the Bible, motivated by and combined with an overwhelming conviction that everything is hinted at or solved by the biblical verses, became the main intellectual activity of Jewish spiritual leadership. The whole of its literary output in the Tannaitic and Amoraic periods was aimed at elucidating the legal part of the Bible and explaining its narrative portions. The authoritative rabbinic Jewish texts were regarded as but pleiades of stars rotating around the Bible, while the other kinds of texts (apocalyptic, magical, mystical, or mere belles lettres) were successfully excluded from the rabbinic universe and condemned to total oblivion. The remnants of the non-rabbinic Jewish literary creations that did survive became planets in Christian literatures; only seldom did they penetrate the rabbinic firmaments. Other texts were simply suppressed, though they continued to be esoterically transmitted among select groups. Such was the case with various types of mystical treatise (the greatest of these coming to comprise the so-called *Heikhalot* literature) as well as with certain magical texts which remained in usage in more popular circles.

This "purification" of Jewish literature contributed to the emergence of the relatively uniform attitude toward the biblical text. But the apocalyptical, magical, mythical, and mystical perceptions of this text, which, naturally, could not be totally eradicated, continued to survive as vague hints or fragments incorporated into classical rabbinic literature. This literature, which was intended as a vast interpretation of the canon for the large Jewish public, was consumed by a community who sought in it the guidance and instruction which it was once the role of the prophet or priest to supply.

I shall now delve briefly into the main components of the midrashic experience. Its disseminators were leading figures in Jewish communities or academies who delivered their homilies before an open audience, without any restrictions regarding the age or the competence of the participants. The language of their discourses was generally perspicuous and aimed at explaining relatively simple items related to the biblical texts. Such explanation was usually achieved without resort to complex theological concepts. Further, these homilies took the form, it seems, of primarily oral speeches, delivered as part of the oral religious service. The language of these homilies, I should like to emphasize, served a highly social function, its central feature being its public or collective communication. Indeed, there is a strong affinity that links the ancient Jewish interpreter, using authorized hermeneutic devices and perceiving the text as mainly speaking to the Jewish community, and the plain, public language he used in order to deliver his message. In effect, one implies the other.

As long as Jewish culture was given the chance to develop more or less autonomously, it generated mostly self-interpretative literature of this type. However, when attacked either by sectarians, like the Karaites, or by outsiders, like the Islamic theologians, the tradition reacted by absorbing the theological positions of its opponents, trying thereby to evidence the complete compatibility of Jewish texts with the intellectual standards of other traditions, such as Islamic Kalam or Aristotelianism. One of the heaviest prices of this apologetic reinterpretation of Judaism was the further suppression of apocalyptic, magical, mythical, and mystical elements which, as I have already suggested, survived in a diluted fashion in rabbinic sources, or in their primary form in Hebrew texts existing outside the authoritative Jewish literature. But just as the purification of Jewish literature caused a relocation of the mysterious, mystical, or magical elements in midrash, so the rationalistic reconstructions of Judaism prompted, in turn, a powerful reaction wherein an amalgam of older traditions, including the same mystical, mythical, and magical elements, came to the surface in more overt and more crystallized forms.[3]

The beginnings of kabbalah offer evidence of this reaction. The emergence of this literature was not only a decisive development for Jewish theology; it also had the utmost influence on the subsequent unfolding of Jewish hermeneutics. Underground myths and symbols surfaced in plain view and hermeneutic methods which were rarely used by rabbinic authorities, as well as entirely new perceptions about the biblical text, came to the forefront.[4] With this theological shift came also powerful new exegetical devices which enabled Jewish mystics to revolutionize conventional understanding of the biblical message. I should like to describe the nature of some of these "re-newed" or, better, really new hermeneutics.

Under the impact of ancient magic and mysticism, kabbalah was able to generate a relatively unique theory of language that applied to the Bible and its interpretation. The Hebrew language was no longer considered the exclusive instrument of divine revelation of sacred history and the Jewish modus vivendi. It was conceived rather as a powerful tool which, used by God in order to create the world, could also be used by the kabbalist masters in imitation of God, in their own marvelous creations,[5] or in the achievement of mystical experiences or sometimes even of *unio mystica*.[6]

Another decisive change in medieval Jewish hermeneutics was the ascent of a far-reaching assumption, expressed almost exclusively in kabbalistic texts,[7] regarding the nature of the interpreter. As already mentioned, the Divine Spirit was categorically excluded from the interpretative process as that process was viewed by the rabbis.[8] Ecstatic states, prophetic inspirations, angelic revelations, or oneiric messages were unacceptable as exegetical techniques or reliable testimonies. It is true that such experiences never ceased to attract some rabbinic masters, and accounts of sporadic occurrences of altered states of consciousness in connection with particularly knotty interpretative quandaries certainly exist. Nevertheless, it was the kabbalists alone who went so far as to condition the attainment of the sublime secrets of Torah on paranormal spiritual experiences. In certain kabbalistic commentaries on the Bible we find indications that a prophetic state of mind is believed necessary to the proper decoding of the Bible. And in a more general way the kabbalists' reaching for a transcendent interpretative dimension even assumed categorical significance. Indeed, we come now to an issue of central importance in kabbalistic interpretation. This is the direct relationship between the notion of the transported interpreter and the growing perception of the Torah as infinity. The kabbalistic blurring of the distinction between God and man[9] in prophetic experiences is coextensive, I believe, with the blurring of the difference between infinite God and infinite Torah.

In the rabbinic sources the Torah is, of course, given a unique status, unparalleled by all but the Divine Throne. The Torah predates the creation of the world. It is considered God's daughter and its way is the single way to contemplate the Godhead, and so on. However, whereas in the non-mystical texts there is a clear reticence to identify Torah with God Himself, there is a tendency in the Heikhalot literature to conceive Torah as inscribed on God's "limbs," thereby minimizing the difference between it and God. The rabbinic opinion, that Torah is not to be found in heaven since it was delivered to Moses in its entirety and is thus completely, finitely, in our possession, seems to be rejected by earlier Jewish mystical groups. Nevertheless, it fell to the kabbalists to take the decisive step toward the explicit identification of Torah with God.

To suggest how this was done, I turn to two intriguing descriptions of the Torah. The first occurs in a long-forgotten kabbalistic work, entitled The Book of [Divine] Unity:

All the letters of the Torah, by their shapes, combined and separated, swaddled letters, curved ones and crooked ones, superfluous and elliptic ones, minute and large ones, and inverted, the calligraphy of the letters, the open and closed pericopes and the ordered ones, all of them are the shape of God, Blessed be He. It is similar to, though incomparable with, the thing someone paints using [several] kinds of colors, likewise the Torah, beginning with the first pericope until the last one is the shape of God, the Great and Formidable, Blessed be He, since if one letter be missing from the Scroll of Torah, or one is superfluous, or a [closed] pericope was [written] in an open fashion or an [open] pericope was [written] in a closed fashion, that Scroll of Torah is disqualified, since it has not in itself the shape of God, the Great and Formidable, because of the change the shape caused.[10]

According to this passage, the exact form of the authorized writing of the Bible is equivalent to the shape of God. The Bible, therefore, in its ideal form, constitutes an absolute book, including in it the supreme revelation of God, which is offered anthropomorphically and symbolically, limb by divine limb, within the whole text.

Even more striking is another description of this formal aspect of the Torah by a certain R. Isaac, apparently a late thirteenth or early fourteenth-century kabbalist:[11] "The form of the written Torah is that of the colors of white fire, and the form of the oral Torah has the colored forms of black fire."[12] This text implies, as Scholem has emphasized, that the real "written Torah" consists in the white background enveloping the black letters which, paradoxically enough, are said to form the "oral Torah." The superiority of the white medium, its existence as an element in itself,[13] recalls the view of white and black that Stéphane Mallarmé offers in "Le Livre," where metaphysical status is attributed to the white space.[14]

II

Aside from these two kinds of contrasting identification of Torah with God or Divine Manifestations, kabbalah views the Bible as encompassing an infinity of significances.[15] The Bible therefore is regarded by kabbalists as being akin to, and in several texts identical with, aspects of Godhead itself. I should now like to survey four significant kinds of infinity of the Torah[16] which are, in my opinion, consonant with various modern literary theories of writing, reading, and/or interpretation.

Indeed, some of the kabbalistic views of Torah discussed below were known to Christian theologians and could, at least theoretically, have influenced the subsequent unfolding of European culture. One of them, as we shall note, is explicitly cited by Jacques Derrida.

A. The nature of the Hebrew language, in which the consonants can be written with the vowels as well as without them, is the starting point of an important remark by one of the first kabbalists. According to R. Jacob ben Sheshet (middle thirteenth century),

it is a well-known thing, that each and every word of the Torah, will change [i.e., its significance] in accordance with the change of its vocalization, though its consonants will not be changed . . . and see: its significance changed . . . the word [i.e., the consonants constituting it] will not change its order. Likewise, we may state that the Tetragrammaton will be used [during the prayer] with [kabbalistic] intentions, in accordance with its vocalization; if someone who knows how to construct its construction will direct [his attention] to the construction which that [peculiar] vocalization points out, his prayer will be heard, and his request will be announced by God.[17]

The Torah scroll, written without vowels, is therefore pregnant with a variety of vocalizations, all of them possible without any change in the canonical form of the sacred text.[18] The fluctuation of the vocalization, as it causes shifts in the meaning of a given combination of the consonants, also alters the meaning of the sentence and of the Torah itself. Interestingly enough, the kabbalist indicates that this process is his own discovery, or one that stems directly from the Sinaitic revelation itself.[19]

A long line of kabbalists copied this text and expanded upon it. I should like to cite and analyze only two of them, wherein the implications inherent in R. Jacob ben Sheshet's observation are framed more explicitly. An anonymous kabbalist, writing, we believe, at the end of the thirteenth century, asserts:

Since the vowel [system] is the form of, and as soul to, the consonants, the scroll of Torah is written without vowels, since it [the scroll] includes all the facets [i.e., aspects] and all the profound senses, and all of them interpreted in relation to each and every letter, one facet out of other facets, one secret out of other secrets, and there is no limit known to us and we said: [Job 28:14] "The depth said, It is not in me." And if we should vocalize the scroll of Torah, it would receive a limit and measure, like the hyle that receives a peculiar form, and it [the scroll] would not be interpreted but according to the specific vocalization of a certain word.[20]

Freedom of interpretation is presented here not as sheer accident, arising from the special nature of the Hebrew language; rather, this freedom is implied, according to the kabbalist, in the very prohibition to vocalize the scroll of Torah, a prohibition which permits an unlimited range of possible understandings. The biblical text, in this view, is the touchstone of man's capacities. Its potential infinity, however, is not wholly dependent upon our capacity to actualize it. It is inherent in the peculiar structure of the biblical text itself. All perfections are encompassed by the Torah, as each and every word of the Torah is pregnant with an immensity of meanings.[21]

Another formulation of this mystical explanation of the non-vocalized form of the Torah should be noted here since it serves as a conduit between Jewish kabbalah and Christian culture. According to R. Menaḥem Recanati (early fourteenth century) in his Commentary on the Torah, "it is well-known that the consonants have many aspects when unvocalized. However, when they are vocalized they have only one signficance, in accordance with the vocalization, and therefore the scroll of Torah, which has all the aspects, is unvocalized."[22] Recanati's Commentary was translated into Latin by Flavius Mithridates for the use of Pico della Mirandola.[23] The translation is apparently lost, but its impact is registered in one of Pico's Kabbalistic Theses: "Per modum legendi sine puncti in lege, et modus scribendi res divinas . . . nobis ostenditur."[24]

I will conclude my brief survey of this aspect of the infinity of Torah with one more point. Despite the fact that these kabbalists maintain the traditional order or morphe of the Torah, they still conceived its meaning as amorphous, allowing each and every interpreter an opportunity to display the range of his exegetical capacities.

B. Another expression of the infinity of Torah overtly connects it to God's infinity in His infinite Wisdom.[25] According to R. Moshe de Leon, God

has bequeathed to Israel, this holy Torah from above in order to bequeath to them the secret of this name and in order to [enable Israel to] cleave to Him [or to His name] . . . in order to evince that as this name [or He] is infinite and limitless, so is this Torah infinite and limitless . . . since the Torah being longer than the earth and broader than the sea [cf. Job 11:9], we must be spiritually aware and know that the essence of this existence is infinite and limitless.[26]

Thus, not only does the infinity of the Torah reflect God's infinity, but apprehension of this infinity offers now a way to cleave to Him. How precisely this happens, we do not know. However, from a different starting point, we observe another kabbalist reach a similar conclusion:

"Since God has neither beginning nor end, no limit at all, so also His Perfect Torah, which was transmitted to us has, from our perspective, neither limit nor end and David therefore said (Ps. 119:96)[27] I have seen an end of all perfection, but thy commandment is exceeding broad."[28]

This kabbalist learns about the infinite Torah through God's infinity. Another kabbalist, a contemporary of the authors quoted above, specifically identifies Torah with God's infinite wisdom. Treating God's "unchangeability," R. David ben Abraham ha-Lavan maintains that as all measure is a result of boundaries or limits, so is the wisdom of a man limited by the peculiar science he knows; and yet "the science which has no measure [i.e., is infinite] has no measure for its power; this is why the Torah has no limit since its power has no measure, because it is the Primordial Wisdom. . . . the Wisdom has no limit since this Wisdom[29] and His Essence are one entity."[30] Here, the essential identity between God and Torah is quite explicit.

C. Torah is infinite, again, because the number of the combinations of its letters—according to the complex kabbalistic techniques of permutations—is infinite.[31] These techniques of combination, developed in works written under the impact of prophetic kabbalah,[32] are described by R. Joseph Gikatilla, a student of R. Abraham Abulafia:

By the mixture of these six letters [the consonants of the word *Bereshit*[33]] with each other, and the profound understanding of their permutation and combination, the prophets and visionaries penetrated the mysteries of the Torah, and . . . no one is capable of comprehending the end of these things, but God alone . . . it is incumbent on man to meditate upon the structures of the Torah, which depend upon the Wisdom of God and no one is able to [understand] one [parcel] of the thousands of thousands of immense [secrets] which depend upon the part of one letter[34] of the letters of the Torah.[35]

The "ars combinatoria" is perceived here as the path toward the partial comprehension of the secrets of the Torah. Its affinity to Abulafia's sixth path of interpretation of Torah is clear.[36] Still, we can discern here two different, though possibly complementary, views of infinity. The first is a mathematical infinity resulting from the application of complicated exegetical methods to letters of Torah and from the attempt to understand the significance of each combination. However, the monadic infinity inherent in each and every letter adds a further dimension to the mathematical infinity. The former is achieved by the destruction[37] of the order of the letters of the Torah by the combinatory process.[38] The latter, however, is quite independent of such permutations and, indeed, meditation upon the infinite significances depending on each letter is recommended when the "structures" of the Torah—ostensibly including also the order of the letters—remain unchanged. Yet the very concentration upon one separate letter is said to have a destructive effect upon the plain meaning of the text (or of the sentence) as a whole. Gikatilla seems to have combined Abulafia's two last paths of interpretation of the Torah into one way. Permutation and monadization both lead away from the significant text toward an incommunicable or asocial perception achieved in a paranormal state of consciousness. The monadization is instrumental, according to Abulafia, in bringing on the kabbalist's *unio mystica*. The path of permutations, the sixth one, is intended for those who attempt the *imitatio intellecti agentes*, persons who practice solitary concentration-exercises and are presumed to invent novel "forms," namely, meanings, for the combinations of letters.[39]

This effort of imitation of the Intellectus Agens is apparently a transition from a limited state of consciousness to a larger one.[40] Interestingly enough, according to Abulafia each higher path of interpretation is described as a larger sphere or circle;[41] the expansion of the intellect is therefore tantamount to the use of ever more complicated hermeneutic methods bent on achieving increasingly comprehensive understandings of the Torah.[42]

Indeed, Abulafia is interested here in transcending the natural understanding of reality which was closely connected, in medieval philosophy, with Aristotle's logic. While Aristotelian logic is based upon coherent sentences which generate conclusions significant in the natural world, kabbalah—specifically prophetic kabbalah—has a special logic which is the only suitable exegesis to the biblical text. To decipher the message of Torah, kabbalah relies upon what it calls an "inner higher logic" which employs separate letters in lieu of concepts, as well as the combination of these letters. This method is deemed superior to Greek logic inasmuch as it returns the text to its original state, when it was but a continuum of letters all viewed as names of God.[43]

In this context it is worth noting that Derrida has combined Abulafia's view of logic with Stéphane Mallarmé's definition of the role of poetry. In his *La Dissémination*, he writes, in reference to kabbalah: "La science de la combinaison des lettres est la science de la logique intérieure supérieure, elle coopère à une explication orphique de la terre."[44] We might also mention here that Umberto Eco refers to Lullian techniques of combination of letters in describing Mallarmé's method of combining pages.[45] As we have learned from Pico,[46] the kabbalistic "ars combinatoria" is closely related to Lull's practice. Not without interest, then, is the fact that in Pico's Theses[47] orphic issues were compared to and connected with kabbalistic discussions, particularly those of Abulafia's school.

Thus the concept of infinity of meaning transforms the Torah from a socially motivated document into an instrument employed by mystics for the sake of their own self-perfection. Moreover, the Torah is perceived by certain kabbalists as a divine and cosmic entity, variously interpreted in the infinite series of universes. According to Gikatilla,

The scroll [i.e., the Torah] is not vocalized and has neither cantillation-notes, nor [indication where] the verse ends; since the scroll of Torah includes all the sciences, the exoteric and esoteric ones, [it] is interpreted in several ways, since man turns the verse up and down,[48] and therefore our sages said:[49] "Are not my words like as a fire? Saith the Lord" (Jeremiah 23:29) like the forms of the flame of fire that has neither a peculiar measure nor peculiar form,[50] so the scroll of Torah has no peculiar form for [its] verses, but sometimes it [the verse] is interpreted so and sometimes it is interpreted otherwise, namely in the world of the angels it is read [as referring to] one issue and in the world of the spheres it is read [as referring to] another issue and in the lower world it is read [as referring to] another issue, and so in the thousands and thousands of worlds which are included in these three worlds, each one according to its capacity and comprehension,[51] is his reading [i.e., interpretation] of the Torah.[52]

Therefore, in Gikatilla's view, there is also another infinity: that stemming from the fluctuation of the vocalizations. It is interesting, though not surprising, that the view of Torah as an entity read or deciphered differently on the different levels of reality, found its way into Christian thought. According to Emmanuel Swedenborg,

The whole sacred scripture teaches that there is a God, because in its inmost content there is nothing but God, that is, the divine which proceeds from time; for it was dictated by God, and nothing can go forth from God, but what is Himself, and is divine. The sacred scripture is this in its inmost content. But in its derivatives, which proceed from the inmost content but are on a lower plane, the sacred scripture is accommodated to the perceptions of angels and men. In these also it is divine, but in another form, in which it is called the divine celestial, spiritual, and natural, which is the inmost and is clothed with such things as are accommodated to the perception of angels and men, shines forth like light through crystals, but with variety according to the state of mind which a man has acquired, either from God or from himself.[53]

It is not unlikely that the similarity between this Christian visionary's perception of the sacred scripture and the kabbalistic one is the result of the influence of Jewish texts.[54]

D. Last but not least, another facet of infinite meanings of Torah is expressed in kabbalistic symbolism.[55] According to some important kabbalists,[56] an infra-divine dynamic is reflected by biblical verses, wherein each word serves as a symbol for a divine manifestation[57] or sefirah.[58] The relationship between a given word and its supernal counterpart is relatively stable in earlier kabbalah. Toward the end of the thirteenth century, however, greater fluctuation in this relationship is perceptible. In the very same treatise a word may symbolize more than one sefirah. The theoretical possibility thus emerges of decoding the same verse in several symbolic directions. Indeed this possibility is fully exploited in the central mystical work of kabbalah, the Zohar.[59] Therefore, the supernal dynamic is reflected not only in a symbolic rendering of the theosophic content of a particular verse, but also by the very fact that the same verse can be interpreted again and again, all interpretations bearing equal authority. According to this perception, discovery of new significances in the biblical text is yet another way of testifying to the infinite workings of the sefirotic world.

The kabbalistic transformation of words and whole sentences into symbols has a deep impact on the perception of language itself. For even as the individual word retains its original forms, even as its place in the sentence or its grammatical function remain stable, its status as a lower projection of an aspect of the Godhead renders it an absolute entity. The result is a mystical linguistics forged into a skeletal grammar. Rather than being understood as mundane and conventional units of communication or representation, the words of the Bible, grasped as moments of God's enacted autobiography, become instruments for His self-revelation in being.

The primary unit then remains the word which, in contrast to Abulafia's text-destructing exegesis which annihilates the "interpreted" material in order to reconstruct it in a new way, is viewed as a monadic symbol.[60]

To summarize: all of the important components of the interpretative triangle undergo decisive transformation in kabbalistic hermeneutics. The kabbalistic interpreter is interested in the subleties of Divine Life. He decodes the Bible as a mystical biography of the infra-divine infinite processes and of the regulations which influence the function of these processes, rather than as a humanly directed document. Or, as in the prophetic kabbalah, he views the highest interpretation of the Torah as the actualization of its infinite mathematical potentialities as they may assist in the expansion of the interpreter's consciousness of the Godhead. Therefore, Torah is either pushed in the direction of revealed Divinity and sometimes even identified with It; or, attracted in the opposite direction, Torah becomes an instrument by which is achieved the union of man's intellect with God. The status of the Torah as an independent entity—such as we find in the talmudic-midrashic literature—standing between man and God and separated from both, vanishes.

Likewise, in kabbalah man's separate identity or self is jeopardized. The divine source of his soul, according to the sefirotic kabbalah, or of his intellect, according to the prophetic brand, endows him with a spiritual affinity to the Godhead. This affinity authorizes, as it facilitates, the emergence of a pneumatic exegesis to be defined against talmudic-midrashic philologically oriented hermeneutics. The text becomes a pretext for innovating far-reaching ideas which are projected onto the biblical verses. The hermeneutic methods whereby these innovations are injected into the text differ considerably from the talmudic-midrashic rules of interpretation. Combinations of letters, gematria, and symbolistic exegesis are wholly indeterminate and superflexible techniques. Hence they are liable to produce radically heterogeneous results. The looseness of these hermeneutic methods is counterbalanced solely by doctrinal inhibitions. When these inhibitions disappear or are replaced by others, the Christian kabbalist, using highly similar kabbalistic hermeneutics, can easily conclude that kabbalah adumbrates Christian tenets.[61]

The kabbalistic perception of the Torah, as an absolute book which is both identical with and descending from Divinity, supplies a point of departure from which the pneumatic exegete is able to discover its infinite significance. Torah is viewed as an "opera aperta" par excellence, wherein the divine character of man finds its perfect expression even as it discovers God's infinity reflected in the amorphous text. To put it another way: the Torah is a divine chef d'oeuvre, while kabbalistic exegesis, and kabbalah in general, is the unfolding of both Torah's infinite subtleties and (paradoxically, to some extent) the kabbalist's inner qualities.[62] The innovative techniques of kabbalistic interpretation are part of a profound transformation that goes on at the heart of Judaism, culminating in what Jacques Rivière calls "a kind of assault on the absolute"[63] which changes the Jewish view of man as well as its view of language. Like many phenomena in modern literature, kabbalah is an attempt to transmute reality through the power of words.[64] Both activities are part of "a vast incantation towards the miracle."[65]

NOTES

1. We may fairly apply Roland Barthes's description of the affinity between the *langage classique* and nature to the attitude of midrashic interpreters toward the Bible: "Que signifie en effet l'economie rationelle du langage classique sinon que la Nature est pleine, possédable, sans fuite et sans ombre, tout entière soumise aux rets de la parole?" *Le degré zero de l'écriture* (Paris: Editions Gonthier, 1964), pp. 45–47. Midrashic language may well be viewed as a *langage classique*, whereas the kabbalistic language accords in principle with Barthes's description of *langage poétique*.

2. See Joseph Blenkinsopp, *Prophecy and Canon* (London: University of Notre Dame Press, 1977), pp. 132–38.

3. On this view of the emergence of kabbalah as a historical phenomenon see my "Beginning of Kabbalah," forthcoming in *The World History of the Jewish People* (Hebrew), ed. Joshua Prawer (Tel Aviv: Massada).

4. I should like to stress that for more than one reason kabbalistic hermeneutics follows earlier midrashic methods of exegesis: see, e.g., Joseph Dan's essay, "Midrash and the Dawn of Kabbalah," in this volume. I am interested in concentrating here, however, upon non-midrashic, and in my view even anti-midrashic, trends in kabbalistic hermeneutics, without denying the existence of "conservative" kabbalistic exegesis. On the split between "innovative" kabbalah, described herein, and "conservative" kabbalah, which in principle rejected the perceptions of Torah described, see M. Idel, "We Have No Kabbalistic Tradition on This," in Isadore Twersky, ed., *Rabbi Moses Naḥmanides (Ramban): Explorations in His Religious and Literary Virtuosity* (Cambridge: Harvard University Press, 1983), pp. 63–73.

5. Cf. G. Scholem, "The Name of God and the Linguistic Theory of the Kabbalah," *Diogenes* 79 (1972), 59–80; 80 (1972), 164–94.

6. See M. Idel, "Abraham Abulafia and *Unio Mystica*," forthcoming in Isadore Twersky, ed., *Studies in Medieval Jewish History and Literature*, vol. 3.

7. The single significant exception is R. Jehudah ben Moshe Romano, a fourteenth-century Italian writer, whose doctrine has recently been the subject of a series of studies by Joseph B. Sermoneta.

8. I have deliberately avoided any discussion of Qumranic exegesis, although the phenomenological affinity to the subject under discussion here is indeed interesting, because I cannot find any significant historical relationship between the inspired eschatological interpretation in Qumran and the late medieval examples analyzed here. It is worth remarking that rabbinic sources acknowledge that the study of the Torah may open the way for paranormal spiritual experiences: see M. Idel, "The Conception of the Torah in Heikhalot Literature and Kabbalah" (Hebrew), *Jerusalem Studies in Jewish Thought* 1, (1981), 35–37.

9. There are significant pantheistic elements in kabbalah: see G. Scholem, *Kabbalah* (Jerusalem: Keter, 1974), pp. 144–52. The pantheistic view is evident also in Abulafia's works. See Idel, "Abraham Abulafia," and Joseph ben Shelomo, "Gershom Scholem's Study on Pantheism in Kabbalah" (Hebrew), in *Gershom Scholem—On the Man and His Activity* (Jerusalem: Israel Academy of Sciences and Humanities, 1983), pp. 17–31.

10. Ms. Milano-Ambrosiana, 62 fol. 113v, printed and discussed in Idel, "Conception of the Torah," pp. 62–64; see also G. Scholem, *On the Kabbalah and Its Symbolism* (New York: Schocken Books, 1969), pp. 43–44.

11. Scholem, "Name of God," pp. 48–49, identifies the R. Isaac the Old, the author of the text, with R. Isaac Sagi-Nahor (the Blind), one of the founders of Provençal Kabbalah. However, this assertion is not proven: see M. Idel, "Kabbalistic Materials from the School of R. David Ben Yehudah he-Ḥasid" (Hebrew), *Jerusalem Studies in Jewish Thought* 2 (1982–83), 170, n. 9.

12. Scholem, *On the Kabbalah*, p. 49.

13. Ibid., pp. 49–50. On the significance of the encompassing white page and space in kabbalah see Idel, "Kabbalistic Materials," pp. 174–75, 182, 206–07; cf. also Jacques Derrida, *La Dissémination* (Paris: Editions de Seuil, 1972), pp. 283ff., 383–84.

14. Cf. Jacques Scherer, *Le "Livre" de Mallarmé* (Paris: Gallimard, 1977), pp. 49–53.

15. The rise of the notion that Torah has an infinite number of significances is a major development in kabbalistic thought of the last third of the thirteenth century. See Idel, "No Kabbalistic Tradition," p. 71.

16. On this issue see the important discussion of Scholem, *On the Kabbalah*, pp. 50–63, whose remarks deal in general with other facets of the subject.

17. See *The Book of Belief and Faith* (Hebrew), chap. 5. Cf. the edition of Ch. D. Chavel, *The Works of Naḥmanides* (Hebrew), vol. 2 (Jerusalem: Mossad Harav Kook, 1964), p. 370.

18. Compare R. Jacob's view in another kabbalistic treatise: *The Book of Correct Answers* (Hebrew), ed. Georges Vajda (Jerusalem: Israel National Academy of Sciences, 1968), p. 107: "The scroll of the Torah may not be vocalized, in order to [enable us to] interpret each and every word according to every significance we can read [i.e., to apply a certain vocalization to the Word]."

19. The very mention of innovation in connection with this view, which will generate an important aspect of the infinite Torah, is highly significant and constitutes a decisive departure from the previous conservative kabbalistic view: see Idel, "No Kabbalistic Tradition," p. 68, n. 58.

20. This text is cited by Gershom Scholem, "The Authentic Commentary on Sefer Yeẓirah of Naḥmanides" (Hebrew), *Kiryat Sefer* 6 (1930), 414. On the infinite Torah in another passage of this text (p. 9) see below, n. 35.

21. Ibid., p. 44.

22. Jerusalem, 1961, fol. 40b.

23. See Chaim Wirszubski, *Flavius Mithridates—Sermo de Passione Domini* (Jerusalem: Magnes, 1963), p. 61.

24. Conclusio 70: "We are shown, by the way of reading the Law without vowels, the way divine issues are written." On this thesis see the comments of Wirszubski, *A Christian Kabbalist Reads the Law* (Hebrew) (Jerusalem, 1977), pp. 36–37.

25. On other identifications of Torah with the Sefirah Ḥokhmah (Wisdom), without attention however to the notion of infinity, see Scholem, *On the Kabbalah*, pp. 41–42.

26. Cf. *Book of the Pomegranate* (Hebrew), Ms. Cambridge, Add. 1516 fol. 29r.

27. This verse is the classical *locus probantes* in the discussion of the infinite Torah. Compare Gikatilla's text printed in Efraim Gottlieb, *Studies in the Kabbalah Literature*, ed. J. Hacker (Tel Aviv, 1976), p. 153.

28. Printed in Scholem, "Commentary on Sefer Yeẓirah," p. 410.

29. Compare to the view quoted by Henri de Lubac: "Mens divina liber grandis est," in *Exégèse médieval: Les quatres sens le l'écriture* (Paris: Aubier, 1959), vol. 1, pt. 1, p. 326; and Annemarie Schimmel, "Sufism and the Islamic Tradition," in *Mysticism and Religious Traditions*, ed. S. T. Katz (Oxford: Oxford University Press, 1983), pp. 130–31. See also

R. Moshe Cordovero, *Shiur Komah* (Jerusalem: Aḥuzat Israel, 1966), fol. 13v: "and the Torah is in the Wisdom, which is the wisdom of God, and as this Wisdom is infinite, so is our Torah—infinite." See also Gikatilla's passage quoted below, and R. Pinḥas of Korez's view, adduced by Scholem, *On the Kabbalah*, pp. 76–77.

30. *The Book of the Tradition of the Covenant* (Hebrew), ed. G. Scholem in *Koveẓ al Yad—Minora Manuscripta Hebraica* n.s. 1, 11 (1936), 35. On this work and its author see Scholem, "David ben Abraham ha-labhan—ein unbekannter jüdischer Mystiker," *Occident and Orient . . . Gaster Anniversary Volume*, ed. B. Schindler and A. Marmorstein (London: Taylor's Foreign Press, 1936), pp. 505–08.

31. See Scholem, "Name of God," p. 189, n. 74. It is pertinent to remark that the kabbalistic view of the infinite potentialities of the Torah is significantly different from the midrashic conception that there are seventy facets of the Torah. On the seventy facets see Wilhelm Bacher, "Seventy-two modes of expositions," *JQR* 4 (1892), 509, Scholem, *On the Kabbalah*, pp. 62–63, Idel, "Kabbalistic Materials," p. 199. The figure 70 stands for the totality of the aspects of a certain limited phenomenon, as we discover by comparing phrases closely related to the phrase "seventy facets": "seventy languages," "seventy nations," "seventy angels," etc. Though pointing to a comprehensive conception of the meanings inherent in the biblical text, the phrase "seventy facets" did not even hint at an infinity of significances.

32. Though none of Abulafia's combinatory techniques was his own innovation and he explicitly refers to the earlier books in which they were introduced, he seems to be the first Spanish kabbalist who presents them as exegetical methods, rather than mere sporadic ad hoc usages.

33. "In the beginning."

34. Cf. R. Isaiah Horowitz, *The Two Tablets of the Covenant* (Hebrew) (Jerusalem, 1969), vol. 2, fol. 98r–v: "you shall know and understand that even one letter has infinite permutations . . . man can comprehend that this thing [i.e., combinatory practices] has no end, and all this is because the Torah is the reflection of the godhead which is infinite." Cf. vol. 3, fol. 87r.

35. *The Gate of Punctuation*, printed in *The Cedars of Lebanon* (Hebrew) (Venice, 1601), fol. 39v–40r. Cf. also R. Moshe Cordovero's view in Pardes Rimmonim, introduction to Gate 30, and Gate 8, chap. 4. Compare also to R. Abraham bar Ḥiyya's view that "every letter and every word in every section of the Torah has a deep root in wisdom and contains a mystery from among mysteries of [divine] understanding, the depths of which one cannot penetrate. God grant that we may know some little of his abundance." Cf. Scholem, *On the Kabbalah*, p. 63.

36. See M. Idel, "Abraham Abulafia's Works and Doctrines" (Hebrew) (Ph.D. diss., Hebrew University, 1976), pp. 226–28.

37. No wonder that Abulafia's exegetical methods were sharply criticized by a representative of the rabbinic authority, R. Shelomo ben Abraham ibn Adret. Abulafia, as R. Shelomo remarked, interpreted in his peculiar way not only the Bible but also non-biblical texts, such as Maimonides' *Guide of the Perplexed*.

38. The transformation of the text into a heap of letters may have its restorative aspects. Cf. the striking passage discussed by Scholem, *On the Kabbalah*, pp. 74–75, where the Torah is described as a chaotic series of letters before it received its present canonic form. Though the sources quoted by Scholem are relatively late eighteenth-century passages, the conception seems to be earlier, and probably stems from the circle of Abulafia or his disciples. Cf. Johannes Reuchlin's version regarding the order of the letters of the Torah as "confusae ac inglomerate" before Moshe arranged them: "De Arte Cabalistica," in J. Pistorius, *Ars Cabalistica* (Basel, 1587), p. 705. See below, n. 55.

39. Cf. Idel, "Abulafia's Works," pp. 227–28.

40. Cf. Abulafia's recurrent motif of unknotting the knots of the soul as part of the mystical progress, in ibid., pp. 329–31.

41. Abulafia uses the term *Galgal* (circle or sphere) in order to refer to "path": *nativ*, i.e., way of interpretation. He starts with the smallest sphere and progresses toward the largest one. Compare Gregorius's interpretation of Ezekiel's *ofan* as referring to exegetical method, hinted at in Henri de Lubac, *L'Écriture dans la tradition* (Paris: Aubier-Montaigne, 1966), p. 276.

42. This is an interesting parallel to Origen's view: "extenditur anima nostra, quae prius fuerat contracta, ut possit cappax esse sapientia Dei" (we enlarge our soul, which was previously contracted, in order to be capable of receiving the Wisdom of God). See *Patrologia Latina*, vol. 25, fol. 627c and de Lubac, *L'Écriture dans la tradition*, p. 285.

43. See M. Idel, "On the History of the Interdiction against the Study of Kabbalah before the Age of Forty" (Hebrew) *AJS Review* 5 (1980), 17–18.

44. *La Dissémination* (Paris: Editions du Seuil, 1972), p. 382. Abulafia's text, discussed in detail in my study referred to in n. 43, reached Derrida through the French version of Scholem's *Major Trends in Jewish Mysticism*: see *Les grands courants de la mystique juive* (Paris: Payot, 1950), p. 390, n. 50, for the same statement made by Derrida. See also George Steiner, *After Babel* (New York–London, 1970), pp. 60–61.

45. See *Opera aperta*, chap. 1. An intriguing and important subject is the probable influence, briefly discussed here, of kabbalistic theories on the peculiar structure of Mallarmé's *Le Livre*. Mallarmé seems to be aware of kabbalistic issues: see Thomas A. Williams, *Mallarmé and the Language of Mysticism* (Athens: University of Georgia Press, 1970), pp. 55–56.

46. See Pico della Mirandola, "Apologia," in *Opera Omnia* (1557), p. 180.

47. See Chaim Wirszubski, *Three Studies in Christian Kabbalah* (Hebrew) (Jerusalem, 1975), pp. 39–51.

48. In Hebrew *le-ma'alah u-lematah*: compare Reuchlin's text referred to in n. 38 above.

49. Shabbat, fol. 88v.

50. In Hebrew *gavvan* means commonly "nuances" and "colors" but also "appearance," "example," and "form."

51. There may be an echo here of the Proclean view that everything receives the qualities of the world in which it exists.

52. Printed in Gottlieb, *Studies in the Kabbalah*, p. 154. See also Scholem, "Name of God," pp. 179–80. A similar anonymous passage possibly authored by Gikatilla is extant in two manuscripts: Paris (BN) 839 fol. 4r–v; Jerusalem, National Library 8°, 488 fol. 45v.

53. *The True Christian Religion* (London–New York, 1936), para. 6, pp. 6–7; cf. para. 212, p. 288; and *Apocalypse Explained*, para. 1074.

54. On the influence of another kabbalistic view on Swedenborg see my paper, "The World of Angels in Human Form" (Hebrew), *Studies in Jewish Mysticism Presented to Isaiah Tishby* (Jerusalem, 1984), p. 66, n. 251, where I present evidence supporting the thesis that Swedenborg studied kabbalah at Uppsala University.

55. On the nature of kabbalistic symbols, see Scholem, *Major Trends in Jewish Mysticism* (New York: Schocken Books, 1967), pp. 27–28; Isaiah Tishby, *Paths of Faith and Heresy* (Hebrew) (Ramat Gan: Massada, 1964), pp. 11–22; and n. 65 below.

56. Although most kabbalists share the symbolistic perception of Godhead and reality, this perception was not, as some scholars have maintained (see n. 62 below), universally accepted, as is evidenced, for example, in Abulafia's Kabbalah.

57. In contrast to Abulafia's view of the Torah as allegorically rendering the processes of human consciousness: cf. Idel, "Abulafia's Works," pp. 239–40.

58. See Scholem, *Major Trends*, pp. 13–14.

59. On the Zoharic symbolism in particular see Isaiah Tishby, *The Wisdom of the Zohar* (Hebrew) (Jerusalem, 1957), vol. 1, pp. 144–61; and Daniel Ch. Matt, *Zohar—The Book of Enlightenment* (Paulist Press, 1983), pp. 32–38.

60. Compare Barthes's description of "Mot poètique," *Le degré zero*, pp. 43–45.

61. See Chaim Wirszubski, *Three Studies in Christian Kabbalah* (Hebrew) (Jerusalem, 1975), pp. 23–27.

62. It is noteworthy that only those kabbalists who belong to what I call "innovative kabbalah" (see Idel, "No Kabbalistic Tradition," pp. 71–73), i.e., R. Abraham Abulafia, R. Moshe de Leon, R. Joseph Gikatilla and partially also R. Baḥya ben Asher, formulate the principles of kabbalistic hermeneutics. Moreover, there is a latent contradiction between kabbalah, perceived as a corpus of esoteric theurgical-theosophical lore, and the existence of a body of hermeneutic rules which tacitly assumes that the details of the kabbalistic lore are not in the possession of the kabbalists who are presumed to apply those exegetical rules in order to reconstruct the kabbalistic system.

63. "La crise du concept de littérature," *Nouvelle Revue Française*, February 1, 1924.

64. See the view of Jacques Maritain, *Creative Intuition in Art and Poetry* (New York: New American Library, 1953), p. 150.

65. Cf. Rivière, ibid.

BETTY ROITMAN

Sacred Language and Open Text

Traditional Jewish exegesis seems to be characterized by its ambivalent position between two systems of reading. On the one hand, since it is bound to a religious tradition, it supposes a standard of truth, in the logical and metaphysical sense of the term, which is alien to most modern theories of interpretation. At the same time, its extreme responsiveness to elements of textual play earns for it a special standing in contemporary critical circles. None of the games, reversals, and anagrams of contemporary criticism are foreign to it. Such exegesis is thus essentially ambiguous in nature. If the Torah represents the divine word, it conveys a particular message, the sense of which it would be heresy to falsify. The role of the oral law, accordingly, must be to stipulate the contents of the written law, by tradition and prior to any act of reading.[1] Yet that act of reading is remarkably free—for the initiate or *talmid vatik*, that is, he who has assimilated the logic of a selective principle and who is therefore entitled to render new perspectives and new understandings of the text. Though some laws of interpretation have been formulated by tradition, these are not prescriptive and are themselves constituted a posteriori from existing midrashim.

The mobility and indeterminacy of midrash no doubt explain its attractiveness to present-day theoreticians who understand midrash in a way that feeds their faith in an infinite unfolding of textual signification. But this contemporary understanding of midrashic interpretation involves some considerable adaptation of the données of midrash. The opening of a text, to a western mind, presupposes an a priori renunciation of any "truth" of meaning. For many contemporary critics it is in the very gap between writing and its object, or between writing and its intent, that the plurality of meaning is said to establish itself, whereas in midrash the alignment of some of the same elements that go into this contemporary attitude produces a significantly different perspective. To describe midrash accurately it is important to acknowledge the force of the paradox represented by the classic midrashic position, which enacts at the level of interpretation a dialectic formulated on the ontological plane by Rabbi Akiva: "All is foreseen, but freedom of choice is given."[2] All is determined, and yet all is open.

In order to explore this paradox and this dialectic, I have chosen the example of demonstrative pronouns, which, in the classificatory system of contemporary linguistics, belong to the category of deictics. Deictics are defined by the variable character of their reference, that is to say by their context-dependence (whether it is the context of statement or of utterance). Their interest for the present discussion is that they possess the particular and to some extent emblematic property of involving no fixed signification (in the broad sense of the term). Consequently they may represent possible parameters of midrashic interpretation, according to the ways in which exegesis may invest their semantic indeterminacy. I will proceed by comparing midrashim with varying levels of interpretative activity which, however, share the common denominator of being centered on the demonstrative. By scrutinizing and comparing the thematic lines developed by the various commentaries at their several levels of interpretation, I hope to disclose an unanticipated convergence.[3] An understanding of this convergence can significantly illuminate the interpretative value of semantic indeterminacy in midrash.

I

In its textual dimension, the Bible (and more specifically the Torah or Pentateuch) presents itself to the midrashic interpreter as a global corpus, a vast labyrinth of meaning in which all paths are possible. The fundamental ambiguity of the text's signification[4] is in no way diminished by the exegetical hypothesis of the semantic plenitude and perfection of a writing inspired or directly dictated by God, a hypothesis which itself stimulates subtlety of analysis and inexhaustible methodological inquiry. Between the *dibbur* and *amira* of God,[5] between speech at its origin and each specific formulation, there is something like an essential split which conditions the dissemination of the unique source and makes the semantic plurivalence of the text a matter of theoretical necessity.

With regard to this open structure, let us consider two general forms of midrashic interpretation, one based on the text as a whole and its conditions of contextualization or intertextuality, the other based on an existential criterion of actualizing the biblical model in accordance with a given historical or moral scheme, which is projected by the reader onto a specific segment. Under the general heading of the text-oriented form of midrash we must examine those midrashim which interpret the sense of the demonstrative in the local text and those which seek to determine its reference in an extended textual field.[6]

The pertinent traits of the sense of the demonstrative in the local text, which represent what O. Ducrot calls the "instructions which are connected with it in the language," are curiously thematized by midrash, and from them may be inferred a reference which is independent of context. As the demonstrative pronoun (or adjective) normally serves to designate a proximate and concrete object in the environment of the speaker, the mere fact of its occurrence in the text, prior to any signifying relationship, permits the marking of a sememe of concretization, of recognition, and of singularity—as well as, in a general way, a presumption of existence and immediacy normally tied to the phenomenon of deixis.[7] Here are a few examples of this use of the demonstrative by midrash:[8]

And such [zeh] is the work of fabrication of the candelabrum ... (Num. 8:4)

You will find that Moses met with more difficulties in the making of the candelabrum than with any of the other objects of the sanctuary, until the Holy-One-Blessed-Be-He pointed to it for him. Likewise, regarding the form of the hooves of the impure and pure animals [Moses was in difficulty], as it is written (Lev. 11:2): "Such [zot] is the animal which you may eat" [and God pointed to them for him]. Likewise for the moon[9] ... [God showed it to Moses], as the verse indicates (Exod. 12:2): "This month will be for you." (Numbers Rabbah XV 4)

Ha-ḥodesh ha-zeh [this month]: The month is a concept, the moon is a visible object. Here we find a typical effect of concretization.

My next example focuses on the account of Jacob's burial in the land of Canaan, with its imposing procession from the land of Goshen down to the banks of the Jordan:

Having reached as far as the Place of the Thicket situated on the banks of the Jordan, there they celebrated solemn and imposing obsequies, and Joseph ordered, in honor of his father, seven days of mourning. The inhabitants of the land, the Canaanites, saw this mourning of the Place of the Thicket, and they said: "Here [zeh] is a great mourning for Egypt." (Gen. 50:10–11)

"Here is a great mourning": Rabbi Yudan ben Shalom taught: this instructs us that they *pointed* [at Jacob's corpse] saying: This one is the cause of a great mourning for Egypt. (P. Sotah I 10)

Mourning is an inner feeling which cannot be designated. What the Canaanites speak of is Jacob as a person and the manifestations of mourning which are consecrated to him.

I cite one more example of this kind of midrash:

The people, seeing that Moses was slow to descend from the mountain, crowded about Aaron and said to him: "Come! Make us a god who goes at our head, since this one [*zeh*], Moses, the man who brought us out of Egypt, we do not know what has become of him." (Exod. 32:1)

The midrash relates that at the moment of his going up to Sinai to receive the Tables of the Covenant, Moses promised the children of Israel that he would return after forty days:

At the end of forty days, as Moses did not come, the satan said to Israel: "Moses is dead." As they paid him no attention, he *showed* them the form of his death bed. This is why one finds it written: "since this one, Moses." (Numbers Rabbah XV 21 and B. Shabbat 89a)

Such use of the demonstrative sense for the sake of indexation is quite frequent in midrash. It reveals a sensitivity to the terms of the language as elements of a system, prior to their entry into a contextual "orbit."

Our second group of midrashim seeks to locate in the extended biblical text the specific references associated with the demonstrative, or to specify its semantic value. This undertaking is distinguished from that typical of the first group in that it clarifies a problematic context by means of the recurrence of *zeh* (this) in other contexts and seeks to reconstruct significations by examining situationally the semantic distribution of the demonstrative in the discourse. One may recognize here in outline the allusive technique of *gezerah shavah* (the technique of contextual inference from identity of expression) expanded to haggadah and often extended to an entire class of occurrences, as in the following midrash on Exodus 12:2: "This month [*ha-zeh*] will be for you the beginning of the months":

This month: Rabbi Assi taught in the name of Rabbi Yoḥanan: Blessing the month in its time [i.e., at the new moon] is a way of welcoming the Presence; in effect, the expression employed here: "This month [*zeh*]," can be compared with that figuring in another context (Exod. 15:2): "Here is [*zeh*] my God, I render him homage." (B. Sanhedrin 42a).

The redundancy of *zeh* in the first context is explained by recourse to a second verse and by equating their thematic value. The same equation is present in the midrash on Genesis 25:32: "Esau answered: To be sure! I am on my way to death; of what use to me then [*Lamah zeh*: Why this] is the birthright":

Resh Lakish taught: Esau has given over to blasphemy. The text does not read "of what use to me" but "of what use to me then [*zeh*] is the birthright"; from which we deduce that he has denied [the "text"] of *zeh eli*: ["Here is my God"] (Exod. 15:2). (Genesis Rabbah LXIII 13)

This technique of equivalence can also be grammatically precise and even propose a univocal relationship between the demonstrative and the referential concept with which it is associated in the contexts compared, as in the midrash on Exodus 15:1: "Then Moses and the children of Israel sang this hymn [*ha-shirah ha-zot*] to the Eternal":

This hymn: we rendered ourselves worthy of intoning it in purifying ourselves by circumcision. This is why the expression "This [*zot*] hymn" appears here, in which *zot* designates circumcision, on the evidence of the verse (Gen. 17:10): "Here is the pact which you shall observe . . . to circumcise every male." (Exodus Rabbah XXIII 13)

The phenomenon of internal reference is interpreted as a source of coherence and unification; it organizes and hierarchically orders the textual material around foci of signification.

One of the midrashim which could serve as an emblem for this reconstruction, by virtue of its comprehensive character, concerns the following verse of Leviticus 16:3 which poses particular grammatical difficulties: "Here is how [*be-zot*] Aaron shall enter into the sanctuary: with a young bull as expiatory offering, and a ram as a burnt offering." One may read in this verse either a cataphoric redundance, "Here is how" being developed by the rest of the text ("with a young bull"), or a referential indeterminacy, in which case the commentary would find itself presented with an "empty" term, to be invested with meaning according to the play of contexts. The midrash proceeds as follows:

"Here is how Aaron shall enter into the sanctuary": Rabbi Yudan explains this text in applying it to the entry of the High Priest, laden with merits, into the Holy of Holies. And what are these merits? the merit of the Torah, as it is written: "This [*zot*] is the Torah" (Deut. 4:44); the merit of the circumcision: "Here is [*zot*] the pact which you shall observe" (Gen. 17:10); the merit of Sabbath: "Happy is the man who does this [*zot*]" (Isa. 56:2); the merit of Jerusalem, as it is written: "Here is [*zot*] Jerusalem" (Ezek. 5:5); the merit of the tribes: "It is thus [ve-zot] that their father spoke to them" (Gen. 49:28). The merit of Judah: "And here [ve-zot] concerning Judah" (Deut. 33:7); the merit of Israel: "This stature [zot] which distinguishes you" (Song of Songs 7:8); the merit of the terumah [heave-offering]: "And here is [ve-zot] what you will receive from them" (Exod. 25:3); the merit of the tithes: "And count upon me for this [zot] proof" (Mal. 3:10); the merit of the sacrifices, as it is written: "Here is how [be-zot] Aaron shall enter into the sanctuary" (Lev. 16:3). (Leviticus Rabbah XXI 6)

This series of semantic possibilities must be understood as paradigmatic, that is to say, as involving a class of alternative terms. At the same time, one must grant the hypothesis of an inclusive rather than exclusive alternativity, that is to say, the propounding of a general theme called zot, differentiated into elements of meaning or modalities.

The propositions of midrash, its homilies and parables, are not, however, determined only in terms of intralinguistic play. One cannot, in fact, exclude from midrashic exegesis a variable parameter of reading which explicitly includes the cultural conventions of the reader, revealing a projection of a temperament or of a period.

Since this kind of interpretation appears to be arbitrarily imposed on the text, rather than deriving from its own logic, it resists analysis and systemization. Such moral reflections and existential propositions spring from an external ideology, which evolves with time and produces its own myths. Here are a few examples of such thematic projections attached, more or less tenuously, to a linguistic reflection.

In Exod. 2:6 we read, "She opened the cradle, she saw the infant therein, it was a boy crying. She pitied him and said: 'This is [zeh] a child of the Hebrews.' " The midrash comments: "And she said: 'This is [zeh] a child of the Hebrews.' How did she recognize him? Rabbi Yossi ben Rabbi Ḥanina taught: it is because she saw he was circumcised" (Exodus Rabbah I 24). The midrash depends on a function of recognition deduced from the use of the demonstrative. However, it goes beyond this function by indicating a specific chosen theme, namely that of circumcision.

In the following midrash, the commentary develops a semantic feature of proximity (in the sense of immediacy): " 'Because you have performed this thing [ha-davar ha-zeh],' said the angel of God to Abraham, after the (unconsummated) sacrifice of Isaac, 'I will heap upon you my blessing, I will multiply your lineage' " (Gen. 22:16–17). The midrash expresses its wonder at the fact that the divine blessing depends explicitly on this particular test, which is the tenth: "Because you have performed *this thing*—specifically: It must be understood that the injunction to sacrifice represents the last [= zeh] of the tests, and that, in itself alone, it is worth the *whole* of the others together; if he had not suffered to submit himself to it, Abraham would have lost *all*" (Genesis Rabbah LVI 11).

Or consider this interpretation, apparently fairly neutral, based on the locative value of the demonstrative: "And he [Joseph] replied: 'It is for my brothers that I am looking. Kindly tell me where they pasture their animals'; the man said: 'They have departed from here [mi-zeh]' " (Gen. 37:16–17). " 'They have departed from here [mi-zeh]': they have abandoned the virtues of the place" (Genesis Rabbah LXXXIV 14). The usual interpretation of this *zeh* is "place"; the strange allusion to a (moral) quality *specific to the place* is an addition.

At another stage, the semantic determination of *zeh* may become less justifiable in terms of the immediate givens of the text, as in the following:

May this one relieve us in our task and in the labor of our hands. (Gen. 5:28–29)

"May this one [zeh] relieve us": A just man comes to the world, well-being comes to the world. This is what the verse says to us: "This one [zeh] will relieve us in our task and in our labor." (B. Sanhedrin 113b)

One discerns here, underlying the theme of an interdependence between the natural and the moral, the structural correlation of the "just" (zeh) and of "well-being."

In an apparently contingent manner each of these midrashim offers a different thematic translation of the demonstrative (construed as appositive or attributive), according to their chosen formulation.

II

The analyses presented thus far roughly correspond to the first three levels of traditional exegesis. I turn now to a plane of interpretation which is naturally discontinuous with these subordinate levels. The anagogic reading found in kabbalah propounds, in effect, a conventional, systematic deciphering of all the terms of the Torah, determining for each a specific and precise reference which is lexically codified. This reading presents itself then as radically severed from any context; it is autonomous and invariable, chosen from among what the kabbalah considers the values founding the world. At the limit, zeh and zot represent for kabbalah particularized appellations, specific modalities of the Creator's expression, the Name by means of which the absolute reveals itself in a given sphere of spiritual experience. At the same time, for the kabbalist the demonstrative appears to change grammatical category, losing, through this hypostasis, its referential mobility as a deictic. Correlatively, this a priori, original, and systematic decoding seems to trap the infinitude of the text within the confines of its postulated truth. Here we are far indeed from the metamorphoses of meaning which are traced through the usual processes of reading.

Nonetheless, detailed study of the various semantic series constructed around the demonstrative pronoun by the kabbalah brings into relief surprising analogies between the different levels, despite their fundamentally disparate sources of inspiration. The architecture of the kabbalistic universe is crucial here. In order to follow its scheme, it must first of all be understood that each "sphere" or *Sefirah*, considered as a general possibility of reference, is itself subdivided into a cluster of partial representations, and thus constitutes a paradigm of conceptual and linguistic symbolizations, namely the kinuyim (indirect appellations of God) grouped around that Sefirah. I will consider these clusters as semantic series focused respectively on each Sefirah.

Even without going into great detail concerning the determination or derivation of these series, it is clear that their mode of association in the following commentaries obeys distinct, and often contradictory, logics. There is, for example, a conventional principle of order that is based specifically on tradition. Hypothetically self-sufficient as it is, however, it is generally accompanied by heterogeneous justifications of a logical and thematic, literal, figurative, or even textual order.

For example, given that the Sefirah of *Malkhut*, the lowest and the last of the spheres,[10] relates structurally to the figure of the receptacle, a whole class of substitutive appellations bearing this common trait of receptivity—whether functional or figurative—may be derived from this archetypal theme: "sea," "reservoir," "house," anything which has the form or value of a container, anything which can mark the seat of a Presence. But new combinations are then grafted onto this series, based on numerical equivalences between words corresponding to each class, on the form of the letters which enter into their composition, or on lexical derivations which are attached to them: thus berekhah, "reservoir," generates berakhah, "blessing," or bekhorah, "birthright."

For its part, the complex of *Tiferet* defines a total space of twelve dimensions. This symbolic number permits the inclusion of the word *zeh* in its series, by virtue of the equivalent numerical value of the letters, along with thematic figures like that of Jacob (and his twelve sons), or conventional cycles like the twelve months of the year or the twelve signs of the Zodiac.

There is a textual basis for these recombinations to the extent that the juxtaposition of the terms in a single syntagm has an osmotic potential and authorizes their "vertical" classification in a single paradigm. Thus the verse "Here is the land [*zot*] which shall fall to you as an inheritance" (Num. 34:2) associates *zot* and "land," while the verse "They shall build me a tabernacle and I shall dwell among them" (Exod. 25:8) gives a basis for the integration of "tabernacle" and "dwell" in a single semantic series—here that of Malkhut. As for the expression "that good mountain" (Deut. 3:25), its analysis discloses a triple relation to *Yessod*: "that" (*zeh*), "good," "mountain."

This kabbalistic system of exposition presents, then, qualities radically opposed to those exhibited by traditional midrash: in particular, whatever the mode of operation employed here, the determination of meaning obeys symbolic laws which put into play analogies between signifiers or signifieds.[11] Most important, this determination of meaning is not channeled through the linguistic signification of the terms in the utterance. Anagogic interpretation of this kind is dependent on a code which is not linguistic in the sense of natural language, although it integrates in its system certain linguistic elements not actualized in the discourse. This code is itself formed from several concurrent subcodes, with integrable results. This may explain why, despite the principle of a one-to-one correspondence between a word and its "translation," the semiotic network functioning here admits further possible programmations, and why the variability of the latter is guaranteed. The structured language of higher truths is itself open, in perpetual mutation.

On this basis, we can analyze the ways in which the kabbalah treats the question of the semantic rendering of the demonstrative. Bearing in mind those restrictions entailed by the mobility of the codes,[12] I will survey these interpretations, focusing on one or two central perspectives.[13] A comparison of the principal orientations of the *Sod* (anagogic level of interpretation) with the particular thematic propositions of the midrash in its different stages will then be appropriate.

In kabbalistic readings,[14] the feminine and masculine forms of the demonstrative pronoun (*zot* and *zeh*) refer respectively to the last two of the ten Sefirot of the spiritual universe, that of Malkhut, or "royalty," and that of Yessod, or "foundation." The commentators also identify *zeh* with the central sphere of Tiferet, the matrix of Yessod. As the world of the Sefirot is hierarchically ordered, or—more precisely—oriented, moving from a first principle, which is hidden and ineffable, towards the creation in process of becoming, the two last "spheres" should be considered the nearest to our universe, the only ones accessible, through revelation, to human understanding. They correspond to the perception which man is able to have of God's dealings in the world; they are the manifested limit of the divine where representation is still possible. *Zeh* and *zot* thus respectively designate, with more or less perceptible nuances, the modalities through which the absolute discloses itself, its traces inscribed in the concrete world. Under the name *zot* it is Providence, while under the name *zeh* it is the revelation of a saving God.

As regards *zeh/Tiferet-Yessod*, this principle of disclosure is translated by all the modalities of the sign: "holy inscription," miracle, rainbow, or covenant. Particularly recognizable in these usages is the thematic cycle of the exodus from Egypt and revelation at Sinai, comprising the deliverance, the written law, the figure of Moses, and so on. As regards *zot/Malkhut* ("royalty") the reconstructed semantic field is that of a royal dominion. Malkhut represents at the same time the possibility of the Presence and the Presence itself: *zot* is the mark of this openness to presence. Its thematic projections are those of extension and fecundity, of Providence and blessing. Comprised in this field as well are the themes of the oral law as the "ark" of the Torah, of the temple or Jerusalem as place of residence, and of the people of Israel as witness and as fiancée. Finally, we find the theme of the union between these two aspects presented in the form of a mystic wedding. The masculine spheres, placed along the median axis, ally themselves with the feminine sphere Malkhut, which receives their influx. This semantic feature of harmony generates in turn its own series, which includes "temple," "Shabbat," "peace," and so on. Furthermore, as a principle of reconciliation of contraries, it permits an osmosis between the complementary themes of each Sefirah, and it may explain their juxtaposition in certain contexts.

III

Thus far my purpose has been to identify a cluster of parallel symbols associated by exegesis with the occurrence of the demonstrative at each level of interpretation. I would now like to suggest that by collating the specific semantic organizations arrived at by those different procedures (textual *vs.* conventional), one may discern (through the necessary metaphorical transpositions and taking into account the inevitable slippage between categories) a surprising convergence of thematic items. From this convergence one can infer an invisible but powerful "deep structure," built on a conventional and symbolic base of midrashic commentary, which restores to the broken line of exegesis a thematic continuity.

On the linguistic plane, the thematization of the sense of the demonstrative as "knowledge" or "proximity" and the midrashim which this thematization engenders may be read as first steps toward the further thematization of references systematized by the anagogic interpretation. Let us remember that the grammatical meaning of the demonstrative enables it to designate an object present to the existential experience of the speaker which is knowable more than known, that is to say manifest but of indefinite nature. Therefore, it is evidently not a matter of chance that the demonstrative refers at the same time, in the configuration of the spheres which it designates (by way of the complex of Tiferet [Yessod] and Malkhut), to the double experience of Providence and Revelation—manifest but of indefinite nature.

Moreover, within the framework of this general metaphorization, it seems that the particular determinations assigned by midrash to the demonstrative sense often fit in neatly with the constellation of corresponding Sefirot. According to the lexicon of Pardes Rimonim, the "candelabrum," which is multivalent, refers (among other things) to Yessod; whereas "moon" and "animal" relate to Malkhut, "Jacob" and "Moses" to Tiferet. Their relationship to *zeh* and *zot* is as follows:

Zeh	candelabrum	Yessod
Zeh	moon (masc. or fem.)	Malkhut
Zot	animal	Malkhut
Zeh	Jacob	Tiferet
Zeh	Moses	Tiferet

The same phenomenon is much clearer at the level of referential

determination in the discourse. The surveying of contexts, which priv-
ileges certain occurences of the demonstrative rather than others,
points toward an underlying system. The recurrence of the same se-
mantizations within a number of variations indeed only reinforces this
hypothesis.[15] The midrashic decoupage of the text thus reveals a pre-
determining conventional foundation, which we shall assimilate, after
verification, to the large thematic lines of the kabbalah. The majority
of semantic determinations brought out by the technique of contextual
allusion seems in fact to be already codified in the disposition of the
kinuyim.

A table of equivalences cited above would appear thus:

Zeh	God (2 examples)	Yessod
Zot	circumcision	Malkhut
Zot	blessing	Malkhut
Zot	Torah, circumcision, Sabbath, Jerusalem, Judah, Israel, terumah, tithes, sacrifices	Malkhut

The case of homiletic extensions is less clear for our purposes, but
it also leads to suggestive coincidences: the midrash offers "circumcision" as a thematic development of "recognition" (Yessod), and "all"
(Yessod) for the last of the tests of Abraham. Similarly "place" refers
to Tiferet, and "just," like "good" (or "calm"), to Yessod:

Zeh	circumcision	Yessod
Zeh	all	Yessod
Zeh	place	Tiferet
Zeh	just, calm	Yessod

This collocation of schemes and correlations strongly suggests the
need to rethink the criteria of hermeneutic reading. In particular, it
indicates that a division between textual and systematic terms of reference is inappropriate for traditional exegesis and even contrary to its
spirit. The thematic convergence seen above supposes on the contrary
a transitivity of structures, insofar as methodological orders as different
as those of the code and the message, of the langue (that of conventional
derivations) and the parole (that of the biblical text), appear here as
concurrent and comparable. Such a convergence is unique in its very
possibility, at the functional as well as at the thematic level.

IV

To render this indeterminacy and these displacements of coordinates
more salient, I propose, in conclusion, to identify a number of inter-

mediate modes of structuring sense that operate within the techniques of interpretation encountered above. By virtue of their hybrid character, these modes typify the ambivalence of kabbalastic and midrashic exegetic procedures.

In midrash and more so in kabbalah the equivalence delineated between linguistic sign and symbol is crystallized first of all in the transfer of meaning which we have previously called "thematization."[16] In the movement from an existential interpretation to a metaphysical one there is, to be sure, an allegorized transposition which effects a displacement in the use of the demonstrative pronoun from the acknowledgment of a particular presence to the acknowledgment of Omnipresence. To this extent, the two planes of signification are in a symbolic relationship, wherein the semantic feature called designation is metamorphosed into a sememe of revelation. Yet at the same time, since the very technique of hypostasizing the demonstrative turns on the meaning of the word within the language, that is to say on instructions for its use,[17] it is generally understood as an effect of connotation.[18] The first linguistic plane of signification appears then to be embedded within the second, thematic one, according to the principles for deriving the sense of any statement whatsoever.

In consequence thematization can be used to support either a semiotic system in the textual sense[19] or a symbolic system of representation. This structural ambivalence is reinforced by the uncertainty of the axial sense of the derivation. Whereas connotation in the midrashic semiotic system normally starts out from the signified *demonstrative* in order to arrive at the intuition of a transcendence, the process may be reversed in the symbolic ordering of experiences. The latter then manifests, in every reality, a possible revelation, a diluted "sign" of Revelation.

Another noteworthy phenomenon embodied in kabbalistic interpretation is that of the underlining of the anagogic chain of reasoning by means of a return to the text, an operation which we have seen is a projection (in the Jakobsonian sense) of a conventional paradigm onto the biblical syntagm. At first glance, these juxtapositions present themselves as pure contiguities and thereby derive directly from an extratextual code. One can imagine, however, a metalinguistic plane of reading which recognizes these juxtapositions as definitional, that is to say as semantically organized midway between *langue* and *parole*. Insofar as each term of the Bible in each of its occurrences is, from the

perspective of an anagogic reading, used absolutely, the traditional semantic structure is broken open. The words of the text then become
elements of a lexicon and present themselves as independent syntagms
of greater or lesser length, each of which functions as the statement of
a semantic equivalence.

Thus canonical expressions such as *zot ha-berakhah* ("Here is the
blessing") or *zot ha-torah* ("Here is the Torah") may be understood
either as structured linguistic statements, in which the demonstrative
determines a particular reference, or as pure contiguities, which are
"inert" from a syntactic point of view. These two readings are merged
in the metalinguistic perspective which, through the ellipsis of the co-
pula "to be," presents the proper name *zot* as equivalent to "Torah"
or "blessing": "*zot* is the Torah" and "*zot* is the blessing," or again "*zeh*
= God," an equation explicitly recognized by midrash (B. Menaḥot
53b).

To this mode can be linked a form of literal reading which gives
to each context, even when extended to more complex statements, a
value of definition similar to the above. Thus the verse "This one [*zot*]
will be *called* woman" (Gen. 2:33) would be understood as auto-refer-
ential, positing the terminological equivalence of *zot* and "woman."
Every textual qualification would then become necessary and sufficient.
"By this [*zot*] you will know that I am the Eternal" (Exod. 7:17): *zot* is
the intervention which manifests the divine power. "It is thus [*be-zot*]
that Aaron shall enter into the sanctuary" (Lev. 16:3): *zot* is that which
enables Aaron to enter the sanctuary. Here again the points of contact
between heterogeneous systems suggests the existence, at the heart of
each system, of alien formations deriving from the opposite perspective: the reader realizes that there are no irreparable discontinuities
between different exegetic methods or between different thematic
constructions, which are normally understood as being incompatible.

The foregoing inquiry suggests that the synchronic coherence of
the layers of midrashic and kabbalistic interpretation runs contrary to
the expectations of a historicist criticism which posits an arbitrary and
discontinuous evolution of this commentary, even though their coherence accords well with the reiterated rabbinical conviction of an
overall exegetical unity.

In support of an historical viewpoint one could claim, of course,
that the kabbalah involves a subsequent encoding of midrashic mate-

rial, supporting its paradigms upon contextual associations which had already been pointed out. Yet we see that this approach does not cover the totality of observed phenomena as soon as we go beyond mere semantic comparison of units to study the modes of derivation which bind them together. The observed superimposition of distinct and autonomous logics in kabbalah is not consonant with the idea of a subsequent reconstruction of the codes.[20] On the contrary, it compels one to seek a more encompassing principle of integration within which thematic coincidence would be only one particular effect.

This feeling of a general polysemous status in kabbalistic interpretation is reinforced in particular by its frequent recourse to biblical quotations of an ambiguous methodological status between proof and illustration. "As it is said," for example, is indeed a mysterious formula which serves as the pivot between two perspectives. This ambiguity is doubled in the necessary selection of supporting examples, concerning which one does not know with certainty whether they are conditioned by an arbitrary or specific choice. No doubt only a computer, by superimposing the distributional contexts of a term in the Bible and comparing these with the totality of thematic projections which are tied to it in the midrash, could pretend to deduce absolute rules of formation for kabbalah.

The above analysis of exegetical procedures suggests an understanding of signification homologous to the cultural sensibility which produced them. Here we find that hermeneutic activity reproduces and metaphorizes a cosmic conception which is itself based on the concurrence of systems and the ambivalence of categories. It emerges that traditional Judaism corroborates, as congruent with its vision of the world, the principle of convergence we have derived. Its general belief in unity admits concurrent modalities of signification derived from an ontological compatibility. In effect, this structural division-within-unity of Jewish hermeneutics, which synthesizes an orientation toward the code and an orientation toward the text, reproduces an homologous metaphysical paradox, to which the metaphors of writing particularly testify.

This homology could be formulated in the following way: the original paradigm of the ten spiritual spheres (Sefirot) which are, so to speak, the constitutive formula of the universe, is also projected on the syntagm of the world in becoming. Every point of the universe is determined simultaneously by its position in the general dynamics of the created world and by its value in the structural configuration which engendered it. In the kabbalah these two components are unified in one equation: the "vertical" axis of the organization of the world is projected upon the "horizontal" axis of its history. The world in mutation is itself the programmed expansion of an origin and reproduces in the process of its innumerable transformations the archetype of a generative structure. In its arbitrariness, the cosmic emanation marks out, in the space of the living, secretly calculated intervals.

Indeterminacy of meaning thus appears to be compatible with truth of meaning according to Rabbi Akiva. All is determined and yet all is open. This system of thought claims to calculate the metaphysical probability of a radically new act, and poses the dialectic of the unpredictable and the absolute.

Translated by Marsha Hill

NOTES

1. The principle of truth could be thus extended, beyond its legalistic application to the ritual code, to the more general phenomenon of interpretation and reading tradition.

2. Cf. M. Avot III 19. Cited from Herbert Danby's translation of the *Mishnah* (Oxford: Oxford University Press, 1933). Unless otherwise indicated all translations from Hebrew or Aramaic are my own.

3. The limits of this study obviously permit me to indicate only certain lines of force, which I have illustrated for each rubric by one or two examples of an explanatory rather than a demonstrative nature.

4. "Thus," Malbim says, "whenever an expression can be read in [at least] two ways, our Sages have explicated both intentions of the text, for the Torah did not arbitrarily choose an ambiguous form [but rather chose one to indicate that both senses must be retained]" (Malbim, Ayelet ha-Shaḥar, Introduction to his commentary on Leviticus, chap. 24, para. 212).

5. Cf. Maharal, Derekh Ḥayyim, chap. 5, Mishnah 1.

6. By convention, I have chosen to unify under the label *reference* the various "objects of discourse," considered as signifieds, to which the occurrence of the demonstrative refers in the biblical text. I cannot undertake here a discussion of the various schools of thought concerning the notion of reference in its relation to the real world, in particular when the object referred to is an abstract entity.

7. John Lyons, "Deixis and Subjectivity," in *Speech, Place and Action: Studies in Deixis and Related Topics,* ed. R. J. Jarvellah and W. Klein (Chichester, Eng.: J. Wiley, 1982).

8. In this paragraph, I will retain those thematic elements upon which the midrash chooses to focus its demonstration.

9. The Hebrew text here has "*yare'aḥ,*" while other variants employ "*levanah.*" (Cf. Exodus Rabbah XV 28.)

10. Although this translation of Sefirah by "sphere" is inexact, I have used it because of its connotations.

11. Cf. the Dictionnaire Encyclopédique des Sciences du Langage (Paris: Seuil, 1972), p. 134.

12. Any fixation, even at this systematic level, is artificial and deforming.

13. I will adopt a thematic-logical outline as more directly readable.

14. R. Yosef ben Abraham Gikatilla, Sha'arei Orah, chaps. 1–2; and R. Moshe Cordovero, Pardes Rimonim, "Sha'ar Erekei ha-Kinuyim, Erekh Zeh"; R. Yekhiel ben Shlomo Halperin, Sefer Erekei ha-Kinuyim; Sefer Kehilat Ya'akov, and of course numerous passages from the Zohar.

15. Compare for example the previously cited midrash of Leviticus Rabbah XXI 6, with Exodus Rabbah XXXVIII 8 on zeh ha-davar.

16. In a general way, the keys provided by reference to the Sefirah can be understood as metaphorizing the grammatical characteristics of deixis: presupposition of existence, referential openness, primacy of relation.

17. In classical linguistics, this technique is extended to numerous categories (deictics in particular: "the I," "the It," etc.).

18. Furthermore, one should consider that the symbolic relationship is normally instituted between elements of like nature, whereas here metaphorization articulates heterogenous registers—simple vs. complex, grammatical vs. thematic.

19. The semiotic sign is conceived of here in a restrictive sense in the spirit of Saussure, namely a sign negatively defined by its operation in a whole system, which is here textual. It is thus opposed to a semantic sign, functioning within a symbolic system of representation which motivates the relationship between signifier and signified.

20. Let us recall that the internal logic of the kabbalistic series is not purely thematic but admits other systems of derivation: lexical, literal, numerical, figurative, etc. For example, while the connection of the tithe with Malkhut appears to be based upon a contextual relation to zot, the Pardes Rimonim recognizes in it a numerical structure of 1/10 which associates it directly with this same Sefirah, which is of analogous arithmetic value in the disposition of the spheres.

Literature and Midrash

FRANK KERMODE

The Plain Sense of Things

My title is taken from a poem by Wallace Stevens:

> After the leaves have fallen, we return
> To a plain sense of things. It is as if
> We had come to the end of the imagination,
> Inanimate in an inert savoir.
>
> It is difficult even to choose the adjective
> For this blank cold, this sadness without cause.
> The great structure has become a minor house.
> No turban walks across the lessened floors.
>
> The greenhouse never so badly needed paint.
> The chimney is fifty years old and slants to one side.
> A fantastic effort has failed, a repetition
> In a repetitiousness of men and flies.
>
> Yet the absence of the imagination had
> Itself to be imagined. The great pond,
> The plain sense of it, without reflections, leaves,
> Mud, water like dirty glass, expressing silence
>
> Of a sort, silence of a rat come out to see,
> The great pond and its waste of lilies, all this
> Had to be imagined as an inevitable knowledge,
> Required, as a necessity requires.

This is a late poem by Stevens, but it continues a meditation that began much earlier. In its own very idiosyncratic way that meditation echoes a central theme of modern philosophy. The plain sense is itself metaphorical; there is no escape from metaphor; univocity in language is no more than a dream. The position is familiar, and the interest of Stevens's poem is that he is not so much affirming it as suggesting the movement of mind that accompanies its consideration. He is especially conscious of the extraordinary effort required even to imagine, to find language for, the plain sense of things and hold the language there for

179

the briefest moment: worth trying, he seems to say, but impossible, this attempt to behold "the nothing that is not there and the nothing that is." To make the attempt, he said in the earlier poem I have just quoted ("The Snow Man"), is "to have a mind of winter." Only such a mind, a snowman's mind, could attend to the frozen trees without adding to them some increment of language, of humanity, even if that increment is misery.

Such a moment, of unattainable absolute zero, is anyway only to be imagined as a phase in a cyclical process. Language, always metaphorical, falsifies the icy diagram, corrupts by enriching the plain sense, which can only be thus corruptly or distortedly expressed. "Not to have is the beginning of desire" ("Notes toward a Supreme Fiction"); and so metaphor, like spring, adorns the icy diagram; only when that desire is satisfied do we grow tired of summer lushness and welcome the fall and winter again. So the plain sense continually suffers change, and if it did not it would grow rigid and absurd. It must change, or it will simply belong "to our more vestigial states of mind" ("Notes"). But change is inevitable anyway, since the effort we make to attend to plain sense itself takes away the plainness. That this is the case may distress philosophers who want to be able to distinguish the literal from the metaphorical, but it is nevertheless a source of poetry: "Winter and spring, cold copulars, embrace, / And forth the particulars of rapture come" ("Notes"). The imagination's commentary is a part of the text as we know it—that is, distorted by metaphor, by secondary elaboration. This is what Stevens means when he speaks of the effect of the gaiety of language on the natives of poverty ("L'Esthetique du Mal"): the games, fictions, metaphors which accommodate the plain sense to human need. Without such "makings," as he calls them, the world is just "waste and welter" ("The Planet on the Table"). And the makings are themselves part of a reality more largely conceived, of a whole which is not merely or not always poor; the words of the world are the life of the world.

In the poem before you there is a winter, a due season, a world stripped of imaginative additions, so cold that it resists our adjectives. The summer world made by our imagination is now a ruin; the effort has ended in failure. So, difficult though it may be, one tries to find an adjective for blankness, a tropeless cold. But to say "no turban" is to introduce a turban, something exotic, a gift of imagination; the floors, though lessened, are still fully there; the structure is still a house. Imagination wants a decrepit greenhouse, a tottering chimney; blankness itself becomes a pond, and the pond has lilies and a rat. "The absence of the imagination had / Itself to be imagined." The pond has reflections, leaves, mud, as real a pond as imagination at the best of times could imagine. All these things have to be added to the plain sense if we want it; it is not to be had without comment, without poetry.

It may seem that I have begun this essay at a great distance from any topic that might be thought appropriate to its occasion. But we know that *midrash* and *peshat* are also an intrinsic plural; that the play, might one say even the gaiety, of the one is required to give a human sense to the inaccessible mystery of the other. And it is on the other instances of this collaboration that I shall be expatiating. So it seems sensible enough to begin with a poet who saw so well the relations between plain sense and human need—saw it not as a philosopher or a hermeneutician, but rather as his own major man might, though the major man would understand wholly the supreme fiction in which plain sense and trope, truth and fiction, are finally apprehended as a unity, and the world stops. (Stevens sometimes thought of this major man as a rabbi.) For him the kind of poetry Eliot said he wanted would be a part, but only a part, of poetry: "poetry standing in its own bare bones, or poetry so transparent that we should see not the poetry, but what we are meant to see through the poetry."[1] Note that in speaking of this impossible nakedness or transparency the poet has to imagine a skeleton and a window. The most arduous effort to express the poetry of plain sense brings with it its own metaphors, its own distortions. There are, as Freud would have said, considerations of representability, there are secondary elaborations, there are fortuitous inessentials, day's residues; he might have agreed with Augustine that some things are there for the sake of the sense but not constitutive of the sense. And our only way to catch a glimpse of the sense is by attending to the inevitable distortions.

Northrop Frye remarks that the literal sense of a poem is the whole poem.[2] And the whole which constitutes the literal sense may not be a single poem; nor need that whole be the same for everybody. A canon may define the whole, and the same parts may figure in different canons. For Christian commentators the Psalms belong to a whole different from the whole to which they belong for Jewish commentators; they may agree that there are messianic psalms, but the plain sense of such psalms must be different for each, since the whole text of the Christian shows the fulfillment of the messianic promises. Herbert's poem "The Holy Scriptures (II)" compares the separate texts of the Bible to a constellation, and remarks on the remote interactions of the verses:

> This verse marks that, and both do make a motion
> Unto a third, that ten leaves off doth lie . . .

But for some, though they might accept the principle, those ten leaves are not in their copies. The expression *Son of man* occurs in Ps. 8:4, and modern scholars agree that it means simply "man", and that it ought not to be thought of in relation to the apocalyptic sense of the phrase in Daniel or the passages in the New Testament which seem to derive from Daniel. But, as John Barton says, the case would be different if the New Testament had happened to cite the passage from the psalm for christological purposes;[3] and in any case it seems unlikely that less scholarly Christians, coming upon these words or hearing them sung in church on the first day of the month, will quite exclude from their thoughts the resonances of New Testament usage.

So the whole, by which the sense of the part is to be determined, varies between the religions and the canons. And there is a further extension of context, which, since it will recur in my argument, I shall mention now. The Roman Catholic Church affirms the authority of the magisterium over all interpretation, and the Church is the custodian of a Tradition; so that to the two parts of the Christian Bible one adds a third contextual element, and the whole that determines the plain sense of the part is thus extended.

However, we need not confine the question thus; for it is clear that different people at different times will form their own notions of the relations between parts, and between parts and wholes. For example, some will maintain that christological interpretations of Old Testament texts are valid only when they have been made in the New Testament; others, a great army of them over the centuries, think otherwise. And the language in which each person or party expresses the sense of the text will necessarily be figurative. The plain sense is not accessible to plain common sense. That is why it has been possible to say, "The plain sense is hidden." Luther believed that "the Holy Spirit is the plainest writer and speaker in heaven and earth," but we may well sympathize with Erasmus, who wanted to know "if it is all so plain, why have so many excellent men for so many centuries walked in darkness?"[4]

The expression *plain sense*, as I am using it, covers the overlapping ideas of literal sense, grammatical sense, and historical sense. It is also a usual translation of *peshat*. The most obvious indication that the plain sense is not a universal and unequivocal property of mankind is that it resists translation from one language into another. A well-known example is John Lyons's demonstration of the difficulty of finding a French equivalent for "the cat sat on the mat"; the nouns are troublesome but the verb is worse, since English does not adjudicate between the senses, in French, of *s'assit, s'est assis(e), s'asseyait*.[5] I shall return to the cat in another connection, but the present point is that plain senses can be tricky to translate. Bruno Bettelheim laments that Freud's English translators alter his sense by refusing to use the word *soul*.[6] But the senses of that word in English are very different from those of its German cognate; *soul* would often be wrong in English. Bettelheim is especially bitter that the translators of the Standard Edition have smuggled in a new word, very technical sounding, to translate *Besetzung*, namely "cathexis." But would "occupation" or "investment" really do the work? And how should we deal with *Überbesetzung*? No doubt "hypercathexis" gives a different idea, but it is probably closer to Freud's sense than "overinvestment," and the same must be true of "anticathexis."

These minor discrepancies are perhaps emblematic of much larger ones. Psychoanalysis changed when it moved from the Viennese into other cultures, and it can never again be what it was in prewar Europe; like other religions it was fissile even in its early stages, and different sects and individuals have always found different plain senses in the original deposits of doctrine. There are obvious parallels in Christianity. Jerome began it, offering *hebraica veritas*, and Greek truth also, but in Latin. Thereafter *logos* became *verbum*, and *verbum* became so firm a part of the theological tradition that when Erasmus, with good philological justification, translated *logos* as *sermo* he got into trouble; for *verbum* seemed to match the required plain sense as *sermo*, a surprising novelty, could not. On the other hand More attacked Tyndale for giving "love" instead of "charity" for *agape*; but now "charity" has changed its contexts and "love" is preferred.[7] The naive desire of the New English Bible translators to provide plain-sense equivalents for the Hebrew of the Old Testament sometimes leads them into what can fairly be called mistranslation, as in their version of the rape of Dinah by Shechem (Gen. 34.3): "But he remained true to Dinah." The sense of the Hebrew *nefesh* is lost, though the King James version, which has "And his soul clave unto Dinah," conveys, as Hammond observes, the intensity of Shechem's erotic feelings. " 'Remained true' is exactly the wrong phrase since it implies fidelity and honour; the point of the story is that Shechem's lust is not fulfilled by one act of rape."[8] No doubt this view could be disputed, since *nefesh*, according to the Lexicon, is a tremendously complicated word, and no translation could do it justice. But King James wins by not seeking a commonplace equivalent.

When whole systems of belief are involved, as in the case of the Bible they always are, the difficulties are multiplied. Christianity decided to reject Marcion and keep the Jewish Bible, and thenceforth the question of the nature of its relevance to a non-Jewish religion became a permanent problem, with much bearing on the matter of plain sense. If the Law was abrogated the relevance of the Old Testament lay primarily in its prefigurative relation to the New; it became, more or less, a repository of types. But it contained other elements not easily given up—moral instruction and a history of God's providence and promises. And from quite early times there was some resistance to the copious allegorizing of the Alexandrian tradition, some respect for the *sensus historicus*. The school of Antioch limited allegorical interpretation to the sort of thing licensed by Paul, for example in his reading of the story of the sons of Sarah and Hagar. Theodore of Mopsuestia sought to understand the Old Testament historically; for instance, he rejected the usual (and, in the circumstances, obvious) reading of the Suffering Servant in Isaiah 53. But Theodore was posthumously condemned, and the majority of Antiochenes were in any case less rigidly historicist, as D. S. Wallace-Hadrill explains.[9]

And yet, despite the success of allegory, the importance of the literal sense was habitually affirmed, most influentially by Augustine, a contemporary of Theodore but working in a different tradition. Augustine was a historian, and as an exegete he held that an understanding of historical reality must be the foundation of any attempt to provide spiritual interpretation. His emphasis on Jewish history as continuous with Christian was influential. But he also ruled that no interpretation should transgress against "charity": any literal-historical sense that was inconsistent with virtuous conduct and the true faith should be treated figuratively. And he provided for the frequent occurrence of texts that appeared to have no particular Christian relevance; they were there for the sake of the others, as ploughs have handles.[10] Thus the typical quality of the historical sense is maintained, and the position is as Preuss describes it: the plain sense of some of the Old Testament is edifying in itself, but the remainder has value only because it means something other than it seems to be saying; the literal, grammatical, and historical senses include what should not be figuratively interpreted and also what must be so interpreted. But that which is edifying is so only because it already conforms with the New Testament, and the unedifying has to be made edifying by figurative reading in New Testament terms. Thus the extended context determines the plain sense, which, in the case of the Old Testament, resides effectively in the text of the New. There was a Jewish or carnal sense, to which one might attribute more or less importance; but the true sense was Christian and spiritual, and that sense could be represented as the plain sense. The figurative becomes the literal.

So, although the warning that the *sensus historicus* must be the foundation of exegesis was frequently repeated, it appears that a really active concern for the historical sense of the Old Testament did not recur until the later years of the eleventh century, when it was in large part the result of intercourse between Jewish and Christian scholars. It was at that moment that peshat entered, or reentered, Christian thought. Erwin Rosenthal has explained with great clarity the position of Jewish scholarship after Saadya Gaon; how the distinction between *peshat* and *derash* now grew sharper, how peshat served as a weapon against christological interpretations, and how Rashi, by his more correct understanding of the relation between the two, influenced not only his Jewish but his Christian contemporaries.[11] The conflict between extreme adherents of peshat and derash, between the literal sense and the tradition, the literal sense and the mystical kabbalistic sense, continued within the Jewish tradition. But meanwhile a new respect for the Hebrew text and the *sensus Judaicus* was once again altering the context of Christian interpretation.

Beryl Smalley established the influence of Jewish scholarship on the work of the Victorines.[12] Relations between Jewish and Christian scholars were never wholly cordial, but they were productive, for the "Hebrew truth" of Jerome was now taken back into its own language. Hugh of St. Victor had some Hebrew, and he consulted Jewish scholars and reported their interpretations. There was a new emphasis on the historical sense as Jews understood it. Hugh anticipated Aquinas in arguing that to be ignorant of the signs was to be ignorant of what they signified, and so of what the signified, itself a sign, signified. It will, however, be noticed that this formula does nothing to alter the position that a true understanding of the Jewish Bible depends upon and is subsequent to a true understanding of the New Testament; for the Jewish reading, though it accurately carries out the first stage of the process, the establishment of literal, grammatical, and historical sense, plays no part in the second, which is to determine what the signified signifies. The Jewish sense is still the carnal one, and preliminary to the spiritual reading.

It would seem that Jewish scholarship was bolder, in that it sometimes risked everything on the plain sense. Joseph Kara, early in the twelfth century, could remark that "whosoever is ignorant of the literal meaning of the Scripture and inclines after a Midrash is like a drowning man who clutches at a straw to save himself."[13] Masters of Haggadah may mock him, he says; but the enlightened will prefer the truth. Nevertheless, we are told, he himself frequently inclined after midrash. It was the next generation of Jewish scholars, contemporaries of Andrew of St. Victor, the hero of Beryl Smalley's research, who installed the literal sense more firmly. Andrew ecumenically devised a dual method of interpretation, giving the Vulgate text with a Christian explanation, and the Hebrew text with a Jewish. The literal sense was that of the Jews. For example, on Isa. 7:14–16, "Behold, a virgin shall conceive," Andrew cites Rashi to the effect that the literal sense is this: the bride of the prophet will conceive a son to deliver Israel. Though he rejects this interpretation with some vehemence, Andrew allows it the title of the literal sense.[14] But Christians live by the spirit, and their reading of the passage, based on the *virgo* of the Vulgate, is the true if not the literal one.

In using the Jews, to quote Smalley, as "a kind of telephone to the Old Testament,"[15] Andrew naturally annoyed some contemporaries. He was accused of "judaizing." But judaizing gave a new turn to the speculation about literal sense and its relation to spiritual sense. Henceforth the argument of Hugh of St. Victor, as restated and given authority by Aquinas, prevailed. The words mean one thing only; but that thing may be a sign of other things, and it is from those second-order things that the spiritual sense derives. The historical sense, the sense of the human author, is what he says; but there is a divine author whose intentions are other than his. "Truly, the literal sense is that which the author intended; but the author of sacred Scripture is God, who comprehends in his *intellectus* all things at once."[16] So the spiritual or symbolic or typical interpretation is more faithful to the *mens auctoris* than the literal; and regardless of what is properly to be called the literal sense, the true sense is to be found in the New Testament.

There were various attempts to resolve the ambiguities of this position, as when the extremely influential commentator Nicholas de Lyra also spoke of the literal sense itself as dual; the symbolic interpretation was to be regarded as the literal one if expressly approved by the New Testament (a partial return to the Antiochan doctrine). When God says of Solomon (I Chron. 11): "I will be a father to him, and he will be like a son to me," the application to Solomon is literal; but because the author of the Epistle to the Hebrews uses the text to show that Christ is higher than the angels, it has a second literal sense, which is also mystical. Preuss thinks this is the "first time . . . a New Testament reading of an Old Testament passage is dignified with the label 'literal' "; though the general idea is of course not new.[17]

It seems, then, that throughout this period there grew up a desire to narrow the gap between the Christian and the literal sense. But since the literal sense could still be referred to the New Testament, some Jewish scholars now abandoned their own messianic interpretations and clove to the *sensus historicus*, in order to avoid any suggestion that might give support to the christological reading, for example of Psalm 2. Once again it is apparent that the Christians, however devoted to the *hebraica veritas*, could not be so bold as the Jews; for their interpretations were always subject to censorship by the custodians of an infallible tradition that was partly independent of Scripture. Of course Jewish interpreters had to steer a course between the fundamentalism of the Karaites and the allegories of the Kabbalah; but the institution controlling Christian interpretation was very powerful, and the authority of the tradition, which in some ways stood to the New Testament as the New Testament did to the Old, could be enforced by the Inquisition; these were not merely erudite arguments.

By the fifteenth century the matter of literal sense called for formal discussion, as in Jean Gerson's *De sensu litterali sacrae Scripturae* of 1414, which decided that the Church alone had the power to determine the literal sense. It derived its authority to do so from the promise of Christ in the New Testament; that is, the literal sense of the New Testament confers on the Church the right to declare the true sense of any text. Preuss comments on the importance and timeliness of this pronouncement. Heretics claimed that their doctrines were founded on the literal sense of Scripture; but if the literal sense is by definition the "literal sense of the Church," and not anything more generally available, then merely to affirm a different sense from that of the Church was proof of heresy. "The possibility of argument from Scripture against the *magisterium* is for the first time . . . programmatically and theoretically eliminated."[18] There would no longer be any point in asking Jews about the plain sense of an Old Testament passage; that sense was first revealed through Christ and the apostles, then protected and studied by the Church, and subsequently enforceable with all manner of sanctions.

So the lines were drawn for the struggle between Luther's plain sense, his *sola scriptura*, and the authority of Rome, only possessor of the sense of Scripture. Luther was speaking no more than truth when he accused the Popes of setting themselves up as "lords of Scripture"; that was exactly what they had done. Of the religious, political, and military consequences of this hermeneutic disagreement it is unnecessary to speak. Curiously enough, in our own time it is a Protestant hermeneutics that has insisted upon the necessity of understanding tradition as formative of the horizon from which we must seek some kind of encounter with ancient texts, denying at the same time any immediacy of access to those texts. It seems that Gerson and the popes had grasped an important point, namely that all interpretation is validated in the end by a third force, and not by the unaided and unauthoritative study of isolated scholars; and they wished to be sure that the third force was the Church.

Luther, as a matter of fact, opposed enthusiastic reading also; as far as he could see Müntzer and the Pope were both arrogating to themselves an improper authority over Scripture. But in the next century the Council of Trent made equivocation and compromise impossible by giving renewed emphasis to tradition and authority. The subsequent history of the Catholic view was determined by the Tridentine decisions.

It seems reasonable to conclude this brief anthology of disputes about plain sense by glancing at some exegetical problems which had to be settled at the time of Catholic Modernism. The intellectual atmosphere of the late nineteenth century, including the success over a generation or so of Darwinism and, perhaps even more threatening, the achievement and the fame of German Protestant biblical scholarship, made both Authority and Tradition subject to question. There arose within the Church scholars who thought the official position needed revision. An early hint of the new kind of hermeneutic understanding recommended to the Church is to be found in the work of the Tübingen Catholic theologian Johann Evangelist von Kuhn. He agreed with the Protestants that the Bible is privileged over all other documents, but said that they failed to understand this: Tradition, as distinct from traditions, is the preaching and consciousness of the Church in the present moment. "Tradition is the *kerygma* of the present; Scripture, the *kerygma* of the past, is the *doctrina*-source of the present."[19]

This new formulation places the sense of Scripture firmly in the here and now; it denies that application can be divorced from understanding. A related idea, very characteristic of its time, is that religion has undergone an evolutionary development, and that the old texts and forms might be thought of as types of later doctrine, an idea prevalent in the thought of the period, and given expression in literature (by Hawthorne, for instance) as well as in Catholic theology (by Newman, who said that "the earlier prophecies are pregnant texts out of which the succeeding announcements grow; they are types"[20]).

Such views were condemned in 1870, but a generation later they appeared again in a rather different form with Modernism proper. Its proponents favored Tradition over Scripture, seeing Tradition as a process of inspired development. The reflex of the Church, inevitably conservative, was to retreat to a scriptural position. This is not surprising; it must have been rather horrifying to hear Von Hügel, a man of impeccable piety (Yeats praised him because he accepted the miracles of the saints and honored sanctity) proclaiming that even if the Gospel narratives were unrelated to historical events they would still be true as "creations of the imagination"—a position not really very far from that of some modern Protestants. The English convert George Tyrrell was shocked to find in the Roman Church the sort of bible religion he had thought he was leaving behind. He believed that God was the First Cause, and so the author of Scripture only in the sense that he was the author of everything. He was aware of the difficulty of steering a course between the two positions, one holding that the deposit was perpetually valid, the other that doctrine developed progressively. Here again is the hermeneutic problem about original and applied sense. Tyrrell failed to solve it and was disgraced. In France Alfred Loisy expressed similar views and with more force, remarking in a very modern manner that a book absolutely true for all times would be unintelligible at all times; he too saw the danger of reading back a modern idea of religion into the Scriptures. Caught between these positions he too fell foul of the Church and was excommunicated.[21]

The plain sense of Scripture, as of anything else, is a hermeneutical question, and we have seen how different are the hermeneutics of Augustine, the medieval Jewish scholars, Gerson, and Loisy. One concept that was rigorously developed was that of the role of authority, the institutional power to validate or to invalidate by reference to Tradition; but when Tyrrell and Loisy were purged authority was acting as it were politically, for to the outsider it might have seemed that they were trying to give the idea of Tradition new force. Their proposals, like those of von Kuhn, offered the Church a plausible modern hermeneutic, with an acceptable view of the relation between the origin and the here and now; but the idea of development, though supported by the whole history of dogma, was too frightening.

Modernism was revived in a modern form in the 1940s and partly endorsed by Vatican II. The principal effect has been to allow Catholic scholars to engage in the sort of historical research formerly associated with Protestant scholarship; and this may seem belated, for elsewhere there is a strong shift away from the objectivist assumptions of that scholarship and toward a newer hermeneutics. It is now often maintained that the plain sense, if there is one, must be of the here and now rather than of the origin.

One thing is sure: the body of presuppositions which determines our notions of the plain sense is always changing, and so is the concept of the validating authority. As the new canonical criticism demonstrates, there are new ways of establishing relevant contexts, and new extratextual authorities, like the idea of canon in this case. And a hermeneutics that allowed for possibilities of change and adaptation might have suited the Church, as the defender of Tradition, very well, as— or so it appears—the Jewish tradition has accommodated change and adaptation without sacrificing the original deposit. What the Modernists saw was that if Tradition entailed change, there was a need for a theory of interpretation which could close the widening gap between doctrine and text and require newly licensed plain senses. In practice the means has always been available; the dogma of the Assumption of the Virgin, promulgated in 1950, depends on Tradition and not on Scripture, and on a tradition that can only with difficulty be traced back as far as the fourth century. It would have been particularly surprising to St. Mark. But if we think of Tradition as the third part of the Catholic canonical context it is possible to suppose that the Assumption is part of the plain sense of the whole; and, after all, assumptions occur in both the other parts.

My purpose has been to suggest that the plain sense of things is always dependent on the understanding of larger wholes and on changing custom and authority. So it must change; it is never naked, but, as the poet says, it always wears some fictive covering. Time itself changes it, however much authority may resist. It must, of course, do so. And it cannot do so if it fails to preserve its foundation text; and, short of keeping that text out of unauthorized hands, it cannot prevent readers from making their imaginative additions to the icy diagram.

Finally, the plain sense depends in larger measure on the imaginative activity of interpreters. This is variously constrained, by authority or hermeneutic rules or assumptions, but it is necessary if the text is to have any communicable sense at all. Given plausible rules and a firm structure of authority, change may not be violent. One recalls Raphael Loewe's magisterial essay on "The 'Plain' Meaning of Scripture in Early Jewish Exegesis."[22] The word *peshat* itself is metaphorical; its plain senses have to do with flattening, extending, and derivatively with simplicity and innocence and lack of learning, with the popular, the read-once-only, the clear, the generally accepted, the current, and so on; but the central sense, Loewe maintains, is authority. It is used to describe readings by no means literal, and applications "entirely arbitrary." Loewe concludes that the best translation of the word, at any rate up to the end of the period of the Talmuds and the midrashim, is "authoritative teaching," which covers both traditional teaching and teaching given by a particular rabbi of acknowledged authority. And, says Loewe, "the conventional distinction between *peshat* and *derash* must be jettisoned." In times later than those of which Loewe speaks, the identification of peshat with plain sense became firmer, with important results. But its historical association with authority, and its inescapable association with derash, point clearly enough to the conclusion that our minds are not very well adapted to the perception of texts in themselves; we necessarily provide them with contexts, some of them imposed by authority and tradition, some by the need to make sense of them in a different world.

It is possible for some philosophers of language to speak of a "zero context"—to maintain that "for every sentence the literal meaning of the sentence can be construed as the meaning it has independent of any context whatever." In expressing his dissent from this opinion, John Searle argues that the meaning even of "the cat sat on the mat" depends upon "background assumptions"; there is, he believes, "no constant set of assumptions that determine the notion of literal meaning."[23] Some of these assumptions are silently at work when we make the statement about the cat. Its plain sense depends, among other things, on the assumption that the cat and the mat are within the gravitational field of the earth; and Searle is able to fit out the sentence with speculative contexts which give it quite other senses. But this fascinating sentence invites other potentially interesting considerations. For example: the sentence is felt as somehow infantile, as belonging to a reading primer, perhaps; it owes its memorability to a triple rhyme—a phonetic bond which solicits our attention to the code rather than the message. That the procedures are metaphoric rather than metonymic gives the sentence a poetic quality and more potential intertext (so long as we have it in the original language). There is the further consideration that the sentence must almost always have a citational quality—Lyons and Searle both cite it as an example, and I have cited them citing it. Since it lives in such rarefied contexts its simplicity is certainly bogus, and its use variously colored by pedantry and archness. It has no plain sense; it merely serves as a lay figure, like the poet's icy diagram, his lake with its shadows, rats, and lilies.

And that takes me back to the imaginary zero context where I began. There is no "inert savoir"; to speak as if there were is already to speak "as if." Metaphor begins to remodel the plain sense as soon as we begin to think or to speak about it. If Stevens is right in saying that the words of the world are the life of the world, then metaphor runs in the world's blood, as if derash and peshat were the red and the white corpuscles, intrinsically plural.

I have taken most of my examples from exegesis as practiced in religions which maintained over very long periods an extreme veneration for their sacred texts, and which certainly abhorred the idea of deliberate interference or distortion. The place of rule-governed imagination was clearly established in midrash. In the Christian tradition, with its basic belief that the sense of the Jewish Bible must be sought in another book, there is a quite different imaginative challenge. All such result in Entstellung, not Darstellung. Among the thousands of commentators there have been literalists of the imagination and also extravagant poets. But all have in their measure to be creators, even if they wish to imagine themselves at the end of imagination when the lake is still, without reflections; there may be silence, but it is silence of a sort, never zero silence.

NOTES

1. See F. O. Matthiessen, *The Achievement of T. S. Eliot*, 3d ed. (New York: Oxford University Press, 1958), p. 90.

2. Northrop Frye, *Anatomy of Criticism: Four Essays* (Princeton: Princeton University Press, 1957), p. 76.

3. J. Barton, *Reading the Old Testament* (London: Darton, Longman and Todd, 1984), p. 85.

4. *De libero arbitrio*, quoted in *Cambridge History of the Bible*, vol. 3, *The West from the Reformation to the Present Day*, ed. S. C. Greenslade (Cambridge: Cambridge University Press, 1969–70), p. 28.

5. John Lyons, *Semantics*, vol. 1 (Cambridge: Cambridge University Press, 1977), p. 237.

6. Bruno Bettelheim, *Freud and Man's Soul* (1983).

7. *Cambridge History of the Bible*, vol. 3, p. 11.

8. Gerald Hammond, *The Making of the English Bible* (Manchester: Carcanet Press, 1982), p. 10.

9. Beryl Smalley, *The Study of the Bible in the Middle Ages*, 2d ed. (Oxford: Clarendon Press, 1952), p. 15; D. S. Wallace-Hadrill, *Christian Antioch: A Study of Early Christian Thought in the East* (Cambridge: Cambridge University Press, 1982), chap. 2.

10. *City of God*, XVI, 2.

11. *Cambridge History of the Bible*, vol. 2, pp. 252ff.

12. Smalley, *Bible in the Middle Ages*, chap. 4.

13. Ibid., p. 151.

14. Ibid., p. 163.

15. Ibid., p. 362.

16. J. S. Preuss, *From Shadow to Promise: Old Testament Interpretation from Augustine to the Young Luther* (Cambridge: Harvard University Press, 1969), p. 53.

17. Ibid., p. 69.

18. Ibid., p. 81.

19. J. T. Burtchaell, *Catholic Theories of Inspiration since* 1810 (London: Cambridge University Press, 1969), p. 32.

20. Ibid., pp. 69–70.

21. Ibid., chap. 5.

22. *Papers of the Institute of Jewish Studies,* London, vol. 1, ed. J. G. Weiss (Jerusalem: Magnes Press, 1964), pp. 141–85.

23. John Searle, "Literal Meaning," in *Expression and Meaning: Studies in the Theory of Speech Acts* (Cambridge: Cambridge University Press, 1979).

SANFORD BUDICK

Milton and the Scene of Interpretation: From Typology toward Midrash

In this essay I would like to use the medium of Milton's poetry to explore the relationship between typology and other forms of exegesis. Milton, I believe, not only makes use of a multiplicity of interpretative modes; he also expands the typological category of interpretation to include something that corresponds closely to one form of midrash. With a preternatural grasp of the historical inner workings of his materials, Milton put his finger on some of the ways in which the New Testament paradigms of typology had themselves derived from this other exegetical model. This model had been made available to Christian writers at the beginning of the common era by Philo of Alexandria and had thence been borrowed and injected into one mainstream of Christian thought by the author of the Epistle to the Hebrews and by Clement of Alexandria and his successors. Building on this tradition, Milton revises and supplements conventional typology to reveal a hermeneutic reality of a different sort. Most particularly in *Paradise Lost*, he demonstrates that a Christian exegetical poetry can forcibly express interpretative necessities in which the fulfillment associated with one kind of typology is significantly deferred.

I

Interpreting the opening lines of Book Eleven is one of the most difficult tasks confronting the reader of *Paradise Lost*. Half-formed image and half-expressed idea seem to set the reader poetic tasks that are beyond human doing—tasks which have vexed many a reader of Mil-

195

ton's verse. Since I will be commenting below on various aspects of these lines, I will cite them whole at the outset:

> Thus they in lowliest plight repentant stood
> Praying, for from the Mercy-seat above
> Prevenient Grace descending had remov'd
> The stony from thir hearts, and made new flesh
> Regenerate grow instead, that sighs now breath'd
> Unutterable, which the Spirit of prayer
> Inspir'd, and wing'd for Heav'n with speedier flight
> Than loudest Oratory: yet thir port
> Not of mean suitors, nor important less
> Seem'd thir Petition, than when th' ancient Pair
> In Fables old, less ancient yet than these,
> *Deucalion* and chaste *Pyrrha* to restore
> The Race of Mankind drown'd, before the Shrine
> Of *Themis* stood devout. To Heav'n thir prayers
> Flew up, nor miss'd the way, by envious winds
> Blown vagabond or frustrate: in they pass'd
> Dimensionless through Heav'nly doors: then clad
> With incense, where the Golden Altar fum'd,
> By thir great Intercessor, came in sight
> Before the Father's Throne: Then the glad Son
> Presenting, thus to intercede began.
>   See Father, what first fruits on Earth are sprung
> From thy implanted Grace in Man, these Sighs
> And Prayers, which in this Golden Censer, mixt
> With Incense, I thy Priest before thee bring,
> Fruits of more pleasing savor from thy seed
> Sown with contrition in his heart, than those
> Which his own hand manuring all the Trees
> Of Paradise could have produc't, ere fall'n
> From innocence. Now therefore bend thine ear
> To supplication, hear his sighs though mute;
> Unskilful with what words to pray, let mee
> Interpret for him, mee his Advocate
> And propitiation, all his works on mee
> Good or not good ingraft, my Merit those
> Shall perfet, and for these my Death shall pay.
> Accept me, and in mee from these receive
> The smell of peace toward Mankind, let him live
> Before thee reconcil'd, at least his days
> Number'd, though sad, till Death, his doom (which I
> To mitigate thus plead, not to reverse)
> To better life shall yield him, where with mee
> All my redeem'd may dwell in joy and bliss,
> Made one with me as I with thee am one.[1]

The interpretative problems presented by these lines are wholly characteristic of Milton's poetry, though they are exhibited here in somewhat acute form. In large part, they derive from the startling elusiveness
of Milton's images, the evaporating visual properties with which Milton
endows his verse. Can any human reader be expected to attain the
divine optics necessary to *see*, with God the Father, in a single field of
vision, fruits and implanted grace, sighs and prayers, and golden censer
"mixt" hazily not only with incense but with transcendent doctrines
of Christian sacrifice? Milton's mercy seat and burgeoning tree—indeed, the entire scene set before us—are deeply rooted in the concrete.
Yet the prevenient grace which controls that scene and which can
remove the stony from human hearts and cause regenerate flesh to
grow instead, defies visual imagining. According to Eliot, "Milton may
be said never to have seen anything"; Milton's verse, he claims, suffers
from a "dissociation of sensibility."

But as I have argued elsewhere, Milton's poetry is intended to
produce an extraordinary kind of visualization.[2] His poetic imagery
does not offer tableaux of completed meanings. Rather it represents a
process of continuous perception which is visual and conceptual both,
and which displaces the emphasis from either stark percept or bare
concept to the interpretative process that relates them. The scene's
constituent visual elements, in other words, are intentionally separated
and held in intellectual suspension so that their total force may be
directed toward producing, not a mere image, but what Coleridge
called a sublime feeling or idea. Instead of a *discordia concors*, in the
tradition of Heraclitus's logos of resolution and plenitude, Milton's
cosmic images constitute a recognizable Christian poetic that reconciles
extremes by keeping them apart: sinful man from angry God, death
from life, earth from heaven. "Accept me . . . let him live / Before thee
reconcil'd . . . till Death . . . To better life shall yield him," declares
Christ. In these verses, as in the passage as a whole, Milton renders the
essential paradigm of this Christian disposition. Indeed, Christ himself
appears in person as the preservative logos, the "great Intercessor,"
who is the omnipresent buffer zone within created being.

To understand Milton's poetry in this way is to learn what Milton
calls the discipline of "mental sight" (XI. 418). It is to "interpret" according to an exegetical pattern which is not only of singular artistic
power but is the essence of the redeemed imagination toward which
the poem as a whole is striving. One of the reasons for the remarkable

impact, not to mention complexity, of these opening lines of Book Eleven, is the way in which they center on the subject of interpretation qua interpretation. The lines, punctuated by rational or analytic as opposed to visual images, solemnly announce a divine requirement to "interpret," and they proclaim that necessity in a scene of redemption which is itself constituted as nothing less than a network of interpretation. Furthermore, and almost as if to emphasize its status as interpretation, the scene itself is depicted twice, both times drawn from scriptural sources, first by an observer outside the scene and then by a great insider.

As we consider the importance of interpretation in these lines, we can note with satisfaction the difference that modern scholarship of a typological orientation has made in the appreciation of Milton's verse. Only in the last half-century have we begun to understand Milton's typological discipline, "From shadowy Types to Truth, from Flesh to Spirit" (XII. 302–03).[3] Of course, it may be argued that even without some knowledge of the tradition of figural or typological interpretation we could ascertain Milton's principal doctrines. We could make out readily enough that the Son comes to enact prophetic meanings stored up in the Old Testament. If we have our Bible down pat (or if we have a well-glossed *Paradise Lost* on our desks), verse after verse of Milton's page necessarily springs at us from the pages behind that page—from Exodus and Hebrews, Ezekiel and Romans, Psalms, Revelations, Mark, and John. We recognize without external prompting that Milton rehearses the Pauline relationship of type to antitype that is spelled out in the New Testament itself, especially in the texts from Hebrews 8 and 9 that provide Milton with a large part of the scene described above. We acknowledge, for example, that Milton has summoned up the mercy-seat blueprint of Exodus 25, fused it with an image of re-edification from Ezekiel 11, and then made it issue in the architecture of new meanings described in Hebrews 8 and 9. When we read "thir great Intercessor, came in sight / Before the Father's Throne" we recall Hebrews 9:24: "Christ is not entered into the holy places made with hands, which are figures of the true; but into heaven itself, now to appear in the presence of God for us."[4]

But the achievement of modern commentary of the typological kind goes beyond this annotation of types and antitypes. It isolates typology as an interpretative activity, and it recognizes that by employing the resources of figural interpretation a poet like Milton (or Dante) could create something very like a hermeneutic reality, a world of interpretation that is not gloss or veneer to something else but which acquires the independent status of what Auerbach calls "dramatic actuality."[5] In a moment I shall try to explain why I believe Auerbach's description of figural interpretation covers something less than the interpretative reality presented in *Paradise Lost*. But in spite of the many attempts to improve on his formulations, Auerbach's account still represents the most significant crystallization in our understanding of typology as interpretative mode:

Figural interpretation establishes a connection between two events or persons, the first of which signifies not only itself but also the second, while the second encompasses or fulfills the first. The two poles of the figure are separate in time, but both, being real events or figures, are within time, within the stream of historical life. Only the understanding of the two persons or events is a spiritual act, but this spiritual act deals with concrete events whether past, present, or future, and not with concepts or abstractions; these are quite secondary, since promise and fulfillment are real historical events, which have either happened in the incarnation of the Word, or will happen in the second coming.[6]

It cannot be doubted that in the opening of Book Eleven of *Paradise Lost* the poet and the Son speak to us from an integral imaginative construct that is significantly related to interpretation of this kind. That is why it can make good dramatic sense for the Son to appear in a *scene of interpretation*. In the moment of redemptive crisis—which, after the fall, is now every moment—the whole cosmos has become an interpretative engine. If we do not grasp the hermeneutic order of reality expressed by the characters and the actions of this text, the lines, which are already marked by their rational as opposed to descriptive images, evanesce into ghostly phrases that have no effectual poetic life: "Grace descending," "Spirit of prayer," "great Intercessor," "better life." Without the visual sight demanded by an Eliot, and uninstructed by the insight provided, at least incipiently, by Auerbach, we may think we are dealing here with a false poetry of statement, one that is grandly sacerdotal in sound but which lacks a cultus that is made meaningful as art. What we need for lines like these, therefore, is a full account of the rites of interpretation within the text, the mediatorial rites which are said to be of climactic significance for mankind. An understanding of typology such as Auerbach gives us makes possible a first quantum leap in our grasp of poetic elements which, as we shall now see, are being accelerated to a new track of meaning.

II

It is with typological structuring, then, that we necessarily begin to define Milton's interpretative order. But the verses summoned up and arranged by Milton in typological relation harbor inner correspondences that are so minute and that suggest a succession of such rapid changes—wheels within wheels whirling in tandem with other wheels within wheels—that we begin to glimpse a pattern of interpretative process that conventional typology alone cannot sustain. Let us examine, for example, Milton's use of the images of the mercy seat, the reedified heart or inner temple, and the heavenly temple—the images from Exod. 25:22, Ezek. 11:19, and Heb. 9:24, respectively, which, as I have suggested, initially open the passage to traditional typological probing. The relevant phrases in Exodus are "And there I will meet with thee, and I will commune with thee from above the mercy seat, from between the two cherubims" (25:22). Milton's rendering of the mercy seat, with "Prevenient Grace descending" from above emplaced as an integral part of the sacred image, brings to bear upon this image a long tradition of exegesis. Understood or, more properly, *seen* from the vantage point of these inherited meanings, the communing voice is the sacrificial logos which stands "between" opposite poles of symbolized being and thus both mediates between the two Covenants and interposes itself between fallen man and the penalty required by the Law.[7] The presence of this particular logos is paradoxically felt in its self-obliteration—in its crucifixion on earth, as earlier in its kenosis in heaven. In Milton's lines the cogency of the logos in "the Mercy-seat above" is pressed into service as an inference from such functioning of the logos in the earthly mercy seat. Thus the same incarnate logos which perfects the structure of the stone temple by standing as sacrifice between its material elements now exercises a similar warrant made clear by Ezekiel. It removes "the stony" from human hearts, and causes flesh-made-spirit or "new flesh Regenerate" to be shaped into the enfolded sanctuary which is the heart of man. Among other things, this deconstruction and reconstruction of the "edified" heart represents in *Paradise Lost* a partial fulfillment of the destiny of "the' upright heart and pure" which in the first moments of the poem the Holy Spirit is said to "prefer / Before all Temples" (I. 17–18). Here in Book Eleven the "new flesh" breathes sighs that accord with the breath of prayer and ascend invisible ("Dimensionless") by the same logos route and in the same medial position ("through Heav'nly doors") to "the Father's Throne" which has now become, as in Heb. 9:24–28, the seat of intercession, sacrifice, and mercy. The Son explains that "these Sighs / And Prayers" of man are the effect of prevenient grace descending, which we know from Paul (Rom. 8:30 and 2 Tim. 1:9) is the Son's being itself. His being as sacrifice or intercession causes the "contrition" (perhaps in the seventeenth-century sense of pulverization) or removal of the stony in man's heart, now once again rendered a fit soil or garden-like sanctuary for God's word.

At this point some readers may be inclined to balk at the superimposition of so many layers of required correspondence. Interpretative mapping of this kind may seem to pin down or seal off Milton's meanings in a way that seems opposed to the liberation of significance effected in Milton's opening of the garden and the temple to the world. Yet, in fact, the immensely intricate structure of interpretation in these lines is calculated to achieve just such a liberation and even to avoid the liability of closure or finite meaning that may be incurred by conventional typological constructions. Before we can see this, however, we must further extend rather than curtail our awareness of the filiations created by the images of mercy seat and reedified heart in the remainder of Book Eleven and in Book Twelve. I will try to do this as succinctly as possible.

III

If we retain a clear memory of the opening of Book Eleven as we read through to the conclusion of *Paradise Lost* (all one massive book in the first edition), we realize that the symbolism of those inductive lines is moved outwards to ever wider spheres of human relevance, very like the mount of Paradise pushed "by might of Waves" to "the op'ning Gulf" of history (cf. XI. 829–33). Milton produces this enlargement primarily in the extended figure of the edified heart.[8] The Son's concluding words in the mercy-seat scene, for example, fulfill and yet suggestively open a related figure that has been held in abeyance until this final moment, which is also the moment of commencement. This is the initial topos of the verse from Ezekiel concerning the removal of the stony from man's heart: "And I will give them one heart." In *Paradise Lost* the Son declares that, having now made his new beginning "with contrition in his heart," mankind shall be "Made one with me as I with thee am one."

This is the Son's prophetic interpretation of the destiny of the heart which has now begun to be renovated. But that final destiny, we know, is far from fulfilled in the poem. Books Eleven and Twelve give us only what Milton calls "wand'ring" motions toward such fulfillment. The most Milton will say about how the mercy of the divine interpreter might redeem the heart of man is to offer us Jeremiah's assurance, transcribed by the author of Hebrews: "this is the covenant that I will make with the house of Israel after those days, saith the Lord; I will put my laws into their mind, and write them in their hearts" (Heb. 8:10; cf. Jer. 31:31–34). Milton further interprets this writing in the heart as being the work of the Comforter and Spirit described by John (14:18; 15:26). And the laws which they inscribe on the heart, Milton believes, are those affirmed by Paul: they represent the law of faith, not works (Rom. 3:27; Gal. 5:6). Thus Michael explains to Adam that

> from Heav'n
> Hee to his own a Comforter will send,
> The promise of the Father, who shall dwell
> His Spirit within them, and the Law of Faith
> Working through love, upon thir hearts shall write.
>
> (XII. 485–89)

"What the Spirit within / Shall on the heart engrave," he adds, itself creates God's "living Temples" (XII. 523–27).

Of course, Milton does not make these late announcements without having given ample notice. Adam's heart is being engraved throughout the course of the prophesied events that lead from the scene of interpretation to mankind's "wand'ring" exit from Eden. Bit by bit, granule by granule, the human heart of stone is being reworked into flesh. After Adam has seen the lazar-house vision, for example, the poet makes this work of transformation quite explicit. "Sight so deform," he exclaims, "what heart of Rock could long / Dry-ey'd behold? *Adam* could not, but wept" (XI. 494–95).

Ultimately the heart within that is being inscribed with redemptive knowledge is commended to Adam as "a paradise within thee, happier far" than the geographical Paradise (XII. 586–87). And this assertion is itself Michael's follow-up to his earlier comment after showing Adam the bodily displacement of the mount of Paradise:

> God attributes to place
> No sanctity, if none be thither brought
> By Men who there frequent, or therein dwell.   (XI. 836–38)

The unusually long telling of Noah's story (almost two hundred lines), which forms the structural center of Books Eleven and Twelve, makes many theological points, but the portability of God's sanctity is one of the most important. The "wondrous Ark" (XI. 819) sent floating through the world is a figure of God's reedified place of sanctity; and the lines quoted above apply equally to the ark and to the mount of Paradise, both wave-borne.

Milton confirms this point (and associates the ark figure with the new Covenant and the renovated human heart) in lines which recapitulate elements of the scene of grace descending to suppliant man. He shows that grace and sanctity have indeed been brought thither by a man who therein dwells:

> from his Ark
> The ancient Sire descends with all his train;
> Then with uplifted hands, and eyes devout,
> Grateful to Heav'n, over his head beholds
> A dewy Cloud and in the Cloud a Bow
> Conspicuous with three listed colors gay,
> Betok'ning peace from God, and Cov'nant new.
> Whereat the heart of *Adam* erst so sad
> Greatly rejoic'd.   (XI. 861–69).

Clearly Adam's heart has now been further inscribed with the message of the new Covenant that is the law of faith. But the rest of his interview with Michael indicates just as clearly that this new writing not only remains incomplete but full of error. Here too the mercy seat defined by the median logos and the heart of man inscribed by God's Word function as precise counterparts to each other. Throughout the last two books the figure of the sanctified temple or ark or mercy seat, which holds out the promise of ultimate fulfillment, does not abide in fixed or fulfilled form. Rather the ark is continually *wandering* and recurringly *exposed* (cf. XII. 333ff.). So too "long wander'd man" is sure to be brought, one day, "Safe to eternal Paradise of rest" (XII. 312ff.). But for the long moment of human history he is still only in the wandering condition of Adam and Eve in the poem's last verses. Wandering or error is a constant feature of the writing of man's heart, as it is an aspect also of the destiny of God's reedified temple. By the end of the poem the two sanctuaries are indistinguishable from each other.

At this juncture it is worth recalling in greater detail that the Spirit which prefers "Before all Temples th' upright heart and pure" is specifically invoked to reconstruct the poet's inner being ("What in me is dark / Illumine, what is low raise and support") so that he may write "to the highth of this great Argument" (I. 17–24). This great argument is not only universal in theme; it is also heavily interpretative. And it has a shape which matches well the high space of the poet's upright heart. This is an entirely appropriate climax to an invocation which begins with the exegetical preposition "Of." The poem's very last words on the human condition, "solitary way," similarly suggest the individual interpretation of the world—guided by Providence and, intermittently, the interlocking of mortal hands—by which each of us necessarily lives. Writing of this tentative, argumentative kind—the only fulfillment of the interpreting Word that Milton gives us—is interminable interpretation as well as misinterpretation and reinterpretation. When we register the facts of the situation as Milton gives them, we realize with something of a shock that even the Son's offer to "interpret" for man suggests only something conditional and continuous. This kind of interpretation is built on meanings which are always open to appeal and to the revisions of mercy. Rather than fix facts here and now, it elucidates potentialities that will develop hereafter and elsewhere.

IV

I return now to Auerbach and typology. The limitations of Auerbach's figural model for the description of Milton's interpretative poetry have been at least implied by some of Milton's typology-oriented commentators, especially those who distinguish Protestant typology from Roman Catholic varieties. Barbara Lewalski, for example, points out that in Books Eleven and Twelve "Adam, in good Protestant fashion, is to do more than simply learn . . . typological theory and the role of Christ as antitype: he . . . lives through, as it were, the experiences of his progeny, exhibiting in himself their miseries, mistakes, and misapprehensions."[9] The errant or erroneous nature of Adam's interpretations is, in fact, part of the poem's core meaning. Adam rises higher and higher in the discipline of shadowy types to truth by a process of trial and error—and further error and further trial. He does not perfect or fulfill truth in the narrative space of the poem, which includes the entire panorama of prophesied human history. Typological fulfillment of the kind described by Auerbach is not Milton's province. Rather, Milton's scene of interpretation resembles the activity of inscription described by Jacques Derrida in "Freud and the Scene of Writing." Derrida devotes his essay to answering the question "what must the psyche be if it can be represented by a text?" In effect Milton, we may say, asks the question, "what must the regenerate heart be if it must be represented by the Word's inscription?" Freud, according to Derrida, reveals "the danger involved in immobilizing or freezing energy within a naive metaphorics of place" and "the necessity not of abandoning but of rethinking the space or topology of this writing." Derrida would have us reenter "a landscape of writing. Not a writing which simply transcribes, a stony echo of mute words, but a lithography before words." Derrida too has Ezekiel in mind.[10] The psyche or the heart as text is in *Paradise Lost* endlessly written. Like the writing described by Derrida, it has spaces and discontinuities and stops; no endings, no fulfillments.

I am suggesting, in still other words, that when we try to see Milton's interpretative figurations through the spectacles of concrete type and concrete, fulfilling antitype we experience a sense of what might be called parallax, of the object displaced in another direction. There cannot be any doubt that typology provides the correct general approach to Milton's interpretative meanings. Typology, as I have tried to suggest, is the living tissue of Milton's philological reality. But we must specify with yet greater exactitude the kind of typology Milton actually assimilates and builds. H. R. MacCallum notes helpfully with regard to Books Eleven and Twelve that the "Protestant bias" of Milton's thought causes "him to emphasize the inward and spiritual nature of the antitype."[11] But how can we describe the special characteristics of this "inward and spiritual nature"? Where is inward? And what is its spiritual force? Milton is not vague on these points. Not only does he place his antitype inwardly and spiritually in the temple-like heart, but he also gives it a specific name, interpreter or interpretation, and he imagines it as an identifiable process, a writing or engraving of the heart which is significantly different from a typology of fulfillment and closure.

Before describing Milton's specific kind of typology let me suggest how it recapitulates a recognizable phenomenon in the historical genesis of typology itself. Auerbach, we recall, speaks glowingly of figural

interpretation as a "fresh beginning and rebirth of man's creative powers." He contrasts this rebirth sharply with what he calls the "spiritualist-ethical-allegorical" method of Philo and Origen. This latter
method, he believes, was imaginatively ineffectual and moribund even
in antiquity.[12] Yet, great and informative as Auerbach's account of figura
surely is, it is also significantly reductive. For not only does the "spiritualist-ethical-allegorical" method manifest its own creative powers in
later poetry (Spenser is perhaps its most forthright exemplar in English
poetry), but it too experienced one of many fresh beginnings in at least
one of the very same texts which are the birthplace of Christian figural
interpretation. This other method supplies the supplementary interpretative factor which we will now try to locate within Milton's typology and its traditions.

We should remind ourselves now that Milton's emphases on the
spatial intervention of the logos within the mercy seat and on the
correlative inscription of the human heart have their origins in the
Epistle to the Hebrews, a work generally regarded (not least by Auerbach) as one of the most typological or figural of New Testament texts.
The logos of Hebrews is the great differentiator and mediator before
the heavenly mercy seat: "For the word of God is quick, and powerful,
and sharper than any twoedged sword, piercing even to the dividing
asunder of soul and spirit, and of the joints and marrow, and is a
discerner of the thoughts and intents of the heart . . . Seeing that we
have a great high priest that is passed into the heavens . . . Let us . . .
come boldly unto the throne of grace, that we may obtain mercy"
(4:12–16). In chapter nine the classic typological model of what is usually called *fulfillment* is itself offered only as a further elaboration of the
interpretative characteristics of the logos that intervenes between the
cherubim. The loud silence of the author of Hebrews about the central
feature of the mercy seat—the logos intercessor—is itself a species of
deferred meaning, a rhetorical *occupatio* or *occultatio* which only emphasizes the invisible activity of the divine intercessor. In verse five we
hear that the author "cannot now speak particularly" of the cherubic
installation on the mercy seat. But as Milton's acquaintance John Diodati recognized (quite conventionally in Milton's age), it is just this
unspoken emplacement which bespeaks the Word's sacrificial efficacy
as claimant on God's mercy.[13] The elaboration of sacrificial types and
antitypes which is the chief business of Hebrews 9, and which Milton
invoked extensively in Book Eleven, is marked by fulfillment of a par-

ticularly absent kind, fulfillment as self-obliterative "mediator" (9:15), sublimed into spirit "now to appear in the presence of God for us" in the mercy seat above (9:24). We must try to go still further in specifying the peculiarly unfulfilled and open (or opened) nature of this spiritual fulfillment. There is an interpretative factor here that still eludes us, both in Hebrews and in Milton's verses.

In *The Philosophy of the Church Fathers* Wolfson significantly revises our picture of the provenience of figural interpretation. He records a dimension of typology that seems to have been unknown to Auerbach by explaining that "the non-literal interpretations of the Old Testament found in the New Testament ... belong to that kind of midrashic interpretation of the rabbis" which is of the "predictive variety." And these "predictive interpretations," he adds, "are all described by terms borrowed from Philo's vocabulary, namely, allegory, type, shadow, and parable."[14] In his *Studies in the History of Philosophy and Religion* he further suggests that in the Epistle to the Hebrews "the Philonic term 'shadow' " and "the Philonic term 'parable' " are used to describe a "Midrashic kind of predictive interpretation."[15] But Wolfson does not tell us what, in his view, the special characteristics of midrash, as found in the rabbis or in Philo, actually are. So we must still press onwards (or inwards), at least one more step.

It may be that in our particular configuration of historical problems—in the understanding of interrelated aspects of typology in Milton and Hebrews—something like a solution or interpreter's key is actually within reach. In addition, it is possible that the same solution sheds some light on the nature of the midrashic interpretation that Wolfson saw as being continuous with typology. I refer to the facts most recently dusted off for close examination by Goodenough, Spicq, and Williamson: namely, that the dividing Word of Hebrews and the entire remarkable picture of the logos as spiritual intercessor or mediator of the mercy seat derived more or less directly from Philo's picture of the dividing logos in the *Quis Rerum Divinarum Heres* and elsewhere. "To His Word, His chief messenger, highest in age and honor," says Philo, "the Father of all has given the special prerogative, to stand on the border and separate the creature from the Creator":

This same Word both pleads with the immortal as suppliant for afflicted mortality and acts as ambassador of the ruler to the subject. . . . God who cannot be shewn [severs] through the Severer of all things, that is his Word, the whole succession of things material and immaterial whose natures appear to us to be knitted together and united. That severing Word, whetted to an edge of utmost sharpness, never ceases to divide . . . the soul into rational and irrational, speech into true and false, sense into presentations, where the object is real and apprehended, and presentations where it is not.[16]

First recognized emphatically in Milton's age, the profound influence on Hebrews of this and other Philonic passages in the same vein, was detailed by Milton's friend Hugo Grotius, the great Dutch scholar, and even published in London in 1660 just as Milton went into high gear in the composition of *Paradise Lost*.[17]

We have seen that Auerbach believed that Philo's "spiritualist-ethical-allegorical" method was irreconcilably opposed to the living historicity of figural interpretation. The historical evidence, however, suggests that he was mistaken. Auerbach's assumptions were logical enough. After all, typology and Philo's variety of interpretation—whether or not we incline, with Wolfson, to identify Philo with a specific historical type of midrash is for our purposes immaterial—seemed to answer to two different historical necessities. Typology, in the form described by Auerbach, expresses the need to interpret the Old Testament in such a way as to close down the interpretative treadmill and to declare the fulfillment of all prophetic figures in Christ. Philo's writings and/or midrash, on the other hand, are symptomatic of a desire to describe a delayed messianic coming. They affirm the continuity of interpretation and even make its endlessness part of the essence of divine meaning. But these two interpretative conditions are not, as Auerbach supposed, mutually exclusive. The fact is that many Christian typologists (especially Protestants), struggling to understand the radically unfulfilled status of divine reality in the interval between Christ's Comings, could and did make use of both figural modes, one within the other. In so doing they tended to affirm Christ's divinity in his kenotic or crucifixional absence, rather than in his fulfilled, historical presence. (The God of the Puritans, it has been suggested, is Christ of the Passion rather than Jesus of Christmas.)[18] Christ is himself the great discerner or interpreter, the nucleus of interpretation which is itself gloriously fissionable.

Philo's model of the dividing logos, and the use ultimately made of it in Hebrews and *Paradise Lost*, may suggest the nature of the supplementary interpretative factor for which we have been searching. The logos interpreted by Philo is bent on fracturing phenomenality. As divine sword or stylus it inscribes the noumenal into the phenomenal.

Philo explicitly aims his conception of a dividing or differentiating logos, like a wedge, against the Greeks', specifically Heraclitus's, logos of phenomenal coincidence. In that sense it anticipates Derrida's critique of logocentricity (the logos of "presence") and his rehabilitation of "writing." For the Heraclitean, says Philo, "God is in a place, not containing but contained"; for him "all things interchange."[19] If, however, we would approach an understanding of divine reality, Philo believes, we must attempt to grasp the logos of God's power not in things but, as the mercy seat shows, in the space or difference between things. Meaning as difference in Philo's view (in this case, very much unlike Derrida's) is intended meaning, intended by God and his agency of differentiation. God's "place" (Hebrew *Makom*) is identified by Philo with this special kind of logos. This logos is a place of absence-as-presence within phenomenal being. For Philo these are the elements of the divine scene of interpretation.

In order to understand Philo and/or Hebrews and/or Milton as fully as possible, it would be helpful to know whether this intervening logos derives from bona fide midrashic sources and, if so, what the meanings of those sources might be. Louis Ginzberg, Harry Wolfson, Samuel Belkin, and Yitzhak Baer suggest that its sources are indeed in many ways historically midrashic. Ephraim Urbach resists these attributions in a most fruitful way. Interestingly enough he concedes the later influence of Philo's logos on the *Pirkei de Rabbi Eliezer*—the one midrashic work which, it has recently been suggested, Milton himself used directly and extensively—via the 1644 Latin translation of William Vorstius.[20] But for purposes of understanding the meanings embedded in Philo's logos, what is particularly fruitful is Urbach's comparison of that logos with what Urbach expounds as a central religious intuition of the Sages with regard to divine place. Urbach objects to an identification of Philo's logos with midrashic or rabbinic conceptions because, in his view, Philo's logos is only allegorized transcendental (or Platonic) "place."[21] But what happens to Philo's meanings, it must be asked, when in Philo's scene of logos intervention, this "place" of immateriality is inserted, like an infinite furrow, between all material existents? What is the religious intuition thus expressed and what might its relation be to rabbinic and non-rabbinic intuitions in the same or related areas of religious experience? These are enormous, ultimate questions which I can only attempt to address by standing awkwardly on the shoulders of giants; by putting, that is, the elements of possible answers in close proximity to each other while also respecting the differences between them. (Some will recognize this as a midrashic technique, others a Derridean one.) My quotations are from Urbach and Derrida:

[For the Sages there is a] tension between the sense of reverence and exaltation that fills the soul of the believer and the feeling of God's nearness and of being drawn to Him in love. The multiplicity of names and titles is not an indication of the absence of a sense of the strong and living reality that marks God's relation to man, but actually expresses a variegated and multifaceted reality. The tension that we have mentioned found its resolution in the pair of epithets *Shamayim* [Heaven] and *Makom* [Omnipresent]. The primary meaning of *Makom* is not space, and is not to be construed as "the most abstract of all terms." Just as "Heaven" is a metonym for "the God of heaven," so is also *Makom* [literally Place] used metonymically and refers to the God who reveals Himself in whatever place He wishes; this epithet thus expresses God's nearness. ... This difference remains firmly entrenched in the Tannaitic sources. ... In all the accounts of the reciprocal relations between Israel and God and in the dialogues between God and individuals or the people of Israel, the dominant epithet is "Omnipresent," even as "Heaven" expresses God's farness and withdrawal from man.[22]

That the present in general is not primal but, rather, reconstituted, that it is not the absolute, wholly living form which constitutes experience, that there is no purity of the living present—such is the theme, formidable for metaphysics, which Freud, in a conceptual scheme unequal to the thing itself, would have us pursue. This pursuit is doubtless the only one which is exhausted neither within metaphysics nor within science. ...

Concerning this nontranscriptive writing, Freud adds a fundamental specification. This specification will reveal: (1) the danger involved in immobilizing or freezing energy within a naive metaphorics of place; (2) the necessity not of abandoning but of rethinking the space or topology of this writing. ...

We have already defined elsewhere the fundamental property of writing, in a difficult sense of the word, as *spacing*: diastem and time becoming space; an unfolding as well, on an original site, of meanings which irreversible, linear consecution, moving from present point to present point, could only tend to repress, and (to a certain extent) could only fail to repress.[23]

Different as they are, Urbach's and Derrida's commentaries point to an intuition which is radically similar. In Urbach's formulation, neither nearness nor distance (or farness) is an adequate or resolved description of God's being. We move towards grasping the-reality-which-is-God only in a difference of terms. Or, as Derrida would say, we experience not the meaning of space but rather the "spacing out of meaning." Derrida writes: "we have just encountered a permeability and a breaching which proceed from no quantity at all. From what then?"[24] The implication that issues from Urbach's formulation is perhaps that the space of meaning caused by such a breaching (the difference that we encounter) is itself the repetition of an originating *impulse* or *act*, a sacred impulsion. When we rethink the space or topology of writing, that is, one possible outcome is that the space emerges as an interpretative act whose "necessity" is closely identified with the sacred itself. Derrida asks, "From what?" What, we might ask, is the "necessity" of his question?

Urbach and Derrida both illuminate a scene of interpretation such as we find in Philo's elaborations of the dividing logos (that is, in its emplaced form), in the Epistle to the Hebrews, and in the opening of Book Eleven of *Paradise Lost*. Diverse as the theological assumptions underlying these texts certainly are, in such scenes a special kind of writing or interpretation intervenes within reality and makes it wholly different, infinitely open. This is a rebirth of creative power of a different kind from the one described by Erich Auerbach. As Milton presents it, the intercession of the logos, His effort to "interpret," is part of a living faith in and of interpretation. In *Paradise Lost* interpretation of this kind is an example of Milton's belief in the ability of the human imagination to emulate divine rationality and Christian redemption in its own acts of reconciliation through separation. Theological meaning of this kind is not secondary interpretation of divine activities manifested elsewhere. Rather this species of interpretative meaning is repeatedly renewed in the imagination's own place of discrimination. According to this kind of faith the sanctuary of mankind's engraved heart must wander and err—must interpret. Only in that special way, Milton suggests, can the human heart achieve unity or oneness with the divine interpreter.

NOTES

1. All citations from *Paradise Lost* are from *John Milton: Complete Poems and Major Prose*, ed. Merritt Y. Hughes (New York: Odyssey Press, 1957).

2. See my *The Dividing Muse: Images of Sacred Disjunction in Milton's Poetry* (New Haven: Yale University Press, 1985).

3. For a convenient listing of modern scholarship, figural and otherwise, on Books Eleven and Twelve of *Paradise Lost*, see Louis L. Martz, *Poet of Exile: A Study of Milton's Poetry* (New Haven: Yale University Press, 1980), p. 326, n. 2.

4. All citations from the Bible are from the Authorized Version.

5. *Scenes from the Drama of European Literature: Six Essays*, trans. Ralph Manheim (New York: Meridian Books, 1959), p. 51.

6. Ibid., p. 53.

7. See, for example, John Diodati, *Pious and Learned Annotations upon the Holy Bible*, 3d ed. (London, 1651).

8. See John S. Coolidge, *The Pauline Renaissance in England: Puritanism and the Bible* (Oxford: Oxford University Press, 1970), pp. 23–54, for an account of Puritan use of the figure of edification.

9. "Typological Symbolism and the 'Progress of the Soul' in Seventeenth-Century Literature," in *Literary Uses of Typology from the Late Middle Ages to the Present*, ed. Earl Miner (Princeton: Princeton University Press, 1977), pp. 103–04. In *Protestant Poetics and the Seventeenth-Century Religious Lyric* (Princeton: Princeton University Press, 1979), pp. 111–44, Lewalski has set the stage for a large-scale redefinition of Protestant typology against the background of sixteenth- and seventeenth-century theology.

10. Jacques Derrida, *Writing and Difference*, trans. Alan Bass (Chicago: University of Chicago Press, 1978), pp. 212, 207; cf. p. 231, where Derrida concludes the essay with a reference to Ezekiel.

11. "Milton and the Figurative Interpretation of the Bible," UTQ 31 (1962), 407.

12. Auerbach, *Scenes from the Drama*, p. 55.

13. See Diodati's comments on Exod. 25:17.

14. *The Philosophy of the Church Fathers: Faith, Trinity, Incarnation* (Cambridge: Harvard University Press, 1964), vol. 1, pp. 40–41.

15. *Studies in the History of Philosophy and Religion*, ed. Isadore Twersky and George H. Williams (Cambridge: Harvard University Press, 1973), vol. 1, pp. 73–75.

16. Philo, *Quis Rerum Divinarum Heres*, xxvi (130–32). See also *Quis Rerum*, xliv, 215, *De Plantatione*, ii (10), and *De Vita Mosis*, xx (197). I have quoted from Philo, trans. F. H. Colson, G. H. Whitaker, and Ralph Marcus, 12 vols. (London: W. Heinemann, 1929–53). For the relationship between Clement and Philo see R. C. Lilla, *Clement of Alexandria: A Study in Christian Platonism and Gnosticism* (Oxford: Oxford University Press, 1971), especially pp. 5ff.; and *The Dividing Muse*, pp. 25–26, 28–29. On Hebrews and Philo see Erwin R. Goodenough, "A Neo-Pythagorean Source in Philo Judaeus," YClS 3 (1932), 117–64, C. Spicq, *L'Epitre aux Hebreux*, 2 vols. (Paris, 1952–53), and Ronald Williamson, *Philo and the Epistle to the Hebrews* (Leiden: E. J. Brill, 1970).

17. Grotius's commentary on Hebrews was first published (as far as I can tell) in Paris in 1646. It was republished in the seventh volume of *Critici Sacri* (London, 1660).

18. See Boyd M. Berry, *Process of Speech: Puritan Religious Writing and "Paradise Lost"* (Baltimore: Johns Hopkins University Press, 1976), pp. 104ff.

19. *Quis Rerum*, xliii (213–14) and *Legum Allegoriae*, iii (7–8).

20. In *The Legends of the Jews* (Philadelphia: Jewish Publication Society of America, 1968), vol. 6, p. 65, n. 333, Louis Ginzberg states that Philo's symbolism of the ark derives from the midrashim, but he does not give details. For the views of Wolfson, Belkin, Baer, and Urbach on this matter, see Ephraim E. Urbach, *The Sages: Their Concepts and Beliefs*, trans. Israel Abrahams (Jerusalem: Magnes Press, 1975), vol. 1, pp. 74–75 and vol. 2, p. 715, n. 35. Golda Spiera Werman, "Midrash in Paradise Lost: Capitula Rabbi Eliezer," MiS 18 (1983), 145–71, presents the case for Milton's use of the Pirkei.

21. *The Sages*, vol. 1, p. 74.

22. Ibid., pp. 71–72.

23. *Writing and Difference*, pp. 212–17.

24. Ibid., p. 205.

HAROLD FISCH

The Hermeneutic Quest in
Robinson Crusoe

I

Of the origins of the novel we may say not that in the beginning was
the word but that in the beginning was the interpretation of the word.
The novel is rooted in exegesis. The dreaming narrator of *The Pilgrim's
Progress* offers a series of adventures for us to interpret. The pleasure
will be not in the adventures so much as in the interpretation. But not
only do we, the readers, interpret his dream; "the man clothed with
Rags" with whom the dream begins is himself an interpreter. We see
him in the opening sentences with a Book in his hand. "I looked and
saw him open the Book, and read therein; and as he read, he wept
and trembled." His journey is in essence a quest for the meaning of
the words in the book. His wrong turns are essentially misreadings,
his victories essentially sound readings indicated by suitable prooftexts
in the margins. His escape from Doubting Castle is by means of the
Key of Promise—a promise to be found in the same book wherein he
had read of the imminent destruction of his city. All these are events
in a hermeneutic journey. It is no wonder that, in setting out on his
pilgrimage, Christian is early on directed to the House of the Interpreter where he sees signs and wonders and is given instruction in how
to decipher them independently. But the sights he sees are themselves
interpretations of further hidden matters. For if Christian is a man with
a book in his hand, then the figure of the Judge and Savior sitting upon
clouds of whom he hears in the last tableau in the House of the Interpreter is himself a man with a book in his hand. The marginal gloss
here directs us to the verses in Daniel which speak of the Ancient of
Days sitting on high on his fiery throne with the Books opened before
him. The Ancient of Days in judging the world is himself a reader and

interpreter, which reminds us of the midrash which says that God looked into the Torah and created the world.[1] We do not get beyond interpretation.[2]

Don Quixote also looked into his prime texts and created his world. His story begins with the reading (or misreading) of earlier stories, such as Amadis de Gaul, Palmerin of England, and the romances of Montemayor. Whilst the barber and the priest may regard the Don's readings as mere folly, we may be forgiven for treating them as strong readings, for in effect he transforms the romances of the fifteenth century with their deeds of incredible chivalry into the stuff of the novel, setting down the feet of their knights-errant on the soil of everyday. The interpreter, like a magician, rubs his lamps and we have new stories for old.

Fielding's *Joseph Andrews*—another early and seminal example of the novel genre—may be regarded as an extended midrash on the story of Joseph and the wife of Potiphar. In fact, it turns out to be more than that, namely, a midrash on a further midrash of Josephus. In his *Antiquities of the Jews* (first published in William Whiston's translation just five years before Fielding's novel) Josephus had provided Fielding with the novelistic exegesis of the Joseph story that he needed.[3] But Fielding's novel is not only biblical exegesis but, as we are told on the title page of 1743, it is also a work in imitation of *Don Quixote*. The Don had gone to battle with the "Poema del Cid" tucked under his arm; Parson Adams takes his Aeschylus with him. Both rueful knights have the misfortune to see their favorite texts burned. Both Joseph Andrews and Don Quixote urge on us the question of whether their prime texts are subverted by interpretation or whether they are enriched and new meaning discovered in them. Joseph's chastity becomes for Fielding the subject of comic burlesque—to that extent the Bible story is turned upside down—but we also have imaginative exegesis of a more serious kind. Towards the end Joseph is restored to his father who turns out to be Mr. Wilson, the man of sorrows. This is clearly the reunion of Jacob and his son Joseph as mediated through Josephus. But it is also the reunion of many fathers with many lost children, in *Cymbeline*, *The Winter's Tale*, and a hundred other romances: the strawberry mark on Joseph's breast is at one with all the tokens and amulets which had enabled the lost children to be found and so many fables to be marvelously concluded. We may say that not only are father and son here happily reunited but many diverse traditions about the reunion of fathers and son are here united! And there is also the happy recognition of other biblical episodes which are brought to bear, midrash-wise, on this reunion. The words of Parson Adams at the sight of Mr. Wilson embracing his long-lost son draw our attention to two passages from the New Testament:

he entred without the least Regard to any of the Company but *Joseph*, and embracing him with a Complexion all pale and trembling, desired to see the Mark on his Breast; the Parson followed him capering, rubbing his Hands, and crying out, *Hic est quem quaeris, inventus est etc.*

The allusion here to the Prodigal Son (Luke 15) is unmistakable, though perhaps Mr. Wilson is more a prodigal father than Joseph is a prodigal son. But the Prodigal Son blends with another figure—that of Christ himself whom Mary Magdalene had sought in the empty tomb (John 20:15). He had addressed her with words which had echoed down the religious drama of the Middle Ages, "Quem quaeritis in sepulchro?" Whom do you seek in the sepulchre? Joseph Andrews becomes something like the risen Christ. It is low-mimetic to be sure, but then in the Christian typological tradition Joseph in Genesis, being sold and betrayed by his brethren, is a low-mimetic version of Christ also. For a brief moment the novel veers towards Christian typology; a lower-case father and son become upper-case Father and Son as the ending resonates with Apocalypse. But this is not the way the novels really work. The eschaton momentarily glimpsed is bypassed as the novel returns us to a very ordinary happy young couple about to celebrate their nuptials. If the novel begins with Lady Booby in naked bed, it ends with Fanny in naked bed. And Joseph, in joining her there, is eschewing any grander mode of endings. From now on, not the vision of the heavenly Jerusalem as in *The Pilgrim's Progress*, but the gratifications of an everyday marriage will provide the proper consummation of novels. And of course marriage, if it rewards us with the sense of an ending, carries much more the sense of a beginning.

II

All this, it may be argued, is comparable to the direction taken in the rabbinical interpretation of the Bible stories. Midrash points to the *Dinglichkeit* of the world we know; it does not translate the concreteness of the Bible episode into the realm of abstraction. Pharaoh's dream will do as our model here. The seven lean kine and the seven fat kine are not metaphors, symbols, but rather graphic instances of the seven years of famine and the seven years of plenty. That is why the Rabbis said that Pharaoh dreamed the dream together with its interpretation.[4] In like fashion Jacob going down into Egypt is seen by midrash to prefigure future exiles. But he does not *symbolize* those future exiles: he *participates* in them, he acts them out. He and they are felt to belong to the same concrete, historical dimension. Midrash establishes such metonymic relationships.[5] Jacob in exile suffers as his children have done down the generations—they are jacobs with a lower-case j. All chaste youths have a touch of Joseph, and all charitable gentlemen have a touch of Abraham. Fielding understood this in designing for us the story of Joseph Andrews and Abraham Adams. They do not point beyond themselves but are rather concrete, discrete instances of the biblical models to which they have reference. If Christian typology sees the tales of Chaucer pointing up to the region of the Trinity, midrash— at least as one of its functions—does the opposite: it prevents the lives of Abraham and Joseph from escaping in to the stratosphere; it brings those figures down to dwell among men. We remember the midrash which describes Joseph's resistance to the seductions of the wife of Potiphar. He might have failed the test except for some physical embarrassments that he had to contend with at the critical moment.[6] As the midrash says repeatedly, speaking even of God and his doings, "To what may this be compared? To a king of flesh and blood . . ."

III

No novel could be more down-to-earth than *Robinson Crusoe*. Speaking of abnormal verbal states (aphasia) involving extreme metonymy, Roman Jakobson remarks that "the reader is crushed with the multiplicity of detail in a limited verbal space."[7] There surely could be no better definition of the effect on us of reading *Robinson Crusoe* or, indeed, any other major novel of Defoe's. The weight of *Dinglichkeit* is sometimes overpowering. We are always talking about things, not symbols. It is the *things* that Robinson manages to drag off the wreck that hold our fascinated attention, the things that he makes or fails to make with his limited skills. The island itself which constitutes his material environment not only imprisons him but somehow imprisons the reader with its manifest substantiality. We may add that it has imprisoned the critics to the point where they have not been able to see the forest for the trees. They have seen Robinson as *homo economicus;* they have not seen him as spiritual voyager. Only in recent years have commentators become aware of the elements of spiritual biography and biblical exegesis in the book, in particular of the overarching theme of exile and deliverance.[8] There is Robinson's "Original Sin" followed by his trials and tribulations, his conversion and repentance, marked by dreams and biblical prooftexts as in *The Pilgrim's Progress.*[9] Indeed, Bunyan and Defoe shared the same Puritan literary tradition. And yet *Robinson Crusoe* is not allegory. It is something else—a moral pilgrimage presented in biblical language with an immense amount of biblical allusion and yet having reference to a person as ordinary as the man next door and inhabiting a universe as palpable as our own.

If, as we have said, the volume of material facts in the novel is almost overpowering, much the same is true of the volume of reflections on biblical episodes and passages. Our concern is with the way these two sets of signs relate to one another. Since one must begin somewhere, I begin with the story of Jonah. This is evoked in connection with Robinson's first voyage. He had gone to sea in defiance of his father's express warning and command. This had been his Original Sin. Like Jonah fleeing to Tarshish, he remains in his cabin in a stupor while the storm rages, coming up to help with the pumps only after he sees the rest of the ship's company at their prayers. Finally, the ship founders off the Yarmouth Roads and Robinson gets ashore with difficulty to be warned by the captain against ever going to sea again: "Perhaps this is all befallen us on your Account, like *Jonah* in the ship of *Tarshish.*"[10]

We remember Father Mapple's sermon on Jonah at the beginning of *Moby-Dick.* The Jonah story has almost equal significance as a controlling image in *Robinson Crusoe,* except that Defoe's novel remains within the boundaries of the quotidian; it does not, like Melville's novel, engage us with the hunting of a primeval monster, with the mystery of evil, or with the wars of the gods. What attracted Defoe to this biblical story was not the prodigy of the great fish but rather Jonah's essential loneliness. Jonah—alone on board ship, in the belly of the fish, keeping his vigil not inside Nineveh but outside it, set apart from the inhabitants—is a figure of radical loneliness. In that he becomes a key to Robinson's condition on the island. It is worth noting some of the details of the Bible story. After being saved from the sea, Jonah proceeds on his journey to Nineveh. The burden that he carries to the inhabitants is the call to repentance. That becomes his essential task. We see him in chapter four outside the city to the east, in the desert in fact, where, like the children of Israel in the wilderness, he builds himself a booth (sukkah) to shelter himself from the fierce heat of the sun. And something else happens to remind Jonah both of his special protection and his special vulnerability. God prepares a gourd (kikayon) to protect him with its foliage but the next day the plant is struck by a worm and withers to nothing. Jonah is left comfortless, lonely, and exposed.

The story of Robinson's many trials on the island may be read as a kind of midrash on Jonah. The island is normally referred to in the book as a desert or wilderness with frequent, explicit reference to the wilderness in which the Children of Israel wandered for forty years. One of Robinson's major preoccupations is the building of a shelter for himself. He scoops out the earth from the side of a rock, making himself a kind of cave in front of which he erects a pallisade containing a tent covered over with thatch. He has another thatched shelter near the center of the island which he calls his "bower." In Part II of the novel, Will Atkins makes himself a home of basket-work. The vulnerability of these sukkot is dramatized when Robinson's first home is threatened by earthquake and later when he fears he will be invaded by wild beasts and by savages. He feels marvelously protected and terribly endangered in turns, as does Jonah and as do the Children of Israel in the wilderness.[11] Here is the biblical polarity which Defoe establishes as the main aspect of Robinson's desert experience—he is chosen for special protection, but he is also singled out for special punishment. This is the condition of biblical man. And the question which he constantly asks himself is that of Moses, Job, Jonah, indeed all the heroes of the Bible, Why am I singled out?[12]

The biblical resonance is specially notable in the matter of the miraculous growth of the barley. Like the gourd which springs up for Jonah, or like the manna in the wilderness, the green blades of barley and rice which Robinson finds springing up in the vicinity of his hut during his first months on the island strike him as miraculous. He is at first moved to thank God for thus providing him with sustenance in "that wild miserable Place" (p. 63). Later his religious thankfulness begins to abate when he discovers that he himself had accidentally emptied out some grains of barley a few weeks earlier thinking they were merely husks. From these eventually he will reap a magnificent harvest of corn. But, in the meantime, his first attempt at sowing is a failure and, like Jonah's gourd, the entire crop withers by drought—to his great vexation. And it is always threatened by birds and beasts. He has to learn what it means to live by the grace of God; that is the nature of the trial in the desert. The question of the psalmist remains with him to be echoed and interpreted four times, each time with a different emphasis, in the course of his long desert sojourn: "Can God spread a Table in the Wilderness?" (Ps. 78:19). The desert is not Bunyan's metaphorical Slough of Despond but a material wilderness and the "table," by metonymy, is the material sustenance, the food by means of which he hopes to survive. These real privations and this real bounty turn out to be ways of understanding the biblical verse.

Robinson is a modern Jonah in a number of other ways. Like Jonah, he is that man who brings the message of repentance to others and is himself recalled to his duty. In his fever he has a terrible dream; he sees "a Man descend from a great black Cloud, in a bright Flame of Fire, and light upon the Ground." The appearance of the man and the accompanying flashes of fire and trembling of the earth recall the vision of the Ancient of Days described to Christian in the House of the Interpreter. And the purpose is similar. The man threatens Robinson with a spear and cries out to him in a terrible voice, "Seeing all these Things have not brought thee to Repentance, now thou shalt die." Like Jonah and like the people of Nineveh, his conscience that had slept so long now begins to awake and he cries out mightily to the Lord: "Lord be my Help, for I am in great Distress" (pp. 70, 73). This recovery of the power to pray is the turning point of Robinson's moral history, having the same force as the parallel moment in the career of Coleridge's Ancient Mariner when, after blessing the water-snakes, he is for the first time enabled to pray. The following day, finding himself somewhat recovered though still very weak, Robinson walks a little way out of his tent towards the shore and, sitting down upon the ground, he gazes upon the sea and sky. Appropriately enough, his religious education now begins with an avowal which echoes the first words of Jonah to the seamen when they ask him to identify himself. Jonah had replied: "I am an Hebrew and I fear the Lord, the God of heaven, which hath made the sea and the dry land." Robinson's searching of divine knowledge likewise begins with a series of questions regarding his own identity and that of his surroundings:

What is this Earth and Sea of which I have seen so much, whence is it produc'd, and what am I, and all the other Creatures, wild and tame, humane and brutal, whence are we? Sure we are all made by some secret Power, who form'd the Earth and Sea, the Air and Sky; and who is that? Then it follow'd most naturally, It is God that has made it all. (pp. 73–74)

There are of course other biblical sources, such as the New Testament parable of the Prodigal Son, at work in the moral history of Robinson Crusoe. I have tried to isolate the Jonah strand because we are directed to this early on by the narrator himself and because Robinson's lonely ordeal first by sea and then by desert exactly parallels that of the biblical prophet, as does the emphasis placed on repentance and the value of prayer. Robinson Crusoe operates for the Western imagination as more than a fictional hero; he is a near-universal paradigm. His lonely trial becomes a fundamental myth, a means of articulating our search for self-understanding and our understanding of reality. It is also a fundamental paradigm for the genre of the novel as it will develop later. It is therefore of special interest to note that Robinson is not only called upon to withstand trials by sea and land but to communicate them to us in words which relate them firmly to a preexisting biblical source.

IV

So far we have argued that this novel proceeds by means of an exegesis of biblical passages and episodes. We must now go one stage further—to the stage of meta-exegesis. For the story not only interprets, it is about interpretation. It is not only that Robinson's doings and the things that happen to him represent an interpretation: he himself is an interpretant,[13] a hermeneut. In this Robinson goes beyond the Ancient Mariner. In Coleridge's poem it is the marginal gloss which carries the interpretation of the mariner's moral history; here in Defoe it is the mariner himself who performs this role. He is at once the object of divine wrath, the man who repents, the mediator of a saving message, and the interpreter of texts and visions. More than that, he is exercised with the problem of interpretation. This, we should remind ourselves, is the way of midrash; it not only interprets, it is about interpretation. David Stern has shown how, in the king-mashal, midrash mirrors its own interpretive activity.[14] We should note too that in the midrash on Jonah, the prophet in the belly of the fish is taken on a conducted tour of some of the more mysterious texts of Scripture.[15] But we do not need to go to midrash: the Bible itself ascribes to its heroes this hermeneutic function. Joseph is the dreamer and, at the same time, the interpreter of dreams. Jonah is asked to interpret the withering of the gourd; Jeremiah is asked to explain the sights shown him at the beginning of his ministry; Ezekiel is charged not only with performing strange signs but with interpreting them. There is a sense in which interpretation is not only a means but an end, a basic property of the spiritual life.

Defoe's book then is not only about a man who undergoes a moral testing on a desert island: it is about the process of interpretation itself, its pitfalls and menaces. His success in sowing his corn and reaping his crop after many years parallels his success in making old words yield a new crop of meaning. "Can God spread a Table in the Wilderness?"— this verse can be glossed: "Can Robinson by the grace of God succeed in translating the canonical text of scripture into the words of a modern fable?" The island provides him with a unique opportunity for this kind of exercise. The stage set is biblical: there is sea and desert, the vision of angels, storm and earthquake. The Bible is placed in his hand and in Protestant fashion he is free to interpret it at will. Indeed, he is left little alternative but to exercise that function. For if he does not find the words and images to comprehend his extraordinary situation, that situation will confound him. Man does not live by bread alone but by the language which he discovers for signifying what is otherwise unsignifiable. And where else should Robinson find that language if not in such a text as Jonah which gives him a key to his own lonely trials and tribulations? It is rather like what Paul Fussell tells us of the desperate need of the soldiers in the trenches in the first World War. They were in search of a language for dealing with their unparalleled mode of suffering. They found it often in Bunyan's *The Pilgrim's Progress*:

It is odd and wonderful that front-line experience should ape the pattern of the one book everybody knew. Or to put it perhaps more accurately, front-line experience seemed to become available for interpretation when it was seen how closely parts of it resembled the action of *The Pilgrim's Progress*.[16]

In a hundred memoirs and diaries Bunyan's "Slough of Despond" becomes the precise image for the warfare in the mud and filth of the trenches in Flanders. Here is a case of symbolic interpretation being reversed and something more like metonymy being restored. Bunyan had spiritualized the biblical Wasteland, the Valley of the Shadow of Death of David's struggles (which in the biblical source meant simply a valley of deep darkness) treating them as metaphysical locations; the men of the Great War reinterpreted them as physical and concrete. They restored the historical moment. They too were engaged in a kind of midrash.

But to return to Robinson and his assumption of the role of hermeneut. This occurs after his meditation on the seashore mentioned above. As night falls, he walks back to his hut fearful that the fever which had brought on his terrible dream the night before will recur. How was he to treat his fever? It occurs to him that in one of his chests he has a roll of tobacco-leaf used in Brazil as a medicine for all manner of ailments:

I went, directed by Heaven no doubt; for in this Chest I found a Cure, both for Soul and Body, I open'd the Chest, and found what I look'd for, viz. the Tobacco; and as the few Books, I had sav'd, lay there too, I took out one of the Bibles which I mention'd before, and which to this Time I had not found Leisure, or so much as Inclination to look into. (pp. 74–75)

The tobacco is not symbolic tobacco—it is the rank weed itself which he uses, laced with rum, to cure his fever. And the words which he finds as he casually opens the book, have as immediate an application to his present condition. They are from Psalm 50: "Call on me in the Day of Trouble, and I will deliver thee, and thou shalt glorify me." The tobacco, it seems, is the material exemplification of the deliverance spoken of in that verse from Psalms. And the two, text and referent, are literally contiguous! Of course the two do not always rest comfortably side by side as in this instance. Sometimes the Book will supervene and sometimes the Tobacco. We will sometimes forget the one and find ourselves totally absorbed in the other. To see them in relation to one another and to find room for both becomes the aim of the novel—indeed, in a manner of speaking, the aim of the whole genre of the novel which Defoe helped to inaugurate. In Jane Austen's novel *Sense and Sensibility*, Marianne Dashwood is delivered in her day of troubles; she overcomes her Giant Despair and is rewarded with love and marriage and an income of two thousand a year. Our job and hers is to mediate between the realms of moral experience and of material fact.

Robinson's first attempt at interpreting the words from Psalms, "Call on me in the Day of Trouble, and I will deliver thee," is according to their literal signification—what the Rabbis called the *peshat*. And the difficulty of this mode of understanding strikes him at once. Was it conceivable that he would pray and then simply be rescued? "The Thing was so remote, so impossible in my Apprehension of Things, that I began to say as the Children of *Israel* did, when they were promis'd Flesh to eat, *Can God spread a Table in the Wilderness?* So I began to say, Can God himself deliver me from this Place?" (p. 75). To expect the verse to implement itself in that automatic fashion seemed illogical and presumptuous. That was on June 28. On July 4 he takes up the Bible again and now, like a good Calvinist, he begins systematically with the New Testament, reading it "seriously" morning and night. This leads him, as he says, to construe the words of that Psalm differently. The key word is deliverance—a Bible word of course—and this becomes from now on the focus for an intense effort of reinterpretation which continues through the novel:

Now I began to construe the Words mentioned above, *Call on me, and I will deliver you,* in a different Sense from what I had ever done before; for then I had no Notion of any thing being call'd Deliverance, but my being deliver'd from the Captivity I was in; for tho' I was indeed at large in the Place, yet the Island was certainly a Prison to me, and that in the worst Sense in the World; but now I learn'd to take it in another Sense: Now I look'd back upon my past Life with such Horrour, and my Sins appear'd so dreadful, that my Soul sought nothing of God, but Deliverance from the Load of Guilt that bore down all my Comfort: As for my solitary Life it was nothing; I did not so much as pray to be deliver'd from it, or think of it; It was all of no Consideration in Comparison to this: and I add this Part here, to hint to whoever shall read it, that whenever they come to a true Sense of things, they will find Deliverance from Sin a much greater Blessing than Deliverance from Affliction. (p. 77)

Here he has moved in the direction of an evangelical theology. Deliverance has to be understood symbolically as deliverance from guilt. But he is betrayed by the phrase "as for my solitary Life it was nothing." Was it really nothing? If so the very substance of the book he is writing is nothing; the accumulation of the details of desolation and exile, the physicality of his dreary environment—all this is nothing. The neat dichotomizing in the last sentence ("they will find Deliverance from Sin a much greater Blessing than Deliverance from Affliction") does not carry conviction. Neither the reader nor the narrator (for the passage has considerable irony) is taken in by this total spiritualizing of the term "Deliverance."

A little later on, musing on a verse from Joshua, "I will never,

never leave thee, nor forsake thee," Robinson takes the evangelical interpretation as far as it will go:

> I began to conclude in my Mind, That it was possible for me to be more happy in this forsaken Solitary Condition, than it was probable I should ever have been in any other Particular State in the World; and with this Thought I was going to give Thanks to God for bringing me to this Place.
> I know not what it was, but something shock'd my Mind at that Thought, and I durst not speak the Words: How canst thou be such a Hypocrite, (said I, even audibly) to pretend to be thankful for a Condition, which however thou may'st endeavour to be contented with, thou would'st rather pray heartily to be deliver'd from; so I stopp'd there. (p. 90)

He dangles the purely spiritual notion of deliverance before our eyes. But good sense prevails over the radical doctrine of Grace and he pulls himself up in time—"I stopp'd there!" That line of interpretation will not get him off the island nor will it get him to the accomplishment of the kind of bourgeois fiction on which he is embarked. He will pray rather for deliverance in a sense compatible with all his actions on the island—his attempts to grow corn, the building of his house, his yearning for society, the desperate and continued boat-building. In fact he oscillates between two kinds of understanding. In moods of relative contentment with his lot, he embraces the spiritual, transferred meaning of deliverance; he finds comfort in the doctrine of Grace, in the thought that through the Book he will achieve deliverance from sin. At other times, especially when the dangers of his situation press closely on him, he seizes upon the historical sense of the words; he is filled with what he terms "the eager prevailing Desire of Deliverance" which he says "master'd all the rest" (p. 156).

In the twenty-fourth year of his stay on the island, he reviews his condition, mental and physical. In spite of religious comforts, he is now constantly disturbed by thoughts of the unwelcome guests who from time to time visit the island to engage in their cannibal feasts. His mind is set wholly on escape: "I look'd back upon my present Condition, as the most miserable that could possibly be, that I was not able to throw myself into any thing but Death, that could be call'd worse" (p. 154). But how to compass his deliverance from the island without compromising his deliverance from sin? For the only practical plan of escape seemed to him to involve slaughtering a group of natives as they landed on the island and seizing one of their number as his slave. Robinson, we must remember, is now a converted Christian, not a savage nor any longer a blaspheming English sailor. He has discovered not only the Tobacco, but also the Book, and from now on his life will necessarily be guided by the Book. But how was it to be interpreted? He will not be saved by the literal meaning pure and simple. He is not likely to be delivered if he simply calls on God in the day of trouble when the savages step on shore. He must also act. But he must act in response to the right signs, the providential signs. It is a little like Hamlet's mood in the last act of his play. "There is special providence in the fall of a sparrow . . . The readiness is all." He must be ready to take up the prompting of that providence.

Interpretation now takes the form of an active cooperation, an active reading of signs. Robinson must learn to act in accordance with the Book and yet he must adapt the Book to his own particular circumstances. This is akin to the casuistry practiced by seventeenth-century divines such as Jeremy Taylor and Joseph Hall.[17] We see Robinson engaged in weighing the response required of him to the arrival of the cannibals. It was difficult to see how he could manage without killing a great many of them: "and this was not only a very desperate Attempt, and might miscarry; but on the other Hand, I had greatly scrupled the Lawfulness of it to me; and my Heart trembled at the thoughts of shedding so much Blood, tho' it was for my Deliverance" (pp. 155–56). He concludes with the sentence already quoted above: "The eager prevailing Desire of Deliverance at length master'd all the rest; and I resolved, if possible, to get one of those savages into my Hands, *cost what it would*" (emphasis added). The last phrase shows him abandoning for the moment the attempt to find a moral interpretation for his proposed actions or a moral basis for the term Deliverance. He will, like so many of the new colonial settlers in their war against the Indians, give up the attempt to square his actions with his conscience or seek a scriptural warrant for what he wants to do. He will say, with Angelo, "Blood thou art blood" and proceed to act out his desires. But this is only for a moment. In the end he finds Friday being pursued by two men intent on killing him. This solves the problem for him. "I was call'd plainly by Providence to save this poor Creature's Life," he declares. He promptly kills the pursuers and saves Friday. This exercise in casuistry is conducted not without a certain irony on Defoe's part.

Robinson faces a similar casuistical problem later on in his twenty-seventh year on the island when he and Friday, armed to the teeth, go to attack six canoe-loads of Indians. Again he asks himself, "What Call?

What Occasion? much less, What Necessity was I in to go and dip my Hands in Blood?" (p. 181). Friday might act because his tribe was at war with theirs. For himself he knows no personal cause to attack them. This is his problem. He decides he will go as near as he can and observe them, gun in hand, and "act then as God should direct." Defoe's irony is unmistakable. Coming close, Robinson finds them about to kill one of their prisoners who is a white man! This "fir'd all the very Soul within me." It was the sign he had been waiting for and so he and Friday attack. They release the prisoner, who turns out to be a Spaniard, and then the three of them fall upon the savages, killing eighteen out of the twenty-two who had come ashore. Another of the prisoners whom they release turns out to be Friday's father. So all is well, the island is now peopled, the enemy is destroyed, and the problem of dealing with the words in the Book has been solved, though at the cost of some little self-deception and a fortunate, ex post facto justification. It is the history in miniature of the Christian settlement of the New World.

Robinson does not really solve the hermeneutic problem. We are left with the feeling that if the transferred, symbolic meaning of "deliverance" is no answer, the direct appropriation of the word to his own immediate needs may likewise result in distortion. He is impaled on the horns of a dilemma. It is of course the Puritan dilemma resulting from the antinomy of Grace and Nature. When we have separated Grace from Nature, Nature will tend to run away with us, as in Paul's letter to the Romans (7:19), and we will sin no matter how hard we try not to. Robinson strives to bring the two together but does not quite succeed. One thing, however, is clear; as long as he is on the island he does not escape the need to grapple with this antinomy, the need to come to terms with the Book which provides him with the indispensable words and images needed to make sense of his situation. There is no alternative to hermeneutics. It seems sometimes that his imprisonment on the island (the term "imprisonment" is obsessively frequent) is also an imprisonment in the text. His island experience constrains him. The role of interpreter is not a comfortable role: it involves him in agonizing choices and contradictions. He will inevitably oscillate between one reading of the word "deliverance" and another. The need to escape from the island becomes, indeed, at one level, the need to escape from the burden of interpretation, from his confinement to the role of interpreter. If only, Robinson seems to say,

I could get away from this island, I could be an adventurer like any other adventurer, I could get into a different kind of book entirely, without carrying on my back the burden of interpretation.

Indeed this is what happens to a great extent in the sequel. In Part II of *The Life and Adventures of Robinson Crusoe*, published in 1719, Robinson, having been delivered from his island, no longer spends many hours each day musing over texts. He has tucked his religion somewhere out of sight and pursues his adventures with a certain innocent reliance on the guidance of Providence and instinct. There is less agonized self-questioning (and also less narrative tension). The task of preaching repentance to the unbelievers on the island is transferred to a French Catholic priest, the Mr. Great-Heart of this novel.[18] The Bible words now seem to flow easily, together with a certain enlightened self-interest. Of course, there is also the danger of self-betrayal. At one point, ironically, we find Robinson, the hero of the faith, the Christian pilgrim of Part I, being pursued as a thief on a stolen ship. It is only his resourcefulness which prevents him from ending his life in ignominy. In Part II there are also renewed references to that Original Sin of wandering which sent him off to sea in the first place. We are made to feel that, unlike Jonah, he has not quite learned the lesson of his trials at Nineveh. His repentance is less than complete. The dénouement is also unlike that of Jonah. Jonah, we remember, is left in the desert at the end to meditate on the answer to the unanswerable questions of the text—we are denied closure. In keeping with the requirements of a Puritan, middle-class imagination, however, Robinson ends his days in peace with a sizable income from his investments in Brazil and his equally profitable adventures in the Far East.

Defoe oscillates then between at least two exegetical poles. There is a third part to the *Life and Adventures*: his long *Serious Reflections During the Life and Surprising Adventures of Robinson Crusoe* (1720). This little-read work takes us away from metonymy into the direction of symbolism and allegory. Defoe had been attacked for inventing so many of the episodes in the original *Life and Adventures of Robinson Crusoe*. His defense is to say that "the Story though Allegorical, is also Historical" (Preface). He prevaricates a little, never defining precisely the boundary between "allegorical" and "historical." He insists, however, that the dreams and other similar episodes in the account of his lonely hero's stay on the island all have a "higher" meaning, and are "designed . . . to the most serious Uses possible." Faith is always served. He ends his *Serious Re-*

flections—a midrash, if you like, on his own earlier novel—with an account of a visionary journey to the "Angelic World," to the Sun and the Planets, citing the example of Milton before him who had used his imagination to envision things quite other than those found in the world we know. He escapes, in short, into outer space.

Read me, he seems to be saying, for the higher truth. But even whilst Defoe affirms this faith in the higher function of the novel, he seems to have his tongue in his cheek. For it is after all not the vision of the Angelic World that we take away from *Robinson Crusoe*, but the vision of a man like ourselves struggling to find a meaning in his lonely existence and doing so with the Bible in one hand and the Tobacco in the other.

MIDRASH AND THE NOVEL—AN AFTERWORD

Midrashim are not novels; equally, myths are not Shakespearean dramas. But literary critics have long ago taken over myth from the anthropologists and archetype from the analytical psychologists without prejudice to the way those terms are still used by the professional specialists. It is recognized on both sides that there is value in stretching terms like these. The value, it would seem, is not only in providing a language for interdisciplinary communications, but in freeing the categories thus displaced from formal boundaries and restrictions and releasing their phenomenological essence. If the myth of Dis and Persephone is relevant to the tragic death of Juliet, then the model of midrash may legitimately be brought to bear on the novel as it grew in the seventeenth and eighteenth centuries. To put the two side by side is not to say anything about midrash as a localized historical institution, nor is it to say anything, strictly speaking, about "the origins of the novel." Instead, by bringing these two categories together, we may light up something more deeply interfused, something about the way in which key words are scrutinized and rescrutinized in both cases; about the way in which stories or hints of stories are generated by the art of interpretation; and about the way in which, both in midrash and the novel, the authors address themselves to the new whilst adhering to what has been transmitted to them from the past.

Why then the novel? Why not see all literature as one big midrash, and by such a gesture of inclusion abolish all useful parameters of discussion? The reason is not far to seek. The novel was essentially a new European genre, unbound by Aristotelian rules of unity and order. Narrative freedom was matched by a tendency to stop and consider the meaning of the narrative, where it had come from, and where it was going. It was in short, in a special sense, interpretive discourse. In the novel we find that textuality (or rather intertextuality) has come of age. This is by now something of a commonplace. Thus Michel Foucault: "Don Quixote's truth is not in the relation of the words to the world, but in that slender and constant relation woven between themselves by verbal signs."[19] Todorov carries the principle back to Boccacio, remarking that "tout récit renvoie à un récit précédent: le récit est toujours un écho de récits."[20] Novels are interpretations of preceding novels; more than that, the novel genre as a whole represents a reinterpretation of other genres, specifically the romance. It is thus a particular kind of fabling, one that is aware of a relation to earlier modes of fabling. The novel, in fact, as it has grown in Europe is a very reflexive genre: it does not merely tell a story; it is about the act of fabling and about interpretation, sometimes obsessively so. *Robinson Crusoe* is a particular example of this and in this too it is a paradigm for the genre as a whole. Robinson's reflexivity is to be found again in Conrad's Lord Jim. He sees himself "as a hero in a book" (chap. 1). Jim's doings become a kind of interpretation of that book. Marlow, the narrator, sets himself to interpret the narrative of Jim's doings. We, the readers, weigh that interpretation and form our own. We never get to the end of what J. Hillis Miller has called "the self-sustaining motion of an unending process of interpretation."[21] It is the very stuff of the novel, the "yarn" that it spins. That word is Conrad's. Yarn is also the image used by Agnon (as Gershon Shaked reminds us)[22] at the beginning of his very midrashic "Agunot" where he speaks of the "thread of grace" that the Holy One weaves endlessly in the world. It is a way of talking about the working of providence; it is also a way of talking about the composition of fictional texts. Emma Bovary is not only a character in a story: she sees herself constantly in relation to other characters in other stories of which her story is, so to speak, the interpretation. We never escape the magic web of intertextuality. That is the peculiar characteristic of the novel: it is also the way midrash works.

We may take an example from the first midrashic comment on the first word of the Bible. It links that word *bereshit* ("in the beginning") with the word *reshit* in Prov. 8:22, "God created me as the beginning of his way, the first of his works of old." *Reshit* there refers to ḥokhmah or

Wisdom which is identified by the midrash with Torah. Thus the midrash on the first word of the Torah tells us that if we try to get behind that first word we find Torah again; we do not get beyond textuality. This particular midrash has sometimes been understood as a logos-formula on the lines of "In the beginning was the Word" (John 1:1). Torah would then become a kind of Platonic or Philonic idea. Efraim Urbach rejects this reading and insists that Torah in this rabbinic saying is here a written text, a body of words and also, of course, a body of commandments.[23] What the midrash is saying, through its play on the words *reshit-bereshit*, is that we do not get beyond the written word in its inexhaustible significance, whether we go forward or backward. It is not in heaven, so that someone should have to go up to heaven to bring it down to us,[24] but here in the words of a book. We play with these words, we even, in a manner, eat them, as Ezekiel the prophet eats the scroll on which the words of his prophecy are inscribed (Ezek. 3:1–4) and it becomes in his mouth like honey for sweetness.

This midrash on Gen. 1:1, however, goes further. It does not only play with words, it actually talks about playing. In the continuation of the passage from Proverbs, likewise cited in the midrash, Torah is pictured as a nursling (or nurse): "Then I was by him as a nursling: and I was daily his delight, playing always before him (*meshaheket lefanav bekhol et*)." (Prov. 8:30). Thus midrash not only plays with words; it points to the idea of such play at the beginning of the discussion. God takes his delight with the words of the Torah and men are invited to do the same. The very following verse in Proverbs makes this point. Wisdom (or Torah, as the midrash understands it) continues with the words: "Playing with the universe, his earth, and my *delights were with the sons of men*." (Prov. 8:31).

The joy of the text is also bound up with what we may term "interpretive bounty." Rabbinic interpretations of Gen. 1:1, for instance, occupy fifty-two pages in Kasher's great collection.[25] The Midrash Haggadol (a thirteenth-century Yemenite compilation) lists eight alternative interpretations of the butler's dream in Gen. 40:10, all of them different and all of them equally valid.[26] All that the butler is told is that he will be reprieved after three days, but the midrash knows of a great many other interpretations reaching forward with promises of hope to the future generations of Israel. In this paradigm, the text being interpreted is already an interpretation—the interpretation of a dream—but this is treated merely as the excuse for a multiplicity of further interpretations none of which is held to be final or exclusive. Some years ago Max Kadushin drew attention to this non-exclusive character of midrash. Essentially, each midrash implies "that other interpretations are possible." He speaks of this as "the principle of indeterminacy."[27] Midrashic statements are, he says, essentially independent of one another; they do not demand to be related to one another by some Aristotelian principle of form and order; they have a "particularistic, atomic character."[28]

Now this interpretive bounty, this essential fertility in the play of the imagination is surely a feature of novels in their relation to earlier stories. Novels too have a quality of non-exclusivity, of indeterminacy. They do not set themselves up, like Milton's great epic, as something final or absolute. If, as I have suggested, *Joseph Andrews* is a kind of midrash on the story of Joseph and the wife of Potiphar, then it is a reading embodied in one concrete human instance, one contingent situation or tangle of situations and, borrowing Kadushin's phrase, we could say that it implies the possibility of any number of other interpretations, involving other tangles equally human and equally contingent. It implies Thomas Mann's freedom of invention in relation to the same story two hundred years later. *Robinson Crusoe*, a midrash on Jonah, implies Melville's freedom of invention in the following century. In short every novel, like every midrash, is a new beginning. It says, "Read me: I am saying what has not been said before; and read me too because I will remind you of what you have read before; and read me too because you will be reminded of me when you read the next story which reminds you of what I remind you of."

Nevertheless, we must be on our guard. Any attempt to harmonize the theory of the composition of midrash with the practice of modern writers or with modern literary theory faces a difficulty so formidable that all that has been said so far is called in question. For the truth is that midrashic statements, however free, are also constrained. The Bible itself provides us with the essential models. Noah in his ark, Joseph in the pit, Ezekiel lying on his side for three hundred and ninety days, Jeremiah in prison, Jonah in the belly of the fish—all these are images of hermeneutic constraint. Midrash is open and yet it is also not open— an aspect overlooked in Susan Handelman's otherwise helpful discussion of rabbinic interpretation and its bearing on modern literary theory.[29] There is a prime text to which midrash has constant, indeed obsessive reference. It is not a matter of intertextuality merely; what we have rather in midrash is the recognition of the unlimited possibilities but also of the unlimited authority inhering in a prime text. Constraint is not the right word either, for what predominates is the joy of recognition. You give the imagination free rein and then back you come triumphantly to the scriptural verse itself, from which all these inexhaustible readings have been derived, with the phrase *hada hu di-khtiv*—There, that is the meaning of what was written! *Bereshit* shines before us, a word never subverted and magnetically drawing to itself the other uses of *reshit* elsewhere in scripture. This constant and joyful reencounter with the prime text is what gives midrash its excitement.[30] This mode of invention depends on a loving intimacy with the words and letters, indeed with the vowel points and variants (*keri* and *ketiv*) of the written word of scripture. That is what is also meant by applying to Torah the verse from Proverbs: "And I was daily his delight, playing always before him." The written word of the Torah remains always in its place, a delight joyfully renewed at every turn.

All this runs counter to at least one important modern theory of literary influence. Harold Bloom conceives of each "strong" poet as needing to kill the father, that is, the precursor text. Blake needed the authority and power of Milton but also needed to purge himself of his dark influence, to create a space for himself against the power of Milton. "The dead poet," says Bloom, "will not consent to make way for others"; nevertheless, the successor poet seeks to displace him and the relationship becomes one of revolt, of antithesis.[31] Elsewhere Bloom enlists the Kabbalah in support of his antithetical theory of poetic influence.[32] This is an interesting notion which it may be helpful to take up again in the light of the contributions of Joseph Dan and Moshe Idel to this volume. But if we wish to use the classical, rabbinic midrash as a model, we need to oppose to the Anxiety of Influence the category that I have here suggested, namely, the Joy of Recognition. The dialectic legitimated by the midrashic model is that of surprise and recognition—the unlimited possibility of new readings which never annuls the loving adherence to what is already known. Not the attempted killing of the father nor the fear of the father killing the child, but the intimate play of child with father as in the verse from Proverbs with which the midrash on Gen. 1:1 opens.

Seen in this light, midrash proves to be a model not easily reconcilable to neo-Freudian literary theory or even to the practice of a majority of writers from the Enlightenment onwards. However problematical such positions turned out to be, what we find in these writers often enough is the revolt against the father and the affirmation of a radical novelty. In this respect, Defoe defines himself as a liminal figure. In *Robinson Crusoe*, he applies himself to an imaginative exploration of the Jonah story, the Exodus, and the passage of the Israelites through the wilderness. The relevant biblical texts are not there to be overthrown but to be recognized and interpreted. We are reminded that he is said to have written out the whole Pentateuch as a boy, thinking that after the Fire of London there might be no more copies of the Bible available. Nevertheless, with Defoe we sense hermeneutic constraint rather than the joy of recognition. True, Robinson delights in the discovery of the Bible among his possessions and the texts in it that helpfully reflect his situation. But weighing on him throughout is the constraint of the island existence itself. He wishes he were away from that island in a place where his existence would not be so obsessively linked with these Bible stories. Perhaps we may say that, in this, Defoe's novel is prophetic of what is to come. Robinson would be delivered from his island and the novel would be delivered from the burden of a prime text. There will be much intertextuality in the novels of his nineteenth- and twentieth-century followers, but there will not be the same obsessive attachment to the words of a scripture (or of Cervantes) in the hope of finding their significance by interpretation. From now on we have a freer climate, perhaps also a greater range of experience—but the joy of recognition and the loving verbal play which depends on that recognition have been largely lost. That is the price that the Enlightenment had to pay for its freedom.

NOTES

1. Genesis Rabbah I 1.

2. Cf. J. Hillis Miller, with special reference to the novel: "Whenever the interpreter thinks he has reached back to something original, behind which it is impossible to go, he finds himself face to face with something which is already an interpretation." "The Interpretation of *Lord Jim*," in *The Interpretation of Narrative: Theory and Practice*, ed. Morton W. Bloomfield (Cambridge: Harvard University Press, 1970), p. 213.

3. Cf. Harold Fisch, "Biblical 'Imitation' in *Joseph Andrews*," in *Biblical Patterns in Modern Literature*, ed. David H. Hirsch and Nehama Aschkenasy (Chico, Calif.: Scholars Press, 1984), pp. 31–42.

4. *Midrash Haggadol on the Pentateuch: Genesis*, ed. M. Margulies (Jerusalem: Mossad Harav Kook, 1975), p. 709 (on Gen. 41:15).

5. Cf. Susan A. Handelman, *The Slayers of Moses: The Emergence of Rabbinic Interpretation*

in *Modern Literary Theory* (Albany: State University of New York Press, 1982), pp. 76–82, on the metonymic mode in rabbinic thought.

6. See Genesis Rabbah LXXXVII 7.

7. Roman Jakobson, *Fundamentals of Language*, 2d. rev. ed. (The Hague: Mouton, 1971), p. 94 (discussing the style of the Russian writer, Gleb Uspenskij).

8. Cf. G. A. Starr, *Defoe and Spiritual Biography* (New York: Goddian Press, 1971), pp. 81–84, 97.

9. Cf. J. Paul Hunter, *The Reluctant Pilgrim: Defoe's Emblematic Method and Quest for Form in Robinson Crusoe* (Baltimore: Johns Hopkins University Press, 1966), pp. 89–90; see also Edwin B. Benjamin, "Symbolic Elements in Robinson Crusoe," *PQ* 30 (1951), 206–11. I take issue, however, with the overly typological emphasis of both Hunter and Benjamin.

10. Daniel Defoe, *The Life and Adventures of Robinson Crusoe, &c.*, ed. Michael Shinagel (New York: Norton, 1975), p. 14. Subsequent citations are from this edition; page numbers are given parenthetically in the text.

11. On this polarity, cf. George W. Coats, *Rebellion in the Wilderness* (Nashville: Abingdon Press, 1968), p. 16 and passim.

12. Cf. *Robinson Crusoe* (p. 51): "Did not you come Eleven of you into the Boat, where are the Ten? Why were not they sav'd and you lost? Why were you singled out?"

13. This term for the interpreter within the text is usefully proposed by Naomi Schor in "Fiction as Interpretation," in *The Reader in the Text*, ed. Susan R. Suleiman and Inge Crosman (Princeton: Princeton University Press, 1980), p. 168.

14. "Rhetoric and Midrash: The Case of the Mashal," *Prooftexts* 1, 3 (1981), 275.

15. Cf. *Yalkut Shimoni*, on Jonah, 550 (1).

16. Paul Fussell, *The Great War and Modern Memory* (London: Oxford University Press, 1975), pp. 138–39.

17. G. A. Starr deals with this aspect of Defoe's writings (though without particular reference to *Robinson Crusoe*) in *Defoe and Casuistry* (Princeton: Princeton University Press, 1971).

18. There is in general, it would seem, a parallel between pt. 2 of *Robinson Crusoe* and pt. 2 of *The Pilgrim's Progress*. The emphasis in both works is on the history of the salvation of the group rather than that of the lonely individual. In Bunyan's sequel too the role of the mediator of repentance is taken over by a pastor-figure, as in the second part of Defoe's novel.

AFTERWORD

19. Michel Foucault, *The Order of Things* (New York: Random House, 1973), p. 48.

20. Tzvetan Todorov, *Grammaire du Décaméron* (Den Haag: Mouton, 1969), p. 12.

21. Miller, "Interpretation of Lord Jim," p. 227.

22. See his "Midrash and Narrative: Agnon's 'Agunot,' " in this volume.

23. E. Urbach, *The Sages: Their Concepts and Beliefs*, trans. I. Abrahams (Jerusalem: Magnes Press, 1975), pp. 199–201.

24. Cf. Moshe Idel, "Infinities of Torah in Kabbalah," this volume, who points out that here precisely is the difference between midrash proper and the more mystical form of interpretation practiced by some of the kabbalistic masters: "The rabbinic opinion, that the Torah is not to be found in heaven since it was delivered to Moses in its entirety and is thus completely, finitely, in our possession, seems to be rejected by earlier Jewish mystical groups."

25. See M. M. Kasher, *Torah Shelemah* (Hebrew), vol. 1 (Jerusalem: privately published, 5687 [1927]). In the much abridged English version of Kasher's monumental work,

rabbinic comments on Gen. 1:1 occupy fourteen folio pages. M. M. Kasher, *Encyclopedia of Biblical Interpretation*, vol. 1, trans. H. Freedman (New York: American Biblical Encyclopedia Society, 1953), pp. 1–14.

26. *Midrash Haggadol on the Pentateuch: Genesis*, pp. 675–77.

27. M. Kadushin, *The Rabbinic Mind* (New York: JTS, 1952), pp. 131–32.

28. Ibid., p. 112.

29. Handelman, *Slayers of Moses*, pp. 41–42, 80, passim.

30. This kind of excitement is all but lost in L. Ginzberg's great collection, *The Legends of the Jews* (Philadelphia: Jewish Publication Society of America, 1909–38), which, owing to the exigencies of translation, largely irons out the ripples of midrashic word-play and thus loses the closeness of midrash to the verbal texture of the Bible.

31. Harold Bloom, *The Anxiety of Influence* (London: Oxford University Press, 1973), p. 154.

32. Harold Bloom, *Kabbalah and Criticism* (New York: Seabury Press, 1975).

JOSHUA WILNER

Romanticism and the Internalization of Scripture

I

As is well known, the intensity of critical debate in the last ten or twenty years has derived largely from an open questioning of the received distinction between literature and its interpretation. On the one hand, there is a growing interest in the imaginative dimension of exegesis: the freedom of its elaborations, the figurative texture of its own language, its narrative modulations. On the other hand, there is a complementary insistence on the exegetic power of literary texts: the ways in which they "read" other texts, the ways in which they explicate themselves, the ways in which they thematize and sustain reflection on questions of hermeneutic theory. It is, among other things, this concern with the problem of the interpretative imagination which has led to an enlarged interest in midrashic traditions of interpretation.

Why this problematization of the relationship between text and interpretation enjoys at present an institutional sanction is a complex historical question. Certainly the situation is traceable in part to tensions latent in the New Critical emphasis on close reading and the autonomous authority of the literary text. But this partial explanation obviously leads quickly to more fundamental questions. First of all, what are the conditions under which secular literary texts become candidates for this kind of interpretative attention and, second, what are the differences between the kinds of authority ascribed to literature and to scripture?

One habitual answer to these questions, among literary historians, is that literature increasingly assumed autonomous cultural authority in the West as the authority of sacred texts came into question. A crisis in this transitional process is usually located some time in the late eighteenth and early nineteenth centuries and is often defined in terms of a historical dialectic in which Romanticism is the synthesis or outcome of a conflict between belief in the authority of a scriptural tradition and scientific rationalism (or, more generally, "materialism" in the varying meanings of that term). Literature, like religion, in this view, would involve the intrusion into thought and social life of a radical otherness, and the tendency to read more intrinsically would be seen as a response to this radical autonomy. At the same time, the status of the literary text is construed in *opposition* to that of the sacred text, since it apparently abjures both ethical and epistemological claims, retaining only a negative and aesthetic authority—its knowledge of itself as fiction and figure, rather than as positive truth.

M. H. Abrams's encyclopedic and highly influential *Natural Supernaturalism*, which develops and documents an account of Romanticism as a "displaced and reconstituted theology,"[1] may be cited here as representative. In his preface, Abrams first summarizes this view as follows:

It is a historical commonplace that the course of Western thought since the Renaissance has been one of progressive secularization, but it is easy to mistake the way in which the process took place. Secular thinkers have no more been able to work free of the centuries old Judeo-Christian culture than Christian theologians were able to work free of their inheritance of classical and pagan thought. The process—outside the exact sciences at any rate—has not been the deletion and replacement of religious ideas, but rather the assimilation and reinterpretation of religious ideas, as constitutive elements in a world view founded on secular premises. Much of what distinguishes writers I call "Romantic" derives from the fact that they undertook, whatever their religious creed or lack of creed, to save traditional concepts, schemes and values which had been based on the relation of the Creator to his creature and creation, but to reformulate them within the prevailing two-term system of subject and object, ego and non-ego, the human mind or consciousness and its transactions with nature.[2]

Abrams intends, of course, to discredit the idea that Romantic writers simply jettisoned tradition and turned directly to nature and immediate personal experience as their source of imaginative strength. But the force of his own position, I believe, goes beyond the claim that there is a wide-ranging network of correspondences linking Romantic thought to "the centuries old Judeo-Christian culture" out of which it emerged. The thrust of Abrams's account is, more emphatically, to portray Romanticism as *in its very essence* an interpretation or reading of that tradition. The interpretative engagement of Romantic writers with biblical texts and inherited modes of religious thought is, Abrams implies, not simply the *means* by which they arrived at a more or less autonomous system of thought; rather that engagement is the condition of their activity as writers and thinkers.

Given this premise, let us examine now more closely how Abrams distinguishes the Romantic interpretation of biblical tradition from other, prior interpretations of that tradition. His argument, in outline, is that Romanticism is an *internalization* of biblically sanctioned modes of thought and, more specifically, of the historical scheme of creation, fall, and millennial redemption which Abrams presents as definitive of Judeo-Christian thought: in Romanticism, the "design of biblical history"[3] becomes reinterpreted as a drama of consciousness, with the human imagination replacing supernatural intervention as the agency of redemption. Since Abrams is well aware that the history of biblical exegesis offers many instances of comparable interpretative tendencies, he further specifies that the events of the French revolution and its aftermath, in their awakening and betrayal of millennial hopes, played a crucial mediating role in the development of Romantic thought. "Romantic literature," Abrams writes, "differs from [its] theological precedents in that its recourse is from one secular means of renovating the world to another. To put the matter with the sharpness of drastic simplification: faith in an apocalypse by revelation is replaced by faith in apocalypse by revolution, and this now gave way to faith in an apocalypse by imagination and cognition."[4]

As Abrams acknowledges, the clarity of this account may be gained at the cost of oversimplification. Is millennial thinking as distinctive of Judeo-Christian tradition as Abrams claims? Is that tradition internally as homogeneous as he suggests? To raise only the most obvious objection, are Jewish and Christian concepts of biblical history fundamentally equatable, as Abrams implies when he speaks globally of the "biblical design of history"? Is it clear that Romanticism is a *response* to the French revolution rather than the other way around? What of Rousseau, for example, arguably *the* key figure of European Romanticism, who died in 1778, some eleven years before the outbreak of the revolution, and whom Abrams, limiting himself to cultural developments in England and Germany, largely neglects? Has Abrams, in fact, sufficiently distinguished Romanticism as an internalization of the scheme of biblical history from its theological precedents? Insofar as *Natural Supernaturalism* avoids confronting these issues the strength of the book lies in the wealth of historical material which it assembles and collocates rather than in the schematic framework which it uses to organize that material.

At the same time, it must be emphasized that the schematization of intellectual history presented in *Natural Supernaturalism* is by no means peculiar to Abrams. On the contrary, his reliance on the notion of internalization as a principle of historical articulation reflects a view of Romanticism which is both time-honored and widely accepted. In Hegel's historical aesthetic system, for example, which conceptualizes a development from Symbolic through Classical to Romantic art, Romantic art is said to resemble Symbolic art (which includes, for Hegel, representations of God in the Hebrew Bible) in that for both—in contrast with Classical art—the Idea has no adequate material expression; they differ, however, in that for Symbolic art the Idea transcends human consciousness and is therefore abstract and "defective," whereas for Romantic art the Idea is immanent in human consciousness itself. Thus Hegel writes in the introduction to the *Aesthetics*, "In the sphere of the Romantic, the Idea, whose defectiveness in the case of the symbol produced the defect of external shape, has to reveal itself in the medium of spirit and feelings as perfected in itself. And it is because of this higher perfection that it withdraws itself from any adequate union with the external element."[5] The affinities with Abrams's account are limited by the fact, among others, that for Hegel Romantic art comes into being with the advent of Christianity, but this divergence in views is, as will emerge, less decisive than it may seem.

On the assumption that any attitude held in common by Abrams and Derrida is, a fortiori, widely shared, I would also cite, in this connection, the description in *De la grammatologie* of Rousseau's treatment of the relationship between writing and presence as a "modification tout intérieure du schéma platonicien."[6] Rousseau plays an exemplary role in Derrida's historical account precisely because he "repeats the platonic gesture" ("répète le geste platonicien") of subjugating writing to the manifestation of presence in the logos, "en se référant à un autre modèle de la présence, présence à soi dans le sentiment, dans le cogito sensible qui porte simultanément en soi l'inscription de la loi divine."[7] Again the parallel with Abrams is not exact, since the schema which Rousseau's work internalizes is Platonic rather than biblical. But Derrida himself blurs this distinction when he goes on to cite in support of his claims the following passage from Rousseau: "La Bible est le plus sublime de tous les livres ... mais enfin c'est un livre ... ce n'est point sur quelque feuilles éparses qu'il faut aller chercher la loi de Dieu, mais dans le coeur de l'homme où sa main diagna l'écrire."[8]

These accounts differ as to when Romanticism assumes its cultural hegemony, they differ as to what tradition or traditions of thought it assimilates, but they concur in treating Romanticism both as a historical phenomenon and as a particular mode of rhetorical transformation— what we have been calling "internalization." It is this articulation of history and rhetoric which I wish now to examine more closely, in part because it may guide us in further defining Romanticism, but more generally because it conditions the ways in which we think about the distance or difference between scripture and literature.

II

Apart from its associations with a particular historical moment, the schema of internalization, as it is applied by the writers we have referred to, presupposes a certain temporalization of spatial oppositions. In the case of Abrams, for whom internalization is basically a mode of analogical construction, this is not immediately obvious. Since Abrams is primarily interested in exhibiting correspondences and continuities, he tends to alternate between a historical account and a synchronic perspective which examines the structural correspondences between the moments of the historical sequence, while abstracting from the temporal aspect of their relationship. (Thus, for example, the relationship between "secular" and "sacred" in *Natural Supernaturalism* is sometimes a matter of historical derivation, sometimes a matter of structural opposition.) Yet the narrative form of his argument dictates that the relationship between theocentric and psychological interpretative orientations be understood as successive and not simply complementary. The internalized analogical derivative of biblical history is presented not simply as supplementing the account from which it derives, but as taking its place, assuming its authority as a totalizing representation.

The implications of thus temporalizing the relationship between outer and inner may be clarified by way of an example borrowed from Dante's exposition of the fourfold scheme of biblical exegesis in his letter to Can Grande della Scala.[9] Taking as his text the opening verses of Psalm 114, "When Israel went out of Egypt, the house of Jacob from a people of strange language; Judah was his sanctuary, and Israel his dominion,"[10] Dante distinguishes between the "historical or literal" sense, which he defines as "the departure of the children of Israel from Egypt in the time of Moses," and the "moral" sense, which is "the conversion of the soul from the grief and misery of sin to the state of grace." The relationship between these two readings seems analogical: Egypt is to the land of Israel as the state of sin is to the state of grace. There seems to be no intrinsic need to choose between them or to order them hierarchically. The situation is complicated, however, by the inclusion within Dante's interpretative system of an "allegorical" reading (we would speak of a typological reading)[11] which expounds the sense of the passage as "our redemption wrought by Christ." Since Christ's advent marks, among other things and perhaps primarily, the deliverance of the word from its bondage to the historical understanding, this interpretation effectively transforms the text into an allegory prescriptive of its own reading. The relationship of this allegorical reading to the literal meaning of the text can no longer be construed as analogical. (In point of fact, since within the Christian fourfold scheme the moral sense is founded on the allegorical or typological sense, the internalizing analogical reading is based on the allegorical reading and not the other way around, although I have presented them in the reverse order for purposes of exposition.)

The same pattern of complication may be illustrated less anachronistically by reference to Keats's "The Fall of Hyperion," a dream-poem which has usually been read as an allegory of Keats's poetic development.[12] The narrative opens with a description of Keats standing in a bower amid the opulent "refuse of a meal / By angel tasted, or our Mother Eve." Apart from this implicit reference to the garden of Eden, the passage is strongly marked by allusions to *Paradise Lost*, though interestingly, as the lines cited indicate, Keats conflates references to Eve's partaking of the forbidden fruit with references to the meal which Eve serves to Raphael.[13] The most striking aspect of Keats's reworking of his sources, however, is the introduction of the poet himself as a figure within the Edenic enclosure.[14] Keats is not in a garden which is "like" the garden of Eden, but in the very place itself, almost as though he had wandered onto a set after the scene had been shot, but before the props had been cleared away. This powerful act of imaginative appropriation may be considered an internalization of its Miltonic and biblical sources in the sense that it subsumes the epic or mythic scenes within the autobiographical narrative of a dream. The point I wish to emphasize, however, is that the poem not only enacts this transformation, but simultaneously narrates that enactment. No sooner does Keats project himself into this slightly-used-but-in-good-condition paradise, than he repeats Eve's fatal error; Keats eats:

> . . . And appetite
> More yearning than on earth I ever felt
> Growing within, I ate deliciously;
> And, after not long, thirsted, for thereby
> Stood a cool vessel of transparent juice,
> Sipp'd by the wander'd bee, *the which I took,*
> *And pledging all the mortals of the world,*
> *And all the dead whose names are in our lips,*
> *Drank. That full draught is parent of my theme.*
> No Asian poppy, nor elixir fine
> Of the soon fading jealous Caliphat;
> No poison gender'd in close monkish cell
> To thin the scarlet conclave of old men,
> Could so have rapt unwilling life away.
> Among the fragant husks and berries crush'd,
> Upon the grass I struggled hard against
> The domineering potion; but in vain—
> The cloudy swoon came on, and down I sunk
> Like a Silenus on an antique vase.
>
> (ll. 38–56, emphasis added)

Although the language of internalization in these lines is so condensed as to virtually overwhelm interpretation, we can nonetheless discern in them Keats's dramatization of an initiatory and fateful engagement with the potent language of his precursors. Thus, the internalization of a narrative proves to contain within itself the narrative of that internalization.

I have sought by means of these examples to suggest the involuted nature of the relationship between the rhetoric of internalization and the critical discourse about this rhetoric, contrasting this complexity with the seeming clarity of Abrams's historical account, itself a function of his reliance on analogical patterns. Let me now attempt a more general description. The peculiar complexity and power of allegorical readings (and for the moment I will equate allegorizing and internalizing) derives from the fact that they function both as interpretations of a text and as metacritical statements regulating the process of the text's interpretation. The allegorical reading thus effectively confounds the question of its own *interpretative* validity (its truth as a representation of the meaning of the text) with the question of the text's *referential authority* (its truth as a representation of the world). It is as though the authority of the text was such that the rules governing its reading had themselves to be derived from a reading of the text, a reading which would be possible only insofar as it was already guided by the rules which it was seeking to enunciate. The element of circularity or discontinuity implied by this situation is, indeed, to some extent implicit in all interpretation, since statements about what a text means always interact with claims concerning its referential orientation and degree of internal coherence. What distinguishes allegorical readings is the way in which they systematically condense a pervasive hermeneutic condition in a single moment of interpretative crisis. The forcing of this moment of crisis is not intended to resolve interpretative difficulties, which are acknowledged to be insuperable, but to render them, like the leopards in the temple,[15] calculable in advance. The interference of functions which blocks access to the meaning of the text is contained within a narrative which moves from an "understanding" of the text— which is in fact a misunderstanding—via a pivotal moment of inscrutability to its own negative understanding of that inscrutability.

Since the allegorical reading of the text as the narrative of a process of self-understanding is in essence metacritical, it follows that any critical discourse about allegorization will inevitably be implicated, in a more or less coherent manner, in the system of rhetorical transformations which it describes. Thus, for example, in Abrams's account of the historical process by which the biblical story of the fall cedes its place to an internalized, secularized version of that story, one may trace in outline precisely such a secularized version of the fall. And this means that not only the narrative pattern of *Natural Supernaturalism*, but its very historical character, is determined rhetorically (as the transformation of another symbolic structure) before it is determined referentially. More specifically, by portraying the internalization of scriptural authority as an event belonging to a more or less definite historical period, Abrams underscores the contrast on which his account of tradition depends: between a transhistorical core of scripture and the shifting interpretations of that core. Yet, at the same time, the story which he tells is the story of the undoing of that opposition. The historiography of Romanticism thus both registers the paradoxes of textual authority and contains them by narrativizing and historicizing them. It enacts a supplementary repression of residual problems in the attempt to distinguish sharply between scriptural and literary authority, an attempt which is itself undertaken as a means of adjusting tensions within the more general concept of textual authority.

Up to this point, we have primarily been analyzing a certain critical-historical account of Romanticism, stressing the paradoxes and involutions which that account entails. It remains to be asked, however, whether Romanticism's implicit understanding of itself and of its relationship to scripture poses the same problems. Our brief consideration of a passage from "The Fall of Hyperion" suggested that, within limits, this may be so, but to pursue the question further we must undertake a more detailed reading of a Romantic text.

III

The poem I have chosen to discuss, Wordsworth's "My Heart Leaps Up," offers the advantage, for our purposes, of occupying both a central position in the canon and a marginal position in Wordsworthian criticism. Its centrality is attested to first of all by the fact, noted by Frances Ferguson, and F. W. Bateson,[16] that in all the editions of Wordsworth's collected poems which he himself supervised it is the opening poem and, second, by its hold on the public memory. Its marginality can be confirmed by a survey of the critical literature: it is occasionally referred to in passing, but, with the exception of the concluding three lines, which Wordsworth was to incorporate as the epigraph to the Immortality Ode, it is virtually never *read*. One need not, I believe, look far for the reasons behind this critical neglect. The extreme simplicity, even by Wordsworth's standards, of the diction and statement of much of the poem is not of a kind to invite, some would say merit, further comment. Bateson speaks of "those now almost all too familiar lines," but one suspects that they may have always seemed so. Yet the very discrepancy between the poem's critical and canonical standings is itself of interest to the extent that it may suggest a power of utterance in Romantic writing which the dominant critical understanding has difficulty engaging.[17]

Here is the text:

> My heart leaps up when I behold
>   A rainbow in the sky:
> So was it when my life began;
> So is it now I am a man;

So be it when I shall grow old,
  Or let me die!
The Child is father of the Man;
And I could wish my days to be
Bound each to each by natural piety.

Let me first of all emphasize the sacramental aspects of the poem. Its generic mode, insofar as it can be precisely characterized, seems to be that of a creed, that is to say, an iterable (and easily memorized) testimony of faith. (Here again, its place in the collected poems is relevant.) More obviously, its explicit theme is "natural piety," a locution which invites comparison with "natural supernaturalism," the phrase which Abrams borrowed from Carlyle for the title of his book. At the same time, as the poem's final words remind us, Wordsworth's frame of reference is resolutely natural and subjective. If there is a power which binds together first and last things, it is a power in nature and in human feeling and the first and last things are preeminently those of one person's life. The poem thus indeed seems to naturalize the supernatural and to internalize the transcendent, subsuming inherited religious ideas and patterns within a secular outlook.

This perspective also provides a rationale for Wordsworth's "naturalization" of poetic language, a naturalization of which "My Heart Leaps Up" is a prime specimen. The tendency to avoid salient figuration and, more specifically, the eschewal of allegorical diction (in the Coleridgean sense of allegory in its opposition to symbol) would express the poet's rejection of a prior textual authority interposed between himself and nature or himself and the reader, while the implicit belief in the naturalness and universality of Wordsworth's subjective responses would compensate poetically for the relinquished appeal to scriptural authority. The significance of the poem and the aura of its language would derive not simply from its literal statement, but from the seamless integration of that statement with the expression of a subjective, universal truth.[18]

A reading of the poem along these lines could be pursued in greater detail and could be reinforced by reference to a great many other Romantic texts. Nonetheless, the apparent transparency and availability of the poem's language is riddled by complexities which are not easily resolved within the framework of a reading such as I have so far presented. Most obviously, the famous aphorism of line seven, "The Child is father of the Man," which the poem dramatically foregrounds, has an enigmatic, almost oracular force which persists whatever we may decide the line finally means. Similarly, if less conspicuously, the qualifying force of "I *could* wish my days to be . . ." is puzzling in a way that borders on agrammaticality. Again, the grammatical and rhythmic parallelism of lines 3–5 ("So was it . . . So is it . . . So be it . . ."), articulating the continuity of past, present, and future, while in itself quite natural and simple, is also oddly arch and artful, if we consider that it is intended as a syntactic equivalent for the opening image of the rainbow, a connection reinforced by the latent pun by which the rainbow is made to bind together the poet's days. On a more general level, the rhythm of the poem is highly irregular (consider, for example, the rhythmic condensation of line 6, "Or lēt m̃e dīe!" or the broken-backed pentameter of the final line) and its discursive movement is disjointed. (What, for instance, is the logical force of the "And" connecting lines 8 and 9 to line 7?)

But the most significant, from our perspective, of the factors complicating the texture of "My Heart Leaps Up," is the latent allusion to Genesis 9 which may be said to underlie the entire poem: "I do set my bow in the cloud, and it shall be for a token of a covenant between me and the earth." Indeed, our entire reading of the poem and, more broadly, the theoretical and historical debate in which we are involved may be organized around the assessment of this allusion. I am not going to engage here in argument about whether the allusion is *intended* or not. Given such a blanket acknowledgment of indebtedness as Wordsworth's statement that "The grand store-houses of enthusiastic and meditative imagination . . . in these unfavorable times are the prophetic and lyrical parts of the Holy Scriptures, and the works of Milton,"[19] the burden of proof rests with the critic who wishes to deny the relevance of the allusion and not the other way around. What should concern us here is the nature of that relevance. Although this specific question has until recently[20] been largely neglected by the critical tradition, Abrams himself has commented briefly on the allusion, not in *Natural Supernaturalism*, but in the *Norton Anthology*, where he glosses "natural piety" as follows: "As distinguished from piety based on the Scriptures, in which God makes the rainbow the token of his covenant with Noah and all his descendants. The religious sentiment that binds Wordsworth's mature self to that of his childhood is a continuing responsiveness to the miracle of ordinary things."[21]

In this view, the function of the allusion is contradistinguishing:

the specific meaning of "natural piety" is clarified by the play of analogy and difference operating between the biblical text and the poem, a reading which is obviously congruent with the central theses of *Natural Supernaturalism*. But if this is true, the fact that Wordsworth articulates a creed of natural piety by way of a scriptural allusion becomes highly problematic, since the claim to immediacy of experience and to a power of poetic utterance inspired by that immediacy, rather than by the transmitted authority of a tradition, is itself mediated by a reference to that tradition.

Abrams's reading here again points to complications and ambivalences which it does not confront. Let me try to sharpen the issue by falling back, at first, on a familiar vocabulary of linguistic analysis. We say that the word *rainbow* has, to begin with, a certain denotative value, referring to a certain natural object/event/illusion which appears under certain conditions, is many-colored, shaped like a broken or unbroken arc, and so on. Furthermore, the word has a range of connotative values based on the experiences we associate with seeing a rainbow. While these connotations are subjective—we can imagine, as Wordsworth does, seeing a rainbow and not having these feelings—they may nonetheless be universal. On the other hand, the word has connotations which derive from its inscription within the biblical narrative of the flood; these connotations do not seem to be based on experience, but on a very specific scriptural legacy. From this point of view, the problem of understanding the allusion to Genesis in "My Heart Leaps Up" would be the problem of understanding the relationship between these two potentially conflicting orders of connotation.

We may receive guidance in navigating this problem from Geoffrey Hartman's observation that the untimeliness or excessive force of line 6, which formalizes and dramatizes the poem's status as an oath (and which may be read, I would suggest, as a transformation of the common law formula, "So help me God"), "becomes timely again when we recall [the] utterance . . . of the creator when he makes the rainbow a sign of His bond."[22] As we have noted, there is indeed something slightly "off" about the whole poem and, from this point of view, the scriptural recollection itself is untimely insofar as it interposes itself between the poet and his recollection of a childhood response unmediated by scriptural associations. Yet poem and prooftext never set themselves in opposition: we cannot say that the recollection of the biblical text disturbs the synchronization of the poem's moment of utterance with the impulse it recalls, because this relationship is already disturbed. Rather the recollection accommodates the agitations of Wordsworth's language, not by countering them with a more stable and authoritative power of utterance, but by giving them scope and in particular by relieving the pressure to collapse language and experience into a single authoritative moment.

Seen in this way, it becomes clearer that both texts—Genesis and "My Heart Leaps Up"—challenge the adequacy of the linguistic and cognitive distinctions which we have used to "clarify" the problem and that consequently everything depends here on the nuances of reading as they resist the mastery of this conceptual framework. Consider, first of all, the biblical text. God's covenant with the earth is in fact expressed in two forms; first it is uttered, "And I, behold, I establish my covenant with you, and with your seed after you," and then God decrees that the rainbow will be the sign of this promise. In other words, first there is a verbal promise and then God, as it were, puts it in writing—a kind of magic writing, as ephemeral as the spoken word, yet more persistent, in the unpredictability of its recurrence, than an inscription. Thus the institution of the rainbow as the sign of the covenant is not the institution of an arbitrary mark or sign, the meaning of which is codified by a divine decree preserved in the Bible; rather the institution of meaning is limited or conditioned in a certain way by the physical properties of the sign. This sense of limitation is further underlined by the fact that the rainbow will not only remind man of God's promise, but also God himself: "And the bow shall be in the cloud; and I will look upon it, that I may remember the everlasting covenant between God and every living creature of all flesh that is upon the earth."

The implication that God could, in fact, forget his promise is hardly reassuring, but it is also in keeping with the fragility and intermittence of the rainbow-sign. What our recollection of scripture brings to the reading of "My Heart Leaps Up" is the sense that the speaker's response is a response to a kind of promise and also a tacit awareness of the fragility of both promise and response. The precise origin and meaning of the promise remain unspecified: the speaker's movement of response is as much a sign as the rainbow itself and the promise to which he responds is simply the promise that in the future he will be able to respond to that promise. It has no fulfillment other than in its repetition. The experience with which "My Heart Leaps Up" is concerned, then, is not a moment of unmediated perceptual intensity, but an experience of time as pure repetition in which it is impossible to distinguish sensation, memory, and anticipation, one from the other.

Wordsworth's poem both does and does not offer itself to the reader as a repetition of the scriptural promise it recalls. Formally, the poem is a promise or vow ("So be it when I shall grow old, / Or let me die!"). But, first of all, it is unclear to whom this promise is addressed, and, second, the very need to promise introduces an element of doubt and anxiety which is allowed further expression in the restrained wish and uncertain meter of the closing lines. Shall we say that it is these hesitations which distinguish Wordsworth's poetic affirmations from the authority claimed by scripture? It is precisely this question to which the poem offers its quickening, yet hesitant, response.

NOTES

1. *Natural Supernaturalism: Tradition and Revolution in Romantic Literature* (New York: W. W. Norton, 1971), p. 65.
2. Ibid., p. 13.
3. Ibid., p. 32.
4. Ibid., p. 334.
5. This translation may be found in *G. W. F. Hegel on Art, Religion, Philosophy; Introductory Lectures to the Realm of Absolute Spirit*, ed. J. Glenn Gray (New York: Harper & Row, 1970), p. 117.
6. *De la grammatologie* (Paris: Editions de Minuit, 1967), p. 30. It should go without saying that the questions which are being raised here about the historicizing rhetoric of *De la grammatologie* are questions which Derrida explicitly solicits. Cf. for example, the italicized claim at the end of the first part that "tous les concepts proposés jusqu'ici pour penser l'articulation d'un discours et d'une totalité historique sont pris dans la clôture métaphysique que nous questionnons ici" (p. 148).
7. Ibid., p. 29.
8. *Lettre à Vernes*, cited in ibid., p. 29.
9. The most readily available (although slightly abridged) translation is to be found in *Critical Theory Since Plato*, ed. Hazard Adams (New York: Harcourt Brace, 1971), pp. 121–23.
10. All biblical references are to the King James Version.
11. It should be noted that Dante uses the term "allegorical" to refer to all of the senses of the Bible which are not literal, as well as to a specific modality of sense. It is the latter which is at issue here, though its centrality to the entire system of interpretation is suggested by the ambiguity of the term.
12. For a thoughtful and detailed reading of the poem along these lines see Stuart M. Sperry's "Tragic Irony in 'The Fall of Hyperion'," reprinted in *English Romantic Poets*, ed. M. H. Abrams (London: Oxford University Press, 1975), pp. 470–85.
13. The reader is referred in particular to Miriam Allott's annotations in the Longman edition of the collected poems (London, 1970).

14. Keats's work offers, of course, many instances of this kind of imaginative projection. Compare, for example, the opening stanza of the "Ode to Psyche."

15. I have in mind here not only Kafka's parable, but also Frank Kermode's discussion of that parable in the introduction to *The Genesis of Secrecy* (Cambridge: Harvard University Press, 1979), which may be seen as studying the institutional *regulation* of textual inscrutability.

16. In Frances Ferguson, *Wordsworth: Language as Counter-Spirit* (New Haven: Yale University Press, 1977), p. 40; and F. W. Bateson, *Wordsworth: A Reinterpretation* (London: Longmans, 1965), p. 41.

17. Geoffrey Hartman's recent essay " 'Timely Utterance' Once More" (in *Deconstruction at Yale*, forthcoming) is an important exception to these claims. Although Hartman's comments on "My Heart Leaps Up" are contained within a reading of the Immortality Ode, they stress the paradigmatic status of the shorter lyric and establish it as a focus of interpretative attention.

18. The authoritative discussion of the relationship between allegory and symbol in Romantic writing is Paul de Man's "The Rhetoric of Temporality," in *Interpretation: Theory and Practice*, ed. Charles Singleton (Baltimore: Johns Hopkins University Press, 1969), to which this paper is extensively indebted. A later essay concerned with related issues is de Man's "Sign and Symbol in Hegel's *Aesthetics*," *CIn* 8 (Summer 1982), 761–75.

19. Preface to *Poems* of 1815, reprinted in *Selected Poems and Prefaces*, ed. Jack Stillinger (New York: Houghton Mifflin, 1965), p. 486.

20. See n. 16 above.

21. (New York: W. W. Norton, 1970), vol. 2, p. 212. Abrams is the editor specifically responsible for the Romantic period, as well as the general editor of the anthology.

22. In " 'Timely Utterance' Once More" (see n. 17 above). The remark is part of a longer argument emphasizing the instability, in Wordsworth, of the pastoral "ideal of harmony or correspondence." See also Hartman's "Poetics of Prophecy," in *High Romantic Argument: Essays for M. H. Abrams*, ed. Laurence Lipking (Ithaca: Cornell University Press, 1981), pp. 15–40, in which Hartman discusses how, in Wordsworth's writing, "The *poet* as reader is shown to have discovered from within himself, and so recreated, a scripture text" (p. 37). At the same time, Hartman relates this discovery to the poet's "entanglement in a certain order of sensations" (p. 18), which involves the "violent harmonizing" of conflicting desires and allegiances.

MYRNA SOLOTOREVSKY

The Model of Midrash and Borges's Interpretative Tales and Essays

> A librarian wearing dark glasses asked him: "What are you looking for?" Hladik answered: "I am looking for God." The librarian said to him: "God is in one of the letters on one of the pages of one of the four hundred thousand volumes of the Clementine."
>
> Borges, "The Secret Miracle"

I

Since the aim of traditional biblical interpretation is to understand the divine thoughts embodied in the Scripture, it does not concern itself with the multiplicity of inscribers of the text nor with the circumstances under which these texts were set down. It deals instead with the Scripture as a single unity. Each constituent text is seen as related to the totality of divine revelation, which is understood as being transmitted by all sacred texts simultaneously as well as by the living tradition of exegesis.

Borges's concept of literature as a totality implies an analogous dissolution of individual authorship. "All authors are one," he writes, associating this idea with a pantheistic vision, according to which all the blessed are one blessed, and all Christians are Christ. This impersonal, ecumenical quality of literature is, he adds, "another witness of the profound unity of the Word."[1] In statements of this kind, Borges the interpreter dissolves into all interpreters and moves from a profane level to that of the divine. It is these interpretative moves which put us in mind of midrash and prompt us to consider the model of midrash as a way of illuminating the activity of his imagination.

Borges's works have been well characterized as "a literature of literature and of thought."[2] His writing persistently calls attention to its own textuality by means of its rich intertextual configuration. "At first sight," says Gérard Genette, "Borges's critical work seems possessed by a strange demon of rapprochement."[3] Genette believes that perhaps the *excessive* idea of literature to which Borges leads us points to an underlying tendency of written works which is necessary for the maintenance and the self-justification of literature itself: a totalitarian Utopia in which the fiction attracts all existing (and non-existing) things into its sphere. It is significant that what remains a utopian tendency in literature is, according to the midrash, already actualized by the Bible, the framework within which all reality subsists, as we read in Genesis Rabbah: "Thus God consulted the Torah and created the world."[4]

Commenting upon Borges's work Walter Mignolo has noted: "Writing which is based on reading, texts which are formed by the decomposition of other texts, are proof of a decentralization, a structure with no center—this is writing understood as production and not as reflection or expression."[5] According to Mignolo, to conceive of an impersonal and eternal author means "to question the former system, its upheaval, to affirm writing as production: not as expression or representation, but as modelization."[6] This intertextual and decentralized unfolding in Borges's work reminds us of the decompositional traits of the midrash, which in order to state the meaning of fragments of the Pentateuchal text turns to fragments of yet other texts. In this way the Bible becomes both a self-referential and omni-explicative text. In the homiletical midrashim—for example, the midrash Vayikra (Leviticus) Rabbah—the proem relates the lectionary verse to other biblical verses, either from the Writings, the Prophets, or the Torah itself. Braude points to the significance of this midrashic textuality: "The reader unfamiliar with Midrash may regard such intense analysis of Scripture as a kind of bibliolatry. For the Rabbis it was no such thing. For them it was one of the several ways of worshipping God and of comprehending the mystery of His providence."[7] Interpretation itself, piece by piece, never daring to dream of fully grasped wholes, is itself part of the fulfillment of God's way. Since the midrash is the metatext of a sacred text, it must apparently revolve around a center (the Scripture as the Word of God). Yet the task of deciphering performed by midrash presupposes the disintegration of this very center and thus triggers an infinite play of signifiers in which, as Bloomfield says, signification and significance are by no means discarded. In midrash, this no-center is both absolute presence and Derrida's "sort of nonlocus in which an infinite number of sign-substitutions [come] into play."[8]

Borges's characteristic metatextuality has usually been understood as an expression of his skepticism. Since literature, this logic goes, cannot possibly embrace all of reality, it can only find refuge within itself. Midrash, on the other hand, turns back repeatedly to the Scripture itself, in endless, partial attempts to perceive and to divulge the total truth embedded in the Bible. But in the light of the points of correspondence between midrash and Borges's writing that we have suggested so far, we must be open to the emergence of yet other similarities. We may yet want to revise our understanding of Borges's literarity.

II

Since the aim of midrash is to reveal the unlimited richness of the Word of God, it brings to the foreground the polysemic nature of the biblical text. Each element of the Bible (letters, words, verses, chapters) is allowed to function as an autonomous unit which has endless possibilities of combination with other units. When a strategy of destructurization is applied to this condition, it provokes the polysemic radiation of the text. Frequently, very different or even conflicting interpretations of the same verse or event appear contiguously,[9] and each of these interpretations is granted equal status. Even a single midrashic exegete may explain a verse in more than one way. Sometimes one authority contradicts another with a seemingly decisive argument, but even then the text or redactor lets the first interpretation stand. The objection does not invalidate it.

The concept of the inherent polysemy of the literary text which nullifies the possibility of a univocal interpretation is one of the arch principles of midrash. It is also central to Borges's work, particularly in those writings in which interpretative activity acquires a kind of self-conscious prominence. In order to consider how this polysemic effect works I will divide a number of his interpretative stories into the following categories: I. exegetical writings, of two types, a) texts which diegetically consist of a variety of versions of a certain discourse, for example, the story "Three Versions of Judas," which explicitly identifies itself as an aggregate of interpretations concerning some statements from the New Testament; and b) texts in which different interpretations are incidentally pitted against each other (in these cases it some-times happens that Borges himself, an authorial substitute, or a narrator emerges as an exegete and indicates his own interpretative prefer-ences); and II. stories which are not themselves exegetical but are de-signed to evoke a variety of interpretations on the part of the reader and thus permit a de-anthropomorphized reading.[10]

"Three Versions of Judas" illustrates a kind of story in which uni-vocal perspective is systematically nullified. For example, the text cites another text, by De Quincey, which substantially modifies the tradi-tional view of Judas as a "universal symbol of betrayal and treachery."[11] According to De Quincey, "Judas reported Jesus to the authorities in order to force him to reveal his divinity and thus incite a vast rebellion against the tyranny of Rome."[12] Judas, in other words, acted in the name of a divine cause which justified his behavior. Nils Runeberg, the protagonist, himself a writer of texts, deepens this process. In the first of his two major compositions, he adopts a metaphysical perspective which suggests a parallel relationship between Judas and Jesus. Judas's lowering himself to become an informer is said to correspond to the sacrifice which is implied by the transformation of the Word into a mortal being.

Since Runeberg's text is refuted by all theologians, he abandons his initial perspective and adopts an ethical criterion which leads him to a new interpretation when he rewrites his first work: because Judas is an apostle, God has provided him with a level of dignity which prevents us from attributing his crime to greed, and thus the cause of his treachery must be traced to the opposite ethical pole: "a hyperbolic and even unlimited asceticism" made him vilify and mortify the spirit as he sought out sins "untouched by any virtue: violation of trust . . . and betrayal" (L, p. 127). Judas sought hell because he considered hap-piness and morality divine attributes not to be usurped by man. This idea is carried to an extreme in Runeberg's second major text, "Den hemlige Frälsaren." God's lowering Himself to a mortal in order to redeem humanity was perfect, total, and that is why He Himself chose to become Judas.

The verses from Isaiah quoted in the story not only support this last notion of Runeberg, but also prove to be the source of yet other interpretations and thus constitute a microcosm, a *mise en abyme*, which reflects the procedure that has been discussed. The citation is from Isa. 53:2–3: "For he shall grow up before him as a tender plant, and as a root out of a dry ground; he hath no form nor comeliness; and when we shall see him, there is no beauty that we should desire him. He is despised and rejected of men; a man of sorrows, and acquainted with grief." Borges's story points out that many consider this verse to describe, and predict, the crucified Christ at the moment of his death. For others, like Hans Lassen Martensen, it is a refutation of the beauty attributed to Christ. In Runeberg's view, it is "the punctual prophecy not of a moment but of a whole atrocious future, in time and in eternity, of the Word made flesh" (L, p. 129).

Borges's second kind of exegetical text can be illustrated by his essay "The Dream of Coleridge," in which the author presents a variety of interpretations of the following remarkable symmetry. In the thirteenth century, the Mongolian emperor Kubla Khan dreams of a palace which he then proceeds to build according to his oneiric vision. Then, in the eighteenth century, Coleridge, knowing nothing about the Emperor's dream, dreams of a poem about that same palace. Borges asks, "which explanation shall we prefer?"[13] and replies:

Those who automatically reject the supernatural (I try, always, to belong to this group) will claim that the story of the two dreams is merely a coincidence, a chance delineation. . . . Others will argue that the poet somehow found out that the Emperor had dreamed the palace, and then said he had dreamed the poem. . . . That conjecture seems reasonable, but it obliges us to postulate, arbitrarily, a text not identified by Sinologists in which Coleridge was able to read, before 1816, about Kubla's dream. Hypotheses that transcend reason are more appealing. One such theory is that the Emperor's soul penetrated Coleridge's, enabling Coleridge to rebuild the destroyed palace in words that would be more lasting than marble and metal. (OI, pp. 16–17)

At the end of his essay, Borges incorporates a new interpretation: "After writing all this, I perceive—or think that I perceive—another explanation. Perhaps an archetype not yet revealed to men, an eternal object . . . is gradually entering the world; its first manifestation was the palace; its second was the poem. Whoever compared them would have seen that they were essentially the same" (OI, p. 17).

Apparently in opposition to the model of midrash, in which all interpretations are considered to be equally authoritative, in some of Borges's writings, the author, authorial substitute, or narrator expresses a preference for one of the suggested interpretations, even though it is couched in relativity and uncertainty. Ana María Barrenechea argues in this regard that Borges's style is consistently marked by doubt and conjecture: "Thus, behind the words, there remains a world in which nothing is certain and nothing provides a support to lean back on."[14] Here we apparently find a contrast between the certainty of midrash, which is based on belief, and Borges's lack of faith. On the other hand, we should point out that the reader's automatic initial acceptance of interpretative preferences which are explicitly announced in the text may itself be revised by a concept proposed by Mercedes Blanco in her analysis of "Parable of the Palace." Blanco suggests that the contradictions among the three different versions presented in the story are only apparent, much as Freud describes the contradictions in dreams: "Even though the three versions of the story are presented as disjunctive, they are, in fact, to be considered as conjunctive." Blanco points out that here, just as in the text of the dream, the distinction Benveniste makes between *discours* and *histoire* is not applicable: "Everything in the text of a dream is to be considered on the same level: there is no difference between the content of the images of the dream and the remarks made by the dreamer when he describes it."[15] This leads us to the possibility of proving that what is apparently disjunctive is in fact compatible and even complementary. The difference between the midrashic model and Borges's procedure would therefore be more apparent than real. Indeed, the similarity leads us towards the heart of Borges's methods.

"The South" is a clear example of my final category, a story which generates a variety of diegetic developments, among which the reader must either choose one or accept them all simultaneously in a de-anthropomorphized reading. The story can be schematized as follows: Development 1: Juan Dahlmann suffers from septicemia and is hospitalized in a sanatorium where he endures infernal suffering; he then recovers and leaves for a ranch he owns in the South; the train leaves him off at an unexpected station; he enters a shop and there an aggressive chap invites him to fight; the owner objects because Dahlmann is unarmed; and then "an old ecstatic gaucho, whom Dahlmann saw as a symbol of the South (of the South which was his own), threw him a bare dagger which fell at his feet."[16] Dahlmann does not know how to use it, but it is "as if the South would have decided that Dahlmann should agree to the duel," and Dahlmann goes out to the plain to die. Development 2: Dahlmann never left the sanatorium, but only dreamed about, or longed for, that death in the open field.

The text provides several hints to support the second interpretation, which is preferred, extratextually, by Borges himself. Another reading, however, that of Jaime Alazraki, rejects Borges's explanation: "the attempt to find a realistic logic in [the idea of] the hallucination leads nowhere in Borges's case, because the narration, no matter how realistic it may be, still transmits another meaning, an intuition which the fabulation itself forges and which is not alien to it."[17] Although in fact there is no necessary contradiction between the realistic nature of a story and the possibility of its symbolic interpretation (Alazraki's "another meaning"), it is undoubtedly important that the reader not allow the literal meaning of Borges's text to be overshadowed by its symbolism. Here again, the special qualities of a midrashic approach to the text are most appropriate. What we need here is an exegesis that actively abets the story in generating all possible interpretations, thus revealing the autonomy of its polysemic values.

III

I pause now to describe in more detail the interpretative strategy of midrash which triggers the polysemic radiation we have been discussing. This consists primarily of the notation of symbolic or indirect meanings (derash) which are seen as arising from the literal or direct meanings (peshat) of the text. These symbolic meanings reveal the spirit of the Scripture. The Talmud (Sanhedrin 34a, in reference to Jer. 23:29) compares these symbolic interpretations to a hammer awakening the latent sparks of a rock.

There is no doubt that the rendering of a symbolic dimension, which is so central to midrash, is also a constant feature of Borges's texts. As Alazraki has pointed out, Borges sees reality sub specie aeternitatis, "that is, not by means of the particular, but by the generic, not by individual beings, but rather by archetypes."[18] In Borges's case, this universalizing tendency is exemplified by stories in which characters recapitulate or even rehearse traditional interpretative schemes, as in "The Gospel According to St. Mark," in which the actors offer one version of the Passion of Christ, or "Guayaquil," in which two contemporary historians mirror the confrontation of Weltanschauungs between San Martín and Bolívar. We can say of Borges, then, what Martha Robert has pointed out with respect to Kafka's work, that the constitutive elements of his stories are "instances of interpretation" in which the symbolic dimension functions as a constructive principle of his texts and frequently absorbs their literarity.[19] In Kafka and Borges both we find heroes who are protagonists of exegesis in search of an archetypal significance which forever eludes them, although their quest itself is rich in significance.

The following examples explicitly illustrate Borges's predilection for what we might call the integration universal. In "The Dead One" the narrator alludes to the symbolic configuration of the text, attributing it to "the man who intertwines these symbols."[20] In "Averroes' Search" Borges exhibits his intention to illustrate a universal idea (a device which is clearly part of the game of the text) by using a particular anecdote:

In the foregoing story, I tried to narrate the process of defeat. I first thought of that archbishop of Canterbury who took it upon himself to prove there is a God; then, of the alchemists who sought the philosopher's stone; then, of the vain trisectors of the angle and squarers of the circle. Later I reflected that it would be more poetic to tell the case of a man who sets himself a goal which is not forbidden to others, but is to him. I remembered Averroes who, closed within the orb of Islam, could never know the meaning of the terms "tragedy" and "comedy." (L, p. 187)

The narrator explicitly turns himself into an interpretative symbol by noting that "I felt, on the last page, that my narration was a symbol of the man I was as I wrote it and that, in order to compose that narration, I had to be that man and, in order to be that man, I had to compose that narration, and so on to infinity" (L, p. 188). This spiralling effect of Borges's universalizing interpretation accords well with the universalizing and particularizing tendencies which coexist dialectically in the midrash. The primary concerns of midrash are both man in general and Jewish man in particular, the world in general and the Land of Israel in particular, redemption in general and redemption of Israel in particular.

Another level of Borges's work which is parallel to the exegetical relation of midrash to Scripture and, therefore, of the darshan, to the continuum of interpretation, is seen in those tales in which a character of the story is the interpreter or, to use Naomi Schor's term, the "interpretant"[21] of symbolic messages. "The Garden of Forking Paths" is a particularly good example of this technique. Stephen Albert, the English sinologist, interprets a labyrinth as symbolizing a book when he deciphers Ts'ui Pên's statement "I am withdrawing to construct a labyrinth" (L, p. 50). This statement becomes synonymous with the previous literal assertion: "I am withdrawing to write a book." Reading a fragment of a letter enables Albert to interpret "my garden of forking paths" (L, p. 51) as symbolic of the chaotic novel which Ts'ui Pên has created. Pên's clearly indexical title not only coincides with that of Borges's story but also refers directly to its own labyrinthian nature. Albert reveals the symbolic interpretative character of Ts'ui Pên's story when he interprets it as a "parable, whose theme is time" (L, p. 53). "The Chief," Yu Tsun's superior, is another commentator, who deciphers the statement that is to be added to the news in the papers about Stephen Albert's death at the hand of Yu Tsun. The Chief thus infers that the mention of the anthroponym actually points to a toponym, a city called Albert, the location of the new British artillery park on the River Ancre.

Another example of the same technique appears in "The God's Script." Here the protagonist makes every effort to interpret the magical sentence which the god wrote on the first day of Creation. His repeated attempts are rewarded, but he will not utter the "formula of fourteen random words (they appear random)" (L, p. 207). As a result he cannot be delivered from his prison and the reader is never given the unspoken knowledge. Here as elsewhere in Borges the interpretative game is its own higher significance, part of a universal impulse that cannot be denied. This impulse does not lead to an arrival or destination.

In midrash too, interpretative historiography functions as a source of symbolic expansion. This procedure involves complementing and amplifying available facts by means of the addition of imaginary configurations such as stories, meshalim, and the like which have an explanatory and clarifying function and exhibit a relation of equivalence to the primary subject or nimshal.[22] Each element of the procedure takes on its own sacred significance. This relation is often indicated by formulas such as "this may be illustrated thus," "this may be compared to," "this being comparable to," or "it is like." In these cases the explanation or apparent solution of the mashal corresponds to a nimshal, which frequently begins with the term "similarly," but the process of finding unending equivalence is sufficient unto itself.

The same phenomenon is affirmed rather than denied by Borges's use of the pseudo-parable. An example of this form is "Parable of the Palace," the title of which identifies it, with apparent innocence, as a parable. Mercedes Blanco interprets the following statement from that story—"Such legends, of course, are no more than literary fictions"[23]—as a denunciation of the lie present in the narration. This lie produces the Liar's Paradox and keeps us in a state of endless irresolution. Blanco concludes, "If a parable is defined as a text that includes the last word of the message it transmits, then 'Parable of the Palace' is the denial of the possibility of such a text, since it designates precisely the incessant reference from one word to another, which should guarantee its truth."[24] In other words, we can say that the pseudo-parabolic nature of the story consists in its incapacity to transmit a nimshal that would finally determine its meaning while the process of incessant reference goes on and on. Midrash uses the parable to clarify a previous context which is partially unknown yet fully existent. Since in Borges's case that context is non-existent, "Parable of the Palace" communicates uncertainty as a more radical or even terminal value, yet the process and values of an interminable referentiality are not abridged. (In Borges's work the status of what we might call the apparent parable—as seen in "The Man at the Threshold"—is quite different. Here something very like positive knowledge is made available.)

Like midrash, Borges's works are marked by symbols with a high degree of semantic stability. Many of them, reinforced by the syntagmatic context in which they appear, stem in obvious ways from an idea of collective memory, for example, the labyrinth as symbol of infinity and of chaos, the library as symbol of the universe, the mirror as that which multiplies and reveals the universe, the fire as demiurge, and the aleph, the Kabbalistic symbol which is the first letter of the Hebrew alphabet and spiritual root of all the other letters, as including in its essence all of the alphabet and thus all the other elements of human discourse.[25] And these are not the only features of a totalizing recall in Borges. We could add, for example, Borges's frequently discussed application of the principle of pertinence even to omissions or textual blanks, his disruption of chronological time to liberate the text from historical reductionism, and the authorial playfulness which retrieves that most elusive aspect of remembering, the tricks which memory and its desires play. Varieties of these phenomena clearly have an important place in midrash, as my colleagues in this volume have explained in some detail.

I would like to conclude by emphasizing what seems to me most distinctive and illuminating in the model of midrash and in the interpretative kind of writing that Borges exemplified. Different as their transcendental and intranscendental intentionalities certainly are, their inherent metatextuality and totalizing interpretative functions exhibit a significant convergence. It is possible that this convergence can be explained in historical terms—by careful study, for example, of Borges's exposure to kabbalistic exegesis—but that is not my concern here. What seems to me important are the correspondences between Borges and midrash in the idea of intertextuality, in the concept of reading not as lineality but as a configuration of textual space, in the notion of destructurization of the text as a condition for deciphering it, and in the arch principle, as I have said, of interpretative metatextuality as the basis of decentralization. Further investigations along these lines might elucidate Borges's demon of rapprochement and the utopian ambience it creates in the light of the midrashic language of intimacy described by David Stern. And the creation or liberation of autonomous or monadic meanings in Borges's exegesis reminds us uncannily of Moshe Idel's analysis of kabbalistic developments from midrash.[26]

Perhaps, after all, the differences between transcendental and intranscendental intentionalities is not of particular significance where midrash and Borges are concerned. Midrash, we have seen, is the metatext of an absolute text, both of which can never be fully possessed. Borges's praxis is functionally similar to this. He describes his own work and his own convergence toward a transcendental-intranscendental literarity when he writes, "the practice of literature sometimes fosters the ambition to construct an absolute book, a book of books that includes all others like a Platonic archetype, an object whose virtue is not lessened by the years" (OI, p. 66)—even though, it seems appropriate to add, it can never be grasped or understood.

NOTES

1. Jorge Luis Borges, *Other Inquisitions*, trans. Ruth L. C. Simms (Austin: University of Texas Press, 1964), p. 12. Hereafter referred to as OI. Unless otherwise indicated all translations are my own.

2. Adolfo Bioy Casares, "Los Libros," Sur 92 (1942), 60.

3. Gérard Genette, "L'Utopie Littéraire," in his *Figures* (Paris: Seuil, 1966), p. 123.

4. Midrash Rabbah, vol. 1, trans. H. Freedman and Maurice Simon, "Genesis" (London: Soncino Press, 1961), p. 1.

5. Walter Mignolo, "Borges, el libro y la escritura," CMHLB 17 (1971), 188.

6. Ibid., p. 190. When Mignolo alludes to the "former system," he means the system of author-book-work, which goes back to Romanticism.

7. *The Midrash on Psalms*, vol. 1, ed. and trans. William G. Braude (New Haven: Yale University Press, 1959), p. xix.

8. Jacques Derrida, *Writing and Difference*, trans. Alan Bass (London: Routledge and Kegan Paul, 1981), p. 280.

9. Joseph Heinemann has noted the presence of contrasts in homiletic midrashim. See "Profile of a Midrash," *JAAR* 39 (1971), 141–50.

10. Regarding this term, see Walter Mignolo, "Emergencia, espacio, 'mundos posibles': las propuestas epistemológicas de Jorge L. Borges," *RI* 43, 100 (1977), 357–79.

11. J. A. Pérez Rioja, *Diccionario de símbolos y mitos* (Madrid: Tecnos, 1962), s.v. "Judas Iscariote."

12. Jorge Luis Borges, "Three versions of Judas," *Labyrinths* [hereafter L], ed. Donald A. Yates and James E. Irby (Middlesex: Penguin Books, 1964), p. 126. The translators of the three stories from *Labyrinths* cited in this paper are James E. Irby (for "Three Versions of Judas" and "Averroes' Search") and L. A. Murillo (for "The God's Script").

13. Jorge Luis Borges, *Otras inquisiciones* (Buenos Aires: Emecé Editores, 1966), p. 28.

14. Ana María Barrenechea, *La expresión de la irrealidad en la obra de Borges* (Buenos Aires: Paidós, 1967), p. 192.

15. Mercedes Blanco, "La parabole et les paradoxes," *Poétique* 55 (1983), 280.

16. Jorge Luis Borges, *Ficciones* (Buenos Aires: Emecé Editores, 1956), p. 195.

17. Jaime Alazraki, *La prosa narrativa de Jorge Luis Borges* (Madrid: Gredos, 1974), p. 128. In a subsequent text, *Versiones. Inversiones. Reversiones* (Madrid: Gredos, 1977), Alazraki changes his point of view and accepts Borges's interpretation, pointing out that it escapes the denotative or literal level in order to become a metaphor of a second meaning.

18. Alazraki, *La prosa narrativa de Jorge Luis Borges*, p. 108.

19. An allusion to Martha Robert is found in Todorov's *Symbolisme et interprétation* (Paris: Seuil, 1978).

20. Jorge Luis Borges, "El muerto" ["The Dead One"], in *El Aleph* (Buenos Aires: Emecé Editores, 1957), p. 29.

21. See "Fiction as Interpretation," in *The Reader in the Text*, ed. Susan R. Suleiman and Inge Crosman (Princeton: Princeton University Press, 1980), p. 168.

22. David Stern has pointed out that a trait of the *mashal* which distinguishes it from other similar literary forms is that it enables the audience to understand by itself what we would consider to be the indirect meaning of the *mashal*. "Rhetoric and Midrash: The Case of the Mashal," *Prooftexts* 1 (1981), 261–91.

23. Jorge Luis Borges, *El Hacedor* (Buenos Aires: Emecé Editores, 1960), p. 42.

24. Blanco, "La parabole et les paradoxes," p. 281.

25. With respect to this, see Gershom G. Scholem, *On the Kabbalah and Its Symbolism* (New York: Schocken Books, 1965). Scholem notes: "To hear the aleph is to hear next to nothing, it is the preparation for all audible language, but in itself conveys no determinate, specific meaning" (p. 30).

26. See Stern's and Idel's essays in this volume.

JILL ROBBINS

Kafka's Parables

In Kafka's unfinished novel *The Castle*, K. visits the Mayor to find out about the terms of his employment as Land Surveyor. The Mayor explains to him at length that no Land Surveyor is needed, and that K.'s being summoned was an error.

> "Allow me, Mr. Mayor, to interrupt you with a question," said K. "Did you not mention once before a Control Authority? From your account of the way things are run here, the very idea that the Control could be lacking makes one feel unwell."
>
> "You are very rigorous," said the Mayor, "but multiply your rigor a thousand times and it would still be nothing compared with the rigor that the Authority imposes on itself. Only a total stranger could ask a question like yours. Is there a Control Authority? There are only Control Authorities. Of course, it isn't their function to hunt out errors in the vulgar sense of the word, for errors don't happen, and even if once in a while an error does happen, as in your case, who can say finally that it's an error?"
>
> "This is something entirely new!" cried K.
>
> "To me it is something very old," said the Mayor.[1]

The Mayor's logic is characteristic of Kafka's writing—a double or triple movement of interpretation that cancels itself out: 1) errors don't happen; 2) K.'s being summoned is an error; 3) who can say finally that it's an error? Here, the movement is further complicated by a question that runs throughout the novel: was K. in fact summoned by the Castle at all? (The first words K. utters upon his arrival are: "What village is this that I have wandered into? Is there a Castle here?")[2] The Mayor himself is not sure if K. was indeed summoned. Shortly after this exchange, the Mayor says: "I don't know whether in your case a decision of this kind happened—some people say yes, others no—but if it had happened, then the summons would have been sent to you."[3]

But the authority of the Mayor—the one who names K.'s being summoned an error and not—is in turn discredited by the Landlady ("The Mayor is a person of no importance," she informs K).[4] Perhaps

265

the statement about the possibility of error, a statement made by one who has no authority, is itself in the mode of error. This suspicion is reinforced by K.'s progressive insight throughout the novel that all his perceptions, all his figurations of the Castle bureaucracy, the Mayor, and the Landlady, may be illusory, that is, in the mode of error. But what if, in a kind of infinite regress, this insight that everything is illusory is itself illusory, the statement that everything is an error also an error? The kinds of conclusions that a reader of Kafka might draw from the larger context of the Mayor's statement about error are hardly encouraging. If the putting into question of the Mayor's authority is not authoritative, if the metadiscursive comment on the status of the Mayor's discourse about error is not free of the error it identifies and denounces, then the possibility of an interpretive metadiscourse on Kafka's writing seems to be discredited in advance.

Interpreters of Kafka will at one time or another come up against the two problems we have tried to identify here. The first, which is exemplified by the Mayor's logic, we might call "Kafka's law." We do this to avoid calling this movement of self-cancellation "paradox," as some commentators have done, thereby reducing this movement to a concept at the expense of its distinctive rhetorical features.[5] Indeed, a more felicitous model for the kind of "logic" that is at work here is summoned up by Freud, when he recounts the joke about the borrowed kettle:

A. borrowed a copper kettle from B. and after he had returned it was sued by B. because the kettle now had a big hole in it which made it unusable. His defence was: "First, I never borrowed a kettle from B. at all; secondly, the kettle had a hole in it already when I got it from him; and thirdly, I gave him back the kettle undamaged."

Freud notes that "Each one of these defences is valid in itself, but taken together they exclude one another. A. was treating in isolation what had to be regarded as a connected whole."[6] In such a treatment, says Freud, "there is no such thing as an either-or, only a simultaneous juxtaposition" (kein Entweder-Oder, nur ein gleichzeitiges Nebeneinander).[7] The discourse of the Mayor, like that of A., the borrower of the kettle, involves a paratactic juxtaposition of mutually exclusive claims. Parataxis (from the Greek word meaning "placing side by side") refers to "clauses or phrases arranged independently, a coordinate rather than subordinate construction," "sometimes ... without the customary connectives."[8] The Mayor and A. place contradictory statements side by side. The connectives that are missing between these statements are logical ones, a gap in thought in violation of the principle of noncontradiction, for example. But a closer look at the Mayor's discourse reveals that its juxtaposition is paratactic on the level of logic only. For the Mayor's discourse does employ subordinate construction and connectives: "Of course, it is not their function to hunt out errors in the vulgar sense of the word, for errors don't happen, *and even if* an error does happen, *as* in your case, who can say finally that it's an error?" On what one could call the level of rhetoric, the Mayor's discourse is, if anything, hypotactic.[9] The simultaneous absence of logical connectives and presence of "rhetorical" connectives in the Mayor's discourse signals what could be a potential tension or mutual interference between logic and rhetoric in Kafka's writing. Perhaps the burden of Kafka interpretation—if it is not to reduce Kafka's writing to mere self-contradiction or self-cancellation—is precisely to read the connectives.

The importance of these connectives, these particles of speech, has been noted by at least two of Kafka's commentators. Horst Steinmetz, for example, has pointed to "the high frequency of conjunctions, adverbial modifiers and prepositions. The texts are shot through with *aber, freilich, allerdings, vielmehr, trotzdem, übrigens, vielleicht*" (but, of course, certainly, rather, in spite of, moreover, perhaps). Steinmetz draws on the work of Herman Uyttersprot, who links the use of these particles to "the interplay between hypothesis and fact that can be seen in almost all the argumentative procedures in Kafka. Given facts are reflected on, hypotheses are won out of them, hypotheses are in turn explained into facts, out of which again hypotheses are derived." Says Uyttersprot, "Every known fact . . . often appears in a bright veil of doubt, every hypothesis, on the other hand, contains something of the rigor of certainty." Uyttersprot, whose study of Kafka's use of particles centers on the occurrence of the word *aber* (but), claims statistical support for his observation that "of all German authors, Kafka uses the adversative conjunction 'aber' by far the most. Indeed, he uses it on the average two and three times more often than all other authors. . . . The cause of this lies in the remarkable complexity of a soul which cannot simply see and feel in a straight line, a soul which didn't doubt and hesitate out of cowardice and caution, but rather out of clear-sightedness. A soul which at every thought, every perception, every assertion, instantly heard a little devil (*ein Teufelchen*) whispering to him:

aber. . . . And then this soul had to write down this devilish 'aber' to our greater 'confusion inside of clarity.' "¹⁰

These particles certainly play a role in the confused clarity of the Mayor's discourse. He moves from fact, "of course (*freilich*), errors don't happen," to hypothesis, "and even if (*und selbst wenn*) an error does happen," to fact, "as (*wie*) in your case," to a question, "who can say finally that it's an error?"

A second problem in the passage with which we began is the status of interpretation in and of Kafka's writing. Interpretation is thematized in this passage not only in the kind of unstable reasoning we find on the part of the Mayor, but, as we recall, in the unreliable discovery that the Mayor's discourse is not reliable, in the nonauthoritative putting into question of the Mayor's authority. If the metadiscursive comment on the Mayor's discourse about error is not free of the error it identifies and denounces, if the metadiscourse is subject to the same error that conditions the discourse that it talks about, then the metadiscourse is no *meta*discourse, and there is a certain return to the Mayor's question, "who can say finally that it's an error?"

Many other examples of this thematization of interpretation in Kafka's writing could be cited: the messages that don't get there in "An Imperial Message"; the exhortation to "Go over" (*Gehe hinüber*) in "On Parables," which is followed by a demonstration of the impossibility of going over;¹¹ the commentary that follows the parable "Before the Law," in which each interpretation that is put forth is in turn discredited. In "Before the Law" we also find the priest's (nonauthoritative) reflection on the status of all particular interpretations: "The scriptures are unalterable and the comments often enough are merely an expression of the commentators' despair."¹²

It is no: surprising then that the bewildering multiplicity of incompatible interpretations has become a topos of Kafka criticism, as well as the suggestion that Kafka's work defies interpretation and thematizes its impossibility. Heinz Politzer is exemplary in this regard when he outlines his method of Kafka interpretation with a motto borrowed from Kafka: "Give it up!" (*Gib's auf!*).¹³ Similarly, Stanley Corngold entitles his critical bibliography on Kafka's "The Metamorphosis" *The Commentators' Despair*.¹⁴ This despair certainly demonstrates an attentive first-level reading of Kafka, but all too often it deteriorates into the smug assurance of a negative knowledge. For example, Politzer argues that Kafka developed the form of the paradoxical parable to demonstrate, in Kafka's words, "that the incomprehensible is incomprehensible, and we knew that already."[15] Corngold, reading the same phrase, writes: "At this point, it is clear, the literary enterprise is seen in its radically problematical character."[16] But a reading of Kafka's "On Parables" would "show" that this kind of *negative* knowledge is precisely not available, especially in the form of a generality. The commentator can make the mistake of believing that something like a negative knowledge can be gained from Kafka's writing, only as long as the nonunderstanding that Kafka's work relentlessly explores is conceived within a hermeneutic model, namely, as the opposite of understanding, as its negative. Returning to the priest's remark about the status of particular interpretations and the interpretation of interpretation, "the comments often enough are merely an expression of the commentators' despair," we might ask: is this despair of hermeneutics a despair that is proper to hermeneutics, that is, something that the interpreter can appropriate? Or, to return to the Mayor's question—"who can say finally that it's an error?"—is there anything like an "I" who can say this?

At stake here is the problem of how one can speak about problems in Kafka criticism. Frank Kermode remarks in *The Genesis of Secrecy* that much commentary takes place according to a revelatory model based on the New Testament's relationship to the Old. Former interpreters are seen, Kermode says, "like the Israelites, men in shadow, possessing a text that only *seemed* to be intelligible,"[17] while the present interpreter reveals the text in all its intelligibility and sees the blindness of the former interpreters with a new, spiritual sight. This pervasive revelatory model, which, one may note, has the structure of a conversion experience, is, simply, hermeneutics. We are certainly working within this model when we discuss the limits of former interpretations of Kafka. But can Kafka's discourse—marked by the oscillation between fact and hypothesis, misunderstanding and understanding—be accounted for by such a revelatory model? In order to pursue the question of models for interpretation, we turn to the reading of Kafka in *The Genesis of Secrecy*.

"Leopards break into the temple and drink to the dregs what is in the sacrificial pitchers; this is repeated over and over again; finally it can be calculated in advance, and it becomes a part of the ceremony."[18] Here we will bypass Kermode's discussion of the parable in terms of the assimilation of an intrusion by a cultus and the intrusion's becoming liturgical, as well as other strong interpretations the parable has received,[19] in order to focus on an interpretation of the parable that thematizes its interpretation. This interpretation is not by Frank Kermode. Following his discussion of the parable, he writes:

Here I will interpolate a reading of the parable by another hand, my wife's. "The letter of the parable," she writes, "masters our freedom to interpret it. The words, we know, must mean more and other than they say; we would appropriate their other sense. But the parable serenely incorporates our spiritual designs upon it. The interpreter may be compared to the greedy leopards. As their carnal intrusion is made spiritual, confirming the original design of the ceremony, so is this figurative reading pre-figured; only complying with the sense, it adds nothing of its own and takes nothing away. In comparing himself to the leopards, the reader finds himself, unlike the leopards, free— but free only to stay outside. Thus dispossessed by his own metaphor, excluded by his very desire for access, he repeatedly reads and fails to read the words that continue to say exactly what they mean."[20]

Kermode's wife (not named in any other fashion) offers a reading of the way in which the parable refers to itself which enjoys, much like her denomination, something like a secondary status in the economy of Kermode's book. Kermode (whose book, incidentally, focuses on interpretive exclusions, and which is dedicated, in the words of Mark, "to those outside") inscribes his wife's discourse—the discourse of one outside a proper name, a discourse about the discourse of the outside—in his book *as* outside. Into his own discourse he interpolates her reading—a reading of the parable that thematizes the reader as "outside," as "excluded by his very desire for access"—and excludes it. Appropriately enough, the reading that Kermode's wife offers—let us, for convenience's sake, refer to her as "Mrs. K."—dramatizes most sharply the problem of how one can speak about the interpretive exclusions that Kafka's writing thematizes.

Mrs. K. opposes the letter of the parable (the words that "say exactly what they mean") to its other, figurative sense (the words that "mean more and other than they say"). "The interpreter may be compared to the greedy leopards. As their carnal intrusion is made spiritual . . . so is this figurative reading pre-figured." The leopards' going from carnal to spiritual is a figure for what the reader does, which is making the "literal" figurative. Thus to interpret the parable is to do exactly what the parable says the leopards do—to make the passage from carnal to spiritual, literal to figurative. In this way the parable figures (and pre-figures) its own interpretation. Mrs. K. then reflects on the status of that insight, of the self-referential reading. "In comparing himself to the leopards, the reader finds himself, unlike the leopards, free—but free only to stay outside." The interpreter, like the leopards, comes from outside the text. But unlike the leopards, who make it inside the text, the interpreter remains outside the text which has again become a letter. In other words, the only recognition that the interpreter gains from this self-referential reading is that he was an intruder, an outsider who remained outside, that his interpretation is superfluous (he is "dispossessed by his own metaphor"); he recognizes himself as excluded.

But is Mrs. K.'s reading of the parable as closed and as self-referential as she seems to imply? Is there not an asymmetry within her analogy between the interpreter and the greedy leopards? "As their carnal intrusion is made spiritual . . . so is this figurative reading *prefigured*." The relationship between carnal and spiritual is a *figure* for what the reader does, which is to pass from literal to figurative. The relationship between carnal and spiritual is itself a *figure* for the relationship between literal and figurative. The asymmetry is that the analogy between carnal/spiritual and literal/figurative is itself based on a *figural* relation, that is, the relationship between literal and figurative. Mrs. K.'s reading knows more about this asymmetry than she does. After saying why the interpreters are *like* the greedy leopards, she says: "the reader finds himself, *unlike* the leopards, free—but free only to stay outside."

The leopards are included in the text by being spiritualized. The reader is included in (and excluded by) the text by being *pre-figured*. The leopards get into the text because they pass from carnal to spiritual. The reader stays outside the text because he passes from literal to figurative. Insofar as the reader's activity is *not* like what the leopards do—drinking up what is in the sacrificial pitchers—insofar as the reader is in a relationship of literal and figurative to a text, (the inscription of) his exclusion from the text is far more radical than Mrs. K. lets on. How is this exclusion to be understood?

Frank Kermode argues that the paradigm for the interpreter's exclusion, including the one we find in Kafka, is authorized by a certain reading of Mark 4: "To you has been given the secret of the kingdom of God but for those outside everything is in parables; so that seeing they may indeed see but not perceive, and they may indeed hear but not understand; lest they should turn again, and be forgiven." The scholarly literature and controversy surrounding this statement ranges from discussions of Mark's theology of secrecy to claims of scribal and redactional errors.[21] Kermode summarizes the two predominant readings this passage has been given as follows: 1) "the stories are obscure on purpose to damn the outsiders"; or, 2) a modified version of what Kermode calls Jesus' "gloomy ferocity," the stories "are not necessarily impenetrable, but . . . the outsiders, being what they are, will misunderstand them anyway."[22]

The interpretive exclusion in and from Kafka's writing can indeed be linked to Mark's theory of parable. But Kafka's work is an outsider's rewriting of New Testament parable, that is, from the point of view of the unredeemed. In other words, the nonredemption in Kafka's work is not simply that of the Jew in the gospel who refuses to accept Christ, but a certain return to an older model of interpretation. That the answer to the question of unredemption, exile, and erring may be formulated in terms of old and new is hinted in the Mayor's final exchange with K.

"errors don't happen, and even if once in a while an error does happen, as in your case, who can say finally that it's an error?"
"This is something entirely new!" cried K.
"To me it is something very old," said the Mayor.

A number of critics, among them Benjamin, Blanchot, Buber, and Politzer, have suggested, in different ways, that Kafka be returned to the Jewish tradition. Benjamin draws an analogy between Hasidic parable and Kafka's writing. Buber talks about Kafka's "Paulinism of the unredeemed." Politzer has suggested that Kafka's style resembles that of the Elohist, as analyzed by Erich Auerbach. It is "fraught with background." Blanchot, who uses metaphors from the Jewish tradition to talk about Kafka's work, suggests that Kafka be read not from the perspective of Christianity, but "from the perspective of Abraham."[23]

Kafka's fragmentary writings on Abraham are then of no small interest. But it is perhaps significant that all the writings by Kafka on Abraham that we possess are glosses on Kierkegaard's Abraham. It is as though Kafka, in order to read the Hebrew Bible, had to read the New Testament first. But before we draw any conclusions from this, a little background for Kafka's readings of Kierkegaard is in order.

Kafka first read Kierkegaard in 1913. He notes, in a diary entry: "As I suspected, his case, in spite of (trotz) essential differences, is very similar to mine. . . . He confirms me like a friend."[24] The similarity that Kafka speaks of here (and elsewhere) is the history of the broken engagement.[25] Kafka, who had proposed to Felice Bauer just two months before, was already regretting his proposal. This twice-broken engagement is documented in Kafka's *Letters to Felice*, which are in length equivalent to nearly his entire novelistic output. Kierkegaard also broke his engagement to Regina Olsen, and generated an excess of texts concerning that rupture. But this similarity "in spite of" (*trotz*)—a characteristic Kafkan preposition—sums up the history of Kafka's reading of Kierkegaard as a history of ambivalences. Four years later, Kafka, who has read more Kierkegaard, says of his friend's *Either/Or* that the book's "hatefulness grows under my hands."[26] A problem of proximity and distance is evident in all of Kafka's writings on Kierkegaard.[27] Kafka's earlier fragments about Abraham all take up Kierkegaard's terminology, despite essential differences. Commenting on these obscure and difficult fragments, Jean Wahl writes: "Kafka directs our attention to two traits of Abraham (but is Abraham not Kierkegaard himself? one might ask). . . . Here Kafka draws a portrait of Kierkegaard. . . . But Kafka does not say: Kierkegaard. He repeatedly speaks of Abraham."[28] Against Wahl's weak explanation for this startling insight (namely, that Kafka saw Kierkegaard in the image of Abraham because the first book he read by Kierkegaard was *Fear and Trembling*), against an idea that Kafka was simply "inspired" by *Fear and Trembling*, one could say that this substitution of proper names poses the question: what kind of return to the Jewish tradition is possible for Kafka? This return is neither unmediated nor nostalgic: when Kafka reads Abraham he can't not read Kierkegaard's Abraham.

But who is Kierkegaard's Abraham? In *Fear and Trembling*, Kierkegaard (or rather the pseudonymous author de Silentio) speaks of a man whose sole wish was "to go along on the three-day journey when Abraham rode with sorrow before him and Isaac beside him."[29] The Bible says:

And He [God] said, "Take now thy son, thine only son, whom thou lovest, even Isaac, and get thee into the land of Moriah; and offer him up there for a burnt-offering upon one of the mountains which I will tell thee of." And Abraham rose up early in the morning, and saddled his ass, and took two of his young men with him, and Isaac his son; and he cleaved the wood for the burnt offering, and rose up, and went unto the place of which God had told him. On the third day Abraham lifted up his eyes and saw the place afar off. (Gen. 22:2–4)[30]

Kierkegaard's versions of Abraham are an attempt to fill in the gaps between verses three and four of the biblical story, between Abraham's early rising and "the third day." They are also answers to a question that Kierkegaard poses of the biblical text: did Abraham communicate the purpose of the journey to Isaac?[31] The final answer that Kierkegaard gives to this question is that Abraham cannot speak, because he cannot make himself intelligible. "The ethical expression for what Abraham did is that he meant to murder Isaac; the religious expression is that he meant to sacrifice Isaac."[32] Abraham's willingness to obey God's command involves renouncing the ethical, which is the general, and with it all possibilities of making himself intelligible. That is why Abraham's answer to Isaac's question—"where is the lamb for the burnt offering?" "God will provide the lamb for the burnt offering my son"— is in the mode of irony, "for it is always irony when I say something and still do not say anything."[33] When Abraham sacrifices the ethical, he also sacrifices the finite, the temporal; he makes the movement of infinite renunciation. But he does not lose his faith, he still has faith in God's promise that "in Isaac thy seed shall be called to thee" (Gen. 21:12). He is a "knight of faith" who makes the movement of faith by virtue of the absurd in such a way that, says Kierkegaard, he "does not lose the finite but gains it whole and intact," in such a way that he "who draws the knife gets Isaac" again. Faith, says Kierkegaard, is this "prodigious paradox" "that makes murder into a holy and God-pleasing act, a paradox that gives Isaac back to Abraham again."[34]

In a letter to Max Brod, Kafka remarks of Kierkegaard's *Fear and Trembling*: "He doesn't see the ordinary man ... and paints this monstrous Abraham in the clouds."[35] Kierkegaard's Abraham is perhaps monstrous because Kierkegaard's Abraham is a murderer, and by antiphrasis, a Cain:

In the moment he is about to sacrifice Isaac, the ethical expression for what he is doing is: he hates Isaac. But if he actually hates Isaac, he can rest assured that God does not demand this of him, for Cain and Abraham are not identical. He must love Isaac with his whole soul. ... Only in the moment when his act is in absolute contradiction to his feelings, only then does he sacrifice Isaac, but the reality of his act is that by which he belongs to the universal, and there he is and remains a murderer.[36]

This disclaimer, and the use of the word "murderer," makes one pause. But Kierkegaard does not say: Cain. He speaks of Abraham.[37]

Kafka's most sustained reflection on Abraham is part of a letter he wrote to Robert Klopstock in 1921:

I could think of another Abraham for myself—who certainly would not make it to a patriarch, not even to an old clothes dealer—who would be ready to fulfil the demand of the sacrifice immediately, with the promptness of a waiter, but who could not bring off the sacrifice, because he can't get away from the house, he is indispensable, the household needs him, there is always something more to put in order, the house is not ready.[38]

Like Kierkegaard, Kafka is involved in the project of thinking Abraham (or Abrahams). Kafka thinks another Abraham, who is so capable, so much in the finite, that he is incapable of leaving the house. And, as Kafka reasons, Abraham did have a house: "if he hadn't had a house, where else would he have raised his son—in which rafter would the sacrificial knife have been stuck?"[39] This is another Abraham, other than the biblical Abraham, other than Kierkegaard's Abraham—or is it? This is not "the monstrous Abraham in the clouds"; it is an Abraham whose ordinariness is stressed. But it is also to some degree an extension of Kierkegaard's description of the knight of faith. The knight of faith has, externally, "a striking resemblance to bourgeois philistinism"; he expresses "the sublime in the pedestrian"; "his gait is as steady as a postman's."[40] But, as Kafka will continue his reasoning: Yes, Abraham had a house, but did he have a son? He says: "It was different for the above-cited Abrahams, who stood in the houses they were building and suddenly were supposed to go up Mount Moriah; possibly (womöglich) they don't even yet have a son, and are supposed to sacrifice him already."[41] Kafka's hypothesis (womöglich) is a devastating one because, for Kierkegaard, it was a fact. Kafka has put his finger on a central embarrassment of Kierkegaard's Fear and Trembling, which lies in the autobiographical allegory of Kierkegaard's broken engagement.[42] This autobiographical allegory is based on the analogy: As Abraham sacrificed Isaac, so Kierkegaard sacrificed Regina.[43] The embarrassment here is that Kierkegaard never had any finite to sacrifice. Kafka says, "possibly he didn't even yet (noch nicht) have a son and is supposed to sacrifice him already (schon)." We could read this "not yet" and "already" as an "always not yet" and an "always already," that is, as an unreachable futurity and an unreachable anteriority. He had no present, no temporal, no finite to sacrifice. Neither, for that matter, did Kafka.

Jean Wahl said that Kafka substitutes the proper name of Abraham for Kierkegaard. Could we not also say that Kafka at times substitutes the proper name of Abraham for Kafka? Perhaps Kafka's autobiography—the one he never wrote—is also in the Abraham story. In a letter to Felice, Kafka writes that he is held back from their marriage, their union, "by what is almost a command from heaven" (*ein Befehl des Himmels*).[44] Yet is this "command from heaven" not also ridiculous, something of a joke? Possibly they haven't even yet a son and are supposed to sacrifice him already. Kafka continues: "These are impossibilities and Sarah is right, when she laughs." Who is Kafka's Abraham?

The last part of Kafka's letter to Klopstock introduces yet another "other" Abraham. If the first version of Kafka's Abraham is he who does not yet have a son and already has to sacrifice him, Kafka's second version of Abraham is he who comes unsummoned. The first version questioned the Abraham of Kierkegaard. The second version asks a question of the biblical Abraham and of the biblical text. The ridicule attached to the Abraham who had no son to sacrifice still clings to this other Abraham, and it gets worse. Kafka writes:

> But another Abraham. One who wants to sacrifice altogether in the right way, and who has the right mood in general for the whole thing, but who cannot believe that he is the one meant, he, the repulsive old man and his child, the dirty boy. The true faith is not lacking to him, he has this faith, he would sacrifice in the right frame of mind if he could only believe that he is the one meant. He fears, he will ride out as Abraham with his son, but on the way he will metamorphose into Don Quixote. The world would have been horrified at Abraham if it could have seen him, he however fears that the world will laugh itself to death at the sight of him. But, it is not ridiculousness as such that he fears—of course, he fears that too, and above all his laughing along with them—but mainly he fears that this ridiculousness will make him even older and uglier, his son even dirtier, more unworthy really to be summoned. An Abraham who comes unsummoned![45]

This chain of reasoning recalls Uyttersprot's remark: "every known fact appears in a bright veil of doubt; every hypothesis, on the other hand, contains something of the rigor of certainty." Kafka begins with a fact that the Abraham story presupposes: Abraham was summoned to sacrifice his son. In contrast to Kafka's earlier version of him, this Abraham is perfectly capable of fulfilling the sacrifice, but (*aber*) he cannot believe that he is the one meant. In other words, the fact is doubted and becomes a hypothesis. The hypothesis, perhaps he is not the one meant, in turn becomes a fact. Kafka continues:

An Abraham who comes unsummoned! It is as if at the end of the year, the best student is ceremoniously supposed to receive a prize, and in the expectant stillness the worst student, as a result of an error of hearing, comes forward from his dirty last desk and the whole class explodes. And it is perhaps no

error of hearing, his name was really called, the rewarding of the best is supposed to be, according to the intention of the teacher, at the same time the
punishment of the worst.[46]

The analogy turns on a humiliating pedagogical scene. The worst
student (out of nervousness? overanxiousness? because he is error-
prone?) mishears his name being called. He who always sits in the last
row (because he is the worst) tries to come up to the first row (because
he would like to be better he makes himself even worse?); he becomes
an object of ridicule.

But is it an error of hearing? The whole analogy is in the form of
a hypothesis: it is as if (es ist so wie wenn). The error of hearing is stated
as a fact: (infolge) "due to, as a result of, in consequence of" an error
of hearing, which is in turn doubted. The doubt becomes a hypothesis:
perhaps (vielleicht) it is no error, which becomes a fact: his name was
really (wirklich) called. However, it is not a question of an error of
hearing after all, the teacher merely wanted to teach the worst student
a lesson.

Let us draw out the analogy this distressing pedagogical scene summons up. Abraham's obedience to God's command is like the worst
student's mishearing. (The dirt that attaches to Abraham's son is now
attached to the worst student's desk—because he is always making
errors and erasing them, and never gets the answer right?) If Kafka's
Abraham is the Abraham of Kafka here—the autobiographical allegory—then Kafka's "command from heaven" is like the worst student's
mishearing. The difficulty of deciding whether or not it is an error of
hearing is like the difficulty of not yet having a son and already having
to sacrifice him.

But why not the Abraham of the Bible here? The question Kafka
poses of the biblical text—did Abraham come unsummoned?—is not
without precedent. A midrashic commentator on the binding of Isaac
has asked the same question of the biblical text, although there the
question is more bound to and bound up with the text. The occasion
for the midrashic remark is verse 12 of the biblical chapter, which
begins, "Lay not thine hand upon the lad." This verse marks the peri-
pety of the episode:

And Abraham stretched forth his hand and he took the knife to slaughter his
son. And an angel of the Lord called unto him from the heavens, and said,
"Abraham, Abraham." And he said, "Here I am." And he said, "Lay not thine
hand upon the lad, neither do thou anything unto him, for now I know that

thou art one fearing of God, because thou hast not withheld thy son, thine only son, from me."

Rabbi Aba said: Abraham said to God: "I will lay my complaint before you. Yesterday (on an earlier occasion) you told me 'In Isaac shall thy seed be called to thee' (Gen. 21:12), and then again you said, 'Take now thy son' (Gen. 22:2), and now you tell me 'Lay not thine hand upon the lad!'" The Holy One, blessed be He, said to him, in the words of Psalm 89:35, "'My covenant will I not profane, nor alter that which is gone out of my lips.' When I told you 'Take thy son,' I was not altering that which went out from my lips, namely, my promise that you would have descendants through Isaac. I did not tell you 'kill him,' but 'bring him up' to the mountain. You have brought him up—now take him down again."⁴⁷

In this midrashic unit, Abraham is portrayed as wondering about the contradiction, on the one hand, between God's earlier promise to him, "In Isaac shall thy seed be called to thee," and the command to sacrifice Isaac (the contradiction Kierkegaard wondered about) and, on the other hand and more at issue here, the contradiction between God's first command to sacrifice Isaac, "Take thy son," and God's second command, "Lay not thine hand upon the lad." Abraham is saying to God, you're contradicting yourself here and you've done it before (or, why do you keep contradicting yourself?). God replies that he is not contradicting himself, and that Abraham has, in effect, misunderstood the command.

When, in verse 2, God says to Abraham, "Take thy son, thine only son, whom thou lovest, even Isaac, and offer him up there for burnt-offering," the verb used is *alah*, "to go up, ascend, climb," which appears here in a form where it has a causative force: "Cause him to go up, cause him to be brought up there." The phrase, in its entirety, has the idiomatic meaning "to offer sacrifice," but a more literal (if less obvious) translation would be "bring him up there for a burnt-offering." In other words, perhaps Abraham misunderstood the phrase. God says, "I did not tell you, 'kill him,' but 'bring him up' to the mountain. You have brought him up—now take him down again." In this midrashic unit, the episode has the structure of a misunderstanding, indeed, the structure of a joke (although perhaps not a very funny one). (In a much later document, one midrashist—Woody Allen—has Abraham pose the question to God thus: "How am I supposed to know when you're kidding?")

In short, Kafka's question—did Abraham come unsummoned—is not far from a question that Rabbi Aba, for different reasons, asks of the biblical text. The midrashic reading—the question and its resolution—is bound to the biblical text in a way that Kafka's is not. And, of course, Kafka, in reflecting on a ridiculed Abraham, departs substantially from the dominant rabbinic view that Abraham was exalted by this episode. Perhaps Kafka is again closer to Kierkegaard, who, comparing the distress of Abraham's situation to that of the Virgin Mary ("the one who God blesses he curses in the same breath"), asks in effect: is this what it means to be God's chosen one? But the ugliness of Kafka's Abraham is not quite the same ugliness of Kierkegaard's Abraham. And there is perhaps, in Kafka's analogy, this story and another story to be read.

When the worst student gets up from his grimy last desk, the opposition best/worst, first desk/last desk and the reversal of rank that results from the error of hearing recalls the New Testament reversal: "The last will be first and the first, last." One place in which this phrase may be found is at the close of the parable of the Laborers in the Vineyard. The story goes: the owner of a vineyard pays the same wage to the laborers who worked all day and to the laborers who were hired at the eleventh hour. When the ones hired first see this, they grumble at the owner, saying, "These last worked only one hour, and you have made them equal to us who have borne the burden of the day and the scorching heat." The owner dismisses the complaining workers from his presence saying, "Take what belongs to you, and go ... do you begrudge my generosity?" Jesus concludes, "So the last will be first and the first, last" (Matthew 20:1–16).

The parable is generally understood as an illustration of God's generosity and as a vindication of the gospel against its critics. As one scholar puts it, Jesus' purpose was to "defend his association with the sinners and to attack any legalistic merit doctrine." For, indeed, the grumbling workers insist on just such an application of merit, in which "reward should be exactly proportionate to achievement." Their "flawed self-understanding" is "challenged" by "the surprising payment" to the eleventh-hour workers, by "the graciousness" (or grace) of the owner. Because of this legalist understanding, however, they "exclude themselves from the source of grace,"[48] and, as another critic says, "they reject God's gift," and "cut themselves off from salvation."[49] Joachim Jeremias remarks that "the parable is clearly addressed to those who resembled the murmurers, those who criticized and opposed the Good News, Pharisees for example."[50] The Jerusalem Bible glosses the parable: "Into his kingdom God brings latecomers, sinners and pagans. Those who were called first (the Jewish people who, from Abraham's time, had been privileged with the covenant) have no right to be offended." Another source invokes Irenaeus, who "proposed that the men who worked longer hours represent the patriarchs and the prophets of the Old Testament, while the eleventh-hour servants represent the disciples of Christ."[51]

In Kafka's analogy, there is a reversal of rank: best/worst, first/last. But the reversal of rank (the worst student's coming forward) is the result of an error of hearing. In other words, there is no reversal of rank. Kafka in effect rereads the New Testament reversal and reverses it, unreads it, calls it an error. But perhaps it is no error of hearing, the name of the worst student really was called, and the teacher's intention was at once to reward the best and punish the worst. It is as though Kafka had to unread the New Testament back to the Old—to unread grace back to a legalistic punishing God who says that the first will be first and the last will be last. But this reversion (turn back) to the "Old Tesatment"—a scripture which is defined by its relationship to the Gospel—is followed by another turn, that is, a turn away from the question of an error of hearing ("who can say finally that it's an error?"), and a turn to somebody else's—the teacher's—intention (nach der Absicht des Lehrers). But that intention is not like the intention of a subject, but the kind of intention that is a law of Kafka's writing: the road to the Castle "did not lead up the Castle hill; it only led near it, but then, as if intentionally (dann aber, wie absichtlich), it turned aside, and if it did not lead away from the Castle, it did not lead nearer to it either."[52]

In short, it is as if, in order to read Abraham, Kafka has to read him back through the New Testament (typology, Kierkegaard) and back through the "Old Testament" (an "old" law which opposes merit to grace or justice to mercy) in order to return him to an other law, which is not yet and already the "law" of the Hebrew Bible, which is the law as other, in other words, an other Abraham.

NOTES

1. "Erlauben Sie, Herr Vorsteher, daß ich Sie mit einer Frage unterbreche," sagte K., "erwähnten Sie nicht früher einmal eine Kontrollbehörde? Die Wirtschaft ist ja nach Ihrer Darstellung eine derartige, daß einem bei der Vorstellung, die Kontrolle könnte ausbleiben, übel wird."
"Sie sind sehr streng," sagte der Vorsteher. "Aber vertausendfachen Sie Ihre Strenge,

und sie wird noch immer nichts sein, verglichen mit der Strenge, welche die Behörde gegen sich selbst anwendet. Nur ein völlig Fremder kann Ihre Frage stellen. Ob es Kontrollbehörden gibt? Es gibt nur Kontrollbehörden. Freilich, sie sind nicht dazu bestimmt, Fehler im groben Wortsinn herauszufinden, denn Fehler kommen ja nicht vor, und selbt, wenn einmal ein Fehler vorkommt, wie in Ihrem Fall, wer darf denn endgültig sagen, daß es ein Fehler ist."

"Das wäre etwas völlig Neues!" rief K.

"Mir ist es etwas sehr Altes," sagte der Vorsteher.

Franz Kafka, The Castle, trans. Willa and Edwin Muir (New York: The Modern Library, 1969), with occasional modifications of my own; Das Schloß (Frankfurt am Main: Fischer Verlag, 1979). References will be first to the English, then to the German edition (84, 65).

2. Ibid., 4, 7.

3. Ibid., 89, 69.

4. Ibid., 112, 85.

5. This includes Heinz Politzer, Franz Kafka: Parable and Paradox (Ithaca: Cornell University Press, 1962, 1966), and Nahum N. Glatzer, editor of the volume of Kafka's writings entitled (not by Kafka) Parables and Paradoxes (New York: Schocken Books, 1971). Therapeutic in this regard are: Henry Sussman, Franz Kafka: Geometrician of Metaphor (Madison, Wis.: Coda Press, 1979); and Jacques Derrida, "Préjugés, devant la loi," in La Faculté de juger, ed. Jean-François Lyotard (Paris: Minuit, 1985).

6. "Jede einzelne Einrede ist für sich gut, zusammengenommen aber schließen sie einander aus. A. behandelt isoliert, was im Zusammenhange betrachtet werden muß." Sigmund Freud, Jokes and Their Relation to the Unconscious, trans. James Strachey (New York: Norton, 1963); Der Witz und seine Beziehung zum Unbewussten (Frankfurt am Main: Fischer Verlag, 1971). (62, 50)

7. Ibid., 205, 167.

8. Richard A. Lanham, A Handlist of Rhetorical Terms (Berkeley: University of California Press, 1969), p. 71.

9. To use a rhetorical rather than a grammatical term here, one could also say that the logic of the Mayor's discourse is asyndeton (from the Greek "unconnected"), the "omission of conjunctions between words, phrases or clauses," while its rhetoric is polysyndeton, the "use of a conjunction between each clause." Ibid., pp. 18, 78.

10. Horst Steinmetz, Suspensive Interpretation: Am Beispiel Franz Kafkas (Göttingen: Vandenhoeck und Ruprecht, 1977), pp. 107–19. Uyttersprot's remarks are cited by Steinmetz.

11. See J. Hillis Miller's "Parable and Performative in the Gospels and in Modern Literature" in Humanizing America's Iconic Book (Chico, California: Scholars Press, 1980), pp. 57–71.

12. Franz Kafka, The Trial, trans. Willa and Edwin Muir (New York: The Modern Library, 1956); Der Prozeß (Frankfurt am Main: Fischer Verlag, 1963). (272, 185)

13. Politzer, Kafka, pp. 1–22.

14. Stanley Corngold, The Commentators' Despair (Port Washington: Kennikat Press, 1973).

15. Politzer, Kafka, p. 21.

16. Corngold, Commentators' Despair, p. 7.

17. Frank Kermode, The Genesis of Secrecy: On the Interpretation of Narrative (Cambridge: Harvard University Press, 1979), p. 20.

18. "Leoparden brechen in den Tempel ein und saufen die Opferkrüge leer; das wiederholt sich immer wieder; schließlich kann man es vorausberechnen, und es wird ein Teil der Zeremonie." Kafka, Parables and Paradoxes, p. 92. It was published posthu-

mously in *Hochzeitsvorbereitungen auf dem Lande* (Frankfurt am Main: Fischer Verlag, 1980) and is included in the English volume *Dearest Father* (New York: Schocken Books, 1954). (31, 34)

19. See, for example, Geoffrey Hartman's "Structuralism: The Anglo-American Adventure," in *Beyond Formalism* (New Haven: Yale University Press, 1970), pp. 3–23.

20. Kermode, *Genesis of Secrecy*, pp. 26–27.

21. See ibid., chap. 2.

22. Ibid., p. 32.

23. Walter Benjamin, "Franz Kafka: On the Tenth Anniversary of His Death" in *Illuminations*, trans. Harry Zohn (New York: Schocken Books, 1969); Martin Buber, *Two Types of Faith*, trans. Norman P. Goldhawk (New York: Harper Torchbook, 1961); Politzer, chap. 1; Maurice Blanchot, "Kafka et l'exigence de l'oeuvre" in *L'espace littéraire* (Paris: Gallimard, 1955).

24. Kafka, *Diaries 1910–1913*, trans. Joseph Kresh (New York: Schocken Books, 1965), and *Diaries 1914–1923*, trans. Martin Greenberg (New York: Schocken Books, 1965), with occasional modifications of my own; *Tagebücher 1910–1923* (Frankfurt am Main: Fischer Verlag, 1973). August 21, 1913.

25. See *Diaries*, August 27, 1916.

26. Letter to Max Brod, Zürau, middle or end of January, 1918, in *Letters to Friends, Family, and Editors*, trans. Richard and Clara Winston (New York: Schocken Books, 1977); *Briefe 1902–1924* (Frankfurt am Main: Fischer Verlag, 1975).

27. Kafka frequently claims to be getting away from Kierkegaard, despite the fact that he seems to be unable to get away from him. In 1918 Kafka writes to Max Brod about Kierkegaard's concern with the problem of finding a true marriage: "But (*aber*) I have, in spite of (*trotzdem*) the fact that Kierkegaard is always in some way present to me, truly forgotten this concern, so much am I roaming about elsewhere, yet (*allerdings*) without ever fully coming out of contact with it" (Zürau, mid-March, 1918). And again to Brod, Kafka writes: "Kierkegaard is no longer so present to me, since I have not read his old books for some time . . . you evidently feel as I do that one cannot withdraw from the power of his terminology" (Zürau, end of March, 1918).

28. Jean Wahl, "Kafka et Kierkegaard" in *Esquisse pour une histoire de "l'existentialisme"* (Paris: L'Arche, 1949), trans. Lienhard Bergel in *The Kafka Problem*, ed. Angel Flores (New York: Octagon Books, 1963). The fragments Wahl discusses were published posthumously in *Hochzeitsvorbereitungen auf dem Lande* (Fourth Octavo Notebook).

29. Søren Kierkegaard, *Fear and Trembling*, trans. Howard V. Hong and Edna H. Hong (Princeton: Princeton University Press, 1983), p. 9.

30. Soncino translation, slightly modified.

31. In one version, for example, Abraham "seized Isaac by the chest, threw him to the ground, and said, 'Stupid boy, do you think I am your father? I am an idolator. Do you think it is God's command? No, it is my desire.' Then Isaac trembled and cried out in his anguish: 'God in heaven, have mercy on me, God of Abraham, have mercy on me; if I have no father on earth, then you be my father!' But Abraham said softly to himself, 'Lord God in heaven, I thank you; it is better that he believes me a monster than that he should lose faith in you' " (pp. 10–11).

32. Kierkegaard, *Fear and Trembling*, p. 30.

33. Ibid., p. 118. Against Kierkegaard's conclusions, one midrashic reading settles the question of how to read Abraham's answer differently. For the grammatical ambiguity of "my son" in Hebrew (in the vocative case or in apposition to "the lamb," in the accusative case) allows two possible readings: "God will provide for Himself the lamb for the burnt offering, O my son" or "God will provide for Himself the lamb for the

burnt offering, namely, my son." See Genesis Rabbah LVI. 4, trans. H. Freedman and Maurice Simon (London: Soncino Press, 1977). Geoffrey Hartman plays on this grammatical ambiguity with a difference in "The Sacrifice: A New Biblical Narrative" in *A Jewish Journal at Yale* 2 (Fall 1984).

34. Kierkegaard, *Fear and Trembling*, pp. 27–53.

35. Zürau, mid-March, 1918.

36. Kierkegaard, *Fear and Trembling*, p. 74.

37. The substitution of Cain (murderer) for Abraham goes back to St. Augustine (*City of God* XV, 7–8), and is closely linked, as an exegetical gesture, to typological readings of the Old Testament. The Old Testament, read without reference to the Gospel, is a dead or killing letter. Read spiritually, it bears witness to "the prophecies that were given beforehand concerning Christ" (XVIII, 46). Kierkegaard's emphasis on Abraham's getting Isaac *back* is not unlike Augustine's: "Abraham is to be praised in that he believed without hesitation that his son would rise again (*resurrecturum*) when he had been sacrificed" (XVI, 32). *City of God*, trans. Henry Bettenson (Baltimore: Penguin Books, 1976).

38. "Ich könnte mir einen andern Abraham denken, der—freilich würde er es nicht bis zum Erzvater bringen, nicht einmal bis zum Altkleiderhändler—der die Forderung des Opfers sofort, bereitwillig wie ein Kellner zu erfüllen bereit wäre, der das Opfer aber doch nicht zustandebrächte, weil er von zuhause nicht fort kann, er ist unentbehrlich, die Wirtschaft benötigt ihn, immerfort ist noch etwas anzuordnen, das Haus ist nicht fertig." Matliary, June 1921, translation (modified) from *Parables and Paradoxes*. All subsequent references to Kafka's Abraham are to this letter.

39. "wenn er nicht das Haus gehabt hätte, wo hätte er denn sonst den Sohn aufgezogen, in welchem Balken das Opfermesser stecken gehabt?"

40. Kierkegaard, *Fear and Trembling*, pp. 38–41.

41. "Anders die oberen Abrahame, die stehn auf ihrem Bauplatz und sollen nun plötzlich auf den Berg Morija; womöglich haben sie noch nicht einmal einen Sohn und sollen ihn schon opfern."

42. According to Walter Lowrie, Kierkegaard broke his engagement with Regina Olsen for the last time and fled to Berlin, where he wrote *Fear and Trembling* and *Repetition*. Lowrie writes: "We know that while he was writing these two works the struggle to attain resignation was complicated by the hope that he might yet make Regina his wife. This was so evident in *Repetition*, that the text had to be altered when, on his return to Copenhagen, S.K. learned that Regina was already engaged to another." But, in *Fear and Trembling*, Lowrie continues, the truth is "so thoroughly refracted" that "the reader . . . may need to be told that Abraham's sacrifice of Isaac is a symbol of S.K.'s sacrifice of the dearest thing he had on earth, and that in order to liberate Regina from her attachment and to 'set her afloat' S.K. felt obliged to be cruel enough to make her believe he was a scoundrel who had merely been trifling with her affections." Introduction to *Fear and Trembling*, trans. Walter Lowrie (Princeton: Princeton University Press, 1954), pp. 9–10.

43. Kenneth Burke correctly points out that "this story, as told in the Bible, does not quite serve the purpose. For there is nothing in it to parallel the very important point about Kierkegaard's 'acting like a scoundrel.' The Bible does not say that Abraham lied to Isaac for Isaac's good. However: Kierkegaard, writing in a highly psychologistic century, improvises a 'psychology' for Abraham. And *this improvised psychology, not the Biblical story,* is the element that helps him solve the most crucial problem in the redeeming of his conduct. For it is the part that parallels, in Biblical ennoblement, Kierkegaard's depicting of himself as a scoundrel who had trifled with Regina's affections." *A Rhetoric of Motives* (Berkeley: University of California Press, 1950), p. 246.

44. Franz Kafka, *Letters to Felice*, trans. James Stern and Elisabeth Duckworth (New

York: Schocken Books, 1973); *Briefe an Felice* (Frankfurt am Main: Fischer Verlag, 1976). (288, 426)

45. "Aber ein anderer Abraham. Einer, der durchaus richtig opfern will und überhaupt die richtige Witterung für die ganze Sache hat, aber nicht glauben kann, daß er gemeint ist, er, der widerliche alte Mann und sein Kind, der schmutzige Junge. Ihm fehlt nicht der wahre Glaube, diesen Glauben hat er, er würde in der richtigen Verfassung opfern, wenn er nur glauben könnte, daß er gemeint ist. Er fürchtet, er werde zwar als Abraham mit dem Sohne ausreiten, aber auf dem Weg sich in Don Quixote verwandeln. Über Abraham wäre die Welt damals entsetzt gewesen, wenn sie zugesehen hätte, dieser aber fürchtet, die Welt werde sich bei dem Anblick totlachen. Es ist aber nicht die Lächerlichkeit an sich, die er fürchtet—allerdings fürchtet er auch sie, vor allem sein Mitlachen—hauptsächlich aber fürchtet er, daß diese Lächerlichkeit ihn noch älter und widerlicher, seinen Sohn noch schmutziger machen wird, noch unwürdiger, wirklich gerufen zu werden. Ein Abraham, der ungerufen kommt!"

46. "Es ist so wie wenn der beste Schüler feierlich am Schluß des Jahres eine Prämie bekommen soll und in der erwartungsvollen Stille der schlechteste Schüler infolge eines Hörfehlers aus seiner schmutzigen letzten Bank hervorkommt und die ganze Klasse losplatzt. Und es ist vielleicht gar kein Hörfehler, sein Name wurde wirklich genannt, die Belohnung des Besten soll nach der Absicht des Lehrers gleichzeitig eine Bestrafung des Schlechtesten sein."

47. Cited by Rashi, *Pentateuch with Targum Onkelos, Haphtaroth and Rashi's Commentary*, trans. M. Rosenbaum and A. M. Silbermann.

48. Dan Via, Jr., *The Parables: Their Literary and Existential Dimension* (Fortress Press: Philadelphia, 1967), pp. 147–54.

49. Joachim Jeremias, *The Parables of Jesus* (New York: Charles Scribner's Sons, 1972), p. 34.

50. Ibid., p. 38.

51. *The Interpreter's Bible* (New York: Abingdon Press, 1951).

52. "Die Straße nämlich, die Hauptstraße des Dorfes, führte nicht zum Schloßberg, sie führte nur nahe heran, dann aber, wie absichtlich, bog sich ab, und wenn sie sich auch vom Schloß nicht entfernte, so kam sie ihm doch auch nicht näher." *The Castle*, 14, 15.

GERSHON SHAKED

Midrash and Narrative:
Agnon's "Agunot"

I

From love of our language and adoration of holiness I abase myself before the words of the Torah, and starve myself by abstaining from the words of the Sages, keeping these words within me so that they may be fitted altogether upon my lips. If the Temple still stood, I should take my place on the dais with my fellow poets and daily repeat the song which the Levites used to chant in the Holy Temple. Now, when the Temple is still in ruins, and we have neither priests at their holy work nor Levites chanting and singing, I occupy myself with the Torah, the Prophets, and the Writings, the Mishnah, the Halakhah and the Haggadot, Toseftot, Dikdukei Torah, and Dikdukei Soferim. When I look into their words and see that from all our goodly treasures which we had in ancient days nothing is left us but a scanty record, I am filled with sorrow, and this same sorrow causes my heart to tremble. Out of this same trembling I write my fables, like a man who has been exiled from his father's palace, who makes himself a little booth and sits there telling of the glory of his forefather's house.

("The Secret of Writing Fables. The Sense of Smell")

This is a poetic expression of Shmuel Yosef Agnon's fundamental attitude towards the relationship between modern literature and ancient texts.[1] For Agnon, intertextuality is neither a mere literary device nor an unconscious phenomenon. Rather it is the very source of his creativity, perhaps even its main subject. Modern Hebrew literature, according to Agnon, is nothing less than a substitute for the sacred texts; the absence of sacred literature is the source of his inspiration. Moreover, the author sees himself as the heir of the holy scribes whose works were only a communal creation, and whose anonymity, which foregrounded the texts and hid the identity of the individual authors, was an integral part of their work.

As a modern author, therefore, Agnon continues the ancient tradition in his work because it has become part of his cultural heritage. But as a modern author, who can only imitate the language of the canon and cannot enact its content as part of a living ritual, he cannot be the true bearer of that canon. Therefore, Agnon does not see himself as a transmitter of a great cultural lineage, built layer upon layer, beginning with the Bible and continuing through the Mishnah, the Talmud, and all the works which stem from them. Instead he views himself as belonging to a different culture altogether, one which inherits a multi-textual tradition it can no longer carry on. This culture relates to these earlier texts, but, because of the new social context, these texts can be made real only by means of invented fables—fables, in other words, which are not the sacred fables that the righteous of each generation were accustomed to tell, but which are, rather, secular chambers, in which only the echoes of the canon are heard. Hence the work of the modern writer, claims Agnon, serves as a secular substitute (a "booth") for sacred tradition (the "palace"). In order to understand Agnon's works in general, and the story with which I shall be concerned in particular, this connection between holy origins and secular expression must be kept in mind.

II

To a greater degree than that of any other writer in modern Hebrew literature, Agnon's work is based upon intertextual connections.[2] Indeed, Agnon conceives of an ideal addressee for whom the traditions of sacred literature are totally native, one who can discern the relationship between the fable and the holy canon. Agnon's implied addressee, however, is not simply the reader who is close to those traditions and is able to recognize them. He is one who is able, like the author himself, to distinguish among them and even to create oppositions between them.[3] In order to understand Agnon's work, one must read his text not only as a link in the chain of sacred tradition, but also as an anti-text to this traditional literature.

Agnon's text will be misunderstood, therefore, not only by the addressee who is completely unfamiliar with the textual tradition to which the author is referring, but also by the addressee who credulously reads the text as a link in a chain of sacred texts. The author writes a great many stories which *appear* to be sacred texts or "quasi-sanctified" texts (or even a kind of Apocrypha), stories in which the author, by various devices, hints that his text is indeed a link in the chain of sacred texts. "Agunot" ["Deserted Wives"] (1908), and *Ve-Haya he-Akov le-Mishor* [*And the Crooked Shall Be Made Straight*] (1912) are two such works. The first is prefaced by a kind of pseudo-midrash, while in the second Agnon opens each chapter with quotations from the traditional literature, the narrative as a whole (through the use of the introduction, the style, and the inserted tales) being structured on the frame of "tales of believers" (the name given to traditional religious and moral stories dealing with awe of heavenly power and deep religious faith). The same literary approach can be found in many later stories as well. But whether, in fact, Agnon's works only contain hints pointing towards sacred texts or are actually written "as if" they themselves are quasi-sanctified, it is clear that the tales' creative power arises from the constant tension between the text itself and the sanctified or semi-sanctified literary tradition (if we take into account the later literature of the religious community) which it invokes. To examine this tension in Agnon's work, let us turn to his first story, "Agunot," which in many ways determined Agnon's subsequent literary development, thematically, structurally, and stylistically.[4]

III

"Agunot," by Shmuel Yosef Czazkes, was the first story published by the young author in Palestine, where he had immigrated in 1908. It appeared in one of the first periodicals of the Second Aliyah, *Ha-Omer*, vol. II, no. 1, 1908. It is significant that the author used part of the title of this story for his nom de plume and his surname. This is a symbolic act which, to my knowledge, is without parallel in Hebrew literature. Indeed, Agnon so identified himself with the name of his story that what we have here is an extension of the fictional into the real, the fictional narrative becoming a kind of *perush* (interpretation) on the existential and poetic experience of the author, an interpretation which has forced him to displace the chief element in his identifying sign. The story, then, might be thought of as a form of midrash on the new name of the author.

Taking the name from the deed or the deed from the name is, of course, a well-known technique in Jewish literature: "And Joseph called the name of the firstborn Menasheh; For God, said he, hath made me forget all my toil, and all my father's house. And the name of the second called he Ephraim; For God hath caused me to be fruitful in the land of my afflictions" (Gen. 41:51–52). (The play here is upon *Menasheh* and *nashani*—"made me forget," and *Ephraim* and *hifrani*—"caused me to be fruitful.") The two names are used to summarize two events which happened to the father of the family. The name is a sign of the deed. When, therefore, Agnon relates the title of his story to himself, he continues this tradition of the ancient literature, implicitly declaring that his life is a commentary on the story, just as the story is a commentary on his life. By affiliating what seems to be a legendary or fictional experience with the actual identity of a person who is within and without the fiction at one and the same time, the author, especially through his signature, identifies the text as something which belongs to him, and to no one else.

IV

This phenomenon of the text as commentary, mediating between fact and fiction, is replicated in a number of ways in "Agunot." The most important of these for our purposes is the relationship that is established between the opening or introduction to the story and what the "author" (as he refers to himself) calls "the fable," "a great tale and terrible, from the Holy Land." The opening section is built along the same lines as many Hasidic tales, which open with "a quotation from the writings," pointing, generally, towards the works of the holy Ari, Rabbi Isaac son of Solomon Luria (1534–72), the head of the kabbalistic community in Safad.[5] The Ari's works were left unpublished. But the "quotations" from the Hasidic books which were attributed to him were cited with a show of great authority, even though it was widely acknowledged that their authenticity was quite often doubtful. Agnon revives this form of the "quotation from the writings," what I would call the pseudo-quotation, supporting his fable with words which seem to have a sanctified status, almost an ordination. Furthermore, the sacred authority of these citations extends itself into the fable, the fable becoming a kind of exemplum of the imaginary quotation. The quotation, however, is not reducible to the purely imaginary. Imaginary in *fact*, and yet constructed of similarly "authentic" passages of sacred literature (which are themselves of dubious authority), it is, we may say, a genuine pseudo-quotation because the well-informed reader can grasp not only the authenticity of the unfolding of its elements, but also the spirit in which it is invoked. It is a text derived from sacred texts, which has many of the characteristics of those texts, but which is itself outside the sacred context.

The opening of "Agunot," therefore, continues the midrashic form of writing signalized by Agnon's choices of name and title. The addressee, as he reads, is half-willing to suspend his disbelief and imagine that this is not a secular work by a secular author, but a religious work in which the implied author carries on the midrashic activity of former generations. The pseudo-sacred opening imitates a tradition in which, the relationship between a secular story and the sacred canon having been revealed, the story itself takes on a species of sacred and sanctified significance. The fictionality is self-fulfilling: secular and sacred are interwoven, and we do not know if the sacred sanctifies the secular, or the secular sanctifies the sacred. Indeed, the relationship between secular and sacred, and the fictive or real status of each, are perhaps the central themes of the tale.

Specifically, the opening follows in a tradition of midrashic writing which depended upon the Song of Songs and the midrash on the Song of Songs. It renews the general motif of the relationship between a metaphorical (or symbolic) character who represents the Jewish people and an anthropomorphic image of God, while it recapitulates a particular stage in the midrashic exegesis of that text where, in Song of Songs Rabbah, this connection is made suggestively to express the intimate and even reciprocal relationship between the people and their God. This relationship is made explicit later in the exegetical tradition, as, for example, in the Lurianic Kabbalah where we find a detailed reciprocity between the deeds of the people and the deeds of God.

Now, the midrash that Agnon writes is simultaneously an interpretation of the Song of Songs and of the midrash on the Song of Songs. In the opening of Agnon's midrash the following phrases from the Song of Songs appear: "Behold, thou art fair, my love, behold, thou art fair" (4:1); "they smote me, they wounded me, they took away my veil" (5:7); "my beloved withdrew and was gone" (5:6); "I am lovesick" (5:8). Citations from the Song of Songs, furthermore, appear not only in the opening but also in the body of the story where they take on increasingly complex significance. On the one hand, their application, like the fable as a whole, moves from the abstract or conceptual level of interpretation to a more literal or reified one. On the other hand, they draw into the body of the story the conceptual significance they had possessed in the opening. (I am referring to such verses as "My beloved descended into the garden," as implied in "Agunot," p. 31, "the time of the singing of birds is come," p. 31, "I sleep but my heart waketh," p. 35).[6]

These verses, and phrases close to them, are the central elements of the intertextual connection. By appearing first in the opening and then returning in the body of the tale they suggest that the story as a whole looks in two directions. On the one hand, it refers to the nearer context of its own secular or fictional elements. And, on the other hand, it points toward the more remote context of its pseudo-sacred opening.[7] The more remote context establishes the relationship between the events of the near context and the traditional literature of past generations. It accumulates the interpretive meanings of the generations and causes them to issue in new events and new interpretations.

The introduction, of course, does not remain on the literal level of the love story told in Song in Songs. It quickly proceeds to evoke the midrash of the Song of Songs, which compares the people of Israel to the "fair one," God to the "beloved," and which interprets other elements of the love story in the light of this comparison. In this way, for example, "Behold, thou art fair, my love, behold thou art fair," elicits the following midrash: "Behold, thou art fair with precepts, behold thou art fair with deeds of kindness, behold thou art fair in positive precepts, behold thou art fair in negative precepts; behold thou art fair in the religious duties of the house, with the ḥallah, terumah, and tithes, behold thou art fair in religious duties of the field, with the gleanings, the forgotten sheaf, the corner, etc." (Midrash Song of Songs 4:1). Or another example: "I adjure you, O daughters of Jerusalem . . . what will ye tell him? That I am love-sick. As a sick person yearns for healing, so the generation in Egypt yearned for deliverance" (5:8).

These midrashim do not appeal in their original form in Agnon's text. They are, however, painstakingly implied in a discourse of authorial asides which compounds new expressions out of the interpretative echoes of many different sacred texts. This process begins in the opening of the story, where, for example, the pseudo-midrash being created substitutes the expression "a thread of grace" (which, so far as I have been able to determine, is not found in the traditional texts) for the phrase "a thread of mercy," which is indeed repeated in various well-known midrashic contexts, as, for example, in Ḥagigah 12b:

Look down from heaven, and see, even from Thy holy and glorious habitation. Ma'on is that in which there are companies of Ministering Angels, who utter (divine) song by night, and are silent by day for the sake of Israel's glory, for it is said: *By day the Lord doth command His lovingkindness, and in the night his song is with me.*

Resh Lakish said: Whoever occupies himself with (the study of) the Torah by night, the Holy One, blessed be He, draws over him a chord of loving-kindness ["a thread of mercy"] by day, for it is said: "*By day the Lord doth command His lovingkindness*"? Because "*by night His song is with me.*" And there are some who say: Resh Lakish said: Whoever occupies himself with the study of the Torah in this world, which is like the night, the Holy One, blessed be He, draws over him a chord of lovingkindness in the world to come, which is like the day, for it is said: "*By day the Lord doth command His lovingkindness, for by night His song is with me.*" (Compare also B. Megillah 13a and B. Tamid 29a.)

The motifs of the "prayer shawl, the hangings, and the weaving," which appear in the concrete image of *the prayer shawl* which is woven from the good deeds of the people of Israel by God Himself for *the Congregation of the people of Israel,* are similarly found in various forms in different midrashic sources. For example, the motif of "the apparel of the She-khinah" appears in the Zohar III, Shelach Lecha 163b: "When the She-khinah is in the pale blue she prepares for herself an outer covering of the same pale blue which was found in the Sanctuary, etc." And it appears in earlier and later versions, for example in The Book of Comfort by the tenth-century writer R. Nissim of Kairouan, or in the kab-balistic book of morals, Shevet Musar, by R. Elijah son of Solomon Ha-Kohen from Izmir, where good deeds are compared to a garment which the naked soul is awarded as a consequence of its fulfillment of the commandments and for other praiseworthy deeds:

Precious is the light and the upper (heavenly) garment created by the light of the Torah and the performance of its commandments, for through the com-mandments a precious, spiritual garment is woven, lighting the body of heaven in its clearness; the soul, leaving this world naked of bodily cover, hovering, ashamed, seeing itself naked, immediately puts on this clear, light-giving gar-ment, a garment it had made for itself in the world of flesh through Torah and the commandments, and is overjoyed, seeing itself in the garment of Kingdom. (Shevet Musar 35, 274–75.)

One could present a long list of sources which would show clearly that Agnon's pseudo-midrash is assembled from authentic materials which themselves provide varying contexts and interpretations. Con-cepts such as "grace and mercy," "the Congregation of Israel," "in her youth in her Father's house," "the Temple of her Sovereign and the city of sovereignty," "neither been sullied nor stained," "the power and the glory and the exultation," "the prayer shawl is damaged," "evil winds [spirits] blow," "and they know they are naked," "wandering and howling," "groans and cries," "darkest melancholy-Mercy shield us!"—all these and more acquired different meanings at different moments in sacred literature, from the midrash through to the late mystic literature (of the Hasidim). There is no need to go over each concept, nor to make a detailed analysis of the compounding of several concepts into units. But as these multiple perspectives come together in Agnon's text—indeed, as they exist separately within different midrashim—they hint at a relationship of reciprocity between the heavenly and the secular, between the Congregation of Israel or the Shekhinah (or the heavenly Spheres) and the Holy-One-Blessed-Be-He (or other Spheres in the scheme of Spheres) as He manifests Himself in affairs of this world. As long as the stream flows from below (the stream of commandments and good deeds), the stream from above continues to flow (the testing of immanence) and harmony exists, a harmony which the Congregation as a whole, and every individual in it, feels. When this stream is impeded, generally because of an event in the lower world of flesh, an interruption of the flow occurs. Harmony, which is simultaneously erotic and cosmic, is disrupted, and there is a kind of fall in the lower world, which will not be corrected until, miraculously, the harmony is restored. This disharmony has multiple manifestations: in the area of personal relations (where pairing becomes separation); in the area of the Spheres (where the masculine Spheres are alienated from the Sphere of Kingdom, which is the Shekhinah, while Judgments and the strength of the devil's camp increase); and in the area of the relations between the people and its God (where Exile overcomes Redemption).

Some of these patterns stand out in the quotations cited above (good deeds lead to unification of Creation, to the satisfaction of the Creator, and to the weaving of the garment which clothes the soul in good deeds), while others are to be found in the general store of meanings known to every "ideal" addressee, one who is intimate with this literature. Agnon's pseudo-midrashic opening, therefore, is both a precis of a sacred text and a narrative of a cosmic story. It suggests that a state of harmony, which originates in the reciprocal relations between the two heroes of the drama (God and the Congregation of Israel, or the Sphere of Glory and Majesty and the Sphere of Kingdom), gives way to the destruction of this harmonic state because of some negative, human factor and to a condition of longing for restoration of the original state (very much as in Romantic longings for lost perfection). Agnon accepts the premise that in sacred literature we find the permanent and known laws of the cosmic drama. These laws govern, as well, the strange game played between the midrashic assumption that "all is foreordained" and "we are free to choose." The cosmic process is realized in human action, just as every human action is an expression of the cosmic process. Reciprocal relations between these two processes are themselves expressed in the relationship between the opening and the tale.

V

As I have begun to show, semantic elements which link "Agunot" with sacred literature are found not only in the opening but throughout the story. Some of these are developed into motifs. Others stand on their own and, by virtue of the opening, are rendered open to conceptual glossing, based on the significance of their appearance in combination in the sources. Since the alternatives for explicating them cannot be limited with any certainty, the text's meaning remains unfixed within a field of intelligible significance.[8] The polysemousness of the textual units leads one back to a multitude of integral cultural contexts (such as the Bible, midrash, Talmud, Zohar, kabbalah more generally, the Ari, the Moral Books, Ḥasidic writings). The choice of one specific implied text as the base line of explication (a choice often reflecting the limitations of the addressee) leads to one kind of interpretation, but it does not necessarily eliminate others suggested by other implied texts. Examples of such exegetical quantities are: "ante-room and mansion of glory" (31), "the harp of David" (31), "but all this pride was inwards" (31), "the garden" (31), "the evil one intervened" (32), "a great mansion" (32), "a hall for prayer" (32), "no part of him was free of it" (34), "an empty vessel" (34), "on her couch in the night" (35), "the taper" (35), "like a lyre whose strings are rent" (36), "the Guardian of Night" (36), and many others. Each phrase has a rich and differentiated semantic history in Jewish culture and religion. The intervention of the devil in Job is not the same as the intervention of the devil in the kabbalistic literature and later Ḥasidic works, and so on. In "Agunot" this lattice of cited and pseudo-cited phrases creates an intertextual network, drawing after it entire systems of connotations and values.

The opening implies that the tale reflects back on a paradigmatic situation and leads forward to a paradigmatic meaning (not fully specified or fulfilled) which replicates the evolution of meanings in the intertextual field. The story, therefore, is not only the tale of Ben Uri, Dinah, Ezekiel, and Freidele. These characters express as well a sacred drama of harmony and disharmony, redemption and exile, unity and disintegration, innocence and the fall, all of which unfolds in the ongoing history of Jewish literary forms, where sacred becomes continuous with secular, divine reality with fictional representation. The continuum grows on and on but the principle of its growth—as perhaps of midrash as a whole—is a denial or blockage of fulfillment, what Agnon conceptualized as *aginut*.

VI

To explain this as clearly as possible I turn now to the mysterious concretization of the title, "Agunot," in the tale itself. On the face of it the title may be regarded as a misnomer. *Agunah* is defined in the halakhah as a married woman separated from her husband who may not divorce him because it is not known whether he is dead or alive. Agnon does not apply this halakhic meaning in his story. The four possible couples in the story either do not marry or marry and divorce in accordance with halakhah. Ben Uri does not marry Dinah; Ezekiel does not marry Freidele; Freidele marries a man in the distant diaspora; Ezekiel and Dinah marry and divorce. In other words, there are no clear cases of *aginut* in this story. And yet a condition of disharmony such as might be thought to be created by aginut does exist; and, as is appropriate to the concept of aginut, it seems to be related to the improper pairing of couples. Thus, according to the story, it is not the law which determines proper pairing—and its consequences. Rather it is the emotional relationship of the individuals to these pairings. Had each of the participants found his or her true partner, harmony might have been established. Had Dinah married Ben Uri and Freidele married Ezekiel, all would have been well. The disharmony of the state of aginut, therefore, must be said to be here actually created, and not, as one might expect, palliated, by law and custom, and the major antinomy emphasized by the structure of the tale is thus the conflict between true marriage and marriage arranged by society. It is for this reason that the rabbi, who has been an agent of these disharmonious couplings, must be exiled.

If we return from the tale itself to the opening, it becomes apparent that cosmic order has been deranged because of a disturbance in the emotional order which is itself a faithful account of an order of cosmic coupling. The customs and norms generally accepted in the congregation bring about a tragic shift in the cosmic order, which is also the order of redemption. According to Agnon, the inherent conflict is between the Jewish tradition in its social form and a system of saving values embedded deep within this same tradition.

The tale itself evokes three additional conflicts which might also be likened to the state of aginut: that between Diaspora and the Land of Israel, between Exile and Redemption, and between Life and Art. These conflicts are connected, first and foremost, to the ghostly insubstantiality of the characters' representational value. Each of them beckons onward to a wider circle of meanings. But much as the title of the story, from which the ghostlike author derives his family name,[9] remains without a definite referent in the events of the story, so the ever-widening circles of reference frequently invert or subvert their previously suggested meanings. Clearly, for example, there is a relationship between Ben Uri and the biblical Bezalel Ben Uri, the builder of the Ark, who is a kind of archetypal craftsman in Israel, a craftsman who built for all time—or did he? Ezekiel's name is connected to the Prophet of God's word—and to the doom of Exile. ("But Rabbi Ezekiel? His feet are planted in the gates of Jerusalem and stand on her soil, but his eyes and his heart are pledged to houses of study and worship abroad, and even now, as he walks in the hills of Jerusalem, he fancies himself among the scholars of his own town, strolling in the fields to take the evening air": p. 41.) Dinah's name is related to frivolous behavior between man and woman, as in the story of Dinah and Shechem the son of Hamor, and as in the midrashic commentary on that story: "And Dinah went forth, the daughter of Leah, of whom it is written, 'The king's daughter is all glorious within'" [Ps. 45]—"And Dinah, the daughter of Leah went forth; she was not the daughter of Jacob. The daughter of Leah: as it is written about her mother that she is a gadabout so she, too, is a gadabout, etc." (Midrash Tanḥuma, Vay-ishlakh, 5–7). Freidele's name, while unrelated to any specific textual antecedent, is significant for its Yiddish form. The Yiddish diminutive unquestionably locates her among the Dispersed.

In similar ways the attraction between Ben Uri and Dinah holds out the promise of building the sanctuary and the Ark in the Land of Israel. Ben Uri is a native of the Land. His Ark may bring about the establishment of Sire Ahiezer in the Land, Sire Ahiezer who went up from the Diaspora in order to become established in the Land of Israel and to strengthen both learning and holy work there. But all these hopes are cut off totally. The failure, in fact, of the pairing of Dinah and Ezekiel, whom Sire Ahiezer chooses as her groom, is also the failure of his "redemption." Further, the failure of this pairing also becomes the failure of the return to Zion, just as Ezekiel's return to the land of Israel is the failure of his "pairing" and his failure as a scholar. Students will no longer come to him. The Ark, which is a sort of metamorphosis of the female figure (according to Midrash Song of Songs 4:4, and also 12: "And through whom did he give the Torah, through his two breasts—these are Moses and Aaron"—and later on, they are "the two Tables of the Covenant"), becomes an inverted metaphor. Instead of the woman being compared to the Ark of the Law, the Ark is compared to a woman ("To what might the Ark have been compared at that moment? To a woman who extends her palms in prayer, while her breasts—the Tables of the Covenant—are lifted with her heart, beseeching her Father in Heaven": p. 36).

The pattern of inversion continues. Analogies between Dinah and the Ark appear throughout the story. Thus, it is said of Dinah: "the doves fluttered about her in the twilight, murmuring their fondness in her ears and shielding her with their wings, like the golden cherubs on the Ark of the sanctuary" (pp. 31–32); and of the Ark: "On the hangings that draped the doors of the Ark, eagles poised above, their wings spread, to leap toward the sacred beasts above" (p. 34). The two exist side by side, and Ben Uri imbues the Ark with spirit, until Dinah (after the Ark has been overturned) causes it to lie like "a body without a soul," and she herself becomes "an unspotted soul gone forth naked into exile" (p. 36).

A tragic exchange occurs here: Ben Uri is matched with the Ark in place of the woman who it would seem is intended for him; Dinah harms the Ark as if it were a woman, her rival. The same exchange has other consequences. The sanctuary is not built properly; the grandee from the Diaspora does not establish himself in the Land of Israel; Redemption recedes further into the distance.

In the tale itself we find a concatenation of unfulfilled matches, characters who do not establish themselves in the Land of Israel, Redemption which has been postponed, and the failure to grasp a chance of human fulfillment. The artist, who because of his work does not devote himself to the human connection which might have brought harmony into the world, epitomizes all these. The breakdown of possible harmonious relationships, which does not permit the community to fulfill its social and national objectives, is figured in the reciprocal relationship between the tale itself and intertextual elements that appear in the tale, which, in turn, returns us to the meaning of the opening. The obstruction represented in the paradigm of the fall, which causes cosmic or metaphysical disharmony, also causes social disharmony and the delay of national redemption.

VII

Underlying both opening narrative and the tale there is a text which, even as it does not appear explicitly, is implied both in the opening and the tale. Finally, this text is also rendered implicit in the epilogue, which once again introduces what we might call a superreal component into the story and, in fact, creates the deepest connection between the different elements of the text. In various midrashic commentaries we find a motif of the perfect pairing similar to that which we find in Plato's *Symposium*. Thus, for instance, the development of the well-known parable in Genesis Rabbah 8: "Rabbi Jeremiah, son of Eleazar, said: 'At the hour that the Holy-One-Blessed-Be-He created the first man, he created him as an androgyne, as it is written "male and female created He them."' Rabbi Samuel, son of Naḥman, said: 'At the hour that the Holy-One-Blessed-Be-He created the first man, He created him with two faces, and sawed him through, and made him double-backed, one facing this direction and one in the other.'" And in the continuation of the same chapter: "He said, 'in the past Adam (man) was created from earth and Eve created from Adam (man).' From here onwards it is said: 'in our image and after our likeness.' There is no man without a woman; there is no woman without a man. And both of them do not exist without the Shekhinah." And in chapter 68: "A matron asked R. Jacob son of Halafta: 'In how many days did the Holy-One-Blessed-Be-He create the world?' He said unto her: 'In six days, as it is written (Exodus 31) "For in six days the Lord made heaven and earth."' She said unto him, 'What has he been doing from that hour to this day?' He said unto her: 'The Holy-One-Blessed-Be-He sits and makes matches, this man's daughter with that man. That man's wife with this man, etc.' "

These early sayings are elaborated in mystical ways in later midrash, frequently endowing the relations between man and woman with cosmic meaning. The following well known example of such elaboration is from the Zohar I 5b:

Another explanation refers "His fruit was sweet to my taste" (Song of Songs 2:3)—to the souls of the righteous who are the fruit of the handiwork of the Almighty and abide with him above. Listen to this: All the souls in the world, which are the fruit of the handiwork of the Almighty, are all mystically one, but when they descend to this world they are separated into male and female, though these are still conjoined. And look at this: the desire of the female for the male creates a soul, and the desire of the male for the female, and his clinging to her, bring(s) forth a soul; and he incorporates the desire of the female and takes it in; and the lower desire is taken up into the higher desire and becomes one thing, without separation. And then the female takes in all and is impregnated by the male; their two desires are conjoined. And because of this all is mixed together, this in that.

When the souls issue forth, they issue forth as male and female together. Subsequently, when they descend (to this world) they separate, one to one side and the other to the other, and the Holy-One-Blessed-Be-He mates them— He and no other, He alone knowing the mate proper to each. Happy is the man who is upright in his works and walks in the way of truth, so that his soul may find its original mate, for then he becomes indeed perfect, and through his perfection the whole world is blessed.

And for this reason it is written: "His fruit is sweet to my taste" because He blesses through making whole, and "that the whole world will be blessed through him," because everything depends upon the actions of the human being, if he is righteous or not righteous.[10]

Even without a detailed explication of this passage it is clear that its meaning is based squarely on a quotation from the Song of Songs, and on several of the chapters of midrash which we quoted above. The topics have been transposed from a conceptual exegesis, backwards one might say, to a level of understanding that is concerned with the movements of the Heavenly Spheres. Here abstractive commentary has been recycled into the processions of phenomenal-noumenal being. Thus, for instance, Tishby explains the first portion: "Souls are created in the coupling of the Holy-One-Blessed-Be-He—Glory—with the Shekhinah. And of the over-abundance given to the Shekhinah by the Holy-One-Blessed-Be-He for the creation of souls, she says: 'And his fruit was sweet to my taste.' " In the next section the chapter describes what happens, what results, in the world of human souls as a consequence of the events in the heavenly Spheres. The coupling of the Holy-One-Blessed-Be-He, says Tishbi, brings about the coming-to-gether of the souls which were united above in the world of spirits, but those who are not deserving may lose their rightful partner, the one created with them in the holy coupling. A whole man is one who returns to his former paired-unity. (See above "he becomes indeed perfect.") And the perfect couple brings blessing to the Shekhinah and draws from her blessing to the world in their coupling. Of them the Shekhinah says: "And his fruit was sweet to my taste," which means, the coupling of the souls which are the fruit of the Holy-One-Blessed-Be-He gives me pleasure.[11]

This is a harmonious and phenomenological understanding of the erotic ideal which connects perfection created in the heavenly Spheres with perfection in relations between men and women. In a correctly ordered world, all species should have existed in permanent pairs, but Adam and Eve's sin caused a breakdown of this harmonic order. The coming-together of split souls in this world is fraught with manifold difficulties. Only he whose acts are desirable can be blessed in coming-together with his ancient partner without hardships, with the help of the Holy-One-Blessed-Be-He.[12]

This myth is at the foundation of our story and is perhaps more important than all the other implied texts, both in the opening and in the tale itself. It determines that the ideal coupling is the desired state, while the imperfect coupling is the state of the world. The tale itself does not tell an unusual story; it reflects a given, everyday situation. The need to correct this situation creates the eternal longing for harmony which characterizes all "deserted" souls (agunot). Ben Uri's music, a social order which creates improper matches, the conflict between art and reality—all of these are necessary obstacles through which the myth is concretized, the myth which hints at a desired harmony but points to the reality of disharmony. In Agnon's hands this myth expresses romantic agony and romantic irony: the suffering of deserted souls, those who cannot find their partners, and the irony created by the gap between longings and the frustration of longings. It recreates the internal connection between the opening narrative and "the tale itself," between the paradigm and the concretization of the paradigm, which in itself incorporates the mythic foundation of that same paradigm.

VIII

The unraveling of the tale is important insofar as it establishes the connection between the tale and everything which emerges from the implied paradigm of the opening, which is based upon the kabbalistic coupling myth. The unraveling of the tale begins with the marriage of Ezekiel and Dinah. The saying of the Sages, "When a person takes a wife to himself, all his sins fall away," through which the rabbi absolves Dinah after her confession, is not fulfilled in her own life. The coupling does not take place ("And neither drew near to the other all that night"); the marriage is not consummated because the two souls are not meant for one another. Each was meant for another. The divorce contract presented by the rabbi is nothing more than an halakhic expression of what actually exists in the domestic life of the couple. The match of the two souls fails. It throws up a barrier which causes the community (through the rabbi) to accept responsibility for the breakdown.

The opening narrative and its mythic foundation forge a connection between the tale and the life of the community. Erotic disharmony is a disharmony between parts of the community (the Land of Israel and the Diaspora) which brings about a breakdown in the process of communal redemption. ("It was not long that Sire Ahiezer left Jerusalem with his daughter. He had failed in his settlement there; his wishes had not prospered": p. 42.)[13]

The rabbi who, it would seem, is responsible for the breakdown in the marital order accepts responsibility for the fact that the community, through enforcing its norms (i.e., marrying a rich man's daughter to a scholar), caused a breakdown in the coupling of souls (the erotic attraction of the woman toward the creative figure). Ben Uri, logically then, is exiled to a foreign place because he too has participated in the breakdown of the coupling of souls in his preference for a woman-substitute (the replacement of the soul by the work of art) to the real woman. And so all of the characters in Agnon's story become agunot, lose their rightful partners and places. The rabbi himself becomes a lost soul, searching for that which will restore to the world what has been lost because of him (or because of the community). All of the stories of the rabbi in the epilogue—searching for a young painter (the reincarnation of Ben Uri), wandering across the sea on a red kerchief with an infant child in his arms, or staring into the eyes of little children in the houses of study—all these are stories with a strange messianic character. Whoever imposes upon himself "the obligation of exile" is looking for a way to emerge from the state of exile, inasmuch as he lifts up his eyes to a messianic solution which will bring redemption to the whole world. "Do not touch my messiahs. These are the babes of the house of study" (B. Shabbat 119b). It is possible to understand the search for the lost child as the rabbi's attempt to atone for the sin of placing an obstacle before true coupling, thereby preventing a child from coming into the world (who might have been the messiah). On the cosmic level the obstacle in the path of the coupling creates the universal disharmony which delays the Redemption and increases the burden of the Diaspora in the life of the nation.

IX

There are no direct parallels between the paradigm of the opening or the mythic paradigm which functions as the foundation of the whole story and the "the tale iself." The tale of the pairings which failed (as a consequence of the norms of society and its failure to absorb the creativity of the artist into a pattern of human creativity) stands on its own and is a story of "the deserted souls" who have not found their proper partners and place. The story as a whole is also a concretization of the experience of the author who associates himself with the essence of the tale. By identifying himself as a romantic figure, cast about from Exile to Redemption, and from the Land of Israel to the Diaspora, the author repeatedly hints that he too is engaged in an eternal erotic quest which will never find satisfaction.

On the other hand, the opening and the myth of a mystic coupling that is left unconsummated, as well as the intratextual relationship that is transformed into an endlessly intertextual one, emphasize that the tale is a concretization of a tragic paradigm. This is the paradigm of the text, or of the pseudo-sacred text, which connects the actions of the people of Israel with the Lord of Creation, or connects the coupling in this world with the ongoing coupling in the Spheres. This relationship secures the connection between the concepts of "love," "art," "exile," "redemption," "diaspora," and "the Land of Israel," on the one hand, and such concepts as "the exile of the Shekhinah," "days of Messiah," "the Shekhinah," and "the Holy-One-Blessed-Be-He," on the other.

The extraordinarily complex intertextuality of this story makes it susceptible to a form of criticism which Hebrew literature, with its tradition of midrash upon midrash, invites in a particularly urgent way. In this work, and in other works of Agnon, intertextuality of a special kind is patently the condition and the theme of its literary being. Only an author who declares that he is a kind of heir to the "poets of the Temple," and who "occupies himself with the Torah, the Prophets, the Writings, the Mishnah, the Halakhah and the Haggadot" can write works which extend the continuum of sacred literature, even while those newly composed works stand in direct contradiction to it. Agnon's is the intertextuality of aginut. By actualizing "the holy paradigm" in the tale, he creates a story of frustrated love which profanes the sacred and sanctifies the profane.

Translated by Lois Bar-Yaacov

NOTES

1. On the general question of Agnon's poetics see G. Shaked, *Agnon's Narrative Art* (Hebrew) (Tel Aviv: Sifri'at Po'alim, 1973), pp. 13–29.

2. Many fine scholars have taken up the question of intertextuality in Agnon's writing, whether they give it this name or some other. On intertextuality in "Agunot" see H. Weiss, *Between Open and Hidden Levels of Meaning in Hebrew Short Stories* (Hebrew) (Tel Aviv: Open University, 1979).

3. I clarified this concept in my book, cited above, pp. 89–132.

4. See the important interpretation of Arnold Band, *Nostalgia and Nightmare* (Berkeley: University of California Press, 1968), pp. 57–63.

5. I would like to thank Yehuda Leibes, who kindly assisted me in the identification of these texts and in defining some of their functions.

6. All the quotations in the Hebrew text are from "Agunot," *Elu Ve-Elu* (Jerusalem and Tel Aviv: Schocken, 1953), pp. 406–16. All quotations in the English are from "Agunot," trans. Baruch Hochman, *Twenty-One Stories*, ed. Nahum Glatzer (London: Victor Gollancz, 1970), pp. 30–44.

7. I am using the term intertextuality here according to the propositions described by Jonathan Culler in the work of Lourent Jenny: "he proposes to distinguish intertextuality proper from 'simple allusions or reminiscence': in the latter case a text repeats an element from a prior text without using its meaning; in the former it alludes to or redeploys an entire structure, a pattern of form and meaning from a prior text": *The Pursuit of Signs* (Ithaca: Cornell University Press, 1981), p. 104.

8. We can thus harmonize two different interpretations such as those presented by Isaac Bacon and Orna Golan. Bacon understands the story in terms of the problems of the artist and bases his argument mainly on the connection between "grace and

mercy," art and love, using midrashim which support this interpretation. Golan interprets the story as the failure of the Second Aliyah (Ben Uri!) which built the sanctuary (the place) before the Ark (Jewish values). She cites various midrashim on the "Ark of the Covenant," and on the characters of Dinah (as the daughter of the tribe of Dan) and Ben Uri (the tribe of Judah), who could have been the parents of the Messiah. See O. Golan, " 'Agunot' and the Second Aliyah" (Hebrew), *Mozna'im* 32 (1971): 215–23; and I. Bacon, "On Shai Agnon's 'Agunot' " (Hebrew), *Mozna'im* 46 (1978): 167–79.

9. This is a technique which reaches its peak in the stories "Edo and Enam" and "Ad Olam" ("For evermore"), in which Agnon uses the first letters of his name, *ayin* and *gimmel*, to indicate that the characters in the story are part of his personality. In *And the Crooked Shall Be Made Straight* (1912) he also uses this technique in the character of Menashe (Mashkiah) Chaim (the "Forgetter of Life"), and Kreindel Charny ("Atarah Shehorah" = Black Crown).

10. *Mishnat ha-Zohar*, ed. I. Tishbi (Jerusalem, 1961), pp. 627–28.

11. Ibid.

12. Ibid.

13. Another myth, that of H. N. Bialik in *Scroll of Fire*, also creates a connection between the erotic separation of men and women and Exile.

Contemporary Midrash

JACQUES DERRIDA

Shibboleth

One time only: a circumcision takes place just once. So, at least, it would appear. We are going to circle around this appearance—I speak of an appearance and not a semblance—not so much in order to circumscribe or circumvent some essence of circumcision as to let ourselves be approached by the resistance which "once" may offer to thought. Before we ask ourselves what, if anything, is meant by one time, before interpreting, as philosophers or philosophers of language, as hermeneuts or poeticians, the meaning or truth of what one speaks of in English as "once," we should keep, no doubt, a long and thoughtful while to those linguistic borders where, as you know, only those who know how to pronounce *Shibboleth* are granted crossing and, indeed, life. Nothing, apparently, could be easier to translate than "one time" or "once"—*une fois, einmal, una volta*; think of latinity's *vicissitudes*, of the Spanish *vez*, and of the whole syntax of *vicem, vice, vices, vicibus, vicissim, in vicem*, etc. But these translations and renderings resort to semantic registers which do not translate each other; they are absolutely heterogeneous. One speaks of time in the English "one time," but not in "once," nor in the French, German, Spanish, Italian, or Latin locutions. Nor do these latter share any affinity of, let us say, a conceptual order.

If a circumcision takes place one time only, this time is thus, *at one and the same time*, the first and last time. It is, at least, around this appearance, archaeology and eschatology, that we are going to circle, as around the ring which they trace, carve out, or set off.

I am going to speak then about circumcision and the one-and-only time or, what comes to the same thing, about what marks itself as the one-and-only time and is sometimes called a *date*. My main concern

Editors' note: This essay was originally given as a lecture, in French, at a conference on the works of Paul Celan held at the University of Washington, Seattle, in October 1984.

307

will not be to speak about the date so much as to listen to Celan speak about it or, rather, to watch as he gives himself over to the inscription of invisible dates: anniversaries, rings, constellations, and repetitions of singular and unrepeatable (*unwiederholbar*) events. How can one date the unrepeatable if dating also calls for some form of recurrence, in the readability of a repetition? Having just named the *Unwiederholbar* and having called attention to the borders of translation, I am tempted here simply to cite the poem which Celan entitled, in French, "A la pointe acérée," not because it has any direct connection with circumcision, but because it seeks its way in the night along paths of questions "Nach dem Unwiederholbar." For want of time and of knowing how to read Celan, I will have to be satisfied with these small pebbles of white chalk on a blackboard:

Ungeschriebenes, zu	Something unwritten,
Sprache verhärtet . . .	hardened to language . . .

In what follows, the unwritten switches over to a question of reading on a board or tablet which you perhaps are:

Tür du davor einst, Tafel	Door you before it once, tablet

(And with this *einst* it is again a question of one time, a single time)

mit dem getöteten	with the slain
Kreidestern drauf:	chalk star on it:
ihn	it
hat nun ein—lesendes?—Aug.	a—reading?—eye now has it.

We could also have followed the ever discrete, discontinuous, cae-sured, elliptical circuitry of the hour (*Waldstunde*) and of the trace (*Radspur*), but here what I am *after* is the question which seeks its way *after* (*nach*) the unrepeatable, through beechmast (*Buchecker*), which may also be read as book corners or the sharp edges of a text:

Wege dorthin.	Pathways there.
Waldstunde an	Foresthour along
der blubbernde Radspur entlang.	the spluttering wheeltrack.
Auf-	Up-
gelesene	gathered
kleine, klaffende	small, gaping
Buchecker: schwärzliches	Beechmast: blackish
Offen, von	Openness, asked of
Fingergedanken befragt	by fingerthoughts
Nach—	after—

wonach?	after what?
Nach	After
dem Unwiederholbaren, nach	the unrepeatable, after
ihm, nach	it, after
allem.	everything.
Blubbernde Wege dorthin.	Spluttering pathways there.
Etwas, das gehen kann, grusslos	Something, that can go, greetingless
wie Herzgewordenes,	as what has turned heart,
kommt.	comes.

What is going (*gehen*), coming (*kommen*), going and coming and turning-heart? What coming, what singular (*unwiederholbar*) event is in question? Given this question of turning-heart, and hearing me speak of the date and of circumcision, some might rush on to the "circumcised heart" of the Scriptures. Such haste, at least, and such facility are out of order. Celan's trenchant ellipsis requires more patience and discretion. Discontinuity is the law; discontinuity and that which nonetheless gathers in the discretion of the discontinuous, that which gathers in the ceasura of the relation to the other, in the interruption of address.

It makes no sense, as you may well suppose, to dissociate Celan's writings concerned with the theme of the date from a poetic practice of dating; to divide his writings into a theoretical, philosophical, hermeneutic, even technopoetic discourse concerning the phenomenon of the date, on the one hand, and its poetic implementation, on the other, would be simply not to read him. The example of the *Meridian* is there to warn us against such a misconstruction. It is, as they say, a "discourse," and one delivered on a particular occasion—that is, an address—dating from the conferral of a prize (*Rede anlässlich der Verleihung des Georg-Büchner-Preises*, 22 Oktober 1960). This address deals, in its way, with art or the memory of art, with art as, perhaps, a thing of the past ("Meine Damen und Herren, Die Kunst, das ist, Sie erinnern sich") and as *one* path for poetry, one among others and not the shortest. "I know that there are other, shorter, paths." Now this address, which deals, in its way, with this simple crossways between art and poetry, is traversed throughout by the question of the date. And this question resists all objectification—Celan shows this poetically, that is to say, in a way which I will explain, by a *mise-en-oeuvre* of the date—resists being formulated as a philosophical question or a theoretico-hermeneutic theme. Here the pace must be quickened. Having cited several dates (1909, the date of a work devoted to Jakob Michael Lenz; the night of

May 23–24, 1792, the date of Lenz's death in Moscow, cited in this work), Celan now mentions the date which appears on the first page of Büchner's *Lenz* who, "on January 20th, went into the mountains." He, Lenz, Celan insists, he and not the artist preoccupied by questions of art, he as an I, "er als ein Ich." The singular structure of this syntagm, "he as an I," is going to support the whole logic of individuation, of the sign of individuation, with which the *Meridian* will subsequently be concerned.

There was a 20th of January. Unique, unrepeatable, this date could be written; and yet its property of absolute uniqueness can be transcribed, exported, deported, expropriated, reappropriated, repeated in its utter singularity—and can enunciate, as its sign of individuation, something like the essence of the poem or, as Celan prefers to say, of "every poem," better still, of "each poem." "Vielleicht darf man sagen, dass jedem Gedicht sein '20. Jänner' eingeschrieben bleibt?": "Perhaps one should say that each poem has its own 20th of January inscribed within it? Perhaps what is new in the poems which are written today is just this: that here, most clearly, one seeks to remain mindful of such dates (dass hier am deutlichsten versucht wird, solcher Daten einge-denk zu bleiben)?" This question and hypothesis concerning the date are dated by Celan; they relate *today* to every poem *today*, to what is new in each poetic work of our time, which, at this date, would share the singularity (which I do not dare call modern) of dating, of remaining mindful of dates ("Daten eingedenk zu bleiben"). The poetic today would perhaps be dated by an inscription of the date. Granted.

But—the sentences which I have just read are followed by three *buts*. The first, which is the least strong and the least oppositional, raises again the same questions concerning the traces of the other as I: how can some other irreplaceable and singular date, how can the date of the other be deciphered, transcribed, or appropriated by me? Or, rather, how can I transcribe myself into it and how can the memory of such a date still dispose of a future? Here, then, is the first But: the ellipsis of the sentence is more economical than I can convey and its sobriety admirable: "Aber schreiben wir uns nicht alle von solchen Daten her? Und welchen Daten schreiben wir uns zu?" "But don't we all transcribe ourselves out of such dates? And to what dates to come do we ascribe ourselves?"

Here the second *Aber* arises, but only after a blank space or very marked silence. And its force of opposition reaches the point of ex-

clamation: "Aber das Gedicht spricht ja! Es bleibt seiner Daten einge-
denk, aber—es spricht. Gewiss, es spricht immer nur in seiner eigenen,
allereigensten Sache." ("But still the poem speaks! It remains mindful
of its dates, but—it speaks. To be sure it speaks always only in its own,
inmost concern.") The *but* seems to carry the poem's utterance beyond
its date; it seems to recall that if the poem recalls the date, calls itself
back to its date, to the date at which it is written, of which it writes, as
of which it writes (and the ambiguous force of *von* in the preceding
phrase—"von solchen Daten"—conveys all of this: we write of the date,
about certain dates, but also *as* of certain dates, *at* [à] certain dates, and
this *at* itself carries another ambiguous force, directed *toward* a future
of unknown destination, "Und welchen Daten schreiben wir uns zu,"
turned toward what dates to come do we write ourselves, do we ascribe ourselves? As if writing *at* a date meant not only writing on a
given day, *at* a given hour, but also writing *to* [à] the date, addressing
oneself to it, intending oneself for [à] the date as one is destined for the
other, the one past as well as that to come [l'à venir—cf. l'avenir—
Trans.]. What is this "to" of "to come"—as date?), still the poem speaks.
Despite the date, Celan seems to say, even if it also speaks thanks to
it, of it, as of it, to it, and always in its own inmost concern, "in seiner
eigenen, allereigensten Sache," without ever compromising with the
absolute and singular specificity of that which calls it forth. The date
provokes the poem *but* the latter speaks! How are we to understand
what at first seems surprising, the force of this *but*, of this exclamatory
and, it would seem, by no means rhetorical objection?

If the poem is due its date, due *to* its date, owes itself to its date
as its own inmost concern, it speaks of this date only insofar as it is
freed, as it were, of its debt—and of its date, which is also something
given—releasing itself from the date without disavowing it. It absolves
itself of its debt so that its utterance may carry beyond a singularity
which might otherwise remain undecipherable, mute, and immured
in its date—in the unrepeatable. One must, while preserving its memory, speak the date, that is to say, efface it, make it readable and audible
beyond its singularity. The beyond of absolute singularity, the poem's
chance to speak, is not the simple effacement of the date in a generality,
but its effacement faced with another date, the date of an other
strangely wed or joined in an *encounter* with the same date. I will offer
by way of clarification some examples in a moment. What takes place
in this experience of a date which must be effaced in order to be

preserved, in order to preserve the commemoration of the singular which the poem's utterance nonetheless must transgress, transport, offer to understanding beyond the unreadability of its cipher? What takes place is perhaps what Celan calls a little further on *Geheimnis der Begegnung*, the secretness of encounter; and in the word *encounter* two values come together without which there would be no date: encounter as it suggests the random occurrence, the chance meeting, the co-incidence or conjuncture which comes to seal one or more than one event *once*, at a given hour, on a given day, in a given month, in a given region; and encounter as it suggests an encounter with the other, the other ineluctable singularity for which the poems speaks and which may in its very otherness inhabit the conjunction of one and the same date. It happens.

The third *But*, at this point, opens a paragraph which, beginning with "But I think," "Aber ich denke," closes with "today and here," with the date and signature of a "heute und hier": "But I think—and such a thought will not surprise you now—I think that it has always belonged to the hopes of the poem to speak as well, and precisely in this manner, in some strange—no, I can no longer use this word—precisely in this manner to speak in the concern of an Other—who knows, perhaps in the concern of a *wholly Other*. This 'who knows,' which I see I have come to, is indeed the single thing [*das einzige*] which it is possible for me, today and here, to add to these old hopes." The "wholly other" (*ganz Anderen*) thus opens the thought of the poem to some thing or some concern (*Sache:* "in *eines Anderen Sache* zu sprechen . . . in eines *ganz Anderen* Sache") the otherness of which must not contradict but rather enter into alliance with, in expropriating, the "inmost concern" just in question, due to which the poem speaks at its date, as of its date, and always "in seiner eigenen, allereigensten Sache." Several singular events may conjoin, enter into alliance, concentrate in the same date, which is thus both the same and other, wholly other as the same, capable of speaking to the other, to the one who cannot decipher one or another absolutely closed date, closed like a tomb, over the event which it marks. Celan calls this multiplicity by the very strong and very charged name of "concentration." This is a little further on, when he speaks of the "attentiveness" (*die Aufmerksamkeit*) which the poem seeks to grant all that it encounters. This attentiveness, he specifies, is rather a kind of concentration which remains mindful of "all our dates" ("eine aller unserer Daten eingedenk bleibende Konzentration"). I understand the word *concentration*, which can become a terrible word for memory, *at once* both in that register in which one speaks of the gathering of the soul or of "mental concentration," as, for example, in the experience of prayer (and Celan cites Benjamin citing Malebranche in his essay on Kafka: "L'attention est la prière naturelle de l'âme"), and in that other dimension in which concentration gathers around the same anamnetic center a multiplicity of dates, "all our dates" coming to conjoin or constellate in a single occurrence or a single place. And this is what goes on perhaps in the act of the *Meridian*—an act which, in my eyes, is exemplary—making of it, as I have already said, something else and something more than a meta-discourse about the date: rather, a poem inhabiting poetically its own date and making of a date which is one's own, absolutely one's own, a date for the other, the date of the other, or, inversely, for it comes around like an anniversary, the step by which the poet transcribes and translates himself into the date of the other. One and the "same" date commemorates, in the uniqueness of its constellation, heterogeneous events. You may read this in the lines toward the end of the text:

"Ich hatte mich, das eine wie das andere Mal, von einem '20. Jänner,' von meinem '20. Jänner,' hergeschrieben.
Ich bin . . . mir selbst begegnet."

"I had, both the one time and the other, out of a 20th January, out of my 20th January, transcribed myself.
I . . . encountered myself."

Does one ever speak of a date? Whether one knows it or not, whether one acknowledges it or conceals it, an utterance is always dated. What I am going to hazard concerning the date in general or concerning the dates of Paul Celan will be dated in its turn.

What dating comes to is signing. To inscribe a date, to enter it, is not simply to sign as of a given year, month, day, or hour (all words which obsess the whole of Celan's text), but also to sign from a given place, as we say "dated" Zürich, Tübingen, Todtnauberg, etc. A date consigns to a letter's opening or closing something of the calendar or indeed the clock but also, in their proper name, something of the country, the region, and the house. It marks in this way the provenance of what is given, or, in any case, sent; of what is, whether or not it arrives, *destined. Addressing its date,* what an address or discourse declares about the concept or meaning of the date is not, by that fact, dated, in the sense in which one says of something that it dates in order to imply that it has aged, and poorly; in speaking of a discourse as dated, our intention is not to disqualify or invalidate it, but rather to signify that it is, at the least, marked by its date, signed by it or re-marked in a singular manner.

It is concerning this singular remarking that I am going to hazard in my turn some remarks—in memory of some consignments bearing Celan's date [envois datés de Celan].

What is a date? Do we have the right to pose such a question, and in this form? The form of the question "what is" has a provenance: it dates. That it is dated does not discredit it, but if we had the time, we could draw certain inferences from this fact.

Has anyone ever been concerned with the question "what is a date?" The "you" who is told "Nirgends fragt es nach dir" ("Nowhere is there any asking about you") is a date, of that we may be a priori certain. This you, which may be an I, like the "er als ein Ich" of a moment ago, always figures an irreplaceable singularity—one which is thus replaceable only by another irreplaceable singularity which takes its place without substituting for it. This you is addressed as one addresses a date, as the here and now of a commemorable provenance.

As it reaches me, at least, the question "what is a date?" presupposes two things. First of all, that the formulation "what is . . . etc." has a history or provenance, in other words, that it is signed, engaged, or commanded by a date in relation to whose essence its power is limited, its claim finite, and its very pertinence contestable. This fact is not unrelated to what this Colloquium calls "the philosophical implications" of Celan's work. Perhaps philosophy, at least insofar as it makes use of the question "what is," has nothing essential to say about what bears Celan's date or about what Celan says or makes of dates—while the latter tells us something, perhaps, about philosophy. On the other hand, and this is a second presupposition, in the inscription of a date, in the phenomenon of dating, what is dated *must not be dated* (the date: yes and no, Celan would say). The mark which one calls a date must be marked off in a particular manner, detached from that precisely which it dates—and in this very marking off or deportation it must become readable, readable as precisely a date, wresting or exempting itself from itself, freeing itself from what it nonetheless remains, a date. In it the *Unwiederholbar* must be repeated, that is to say, effaced, ciphered, or encrypted. Like *physis*, a date likes to encrypt itself and thus to efface itself in order to become readable. For if it does not efface in itself the singularity which connects it to an event without witness, it remains intact but absolutely indecipherable. It is no longer even what it has to be, a date.

How, then, can that which is dated, while at the same time marking a date, not date? This question, whether one finds this heartening or worrying, cannot be formulated in this way in all languages—perhaps only in French and English—which is to say that its translatability remains limited. I insist on this because what a date, which is always related, as we will see, to some proper name, offers for our consideration, commemoration, or blessing is, each time, an idiom. And if the idiomatic form of the question may appear untranslatable, this is because it plays on the double functioning, in French, of the verb *to date*: transitively: I date a poem; intransitively: a poem dates if it ages, if it has a history.

To ask "What is a date?" is not to ask about the meaning of the word *date*. Nor is it to inquire into the essence of an established or putative etymology, though this may not be without interest for us. It might, in fact, lead us to think about the given and literality, and, in particular, the giving of the letter. *Data littera*, the given letter: isn't this the first word of the formula for indicating the date? So a letter's first word, its initial, its opening enters into it: the first letter of a letter—but also of something given or sent. The sense of the date as something given or sent will perhaps carry us as well beyond the question given in the form "what is?" A date is not something which *is there*, since it withdraws in order to appear, but perhaps *there are* (*gibt es*) dates. I will associate for the moment, in a preliminary and disorderly way, the values of the given and the proper name (for a date functions like a proper name) with three other essential values: 1) that of the missive [envoi] within the strict limits of the epistolary code; 2) the re-marking of place and time; 3) the signature, for if *data littera* is the initial letter, it may nonetheless come, as date, at the letter's end and in either case, whether at the beginning or the end, have the force of a signed commitment, of an obligation, a promise or an oath (*sacramentum*). In its essence, a signature is always dated and only has value on this account. It dates and is a date.

As the readers of Celan whom I am addressing here know very well, he often dated his poems and in a certain sense dated all of them.

I am not thinking here, in the first place, of a kind of dating which one might—superficially—call "external," namely, the mention of the date on which a poem was written. This mention lies in some ways outside the poem. One certainly is not entitled to push to its limit the distinction between an "external" mention of the date and a more essential incorporation of the date within the poem; in a certain way, it is this very limit which Celan's poetry tends to efface. But, supposing that we maintain it as a preliminary convenience and for clarity of exposition, we will be concerned first of all with that dating which is entered in the body of the poem, consigned to one of its parts, and at times, indeed, with that dating which, leaving nothing over, is utterly confounded with the general organization of the poetic text.

In *Eden*, that memorable reading of the poem from *Schneepart*, "DU LIEGST im grossen Gelausche," Szondi recalls that an indication of date accompanied its first publication: Berlin 22–23–12–1967. We know how Szondi turned to account these dates and his chance to have been the intimate witness of, and at times actor in, or party to, the experiences commemorated, displaced, and ciphered by the poem. We also know with what rigor and modesty he posed the problems of this *situation*, both with regard to the poem's genesis and with regard to the competence of its decipherers. We must indeed take into account, as he did, the fact that, as the intimate and lucid witness of all the chance happenings and all the necessities which intersected at the date of Celan's passing through Berlin, Szondi was able to bequeath us the irreplaceable password of access to the poem, a priceless *Shibboleth*, a luminous, clamorous swarm of *Shibboleth*; and that still, left to itself without witness, without an implicated and informed decipherer, without even the external knowledge of its date, a certain internal necessity of the poem would "speak" to us—in the sense in which Celan says that the poem, beyond its date, "still speaks." Szondi was the first to acknowledge this, to set this enigma before himself with a lucidity to which we must pay homage. I do not want to engage in my own commemorations or provide my own dates (perhaps I will do so *a parte*, outside this somewhat formal session), but permit me to recall here that it was only a few months after this date, in 1968, that I met Szondi in Berlin at his seminar, by his invitation, and that we were already connected by friendship when some months later, thus in the same year, he introduced me to Paul Celan in Paris.

What Szondi recalls, from the very beginning of his reading, is that

Celan suppressed the poem's date for the first collection and that it also does not figure in the *Ausgewählte Gedichte* which Reichert edited in 1971. This conforms, says Szondi, with Celan's customary practice: "the poems are dated in the manuscript, but not in the published versions." But the effacement of what we are calling the "external" date does not do away with the internal dating. And while the latter carries in its turn a force of self-effacement, as I will try to show, what is involved is a structure of self-effacement which is wholly other and which confounds itself with the inscription of the date itself.

We are going to be concerned then with the date as a cut or incision which the poem bears in its body like a memory, like, at times, several memories in one. To speak of an incision or cut is to say that the poem is entered into, that it begins in the wounding of its date.

If we had the time, we should patiently analyze all the modalities of dating. There are many. In this typology, the most conventional form of dating, dating in the so-called literal or strict sense, involves marking a missive [envoi] with coded signs. It entails reference to charts, and the utilization of systems of notation and spatio-temporal plottings: the calendar (year, month, day); the clock (the hours, whether or not they are named—and how often will Celan name them but also restore them to the night of their ciphered silence: "sie werden die Stunde nicht nennen ..." ["They will not name the hour"], "Nächtlich geschürzt" ["tucked up in night"]), toponomy, and first of all the names of cities (Berlin, Zürich, Tübingen, Paris). These coded marks all involve the same shift: while assigning or consigning the singularity of an event to a particular place and time, they must, at the same time, in the possibility of commemoration, mark themselves off from themselves. In effect, they mark only insofar as their readability enunciates the possibility of a recurrence, and the recurrence of that which precisely cannot return, the possibility, let us say then, of the spectral return [revenance] of that which, unique in its occurrence, will never return. A date is a specter. But the spectral return of this impossible recurrence is marked in the date in the sort of ring or anniversary secured by a code such as the calendar. The ring of the anniversary, which may also be the circuit of return to the city whose name dates the poem, inscribes the possibility of repetition from the moment of the date's first inscription. The latter comes to sign and seal what is unique and *unwiederholbar*; but to do so it must offer itself for reading in a form which is coded, readable, and decipherable enough for the ring of the anniversary to be able to consecrate it and the undecipherable to *appear*, be it *as* undecipherable. I would be tempted to associate here all of Celan's rings with this alliance between the date and itself as other. You know how many there are and that they are all unique. Allow me to cite, as imposing itself, the one in "Mit Brief und Uhr":

Fingern, wächsern auch sie,
Durch fremde
schmerzende Ringe gezogen.
Fortgeschmolzen die Kuppen.

Fingers, also waxen,
through strange
painful rings drawn.
The tips melted away.

Or again, the "so leichten / Seelen- / ringen" ("so gentle / soul- / rings") of "Chymisch," the "schönes, lautloses Rund" ("beautiful, soundless Round") of "Erratisch," the "und am Finger erwacht uns der Ring" ("and on our finger the ring awakens") in "ES WAR ERDE IN IHNEN" and especially, since we are speaking of a date which is never without a letter to be deciphered, the ring of the carrier-pigeon at the end of "La Contrescarpe": the carrier-pigeon transports, transfers, or translates a coded message, it departs at its date, that of its sending, and must return from the other place to the same one, to the one from which it came. And the question of the cipher is posed by Celan not only with regard to the message but also with regard to the ring itself: the cipher of the seal, the imprint of the ring *counts*, perhaps more than the content of the message:

Scherte die Brieftaube aus, war ihr Ring
zu entziffern? (All das
Gewölk um sie her—es war lesbar.)

Did the carrier-pigeon sheer off, was its ring
decipherable? (All that
cloud around it—it was readable.)

The date effaces itself in its very readability; it must efface in itself some stigma of singularity in order to outlast, in the poem, what it commemorates; in this lies the chance of assuring its spectral return. And since this annulment in the annulation of return partakes of the very movement of dating, what must henceforth commemorate itself is the annihilation itself of the date, a kind of nothing—or ash.

Let us stay for the moment with those dates which are caught in the grid of the calendar's language, the day, the month, the year. A given date may commemorate an event which, at least in appearance and outwardly, is distinct from the writing itself of the poem and the moment of its signing: "Dreizehnter Feber," for example, "Thirteenth of February," the first line of "In Eins."

What is gathered and commemorated in the single time of this "in eins," at one poetic stroke? And is it a matter, moreover, of *one* commemoration? The "all in one," "all at once," seems to constellate in the uniqueness of a date, but is this date, in being unique, also one? And what if there were more than one thirteenth of February?—not only because the thirteenth of February becomes each year its own *revenant*, but first of all because a multiplicity of events, in dispersed places (dispersed, for example, on the map of Europe), at different periods, in foreign idioms, may have conjoined for the same anniversary.

IN EINS	ALL IN ONE
Dreizehnter Feber. Im Herzmund erwachtes Schibboleth. Mit dir, Peuple. de Paris. No *pasarán*.	Thirteenth of February. In the heartsmouth an awakened shibboleth. With you, Peuple de Paris. No *pasarán*.

Like all the rest of the poem, and well in excess of what I will be able to say, these first lines are *evidently* ciphered. That they are is in evidence in several senses and in several languages: first of all, in that they include a cipher, the numeral thirteen. This cipher marks one of those numbers in which chance and necessity cross and in this crossing are, just one time, consigned. It is the ligament which holds together a fatality and its opposite, in a manner which is at once both significant and insignificant:

DIE ZAHLEN, im Bund mit der Bilder Verhängnis und Gegen- verhängnis. ("DIE ZAHLEN")	NUMBERS, in league with the fatality of images and their counter- fatality. ("NUMBERS")
Und Zahlen waren mitverwoben in das Unzählbare ("Die Silbe Schmerz")	And numbers were interwoven into the numberless. ("The Syllable Pain")

Even before the number thirteen, the one of "In Eins" announces the con-signing and co-signing of a multiple singularity. From the title and the opening on, cipher, and then date, are incorporated in the poem. They give access to the poem which they are, but a ciphered access. These first lines are ciphered in another sense: more than others, they are untranslatable. I am not thinking here of all the poetic challenges with which this great poet-translator confronts poet-translators. I limit myself here to the aporia—to the barred passage: *no pasarán*—this is what "aporia" means—constituted by a multiplicity of languages in a single poem, all at once: four languages, like a series of proper names or signatures. As with the title and the date, the first line is in German. In the second line, a second language, an apparently Hebrew word, arises in the "heartsmouth": "Im Herzmund / erwachtes Schibboleth." This second language could well be a first language, the language of the morning, the language of origin speaking of and from the heart. Language in Hebrew is lip, and doesn't Celan speak elsewhere (we will come to it) of circumcised words, as one speaks of the "circumcised heart"? Leave this for the moment. The word I have referred to as Hebrew, *Shibboleth*, is found, as you know, in a whole family of languages (Phoenician, Judeo-Aramaic, Syriac); apart from the multiplicity of meanings which are grafted on to it (river, stream, ear of grain, olive-twig), *Shibboleth* has the value of a password. It was used during or rather after the war, at the crossing of a border under watch. The word mattered less for its meaning than for the way in which it was pronounced. The Ephraimites had been defeated by the army of Jephthah and in order to keep the soldiers from escaping across the river (*Shibboleth* also means river, though this is not necessarily the reason it was chosen), each person was required to say "*Shibboleth*." As the Ephraimites were known for their inability to pronounce correctly the *shi* sound, this was an "unpronounceable word" for them, so that they would say "sib-boleth" and thus betray themselves to the sentinel at the risk of death. This barred right of passage at the border of the Jordan is repeated, in reverse, so to speak, in the fourth language of the strophe, *no pasarán* (February 1936: this is the challenge to the fascists, to Franco's troops, to the Phalange supported by Mussolini's troops and Hitler's Condor legion: "They shall not pass" is the cry of the Republicans and the International Brigade, what they are writing on their banderoles, just before the fall of Madrid in February). Spanish is allotted to the whole central strophe ("er sprach / uns das Wort in die Hand, das wir brauchen es war / Hirten-Spanisch, darin . . .") ("he spoke / the word in our hand, the one we need there was / Shepherd-Spanish in it . . .") which transcribes, in short, a kind of Spanish *Shibboleth*, a password, a pass-not-word, a silent word transmitted like a *symbolon* or handclasp, a rallying sign, a sign of membership and political watchword. Amidst the German, the Hebrew, and the Spanish, in French, the people of Paris: "Mit dir, / Peuple / de Paris." The multiplicity of languages may concelebrate, at one and the same date, the poetic and political anniversary of singular events, spread like stars over the map of Europe and conjoined by a secret affinity (the fall of Vienna and the fall of Madrid in February of '36, since, as we shall see, Vienna and Madrid are associated in the same line by another poem, entitled "Shibboleth"; the beginnings—precisely in February—of the October Revolution with the incidents connected with the cruiser *Aurora* and with Petrograd, indeed with the Peter and Paul Fortress: this is the last stanza of "In Eins"; and no doubt other singular moments which I will not here undertake to decipher). But even within the same language, French for example, a discontinuous multiplicity of events may be commemorated by *one and the same date*, which consequently takes on the strange, *unheimlich* dimensions of a cryptic predestination. The date itself resembles a *Shibboleth* giving ciphered access to this configuration. The more indeterminate the date, the more ample and, so to speak, populous the constellated series. If Celan says only "February," as in the poem entitled "Schibboleth," one can spend hours bringing together all the demonstrations of the same kind, with the same political significance, which brought the people of Paris, that is, the people of the left, together in the surge of a single impulse to say, like the Republicans of Madrid, *no pasarán*. To take only one example, it is on the twelfth of February, 1934, after the failure of the attempt to form a Common Front of the Right (under Doriot), after the riot of February sixth, that a huge march takes place which spontaneously regroups the masses and the leadership of the parties of the left. This march was, in effect, the origin of the Popular Front. But if Celan specifies, in "In Eins," the "thirteenth of February," one may think (and I consign this hypothesis to those who may know something about or can testify concerning the so-called "external" date of the poem; I am unaware of it, but even should my hypothesis be factually false, it would still designate the power of those dates to come to which, Celan says, we write and ascribe ourselves) of the thirteenth of February, 1962. Celan was in Paris and *Die Niemandsrose* was not published until 1963. Moreover, it is in the later piece, "In Eins," that Celan specifies the "thirteenth of February," whereas in "Schibboleth," the earlier poem, he says only "February." February 13, 1962 is the day of the funeral for the Métro Charonne massacre victims, an anti-OAS demonstration at the end of the Algerian war. Several hundred thousand Parisians, the "people of Paris," are marching, and it is two days after the opening of Franco-Algerian meetings with a view to the Evian accords. The people of Paris are also the people of the Commune with whom Celan wished to ally himself: mit dir, peuple de Paris.

Like the date, and, at once, in eins, Shibboleth is marked several times, and marked just as much by a multiplicity. Within the poem, it names, as is obvious, the password or rallying cry, the right of access to or sign of membership in all the political situations, along all the historical borders which are brought together in the poem's configuration. This, it will be said, is the Shibboleth as theme or thematic meaning of the text. But Shibboleth also marks, in the sense of cryptic or numerical cipher, the anniversary date's singular power of gathering together, as it grants access to the date's memory, its future, but also as it grants access to the poem itself. Shibboleth is the Shibboleth for the right to the poem which is itself a Shibboleth, its own Shibboleth at the very moment that it dates and commemorates others. Shibboleth is its title, as in one of the two poems in which the word appears. This does not mean, on the one hand, that the events commemorated in this fantastic constellation are non-poetic events transfigured by an incantation. No, I believe that for Celan the signifying conjunction of all these dramas and historical actors would have been in itself the dated signature, the dating of the poem. Nor does this mean, on the other hand, that possession of the Shibboleth effaces the cipher, holds the key to the crypt, and guarantees the transparency of meaning. The crypt remains, the Shibboleth remains secret, and the poem unveils this secret as a secret which is withdrawn, beyond the reach of any hermeneutic exhaustion. The secret is not hermetic, but it remains, like a date, heterogeneous to all hermeneutic totalization or radicalization. There is no one meaning, no single originary meaning, from the moment that there is a date and a Shibboleth.

A Shibboleth, the word Shibboleth, if it is one, names, in the broadest extension of its generality or its usage, any insignificant, arbitrary mark, for example the phonemic difference between shi and si, once it becomes discriminative and decisive, that is, divisive. This difference has no meaning in and of itself, and becomes what one must know how to mark or recognize if one is to get on, if, that is, one is to get over a border or the threshold of a poem, if one is to be granted asylum or the legitimate habitation of a language. And to inhabit a language, one must already have a *Shibboleth* at one's command: it is not enough simply to understand the meaning of the word, simply to know how it should be pronounced (*shi* and not *si*, this the Ephraimites knew). One must *be able* to say it as it should be said. There is nothing hidden about this secret, this claim of alliance, no meaning concealed within a crypt, but it is a cipher which one must *share and divide* [*partager*—see below—Trans.] with the other.

Shibboleth is thus not only a cipher, and the cipher of the poem; it is the cipher of the cipher, the ciphered manifestation of the cipher as such. And when a cipher manifests itself as what it is, that is to say, in encrypting itself, it does not say to us "I am a cipher." It may still conceal from us, without even wanting to, the secret which it shelters in its very readability. It moves, touches, fascinates, or seduces us all the more. The ellipsis and caesura of discretion inhabit it, there is nothing it can do about it, it is a passion before it becomes a calculated risk, before it risks a strategy of encryptment, or a poetics of ciphering intended, as with Joyce, to keep the professors busy for generations. Even supposing that this was Joyce's first and true desire, something which I do not believe, I am certain that it was foreign to Celan.

Just as much as it marks the multiplicity of languages, that is to say *Babel* (the last word of the following poem, "Hinausgekrönt," which also names the "Ghetto-Rose"), and the migration of languages ("es wandert überallhin, wie die Sprache"—"it wanders all over, like language"—in "Es ist alles anders"), *Shibboleth* marks the multiplicity within language, insignificant difference as the condition of sense in language. And even if one speaks of a multiplicity of languages, it is proper to specify that Babelian untranslatability is connected not only with the difficult passage (*no pasarán*) from one poetic language to another, but also with the aporia, the impasse beyond all possible transaction, which is connected with the multiplicity of languages within the uniqueness of a poetic inscription. This uniqueness—which is also a date and a *Shibboleth*—forges and seals, *in eins*, in a single idiom—which is the poetic event—a multiplicity of languages and of singular dates. *In Eins*: within the unity, within the uniqueness of this poem, the four languages would nonetheless seem easy enough to translate, or so it appears. But what will always remain untranslatable into any single language whatsoever is the fact or the mark of the multiplicity of languages in the poem. Look at what happens with the excellent French translation, for example. The German is translated into French, as is normal. *Schibboleth* and *no pasarán* are left untranslated, which respects the foreignness of these words in the principal medium, the German idiom of the text. But in preserving the French of the original version in the translation, "Avec toi, Peuple / de Paris," the translation can only efface the very thing which it preserves, the foreign effect of the French in the poem, which places it in configuration with all those ciphers, passwords, and *Shibboleths* which date and sign the poem in *eins*, in the at once dissociated and adjoined unity of its singularities. And there is no remedy to which translation could have recourse here, none at least in the body of the translated poem. No one is to blame. A *Shibboleth* is untranslatable, not because of some inaccessibility of its meaning to transference, not simply because of some semantic secret, but by virtue of that in it which forms the cut of a non-signifying difference in the body of the (written or oral) mark. On both sides of the historical, political, and linguistic border the meaning, the different meanings of the word *Shibboleth* are known, one even knows how it should be pronounced. But there is a test once, in the course of which some cannot pronounce it with the heart's mouth, and they will not cross, they will not cross the boundaries of the country, of the community, or simply of the poem. And from this point of view, the value of the *Shibboleth* may always be tragically inverted: a watchword or password in the struggle against fascism, racism, oppression, and exclusion, it may also corrupt its differential value, which is the condition of alliance and of the poem, making of it a discriminatory limit, a technique of exclusion or screening. We will return to this.

Inserted in the second line of "In Eins," the word *Schibboleth* also forms the title of a longer poem published in 1955 in the collection *Von Schwelle zu Schwelle* (*From Threshold to Threshold*). And *Shibboleth* is indeed the threshold word, the word which permits one to pass or to cross, to transfer and, one could even say, to translate. One finds here more or less the same constellation of events, sealed by the same February anniversary, the linking of the capitals of Vienna and Madrid substituted perhaps for the linking in "In Eins" of Paris, Madrid, and Petropolis. The words *no pasarán* are again in close proximity to *Schibboleth*. No doubt it is again February 1938 which is in question, though this time the day, as well as the year, does not appear; and this, taking into account the fact that references to France and the French language appear to be absent, leads one to think that, in fact, another date is in question, in the otherness of which other Februaries, including a certain thirteenth of February, come together, overdetermining the *Sprachgitter* of the signature. The play of resemblances and differences, that is to say the *Shibboleth between* the two poems, the passage from one to the other, could occasion an interminable analysis which I cannot even sketch here. Apart from its presence in the poem's title, the word *Schibboleth* appears in close proximity to *no pasarán*, as I just recalled, in a strophe which one might call openhearted, opened through the heart, through the single word *Herz*. In "In Eins," it will be *Herzmund*, again in the first line:

Herz:	Heart:
gib dich auch hier zu erkennen,	make yourself known even here,
hier, in der Mitte des Marktes.	here, in the middle of the market.
Ruf's, das Schibboleth, hinaus	Call it out, the shibboleth,
in die Fremde der Heimat:	into the homeland's strangeness:
Februar. No pasarán.	February. No pasarán.
	(trans. Joachim Neugroschel)

Strangeness, estrangement in one's own home, not being at home, being called away from home in one's homeland, the not of "they shall not" [ce pas (step) du "ne pas"] which secures and threatens every border crossing in and out of oneself, this moment of the *Shibboleth* is re-marked in the date itself, by which I mean here in the month of and in the word February. The difference is hardly translatable: *Februar* in "Schibboleth," *Feber* (*Dreizehnter Feber*) in "In Eins" leading, through an archaizing play and an etymology attributed, no doubt falsely, to *februarius*, to a moment of fever.

The two poems thus remain as kindred and as different as possible. They bear and do not bear the same date. A *Shibboleth* secures the passage from one to the other in the difference, within sameness, of the same date, between *Februar* and *Feber*. They speak two different languages. *Shibboleth* is, if one may make use here of a word more common in French than in English, a word of *partage*: *partage* as difference, line of demarcation, parting of the waters, scission, caesura, border, dissociation; but also as participation, as that which is divided because it is held in common, by virtue of partaking of the same. Fascinated by a resemblance which is both semantic and formal and which nonetheless has no linguistico-historical explanation, I will hazard a comparison between *partage* as shibboleth and *partage* as *symbolon*. In both cases, we find S-B-L, in both a token transmitted to another ("er sprach / uns das Wort in die Hand"), a word or piece of a word; the complementary part of an object divided in two comes to seal an alliance. This is the moment of engagement, of signing, of the pact or contract, of the gift, the promise, the ring.

The date, like the signature, plays a role here. It not only marks a singular event of which it would be the detachable proper name, able to outlive and thus to call, to recall what has vanished *as vanished*, even incinerated; it gathers together, like a title (*titulus* includes a sense of gathering) a more or less apparent and secret conjunction of singularities which share and divide [se partagent], and in the future will continue to share and divide [se partageront] the *same* date. There is no limit assignable to such a conjunction. No testimony, no knowledge, not even Celan's, can, by definition, exhaust the deciphering or decrypting of a date and of the events which share, in dividing it [se partagent], a date.

First of all—and here we may all think of that admirable reading of Szondi's which I referred to just before—because there is no external witness who could enable an external deciphering, and Celan may always have concealed one more *Shibboleth* beneath a word, cipher, or letter. Second, Celan himself would not have claimed to have exhausted the possible meanings of a constellation. Finally and above all, the poem is destined to remain alone, it is destined for this from its first breath, alone after all the witnesses and witnesses of witnesses have vanished. The date is a witness, it bears witness, but one may very well bless it without any longer knowing to what and for whom it bears witness. And it is always possible that there may no longer be any witness for this witness. This is where the poem begins—to speak. I will say in a moment why I feel that there is, in this regard, an affinity between a date, a name and ash. You recall the last words of "ASCHEN-GLORIE":

Niemand	No one
zeugt für den	bears witness
Zeugen.	for the witness.

A certain repetition, folded or refolded in the simplicity of the singular, thus assures, paradoxically, the minimal and "internal" readability of the poem, in the very absence of a witness or even a signatory, or of anyone assured of knowledge. And this is what the word or title *Shibboleth* signifies, as it were. It does not signify this or that (river, ear of grain, olive-twig, or all the other meanings which it takes on in the two poems). It signifies: there is *Shibboleth*, there is encrypting, it is not calculated, but destined, it does not conceal a determinate secret, a semantic content waiting behind the door for the one who holds the key. And if this crypt is symbolic, this does not in the last analysis derive from some tropic or rhetoric; there is, to be sure, meaning, a theme, something symbolized. But what the poem marks, what it enters and incises in the form of a date, is that there is *partage* of the *Shibboleth* and that this *partage* is at once open and closed. The date (signature, moment, place, totality of singular marks) always functions as a *Shibboleth*. It marks the fact that there is ciphered singularity which is irreducible to any concept, to any knowledge, and even to a history or tradition, be it of a religious kind; a ciphered singularity in which a multiplicity gathers itself in *eins*, but through whose grill a poem remains readable: "Aber das Gedicht spricht ja!" It reaches and leaves its mark on, and if it does not, at least it calls to, the other. It speaks to and addresses the other. In a language, in the poetic writing of a language, there is nothing but *Shibboleth*. And it permits, like every date, like a name, anniversaries, alliances, returns, commemorations, even if there should be no trace, scarcely an ash of what we thus date, celebrate, commemorate, or bless.

Other poems inscribe in themselves the dating coded in calendars or toponymy. "Tübingen, Jänner" (*Jänner* in the old style, heralding *Feber*) is at one and the same time a title, a date, and a signature, taking into its consignment, like a *Shibboleth*, enigma and memory, citing the enigma:

Ihre—"ein	Their—"a
Rätsel ist Rein-	riddle is pure
entsprungenes"—, ihre	origin"—, their
Erinnerung an	memory of
schwimmende Holderlintürme . . .	swimming Holderlin-towers . . .

"La Contrescarpe" writes, in italics and in parentheses, "(*Quatorze juillets* . . .)." This is in French in the original and thus untranslatable into French. The incorporated date is overdetermined in several ways. For one, it commemorates what, for two centuries now, every fourteenth of July may commemorate. At the same time, the fourteenth of July is the emblem of commemoration itself, the figure of a political and revolutionary anniversary in general, past and to come. In addition, "Quatorze juillets" is written here with an *s*, the mark of the plural in this disorthography insisting on the plurality of rings, of anniversaries which are not only and not necessarily anniversaries of the same original fourteenth of July, but also perhaps of other more or less secret events, of other rings, anniversaries, alliances, other partakings [partages] of the same date. The same parenthesis adds, again in italics: "(*Quatorze juillets. Et plus de neuf autres*)," which one may read as nine other fourteenth of Julys or as 14 + 9 = 23 Julys, 23 months of July, 23 anniversaries. If I say that I don't know what other anniversaries the poem is thus turning towards, this does not mean that "I don't want to know" or that I am foregoing all interpretation which would make use of the resources of hermeneutics, philosophy, historical knowledge, biographical testimony, and so on. What "I don't know" means is that the poem, in what I have elsewhere called its *remnance*, speaks from beyond knowledge; and what it tells me is, first of all, this very fact, that it speaks from beyond knowledge, of dates and of signatures which one may encounter and bless without knowing anymore what they date and what they sign, commemorating through forgetfulness or the unshared [non partagé] secret, sharing in the unshareable [le partage de l'impartageable]. The "Quatorze juillets" form the cut of an *unwiederholbar* singularity, but they repeat the unique in the ring, which is to say the tropic, that sets anniversaries turning around the same. Furthermore, the whole of the poem multiplies the signs of other events associated with the fourteenth of July. One is thus led to think that "Quatorze juillets" is not a listed date, the date of public and political history, but perhaps, who knows, the date which signs in secret, the private seal which, at the least, marks with its initials or flourish the advent of this particular poem. This signature would make up part of the constellation. I will simply recall, without other commentary, that "Conversation in the Mountains," says somewhere "and July is not July." This is in the course of a meditation on the Jew, son of a Jew, whose name is "unpronounceable," and who has nothing of his own, nothing that is not borrowed, so that, like a date, what is proper to the Jew is to have no property or essence. Jewish is not Jewish. We will come back to this. For the Ephraimites too, *Shibboleth* was an unpronounceable name. And we know what this cost them.

I have spoken often of "constellations": several heterogeneous singularities are consigned in the starry configuration of a single dated mark. So then, let me recall here the November-constellation (*Novem-*

bersternen)* associated with an ear, not of grain as in *Shibboleth*, but of corn:

BEIM HAGELKORN, im
brandigen Mais-
kolben,
den späten, den harten
Novembersternen gehorsam.

NEAR THE HAILSTONE, in the
blighted corn-
cob,
to the late, the hard
November stars obedient.

There would be a great deal to recall as well concerning September and March. The return of the month, without mention of the year, offers itself for reading in, among other places, "Huhediblu." In a certain way, the poem signs in this return the demarcation and partaking [partage] of the date, and also its deportation as the ring's condition and the fate of all archival recording. A date marks itself and becomes readable only in freeing itself from the singularity which it nonetheless recalls. It carries forgetting into memory, but it is the memory of forgetting itself, the truth of forgetting; it annuls in the ring's annulation, in the same way that a month annually recalls and annuls a year, as it rounds on itself—by virtue of which a date is always a turnabout, a vicissitude, a "volta," and a revolt or revolution. It replaces itself in its vicissitudes. So that, commemorating what may always be forgotten in the absence of a witness, the date is exposed in its very essence or destination to annihilation, threatened in its very readability; it risks the annulment of what it saves. It may always become no one's and nothing's date, the essence without essence of ash in which one no longer even knows what one day, one time, under some proper name, was consumed. And the name itself shares this destiny of ash with the date. This does not happen by accident; it is incident to the date's erratic essence [il appartient à l'essence toujours accidentée de la date] to become readable and commemorative only in effacing that which it was to date, in becoming no one's date. The possessive *no one's* may be understood in two contradictory senses, which nonetheless form an alliance in the tragedy of the date. Either/Or. *Either* the date remains encrypted, as in the case, for example, that behind the allusion to September in "Huhediblu" ("unterm / Datum des Nimmermenschtags im September"—"under the / date of Nevermansday in September"),

Translator's note: The translation of the poem cited in the French text renders *Novembersternen* as *constellation de Novembre*, a rendering motivated by the allusion to Saggitarius in the poem's last line (Schütze).

and beyond a certain number of identifiable things, the poet has, as one says, sealed and ciphered an event which he alone, or alone but for a few others, is able to commemorate—and those who commemorate are mortals, one must start with that. Now a date which is encrypted in this way is destined, at least to this extent, no longer to signify at all *one day* for those who outlive it, that is to say, for the reader, interpreter, or guardian of the poem, whose condition is always one of finite outliving. In this case, the date, from the moment that it crosses the threshold of this outliving and spectral return, becomes no one's date. The name September arises in a poem, a poem which "speaks"; it is readable to the extent that it is caught up within a network of marks which signify and are, by convention, intelligible; it has its share in the poem's beauty. But to the same extent, it pays for its readability with the terrible tribute of lost singularity; what is encrypted, dated in the date, is effaced in it, the date is marked in marking itself off. Or, in line with an *apparently* inverse hypothesis, nothing is encrypted in the date, it is available to all; in which case, the result is the same, the other's singularity turns again to ash, September's rose is no one's rose. As you know "die Nichts—, die / Niemandsrose" ("the nothing—, the / no one's rose") of "Psalm" belongs, so to speak, to the same generation as "die September- / rosen" of "Huhediblu," "unterm / Datum des Nimmermenschenstags im September." This Either/Or does not constitute a choice, the date's double demarcation does not make two. The two phenomena do not contradict each other, and, above all, they are not juxtaposed, in the poem of the date. The sameness of all dating is gathered and constituted here. This is the possibility of reading and of recurrence, of the ring, of the anniversary and its keeping, of the truth of the poem; it is its very reason, I would say, its essential raison d'être, its chance and its sense, but also, by that very fact, its madness. A date is mad. And we are mad for dates, for those ashes which dates are. But Celan knows that one may praise or bless ashes, that religion isn't needed for this, perhaps because it is here, quite simply, that religion begins, in the blessing of dates, of names and of ashes.

A date is mad because it is never itself or what it says it is, it is always more or less than what it is. What it is is either what it is or what it isn't. It does not take its rise from being, from some sense of being: it is on condition of this that its mad incantation turns into music, "CELLO-EINSATZ / von hinter dem Schmerz" ("CELLO-ENTRY /

from behind the hurt"), as in this poem, which speaks of the undeci-pherable and insignificant ("Undeutbares") and which closes with these, henceforth unforgettable words: "alles ist weniger, als / es ist, / alles ist mehr." ("all is less, than / it is, / all is more.") And if I say that the sense of a date is madness, a kind of *Wahnsinn*, this is not to move you, but to enunciate what there is *to read* in a date, in every injunction or every chance of reading. *Wahnsinn* is the madness of *when*, the delir-ious sense of *Wann*. The madness of this homophony is not a play on words of Celan's, any more than was the resemblance between *shib-boleth* and *symbolon*, between Hebrew and Greek, and, here, Germanic. Madness is this aleatory encounter in absolute heterogeneity which breaks into making sense and dating. Permit me to read (poorly, I'm afraid) a long fragment of "Huhediblu":

> Und—ja—
> die Bälge der Feme-Poeten
> lurchen und vespern und wispern und vipern,
> episteln.

(A certain kind of dating is never far, nor is writing, from these epis-tolary espittles.)

> Geunktes, aus
> Hand- und Fingergekröse, darüber
> shriftfern eines
> Propheten Name spurt, als
> An—und Bei—und Afterschrift, unterm
> Datum des Nimmermenschtags im September—:
>
> Wann,
> wann blühen, wann,
> wann blühen die, hühendiblüh,
> huhediblu, ja sie, di September—
> rosen?
>
> Hüh—on tue . . . Ja wann?
>
> Wann, wannwann,
> Wahnwann, ja Wahn,—
> Bruder
> Geblendet, Bruder
> Erloschen, du liest,
> dies hier, dies:
>
> And—yes—
> the windbags of the poet-proscribers
> toady and vesper and whisper and viper,

epistle.
Croaked things, out of
Hand- and finger-tripe, on which
far from writing the
name of a prophet leaves its traces, as
at- and by- and behindscript, under the
date of Nevermansday in September—.

When,
when bloom, when,
when bloom the, hoomendibloom,
hoohedibloo, yes them, the September—
roses?

Hoo—on tue . . . when then?

When, whenwhen,
frenzwhens, yes frenzy,—
brother
blinded, extinguished
brother, you read,
this here, this:

The date's annulment in the anonymity of nothing or of the ring is its *given*, its very condition, leaving its trace in the poem. Consequently, what the poetic trace comes to is not the same thing as the trace of something which happened, which took place in that it was lived through, in a sense demanding of commemoration. It is this but it is also and first of all trace *as* date, and the date, specifically, of what is bound to mark itself off if it is to mark, to bereave itself if it is to remain, to expose, that is to say, to risk losing its secret if it is to keep it, to blur or cross the border between readability and unreadability. The unreadable is readable as unreadable, this is the madness or fire which consumes a date from within and turns it to ash. In the finite time of incineration, the password is transmitted, passed from hand to hand or mouth to mouth or heart to heart, but it can vanish with those who passed it on and remain as an undecipherable, but nonetheless universal, sign, a token, a symbol, a trope, the circulation of an anonymous code.

Despite appearances, there is no contradiction here which could be organized dialectically. One could cite the beginning of the *Phenomenology of Spirit* to illustrate the paradoxes of this universalization of the *this* or the *wann*. But here, the ellipsis, the discontinuity, the caesura, the discretion with which this incineration of the date ciphers the poem do not allow themselves to be reduced or transcended (*aufge-*

hoben). No dialectic can reassure us in the matter of an archive's safe-keeping. This is the gift of the poem, and of the date, their condition made up of distress and hope, the shift of tones, the "Wechsel der Töne." Annulment, the return without return, is not brought upon experience by the poem, the poem which there isn't ("Ich spreche ja von dem Gedicht, das es nicht gibt"), any more than there is the date which nonetheless is to be given. Annulment is at work everywhere that a date inscribes its *here and now* within iterability, which is to say, everywhere that it consigns itself to oblivion, inscribes itself only to efface itself. This is what I call the trace or ash. These names stand for all the others. A date's destiny is analogous to that of every name, every proper name. Is there another desire than that of dating? of praising or blessing a commemoration without whose enunciation no event would take place? Yet desire gets carried away in praising or blessing the gift of this letter, this date which in order to be what it is must be open to reading in its being or non-being of ash. Of the date *itself*, *nothing* remains of what is dated, *no one* remains—a priori. This "nothing" or "no one" does not come upon the date like an abstract negativity which one could, by calculation, plan or avoid. I use "nothing" and "no one" in the grammatical sense in which they are neither positive nor negative. This corresponds to the grammatical suspension in which Celan lets "Nichts" and "Niemand" resonate, especially when he writes: "Gelobt seist du, Niemand." ("Praised be thou, No one.") I am thinking here, in particular, of the poem "Einmal," in which a virtually untranslatable "ichten" repeats, in some sort, in the "ich," that which is annihilated without negation:

Eins und Unendlich	One and Infinite
vernichtet,	annihilated,
ichten.	ied.
Licht war. Rettung.	Light was. Salvation.
	(trans. Michael Hamburger)

The date is readable only as a *Shibboleth* which says to you: I am a cipher which commemorates that which was destined to be forgotten, destined to become a name, nothing, no one, ash. The desire to date, which is the desire or giving of the poem, is borne, like the movement of blessing, toward this ash. In saying this, I am not presupposing some essence of blessing, realized here in a strange example. Perhaps it is only in poetic prayer, as it faces the incineration of the date, that the essence of blessing enunciates itself. Like the September-roses, no one's rose calls for the blessing of what remains of what doesn't remain and thus for the blessing of the remains that don't remain, the dust or ash. The heart's mouth which comes to bless the dust of ash comes again to bless the date, to say yes, amen, to the nothing that remains and even to the desert in which there would be no one even to bless the ashes.

> Niemand knetet uns wieder aus Erde und Lehm,
> niemand bespricht unsern Staub.
> Niemand.
>
> Gelobt seist du, Niemand. ("Psalm")
>
> No one kneads us again out of earth and loam,
> no one conjures our dust.
> No one.
>
> Praised be thou, No one.

To address no one, in the risk that there is no one to bless, no one for blessing, is also the only chance for blessing as an act of faith. I have suggested that date, ash, and name are the same, as here in "Chymisch":

Grosse, graue,	Great, gray,
wie alles Verlorene nahe	like all that is lost near
Schwestergestalt:	Sisterly shape
Alle die Namen, alle die mit-	All the names, all the
verbrannten	names burnt up
Namen. Soviel	with the rest. So much
zu segnende Asche. Soviel	ash to bless. So much
gewonnes Land	Land won
über	over
den leichten, so leichten	the light, so light
Seelen-	soul
ringen.	rings.
	(trans. Michael Hamburger)

All the rings, all the ashes—there are so many and each time unique—pass through the giving of a blessed date. And each tear as well. I will not cite all the tears, the ashes, and the rings which Celan has ciphered.

We have been speaking all this time of dates coded by the conventional grid of the calendar. I said that the poem could mention these dates while incorporating them into its sentence. The date thus marked was not necessarily that of the poem's writing or even of its event; it was its theme rather than its signature. But, as you can see, while there is a certain necessity to this distinction it is nonetheless of limited pertinence. Precisely because of the ring, the commemorated date and the commemorating date tend to rejoin and conjoin in a secret anniversary. The poem is this anniversary, the giving of this ring, the seal of an alliance and of a promise. It *belongs to* the same date as what it blesses, gives and gives back again the date to which it belongs and for which it is destined. And at this point, the border between the poem's external occasion, its "empirical" date, and its internal geneal-ogy is effaced. The *Shibboleth* also crosses this border and for a poetic date, for a blessed date, the difference between the empirical and the essential, between the contingency of the outer and the necessity of the innermost no longer has any place. This no-place, this utopia, if you wish, is the poem's taking place or occurrence as blessing. And with the distinction between the empirical and the essential, it is phi-losophy's own limit, philosophical distinction itself, which is blurred.

Thus the privilege of what I have called a code (the calendar which permits one to call off [*calare*] the years, months, days, or again the clock and the revolution of the hours). Like the calendar, the clock names the return of the other, of the wholly other in the same. *Uhr* and *Stunde* are not only *that which* many poems speak of, their theme or their object. The hour writes, the hour speaks, it calls the poem, provokes it, convokes, apostrophizes, and addresses it, it and the poet whom the hour claims, it causes it to come at its hour: "Nacht" speaks of a "Zuspruch der Stunde" ("exhortation of the hour"). And in "Selbdritt, Selbviert" we also read:

| Diese Stunde, deine Stunde, | This hour, your hour, |
| ihr Gespräch mit meinem Munde. | its dialogue with my mouth. |

Just as much as a sundial or any other chart, the mark of the hour assigns its place, gives rise to [donne lieu à] the subject, the signatory, the poet, even before he has himself marked and given an hour. The initiative is with the date and the poet is constituted by it. It is thence that he appears to himself.

The turning-to-ash, the burning up or incineration of a date, is the infernal threat of an absolute crypt: non-recurrence, unreadability, am-nesia with nothing left over. Such a risk is no more inessential to the date than the possibility of recurrence which may be a chance as well as a threat. And I will not speak here of the *holocaust*, except to say this: there is the date of a certain holocaust, the hell of our memory, but there is a holocaust for every date, somewhere in the world at every hour. Every hour is unique, whether it comes back or whether, the last, it comes no more, no more than the sister, the same, its other *revenant*, coming back:

Geh, deine Stunde	Go, your hour
hat keine Schwestern, du bist—	has no sisters, you are—
bist zuhause. Ein Rad, langsam,	are at home. A wheel, slow,
rollt aus sich selber / . . . /	rolls on its own / . . . /
die Nacht	the night
/ . . . / nirgends	/ . . . / Nowhere
fragt es nach dir. / . . . /	any asking about you. / . . . /
Jahre.	Years.
Jahre, Jahre, ein Finger / . . . /	Years, years, a finger / . . . /
Asche.	Ash.
Asche. Asche.	Ash. Ash.
Nacht.	Night.
Nacht-und-Nacht.	Night-and-Night.
	(trans. Joachim Neugroschel)

If the date which is mentioned, commemorated, or blessed tends to merge with its recurrence in the mention, the commemoration, the blessing of it, one can in that case not distinguish in a poetic signature between the constative value of a certain truth and that other order of truth or of the non-truth of truth which would be associated with the poetic performative.

We should now go beyond that in language which classifies marks of dating according to the calendar or the clock. Radicalizing and generalizing, we may say, without artifice, that poetic writing is dating, through and through. It is all cipher of singularity, offering its place and recalling it, offering and recalling its time at the risk of losing them in the holocaustic generality of recurrence and the readability of the concept, in the anniversary and the repetition of the unrepeatable. Wherever a signature has entered into an idiom, leaving in language the trace of an incision which is *at once* both unique and iterable, cryptic and readable, there is date, there is the madness of "when," the *Wahnsinn* of "Einmal," "once," and the terrifying ambiguity of the *Shibboleth*, sign of membership and threat of discrimination.

This situation (a date is a *situation*) may give rise to calculations. But in the final analysis, it ceases to be calculable, the crypt ceases to be the result of a concealment on the part of a hermetic poet, one skilled at hiding and anxious to seduce with ciphers. A crypt occurs wherever a singular incision marks language, as one might engrave a date in a tree, burning the bark with figures of fire. The voice of the poem carries beyond the singular cut, it becomes readable for all those who had no part in the event or the constellation of events entered into it, for all those excluded from its partaking [partage]. Seen from the side of this generality or repeatable universality of meaning, a poem counts as a philosopheme; it may offer itself as the object of a hermeneutic labor which, for the purposes of its "internal" reading, has no need of access to the singular secret once shared [partagé] by a few witnesses. Looking at it from the side of universal meaning which corresponds to the date as the possibility of a publicly commemorated recurrence, one may always speak, as in a panel title, of "philosophical implications." But seen from the other side, from the side of irreducibly singular dating and untranslatable incision, not only is there no philosophical implication as such, but the possibility of a philosophical reading encounters here, as does any hermeneutics, its limit. This limit, which would also be the symmetrical limit of a formal poetics, does not signify the failure of philosophical hermeneutics or formal analysis, and even less does it indicate the necessity of their renunciation. Rather it turns us back toward the effaced provenance, toward the *possibility* of both philosophical hermeneutics and of formal poetics. Both presuppose the date, that is to say the mark, incised in language, of a proper name or an idiomatic event. This is what I suggested in a somewhat elliptical way when I began by saying: the question "what is?" dates. Philosophy, hermeneutics, and poetics can only be produced within idioms, within languages, within the body of events and dates, a metalinguistic overview of which I do not say is impossible but, on the contrary, that its possibility is guaranteed by the structure of marking off which pertains to the date's annulment. The effacement of the date, in its very recurrence—here is the origin and the possibility of philosophy, of hermeneutics, and of poetics. It is also the effacement of the proper name, of the signature, of language, in the necessity of knowledge and the transmission of meaning. Annulling it in its repetition, what is sent [l'envoi] presupposes and disavows the date, that is to say, the *Shibboleth*.

Formally, at least, the affirmation of Judaism has the same structure as that of the date. Is this only a formal analogy? When someone says, "We Jews," does he intend the reappropriation of some essence, the acknowledgment of a belonging, of a partaking [partage]? Yes and no. Celan recalls—for this is a common theme and also the title of a question—that there is no Jewish property. "/ . . . you hear me, I'm the one, me, the one you hear, the one you think you hear, me and the other / . . . / because the Jew, you know, what does he have, that really belongs to him, that isn't lent, borrowed, never given back . . ." ("Conversation in the Mountains"). The Jew is also the other, myself and the other; I am Jewish in saying: the Jew is the other who has no essence, who has nothing of his own or whose own essence is not to have one. Thus, at one and the same time, both the alleged universality of Jewish witness ("All the poets are Jews," says Marina Tsvetayeva, cited in epigraph to "Und mit dem Buch aus Tarussa") and the incommunicable secret of the Judaic idiom, the singularity of its "unpronounceable name" ("Conversation in the Mountains"). The Jew's "unpronounceable name" says so many things: it says *Shibboleth*, the word which is unpronounceable—which *can* not be pronounced—by one who does not partake of the covenant or alliance; it says the name of God which *must* not be pronounced; and it says also the name of the Jew which the non-Jew has *trouble* pronouncing and which he scorns or destroys for that very reason, which he expels as foreign and uncouth [comme "un nom à coucher dehors," i.e., a long, unpronounceable name—Trans.], or which he replaces with a derisory name which is easier to pronounce—as has sometimes happened on both sides of the Atlantic. Its unpronounceability keeps and destroys the name; it keeps it, like the name of God, or dooms it to annihilation. And these two possibilities are not simply different or contradictory. The Jew, the name Jew, is a *Shibboleth*; prior even to any use of the *Shibboleth*, prior to any communal or discriminatory division [partage], whether he is master or proscript, Jew and *Shibboleth* partake of each other: witness to the universal, but by virtue of absolute singularity, dated, marked, incised by virtue of and in the name of the other. (And I will add as well, in parentheses, that in its terrifying political ambiguity, *Shibboleth* could today name the State of Israel, the state of the State of Israel.)

The impulse to designate the "Judaic," Jewishness, as yours and not only mine, as always something of the other's, inappropriable, may be read, for example, in the poem dated (this is its title) Zürich, zum Storchen, and dedicated, in the way that every date is dedicated, to Nelly Sachs. The semantics of I and you here appear to be as paradoxical as ever and this paradox is again that of the immeasurable relative to a measure of being, the disproportion or dissymmetry of too much or too little. The "you," the word *you*, may be addressed to the other as well as to oneself *as* other, and each time it overruns the economy of the discourse:

Vom Zuviel war die Rede, vom Zuwenig. Von Du und Aber-Du, von der Trübung durch Helles, von Jüdischem, von deinem Gott. / . . . / Von deinem Gott war die Rede, ich sprach gegen ihn . . .	The talk was of too much, of too little. Of You and Yet-You, of the dimming through light, of Jewishness, of your God. / . . . / The talk was of your God, I spoke against him . . . (trans. Joachim Neugroschel)

(Just as I have abstained on several occasions from interpellating Heidegger or evoking his interpellation, I will say nothing of what might be said here of other thinkers, Buber, Levinas, Blanchot, and still others.)

The *you*, the *yours*, may be addressed to the other as Jew but also to the self as other, as another Jew or as other *than* Jew. And this is no longer a true alternative. "Die Schleuse" addresses you, and your mourning, to tell you that what has been lost, and lost beyond a trace, is the word which opens, like a *Shibboleth*, on what is most intimate; the word which was left me ("das mir verblieben war"), and, what is graver still, if this could be said, the word which opens the possibility of mourning what has been lost beyond a trace: not only the exterminated family, the incineration of the family name in the figure of the sister (for the word is a "sister," *Schwester*), at the moment of her death, and of the final hour which no longer has a sister ("deine Stunde / hat keine Schwester"), but the very word which grants me access to Jewish mourning: *Kaddish*. This word addressed me, sought me, like the hour's interpellation, but then I lost it, "An die Vielgötterei / verlor ich ein Wort, das mich suchte: / *Kaddisch*." ("Amidst / many gods / I lost a word, which sought me: / *Kaddish*.") And lost too was "my Jew's spot" ("wo mein Judenfleck . . . ?" in "Eine Gauner—und Ganovenweise Gesungen zu Paris . . ."), lost, my Jew's curl, which was also my human curl ("Judenlocke, wirst nicht grau / . . . / Menschenlocke, wirst nicht grau," in "Mandorla"). The loss, when it extends to the death of the name, to the extinction of the proper name which a date, a bereaved commemoration, also is, cannot be worse than when we have crossed the boundary where what becomes denied us is mourning itself, the interiorization of death in memory, Erinnerung, the preserving of the other in a sepulcher or epitaph. The date is also a sepulcher which gives rise to [donne lieu à] a work of mourning. Celan also names the incinerated beyond of the date, those words lost without sepulcher, "wie unbestattete Worte" ("Und mit dem Buch aus Tarussa"), the errancy of spectral names, come back to roam (streunend) about the stelae.

There is an event, a rite of passage, which marks the legitimate entry of the Jew into his community and which takes place only once, on a specific date; this event is circumcision. One may translate this word as "reading-wound," as in the end of "DEIN VOM WACHEN," "sie setzt / Wundgelesenes über." I am not claiming that Celan is speaking here about circumcision, literally; I am translating what speaks about the translation or passing over ("sie setzt . . . über") of that which is, if not, as the French translation says, a readable, ciphered, or decipherable wound [blessure lisible], at least read to the quick [lu jusqu'au sang] ("Wundgelesenes").

Circumcision, in the literality of its word (Beschneidung), is rarely mentioned, at least as far as I know. The example of which I am thinking and to which I will return in a moment concerns the circumcision of a word. But does one ever circumcise without circumcising a word, a name? And does one ever circumcise a name without something done to the body? If the word circumcision rarely appears, other than in connection with the circumcision of the word, by contrast the tropic of circumcision disposes cuts, caesurae, ciphered alliances, and rings throughout the text. The wound is also universal, a differential mark in language, precisely that which dates and sets turning the ring of recurrence. To say that "all the poets are Jews," is to state something which marks and annuls the mark of a circumcision. All those who deal or inhabit language as poets are Jews—but in a tropic sense.

What the trope comes to is locating the Jew not only as a poet but also in every man circumcised by language or led to circumcise a language. I am not prepared to confront here the question of the semantic charge of circumcision and of all the usages which the rich lexicon of circumcision may authorize in the Scriptures, well beyond the consecrated operation which consists in excising the prepuce. The "spiritualization," as one often says, or "interiorization" which consists in expanding the meaning of the word beyond the sense of the cut into the flesh does not date from Saint Paul and is not limited to the circumcision of the soul and the heart. Remaining at the level of a minimal semantic network, we can say that "circumcision" involves *at least* three significations: 1) a cut which incises the male sexual member, entering and passing around it, to form a circumvenient ring; 2) a name given to the moment of covenant or alliance and of legitimate entry into the community. This is the *Shibboleth* which cuts and divides in distinguishing, for example, by virtue of language and the name which is given to each of them, one circumcision from another, the Jewish from the Egyptian operation from which it is said to derive, or the Muslim operation which resembles it, or many others. 3) The experience of blessing and of purification.

Now among all these meanings, a certain tropic may displace the literality of membership in the Jewish community, if one could still speak of belonging to a community to which, we are reminded, nothing belongs as its own. In this case, those who have undergone the *experience*—a certain concise experience—of circumcision, circumcised and circumcisers, are, in all the senses of this word, Jews.

Anyone or no one may be Jewish. No one is (not) circumcised; it is no one's circumcision. If all the poets are Jews, they are all circumcised or circumcisers. This gives rise in Celan's text to a tropic of circumcision which turns from the *Wundgelesenes* toward all ciphered wounds, to all cut words (notably in "Engführung," where a whole thread passes through "points of suture," closed up tears or scars, words to be cut off which were not cut off, membranes stitched back together.) And if I spoke a moment ago of "no one's circumcision," this was because the evocation of the exterminated race designates it both by a black erection in the sky, verge and testicle, *and* as the race and root of no one. As uprooting of the race in "Radix, Matrix":

Wer,	Who,
wer wars, jenes	who was it, that
Geschlecht, jenes gemordete, jenes	Race, that murdered,
schwarz in den Himmel stehende:	black in the sky standing:
Rute und Hode—?	rod and bulb—?
(Wurzel.	(Root.
Wurzel Abrahams. Wurzel Jesse. Niemandes	Root of Abraham. Root of Jesse. No one's
Wurzel—o	root—o
unser.)	ours.)

Circumcise: the word appears once in the form of a verb, *beschneide*, a verb in the imperative mode, the mode of command, of appeal, or of prayer. And this word, this word of command, injunction, or supplication bears upon the word, this verb has the word as its object, this verb speaks about an operation to be performed on the *verbum*, on the word, its complement is the word, or rather the Word: "beschneide das Wort." It is a question of circumcising the Word and the interpellation apostrophizes a rabbi, a circumciser. Not any rabbi, but Rabbi Loew:

Rabbi, knirschte ich, Rabbi
Löw:

Diesem
beschneide das Wort

Rabbi, I grated, Rabbi
Loew:

For this one
circumcise the word

This word to be circumcised, this word of someone's to be circumcised, this word to be circumcised for someone, this word is an *open* word. Like a wound, you will say. No, first of all like a door: open to the stranger, to the other, to the guest, to whomever. To whomever no doubt in the figure of the monstrous creature—and I am passing over here what the figure of Rabbi Loew may recall of the Golem, the narrative being given over in the poem to an essential transmutation, a transfigurative translation, meticulous in the letter but totally emancipated, beholden to the narrative but absolved from and having no relationship with this same literality. A word open to whomever in the figure as well, perhaps, of some prophet Elijah, of his phantom or double. He can be mistaken, but one must know how to recognize him, for Elijah is also the one to whom hospitality is owed. He may come, as we know, at any moment. He may happen at each instant. I will situate in this place that which speaks of or summons the *coming* of the event (*Kommen, Geschehen*) in so very many of Celan's poems.

The prophet Elijah is not named by the poem, and perhaps Celan was not thinking of him. But I will take the risk of recalling as well that Elijah is not only the guest, the one to whom, as relationship itself, the door of the word must be opened. Elijah is not simply a messianic and eschatological prophet. He is also, as you well know, the one who, at God's command, according to one tradition, must be present at all circumcisions. He watches over them. The one who holds the circumcised infant must be seated on what is called Elijah's chair (*Kise Eliyahu*).

Here in this very place, in the poem, the monster or Elijah, the guest or the other who stands before the door, at the poem's first step, on the threshold of the text ("EINEM, DER VOR DER TÜR STAND" is its title) stands before the door as before the law. I am not thinking only of Kafka's "Vor dem Gesetz," but of everything in Judaism which associates the door and the law.

And the one who says I, the poet, if you like, one of those poets "all" of whom "are Jews," no doubt opens the door to him, but the door turns into the word. What he opens to him is not the door but the word:

EINEM, DER VOR DER TÜR STAND,	TO ONE, WHO STOOD BEFORE THE DOOR,
eines	one
Abends:	evening:
ihm	to him
tat ich mein Wort auf-:	I opened my word-:

Let us call this, by way of allegory, an allegory, the bearing [portée—cf. porte—Trans.] of a word for the other, to the other or from the other. The allegory follows the revolution or vicissitude of the hours, from evening to morning, the times in their turns (in vicem, vice versa). The vicissitude begins one evening, eines Abends, in any case in the Occident of the poem, and the poet who then opens the door ends by asking the Rabbi-circumciser, the Mohel, to close the door of the evening and to open the door of the morning (die Morgentür). If the door speaks the word, he now, once the word is circumcised, asks it for the word of morning, the oriental word, the poem of origin. Ra, the Rabbi cut in two, is perhaps the Egyptian God as well, the sun or light.

I will not attempt to read or decipher this poem. It is also, as you have just heard, a poem about the poem, it names the becoming-poetic of the word, which amounts to its becoming-Jewish if "all the poets are Jews." It describes the becoming-circumcised of the word of origin, its circumcision. I use the word circumcision to designate both an operation, the surgical act of cutting, and the state, quality, or condition of being circumcised. In this second sense, one may speak of the circumcision of a word or utterance, as one also speaks of the concision of a discourse, its being-circumcised or circumscribed. Blake's Jerusalem, which is also a great poem of circumcision, regularly links circumcision, circumscription, and circumference. For example, that of the four senses which are also four faces turned toward the four cardinal points, from the West ("the tongue") to the East ("the nostrils"), from the north ("the ear") to the South ("the eye": "eyed as a Peacock"):

"... Circumscribing & Circumcising the excrementitious Husk & Covering, into Vacuum evaporating, revealing the lineaments of Man ... /
... rejoicing in Unity in the Four Senses, in the Outline, the Circumference & Form for ever in the Forgiveness of Sins Which Is Self Annihilation; it is the Covenant of Jehovah" (98:745). I have cited Blake
to underline that, in all of what we are calling its tropic dimensions,
circumcision remains a matter of the body, it is on the body that it
offers itself for reading. And it is thus that the body offers itself to
thought and signification. Before Saint Paul, it was a question in the
Bible of circumcised or uncircumcised lips (which is to say, in this
language, of "language") (Exod. 6:12,30), of the ears (Jer. 6:10), and of
the heart (Lev. 26:41). The opposition of the clean and the unclean,
the pure and the impure, coincides often with that of the circumcised
and the uncircumcised. The circumcision of the word must also be
understood as an event of the body, in a way essentially analogous to
the diacritical difference between *Shibboleth* and *Sibboleth*. It was in their
bodies, in a certain impotence of their vocal organs, that the Ephraimites experienced their inability to pronounce what they nonetheless
knew ought to be pronounced *Shibboleth*. The word *Shibboleth*, for some
an "unpronounceable name," is a circumcised word.

    I will have to limit myself in concluding to some remarks or ques-
tions.

    The word which is to be circumcised: here it is, first of all, opened,
offered, given, at any rate, promised to the other. The other remains
totally indeterminate, unnamed in the poem, having no identifiable
face, simply a face. It is *no one*, anyone, the neighbor or the stranger,
for with the other, it comes to the same. The one who is not yet named,
the one who perhaps awaits a name, awaits its bestowal by a circumcision, this one is the one-and-only, the unique, the one toward whom
the whole poem is drawn, inspired toward its own pole in absolute
dissymmetry. The other, this one, is always, as it were, placed at the
head, alone, very much alone on a line. It is *to this one* that one must
open, give, circumcise, *for this one* that the living Nothing must be inscribed in the heart ("schreib das lebendige / Nichts ins Gemüt"): ihm,
Diesem, diesem, Diesem, four times the same word framing a strophe, four
times alone by itself on a line, twice in the grammar of the capital. The
offering of this word for circumcision is indeed the giving of a word,
of one's word, since it is said that "I open my word," mein *Wort*. Promise,
engagement, signature, date, this word of opening permits one to pass

through the doorway. It is yet another *Shibboleth*: given or promised by *me* (*mein Wort*) to the singular other, *this one*. Yet this word, which is given or promised, in any case, opened, offered to the other, also asks, asks intercession, or rather it intercedes with the rabbi—still an other— asking that he bestow, for his part, the value of circumcision on this word. The Rabbi has the knowledge, he is a wise man, and he has the power to circumcise the word and to transmit the *Shibboleth* just as the doorway is crossed: the *Shibboleth* in the form of circumcision, which is to say, the right of access to the legitimate community, the covenant or alliance, the given name of a singular individual, membership, and so on.

But here the knowledge and the power of Rabbi Loew, his knowledge and power to circumcise are annulled. They know how and are able to an infinite degree, but to an infinite degree also to annul themselves. For the writing of circumcision which the intercessor asks of him is a *writing of Nothing*. It performs its operation on Nothing, it consists in inscribing Nothing in the flesh, in the word, in the flesh of the circumcised word: "Diesem / beschneide das Wort, diesem / schreib das lebendige / Nichts ins Gemüt." (Here I would place—to close it forthwith—an immense parenthesis on the question of Nothing and the meaning of being in Celan: here the question of circumcision left unanswered and dated "Todtnauberg," when it was, in effect, put to another kind of wise man.)

No one's circumcision, the word's circumcision by the incision of Nothing in the circumcised heart of the other, of this one, you.

Circumcise the word for him, circumcise his word, what is meant by this demand? More than one can *mean-to-say*, more and less than this or that meaning. The circumcised word is *first of all* written, at once both incised and excised in a body, which may be the body of a language: the word which is entered into, wounded in order to be what it is, the poem's caesura, the word cut into. The circumcised word is, *next of all*, read, "read-to-the-quick," as was said in another place. *By the same token*, as it were, it grants access to the community, to the covenant or alliance, to the partaking [partage] of a language: of the Jewish language as poetic language, if all poetic language is, like all the poets according to the epigraph, Jewish in essence, but according to that expropriated disidentification, in the nothing of that non-essence, of which we have spoken. The Germanic language, like any other, but here with what privilege, must be circumcised by a Rabbi, and the

Rabbi is in that case a poet. How can the German language receive circumcision at this poem's date, that is to say, following the holocaust? How may one bless these ashes in German? Finally, *fourth* and in consequence, the circumcised word, the word turned *Shibboleth*, at once both secret and readable, mark of membership and of exclusion, the shared wound of division [blessure de partage], reminds us also of what I will call the *double edge* of every *Shibboleth*. The mark of an alliance, it is also an index of exclusion, of discrimination, indeed of extermination. One may, thanks to the *Shibboleth*, recognize and be recognized by one's own, for better and for worse, for the sake of partaking [partage] and the ring of alliance *on the one hand*, but also, *on the other hand*, for the purpose of denying the other, of denying him passage or life. One may also, because of the *Shibboleth* and exactly to the extent that one may make use of it, see it turned against oneself: then it is the circumcised who are proscribed or held at the border, excluded from the community, put to death, or reduced to ashes merely on the sight of, or in the name of, the *Wundgelesenes*.

Perhaps Nothing, the annulment of all literal circumcision, the effacement of this determinate mark, perhaps the inscription as inscription of nothing or nothing in circumcision, can guard against this double edge. Perhaps this is what Rabbi Loew finds himself asked or ordered to do. Perhaps, but this would not make nothing of the demand. *There must be* circumcision, circumcision of the word, and it must take place once, each time one time, the one time only. This time awaits its coming, it awaits a date, and this date can only be poetic, an inscription in the body of language. How are we to transcribe ourselves into a date? Celan asked. When we speak here of the date of circumcision, we are no longer speaking of history. We are not speaking of the date in the history of an individual (we know that it was variable before it was fixed at the eighth day after birth) or in the history of Judaism (we know that other peoples practiced it already and still do; a *Shibboleth* passes the blade of a slight difference between several circumcisions. We also know that it is only at a certain date that circumcision became the law. The first codes of Israel did not make of it a ritual injunction). No, the circumcision of the word is not dated in history. In this sense, it has no age, but gives rise to, is the occasion of, the date. It opens the word to the other, it opens history and the poem and philosophy and hermeneutics and religion. Of all that calls itself, of the name and the blessing of the name, of yes and of no, it sets turning the ring, to affirm or annul.

I have kept you too long and ask your pardon. Permit me to let fall, by way of envoy or *Shibboleth*, in the economy of an ellipsis which circulates only in our language, by way of signature here, *today*, this: circumcision—dates.

Seattle, October 14, 1984
Jacques Derrida

Translated by Joshua Wilner

Translator's note: In preparing translations from the German, I have consulted the bilingual editions of Joachim Neugroschel (*Paul Celan, Speech-Grille and Selected Poems*, New York: E. P. Dutton, 1965) and Michael Hamburger (*Paul Celan: Poems*, New York: Persea Books, 1981). In those instances where the balance of a translation has been drawn from one of these sources, this has been indicated.—J. W.

EDMOND JABÈS

The Key

Dedans: deux (fois) dans.
Within: with (another, i.e., twice) in.

It is clear that you expect me to insert the key in the proper keyhole and, once in, to turn it once or twice the right way, then to push the door open which can no longer offer any resistance. You count on crossing after me the threshold which leads to other thresholds, stage after stage of insight which daily put our acquired knowledge to the test.

Nothing can be forgotten unless it was meant to be, from the start.

The book is an invaluable support for death.

Could it be that the impossibility of telling is only an impossibility to be born?
There are no words to report the death of God.
There is only death.

God's strangeness lies in His birth and death, His birth being the astonishment of His strangeness, His death its confirmation.

The death of a word is but another moment in the life of the book.

□ □ □

The keys a writer has at his disposal—a whole set of them—are those which let him enter his books.

Which of all the keys spread out before me will I use?

I opted for the one which had overcome the greatest number of doors and, by opening them, had itself become open, as if openness were also a key, as if, at a given moment, openness could by itself grant passage by opening onto itself.

349

Once what is to be opened is open, it will open other things in its turn.

Into this opening, into this series of openings, I write my name.

□   □   □

Judaism and writing seem to participate in one and the same openness to a word whose totality we are called to live.

Word of a word of horizons to which we have been yoked since the first book, that book outside time which time, though it cannot change it, nevertheless perpetuates and itself with it.

What we read is only what we write daily into the lack of the book: lack which is not its margins, but the traces of words buried within each word, sign on top of sign, which our eyes, dazzled by what is hidden, bleach with excess light, bleach, as time bleaches our hair, even to transparency.

Thus the Jew bends over his book, knowing in advance that the book always remains to be discovered in its words and in its silences.

Then reading would mean exhausting the word's resemblance and breaking the barrier of our appurtenances within it, in order to restore it intact to its initial, limpid purity.

Could it be that God, as tangible proof of the voluntary effacement of His Name, bequeathed to the Hebrew people a blank book?

But how can we read these blank words save with the help of our own words? How hear the silence of these pages save through our own silence?

To discover means, after all, to create.

Readability has its limits.

We can only trust our eyes, our intelligence to try to grasp all that is contained in the text. We can approach the infinite of the word to be read only within the unbearable limits of the words we have read.

So that we always come up against an impossible utterance to which we sacrifice our own.

A word fits within, occupies the space of, a few signs. Inside, it is as large as the universe.

To take in the universe of a single word means, on the one hand, seizing it in its constant expansion required by the vocabulary which inhabits it and, on the other hand, to judge the progress of our reading by its new dimensions.

For reading is perhaps nothing but replacing a word with all those which have deciphered it.

This exemplary kind of reading the Jew has practiced for centuries.

Because the text he bends over contains his truth, he must question it without respite. And it takes his entire life to develop his questioning, not only because of all he can still learn, but also because of all that, once learned, helps him better to formulate his next question.

The word survives words by taking on the empty space which their disappearance has left inside it.

It owes its vastness to the failure of their attempt to circumscribe it.

Is one void like another? They are differentiated by the content their hypothetical space could hold.

And totality? Could it fill up the void?

What we call *All* is only a part of the invisible—and Ungraspable—totality. One of its visible parts: the letter which the void supports as it carries the world.

Thus the void is the kingdom of Thought: the coming of fullness.

Would not the word *God*, in this perspective, be the emptiest word in the vocabulary? So completely empty that man's universe and the infinite of his soul can always find room there?

I am thinking, for example, of how the chanting in the synagogue transforms this word. While we meditate, the cantor intones the Name of God, and through the modulations he draws from each of its letters, from sobs to serenity, from revolt to gratitude, we hear our words fall silent within this word which their silence fashions and which the chant gives back to us.

Chant of resurrected vowels, giving away the sealed other side of the word, word seized even beyond itself by this inner chant: the sound of a life, an alliance, an infinite evoked in an instant.

Perhaps it falls to this chant to express the unsayable, to extend the unsayable within the said into its obliteration. For we never obliterate anything. As fast as we can obliterate we are ourselves obliterated by this eternal process, as keen as the moment which consumes us in making us live.

The meaning of a word is perhaps only its openness to meaning.
The word *God* has no meaning. Not several either. It is meaning: the adventure and ruin of meaning.

In regard to all this, I once proposed that *Judaism and writing are one and the same waiting, one and the same hope, one and the same wearing down.*

In the book, the Jew himself becomes a book. In the Jew, the book itself becomes Jewish words. Because for him, the book is more than confirmation, it is the revelation of his Judaism.

For the writer, to fashion a book means learning to read the book within the book: book of his ambition, his obsession.

What the Jew answers for is, above all, his fidelity to the book which is only his fidelity to himself.
In this perpetual tête-à-tête with writing he recognizes himself: his voice in the voice, his chant in the chant, his word in the word, in the name of a truth whose frail and yet hardy tenant he is: oak and reed at the same time.

Like the writer, the Jew expects his identity from the book. He owes his Jewishness less to the accident of his birth than to the future he strives to shape down to the smallest details. Here lies his genius.

Judaism is a faith based not on faith alone, but on the test to which the text of this faith forever puts it, on every word of this text which it accepts by putting it to the test in turn.
Interminable challenge which only death can terminate.

This is why the seventh day of the week, the day of rest, could also be a day withdrawn from the book. Withdrawn from the book, but no doubt still as an immaculate space between the lines. On this day, the Jew is not in the words of the book, but, as one walking might take refuge from the hot sun under a tree, in their shadow.

The writer tries to close in on the book which has already overpowered him unawares. Its pages cause him an anguish he will never escape.

To be what you write. To write what you are. These are the stakes.

The question which obsesses the Jew is this: "What justifies my considering myself Jewish? What makes my words and actions Jewish words and actions?"

Thus a double questioning forms and develops in him: his certainty challenging his doubt, and his doubt, his certainty.

And if Judaism were only the growth of this doubt filled with certainty?

But is it really a matter of doubt? Or, rather, of the need to weigh every time the pro and con?

Certainty can only come out of this confrontation.

An ideal way for the Jew to deepen his certainty which will fuse with the deepening.

A question asked of Judaism is a question asked of the book. For how could we formulate a question outside language? The words of our questioning confront the words of the answers which the book destines only to its readers.

All dialogue is a dialogue between words. It gives existence to the universe and to man.

Issued from the book, questioning is of primary, burning relevance for both Jew and writer, has been for five thousand years for the one, and is anchored in the future for both.

For what does modernity mean without openness? It is only this.

For the Jew, openness means first of all that of the desert for the Word of his God. Indispensable openness.

Without the desert, for lack of space to unfold, the Judaism which goes through the Word of God, and hence must go through the book, might not have existed.

For the desert is more than an arid stretch of sand. It is above all land desolate with silence and listening, land propitious to silence and infinite listening, where silence is giddy with its own echoes, and listening with all the sounds caught at the heart of this silence. Just as death gets drunk on the words of life and death, on the airy lightness of life, on flint and wind, sand and sky, and nothing, nothing, nothing in between.

Nothing except the burst of authoritative Speech which a sage wrote down.

But in the desert of His absence, on the naked peak of a pulverized world, did God really speak? What if this Word wanted to be more silent than silence in order to be heard, in order to help us perfect our ears, since hearing means only plunging down into ourselves?

Listening to the desert means listening to life and death. Listening to death means not losing a single moment of your life. Taking in the last words of life—each word of life is the last—means having already entered into your death.

God commands His people to listen: "Listen, Israel . . ." But listen to what? *Listen to the words of your God.* But God is absent, His words without voice, distance cutting off their sound. *Listen to silence.*

For it is in this silence that God speaks to His creature. It is with words fed by this silence that the Jew answers his God.

What if God had given up His word in order to put it into the mouth of a receptive people, to share His listening with them?

The imperious word is always still to be born. It leaves free rein to our attentive words.

Waiting is the leaven of questions because it is attentive to the unknown, open to hope.

But what if this daughter of the desert, the question asked of the unknown, were itself only the desert of questions? Then it would only be the solitude of a question put to the question of solitude: from the infinite solitude of God's question to the tragic solitude of man's question.

Facing the text has replaced facing God. *Listen to what is written . . .*

Two solitudes find themselves together: the one *before* and the one *after* the word.

This is why the relation to Judaism is strictly individual before it can, or wants to, be collective.

However, does this importance given to the question not already set up a dialogue? And does this not mean partly escaping our solitude, though without leaving it altogether?

In this freed part reside our ties.

If the Jew stands alone before his Judaism, then every Jew could define Judaism by his original approach, that is, through his reading of his book.

If the book—being open—authorizes his various approaches, it also justifies them at the same time. And this justification inevitably leads to the reader himself being called into question.

A Jewish being is only the Jew of beings.

But what if, in reading himself in his book, he only read his desire to be read by himself, as if he were, before it even existed, the unforeseeable though ineluctable becoming of the letter?

Being only warrants having been. The future takes hold of what is called to be preserved and inscribes it in its duration. It subtly transforms it day after day, so that enduring means nothing but living the amazement of these daily metamorphoses.

Thus Judaism opposes its lack of images to its various self-images.

Perhaps being Jewish, being a writer, means being granted the means to attain this. The far side of words is still on this side of being. Tomorrow is the kernel of their condition.

Do we not, by the way, say of a negligible, uninteresting matter that it has no future?

But to which familiar face should we refer in order to describe its features?

And what is a face which owed its particularity only to all the faces which recognize themselves in it?

And if that face were, all by itself, the book?
Youth of God. Man's old age.

Thus Judaism questions Judaism, staking as much on this interrogation as on its everlasting foundation.

Is the law in the book or, rather, the book in the law?
Does every book have its own law, or every law its book?
In other words, does reading and writing mean bowing to the law of the book or, on the contrary, forging by and by a law to submit the book to?

The law is an invention of the book, invention of a book with the authority of law.

And if the law were the desire for the book, and the book the desire for the law to which it owes its articulation?

And if the beginning were only the Book's desire for a beginning? Could this beginning be God?

Much more than its signs, we question the book's silence: its signs are only the counted traces of this silence.

Traces of the book's desire for the book, like footprints in snow or sand which snow or sand will cover up again.

Then words are only repeated cries of desire, cries of love or distress, at the moment of being engulfed.

Even if not all books have the same origin they still share the same silence.

"If you admit," I wrote in one of my works, "that all that troubles, disturbs, feverishly calls into question is basically profane, then we can deduce that the sacred somehow, in its disdainful persistence, is, on the one hand, whatever freezes us in ourselves, perpetrates a sort of death on the soul and, on the other hand, the disappointing outcome of language, the last petrified word.

"Hence it is in and through its relation to the profane that we can experience the sacred, not as the sacred, but as sacralization of a profane giddy with transcendence, as the indefinite lengthening of a minute rather than as an eternity alien to the moment.

"For death is a matter of time.

"Is it not exactly through seeing the word unable to appropriate speech that eternity realizes it is incompatible with language?"

"Writing, or being written, then means passing, sometimes unawares, from the visible—the image, figure, representation which lasts the time of an approach—to the invisible, the non-representation against which things put up a stoic struggle; from the audible, which lasts the time of listening, to silence where our words obediently come to drown; from sovereign thought to the sovereignty of the unthought, remorse and supreme torment of the word.

"The sacred remains what is unperceived, hidden, protected, ineffaceable. Hence writing is also the suicidal effort to take on the word down to its last effacement where it stops being a word and is only the trace—the wound—we see of a fatal and common break: between God and man, between man and Creation.

"Divine passivity, unshakable silence in the face of the unpredictable, perilous adventure of the word left to itself.

"Prior to the profane, it is the arbitrary excess that ceaselessly pushes back any boundary.

"Sacred, Secret.

"Could the sacred be the same as the eternal secret of life and death?

"There is a day-after, a night-after which day and night must invariably confront.

"They are the promise of dawn and the certainty of the next dusk. Here, life and death, the profane and the sacred, meet and fuse, like sky and earth convinced they form one and the same universe.

"The original taboo gives non-representation its sacred character. God's language is the language of absence. The infinite tolerates no barrier, no wall.

"We write against this taboo, but is it not, alas, only to clash more violently with it? 'Saying' is only defiance of the unsayable, and thought a denunciation of the unthought."

While the law of God made His people a people of priests, His book made them a people of readers.

Giving His creature His book to read, He demanded in return that man teach Him to reread it with human eyes.

So we are perhaps entitled to hold that, if the Jew is a Jew by the choice of God, God is a Jew through the intervention of His creatures.

The Jew lives on intimate terms with God, and God with the Jew, within the same words: A divine page. A human page. And in both cases the author is God, in both cases the author is man.

Hence, the Jew's familiarity with his God, which is never lack of respect but comes out of their singular, specific relation, the punctuality of their exchanges.

God needed man so His Word could be understood beyond its immediate import, understood even where man is alone facing himself and man.

Every reader is a potential writer. He makes the book into his book. He rewrites it for himself. What matter if this book never sees the day. On top of its transparent words, there are lined up the printed words of the book he bends over. So that the book buried in the book is now the dreamed, unequaled, inimitable book I mentioned earlier, now our perishable book which tries in vain to resemble the former in the essence of its manner and statement.

This is why in thinking about my condition as a Jew and a writer,

I was led to note: "First I thought I was a writer. Then I realized I was a Jew. Then I no longer distinguished the writer in me from the Jew because one and the other are only the torment of an ancient word."

From these sentences some people deduced that I had made the Jew into a writer, and all writers into Jews. Whereas I had simply taken the liberty to underline their common relation to the text.

Of nobody can we say with more justice: "*He talks like a book.*" And not as a game or from pedantry, which would justify the irony in such a remark, but because the Jew never leaves the book, even when he thinks he has abandoned it.

Deprived of freedom, deprived of a territory, it was natural that the Jew should take refuge in the book which immediately became the lasting place his freedom could resort to.

The relation between Jews, as that between writers, is made concrete by an exchange of books.

Between self and self there is the other: not the human obstacle, but the ideal mediator.

And if the other were the book? The other as book; the book as the other?

This would not imply that we vouch for one and the same utterance, only that we bear witness to its resonance within us, to our experience of this utterance behind which our own history slips into place.

Vital dialogue. The book of the living can only be a book of dialogue.

Only dialogue can, for a moment, outwit death.

Claimed by two voices, caught between two fires, it half escapes the void. For though they are prey to the same flames, the voices never fall silent together. A moment of survival is always granted the other.

Thus we die of a word torn from the word, and live by the silence to which it restores us.

In a dialogue, the two partners are equal, have the same rank, the same consideration for one another.

Dignity of man—as if God had wanted His creature equal to His message—and also man's need to step in and judge.

What fascinates me about this relation God/man at the heart of Judaism is that man imposes his language on God. What takes precedence is not what God says, but what man says in the silence of the divine Word.

He repeats forever this Word with the words that received it. He tries his best to lose it only to find it again at the end of his losses. Virtue of Jewish commentary which is never a vulgar comment on the text, but a deepening inner speech face to face with the undecipherable text. There, God is silence, allows His creature to talk, and sizes up his listening.

How simple and how difficult to be Jewish. Difficult simplicity, I would say. But how come the Jew does not hesitate a second to answer "Jewish" to the question of his identity? Has he forgotten his trouble to be so with one accord? How come the non-believer as much as the believer can claim, can presume on the same Judaism? Is it because their past and future are alike? Is there such a thing as Jewish destiny?

There is such a thing as the destiny of a book, the past and future of a book which hides an origin so ancient that it is barely a wound, barely a scratch which silence, in a moment of daring, left on the silence which from now on shrouds it.

Origin of the Jewish word.

"Come in with your words," the book seems to tell us in each of my words. "You have a place here, a place to receive you with your past and your future. Because I am old as time and ageless as eternity. Because I am eternity within time and time eternal."

And if this difficulty in being wholly Jewish were the same as everybody's difficulty in being altogether human?

Man's greatness lies in the question, the questions he can ask himself by asking them of his kindred. And his questions to the universe.

There is always, in a text, something unnoticed which haunts us, a key-word which obsesses us.

Death is a whirlwind of words which life labors to give meaning to, forgetting that they will engulf it.

The sea will die of the sea and will, again, be desert.

The history of the Jews is perhaps only the history of the sea turned sand so that out of this sand, out of this vast mass of shifting sand, a word could rise and become a book.

Certainty is perhaps the motive of all questions. In that case it will be formulated with the ultimate question.

Even now, I sometimes ask myself if I ever came out of the gray of the first book, if I ever woke up.

Sleep does not always mean loss of consciousness. God put the world to sleep in order to create it and goes to sleep in Creation in order to be Himself created.

We close our eyes to dissolve into the universe and be reawakened by it.

We can only bet on waking. Man's future lies in his eyes. Perhaps he is nothing but the secret expectation of an infinite look.

And what if, even to the limits of readability, writing, with its dependence on words, meant only espousing this look?

Translated by Rosmarie Waldrop

Reference Matter

Glossary

AGGADAH: (also Haggadah) From *le-haggid*, to tell. Traditionally defined as everything in talmudic literature which is not halakhah (Jewish law), including the amplification of biblical narratives, filling in apparent gaps in the narrative, parables, biblical and non-biblical legends, didactic or ethical exhortations, and allegory.

AMORA'IM: Plural of Amora, literally "speaker" or "interpreter," name designating Sages who flourished in the period following the completion of the Mishnah and whose teachings are largely recorded in the Jerusalem Talmud (redacted in approximately 400–25 C.E.), in the Babylonian Talmud (approximately 500 C.E.), and in midrashim contemporaneous with these sources.

ASHKENAZI: From Ashkenaz (Germany). Pertaining to descendants of early Jewish settlers in northwestern Europe, specifically the German and North French community, and later also the Austrian, Bohemian, Hungarian, and Polish-Lithuanian communities.

BERAKHA: Benediction. There are four kinds of berakhot (pl.): those said as part of the statutory prayers, those said upon performing certain commandments, those of thanksgiving, and those said upon enjoying things of this world. They all begin with the formula, "Blessed art thou. . . ."

BERESHIT: The first of the Five Books of Moses (Genesis), so called for the first word used in the first verse, *Bereshit*, "In the beginning."

DARSHAN: Preacher or speaker of sermons.

EXEGETICAL MIDRASH: Generic term for midrashic collections which are anthologies of interpretations, presenting running commentaries upon entire books of Scripture (like the Sifra on Leviticus or Bereshit Rabbah on Genesis) or large segments of books (like the Mekhilta on Exodus 12:1–23:19), with the interpretive opinions cited verse by verse, often phrase by phrase. All the Tannaitic midrashim are exegetical anthologies, as are many of the Amoraic ones.

GEMATRIYAH: Possibly from the Greek "geometry" or "gamma = tria" (third letter, third numeral). The method by which the values

363

of letters in words are calculated and then interpreted, often by comparison with some other word with the same numerical value.

GEZERAH SHAVAH: Inference by analogy in which two different passages containing similar words are equated for purposes of interpreting them and extending their meaning.

GNOSTICISM: From the Greek *gnosis*, knowledge, this term refers to the beliefs of sects of the first centuries C.E. whose systems (usually dualistic) were based on a mystical view or knowledge of God. Gnostic beliefs derived as much from pagan as from Christian and Jewish sources.

HAGADAH: See AGGADAH.

HAFTARAH: Section from the Prophets read in synagogue after the Torah-reading on Sabbaths and holidays (as well as on fast-days).

HALAKHAH: Jewish ritual and civil law.

ḤASIDISM: A religious movement founded by Israel ben Eliezer, otherwise known as the Ba'al Shem Tov, in the eighteenth century. It is usually organized around the adulation of a Rebbe and characterized by a mystical-emotional view of Judaism.

HEIKHALOT MYSTICISM: Early Jewish mysticism of the talmudic and post-talmudic period in the Land of Israel which described mystical ascensions to divine worlds in terms of a progress from one palace to another in a system of seven celestial palaces. Some of the principal works of this school of mystics (fifth and sixth centuries) include the term *heikhalot* (palaces) in their titles, hence it became a common reference to ancient Jewish mysticism as a whole.

ḤOKHMAH: Literally, wisdom; sometimes identified with the concept of the logos. Denotes the supreme divine wisdom which is the second divine emanation among the ten which comprise the kabbalistic pleroma.

HOLY OF HOLIES: *Devir*, the adytum in the Temple in Jerusalem; in the First Temple it housed the Ark of the Covenant and the Cherubim. Tradition held it was erected on the site of the binding of Isaac and of other divine revelations. It was entered once a year, on the Day of Atonement, by the High Priest.

HOMILETICAL MIDRASH: Midrashic collections of homilies on the Torah portion for a Sabbath or a festival. Generally, portions are devoted to the exposition and interpretation of one or two verses in the weekly Torah-reading. An innovation of the Amoraic period, its earliest examples are Leviticus Rabbah and Pesikta de-Rav Kahana. Later homiletical midrashim include the Yelamdenu-Tanḥuma group.

KABBALAH: The Hebrew term for medieval Jewish mysticism.

KAL VAHOMER: Explicit or implicit inference a minori ad maius and vice versa.

KARAITES: Members of a Jewish medieval sect which rejected the authority of the rabbinic, talmudic Halakhah, preferring instead a direct derivation of law from Scripture.

KEDUSHA: From the Hebrew for "Holy." Shortened form of Kedushat Hashem, "the Holiness of the Name," the term for the third blessing in the main daily prayer. Kedusha specifically refers to verses which the congregation and cantor recite alternately during the repetition of this benediction by the cantor. The Kedusha is believed to be recited by the angels before the throne of the divine glory and is based on texts from Isaiah and Ezekiel.

KING PARABLE: Common form of mashal in talmudic literature, in which the protagonist is a king while the other characters are drawn from the king's court—his consort, children, generals, soldiers, and subjects. The figure of the king in these parables is often modeled upon the Roman emperor.

MALKHUT: In Kabbalah, "kingdom," an attribute or sefirah of God.

MASHAL: Biblical word that becomes a generic name for parables (but also for proverbs). Has bipartite structure of narrative (mashal-proper) and explanation (nimshal).

MIDRASH: From the root meaning "to seek out" or "to inquire": a term in rabbinic literature for the interpretative study of the Bible. By extension the word is also used in two related senses: first, to refer to the results of that interpretative activity, namely, the specific interpretations produced through midrashic exegesis; and, second, to describe the literary compilations in which the original interpretations, many of them first delivered and transmitted orally, were eventually collected.

MIDRASH RABBAH: Two collections of various midrashim, from various periods, one on the Pentateuch and one on the Five Scrolls (Ruth, Esther, Ecclesiastes, Lamentations, Song of Songs).

MISHNAH: "Repetition." An authoritative compilation of rabbinic laws by Judah Hanasi circa 200 C.E. Together with the Gemorah (a later commentary on it) constitutes the Talmud.

NOTARIKON: A method of midrashic hermeneutic in which the letters of a word are taken to be abbreviations of other words (as in acronyms) or in which words reveal new meanings by being divided into two or more parts.

ORAL LAW: That part of the divine revelation which was not written down in the Torah (i.e., Pentateuch).

PESHAT: A term that in medieval Hebrew exegesis designates the plain-meaning or contextual sense among the different levels of interpretation. In talmudic texts it denotes, however, an authoritative interpretation.

PETIḤTA: (Aramaic), or PETIḤAH (Hebrew), literally, "an opening" or "beginning." A midrashic proem. The classical, Amoraic *petiḥta* had a conventional structure beginning with elucidation of one biblical verse and ending with another, the lectionary-verse; the rhetorical function of the proem is to connect the two verses. Classical Amoraic collections of midrash usually begin each section or portion with one or several *petiḥtot*.

PSEUDEPIGRAPHIC LITERATURE: Literature falsely (from the Greek *pseudes*, liar) attributed to ancient personalities. Refers to Jewish works of late antiquity which were pseudo-epigraphically attributed to ancient sages like Rabbi Akivah and Rabbi Ishmael. Many medieval kabbalists followed the same tradition, like the authors of the Bahir, the Zohar, and Iyun circle in the thirteenth century. Others, however, did not hesitate to include their names in their mystical works.

QUMRAN: Wadi flowing into the Dead Sea from the northwest. The Dead Sea Scrolls were discovered in caves nearby.

SEFIROT: A kabbalistic term relating the radiance of God to a continuous process of emanation by epithets or attributes: *Keter Elyon* (supreme crown), *Ḥokhmah* (wisdom), *Binah* (intelligence), *Gedulah/Ḥesed* (greatness/loving kindness), *Gevurah/Din* (power/judgment), *Tiferet/Raḥamim* (glory/compassion), *Neẓaḥ* (eternity), *Hod* (majesty), *Ẓadik/Atarah* (kingdom/diadem).

SEPHARDI: From Sepharad (Spain). Jews whose roots are traced to Spain and Portugal before the expulsion in 1492.

SHEKHINAH: From the Hebrew for "dwell," it is used to indicate the immanent presence of God. In later kabbalah it is associated with the feminine aspects of the godhead.

TAGIN: (sg. *tag*, appendage) Crownlike embellishments used on seven of the twenty-two letters of the Hebrew alphabet in sacramental scrolls (Torah, phylacteries, mezuzah, and megilah). Tagin were occasionally subject to homiletical exegesis.

TANNAIM: Plural of *Tanna*, literally "repeater" or "teacher," name designating Sages who lived between 70 and 220 C.E., in the period that is usually described as mishnaic, in the Land of Israel. Their teachings are preserved largely in the Mishnah, Tosefta, and the Tannaitic midrashim.

TARGUM: Literally, "translation." Targum specifically refers to the Aramaic translations of the Hebrew Bible. Onkelos on the Torah tends to give a straightforward translation, while some of the other targumim are more free and elaborative.

TE'AMIM: In texts of the Hebrew Bible te'amim are signs added to the words to indicate the precise musical and syntactical reading of the verse. The names and forms of the te'amim were themselves midrashically expounded.

TETRAGRAMMATON: The Divine Name which consists in Hebrew of the four letters (transliterated) YHWH.

TORAH: Specifically, the Five Books of Moses, or Pentateuch; known in rabbinic literature as the Written Law, though parts of it are narrative in style and content. Also refers to the entire body of divine knowledge in the Jewish Scriptures and the Oral Law.

ZOHAR: The most important text of Jewish mysticism, spuriously attributed to R. Shimeon bar Yoḥai, but in fact composed in Spain in the thirteenth century.

Selected Bibliography

EDITIONS

Avot de Rabi Natan

Aboth de Rabbi Nathan (Hebrew). Edited by S. Schechter. Vienna: Knöpfl-macher, 1887. Photocopy New York: Feldheim, 1945.

The Fathers According to Rabbi Nathan. Translated by Judah Goldin. New Haven: Yale University Press, 1955.

The Fathers According to Rabbi Nathan, Version B. Translated and edited by Anthony I. Saldarini. Leiden: E. J. Brill, 1975.

Mekhilta de Rabi Ishmael

Midrash HaMekhilta (Hebrew). Constantinople: Asfrok de Toulon, 1515. Photocopy Jerusalem: Makor, 1972.

Midrash HaMekhilta (Hebrew). Venice: Bombergui, 1544. Photocopy Berlin: Sefarim, 1925; Jerusalem: Makor, 1971.

Sefer Mekhilta de Rabi Ishmael (Hebrew). Edited by M. Friedman (Ish-Shalom). Vienna: Halzwarta, 1870. Photocopy New York: Om, 1948; Tel Aviv: Leon Press, 1961.

Mekhilta, ein tannaïtischer Midrasch zu Exodus. Translated and edited by J. Winter and A. Wünsche. Introduction by Ludwig Blau. Leipzig: Hinrichs, 1909.

Mechilta D'Rabbi Ismael (Hebrew). Edited by H. S. Horovitz and A. E. Rabin. Frankfurt am Main: J. Kaufmann, 1931. Photocopy Jerusalem: Bamberger and Wahrmann, 1960.

Mekhilta de Rabi Ishmael. 3 vols. Translated and edited by Jacob Z. Lauterbach. Philadelphia: Jewish Publication Society of America, 1933. Reprint, 1976.

Mekhilta de Rabi Shimon

Mekhilta d'Rabbi Sim'on b. Iochai (Hebrew). Edited by I. N. Epstein and E. Z. Melamed. Jerusalem: Sumptibus, 1955, 1979.

Midrash Mishley

Midrash Mishley (Proverbs) (Hebrew). Constantinople: 1517. Reprint edited by S. Buber. Vilna: Romm, 1893.

Midrash on Psalms (Shoḥar Tov)

Midrash Tehilim, Shoḥar Tov (Hebrew). Edited by S. Buber. Vilna: Romm, 1891. Photocopy Jerusalem, 1966.
The Midrash on Psalms. 2 vols. Translated and edited by William Braude. New Haven: Yale University Press, 1959.

"Midrash Rabbah"

Midrash Rabbah on the Pentateuch (Hebrew). Constantinople: Yosef Gabai and Abraham Yerushalmi, 1512.
Midrash Ḥamesh Megiloth (so called "Rabbah" on the Scrolls) (Hebrew). Pesaro: Soncino, 1519. Photocopy Berlin: Sefarim, 1926.
Midrash Raba al Ḥamisha Ḥumshei Torah Veḥamesh Megilot (Hebrew). 2 vols. Vilna: Romm, 1878. Photocopy Jerusalem, 1961.
Bibliotheca Rabbinica (Midrash Rabba). 12 vols. Translated by Aug. Wünsche. Leipzig: O. Schulze, 1880–85.
Midrash Eicha Rabbati (Hebrew). Edited by S. Buber. Vilna: Romm, 1899. Photocopy Tel Aviv, n.d.
Bereschit Rabba (Hebrew) 3 vols. Edited by J. Theodor and Ch. Albeck. Berlin: H. Itzkowski, 1912; 2d ed. 2 vols. Jerusalem: Wahrmann Books, 1965.
Midrash D'varim Raba (Hebrew). Edited by S. Lieberman. Jerusalem: Wahrmann Books, 1940. 3d ed., 1974.
Midrash Vayikra Raba (Hebrew). 5 vols. Edited by Mordechai Margulies. 1953–60. Reprint (3 vols.) Jerusalem: Wahrmann Books, 1972.
Midrash Raba la Torah (Hebrew). 8 vols. Edited by Elimelech Epstein (A. A.) Halevi. Tel Aviv: Maḥbarot LeSifrut, 1956.
Midrash Raba (Hebrew). 11 vols. Edited by Aryeh Mirkin. Tel Aviv: Yavneh, 1958–67.
Ruth Rabba (Hebrew). 3 vols. Edited by Myron Bialik Lerner. Dissertation, Hebrew University, 1971.
The Midrash Rabbah. 10 vols. Translated and edited by H. Freedman, Maurice Simon. London: Soncino, 1939. Reprint 1951 and 1961. New Compact Edition. London, Jerusalem, New York: Soncino Press, 1977.
Midrash Shmot Raba, sec. 1–14 (Hebrew). Edited by Avigdor Shinan. Jerusalem, Tel Aviv: Dvir, 1984.

Midrash Shmuel

Midrash Shmuel (Hebrew). Constantinople: Afinda Viroti and Judah ben
    Altabib, 1517.
Midrasch Samuel (Hebrew). Edited by S. Buber. Cracow: J. Fischer, 1893.

Midrash Tanḥuma

Midrash Tanḥuma (Hebrew). Constantinople: Solomon ben Mazal-Tov
    and Moshe ben Maimon Maḥbob, 1520. Photocopy Jerusalem: Makor,
    1972.
Midrash Tanḥuma (Hebrew). 2 vols. Jerusalem: Eshkol, 1972.
Midrash Tanḥuma (Hebrew). 2 vols. Edited by S. Buber. Vilna: Romm,
    1885. Photocopy Jerusalem, 1964. *Different midrash from above.*

Six Orders of the Mishnah

Mishnah (Hebrew). Naples: Soncino, 1492. Photocopy Jerusalem: Sifriat
    Mekorot, 1970.
The Mishnah. Translated and edited by Herbert Danby. London: Oxford
    University Press, 1938.
Shisha Sidrei Mishnah (Hebrew). 6 vols. Edited by Ch. Albeck. Punctuated
    by Ch. Yalon. Jerusalem: Mossad Bialik; Tel Aviv: Dvir, 1952–58.
Shisha Sidrei Mishnah (Hebrew). 13 vols. Vilna: Romm, 1852. Photocopy
    Jerusalem: Mekorot, 1976.
Mishnayoth. 7 vols. Translated and edited by Philip Blackman. New York,
    1951–56. 3d ed. New York: Judaica Press, 1965.

Mishnat Rabi Eliezer (Midrash Agur)

The Mishnah of Rabbi Eliezer; or the Midrash of Thirty-Two Hermeneutic
    Rules (Hebrew). Edited by H. G. Enelow. New York: Bloch Publishing
    Company, 1933. Photocopy Jerusalem: Makor, 1970.

Pirkei D'Rabi Eliezer

Pirke de Rabbi Eliezer (Hebrew). Constantinople: Yehuda ben Yosef Sas-
    san, 1514.
Pirkei D'Rabbi Eliezer (Hebrew). Commentary by R. David Luria. Warsaw:
    Bamberg, 1852. Photocopy Jerusalem, 1963.
Pirke de Rabbi Eliezer (The chapters of Rabbi Eliezer the Great). Translated
    and edited by Gerald Friedlander. London: Kegan Paul, Trench, Trubner;
    New York: Bloch, 1916. Photocopy New York: Hermon Press, 1965.

Pesikta Rabbati

Pesikta Rabbati (Hebrew). Prague: Yitzhak Katz, c. 1656.

Pesikta Rabbati Midrasch (Hebrew). Edited by M. Friedman (Ish-Shalom). Vienna: Privately published, 1880. Photocopy Tel Aviv, 1963.

Pesikta Rabbati. 2 vols. Translated by William Braude. Edited by Leon Nemoy. Yale Judaica Series. New Haven: Yale University Press, 1968.

Pesikta de Rav Kahana

Psikta de Rav Kahana (Hebrew). 2 vols. Edited by Dov Mandelbaum. New York: JTS, 1962.

Pesikta de Rav Kahana: R. Kahana's Compilation of Discourses for Sabbaths and Festal Days. Translated by William Braude and Israel J. Kapstein. Philadelphia: Jewish Publication Society of America, 1975.

Seder Olam

Seder Olam Rabbah (Hebrew). Mantuba: Samuel Latif, 1514.

Midrash Seder Olam [Rabbah] (Hebrew). 2 vols. Edited by Dov Ber Ratner. Vilna: Romm, 1894–97. Photocopy New York: Talmudical Research Institute, 1966.

Seder Olam (chaps. 1–10) (Hebrew & German). Edited by Alexander Marx. Berlin: H. Itzkowski, 1903.

Seder Olam: Critical Edition and Introduction (English & Hebrew). 2 vols. Edited by Chaim Milikowsky. Dissertation, Yale University, 1981.

Sifra

Sifra (Hebrew). Constantinople: Solomon ben Mazal-Tov, 1523.

Sifra (Hebrew). Venice: Bombergui, 1545. Photocopy Berlin: Sefarim, 1925; Jerusalem: Makor, 1971.

Sifra (Hebrew). Edited by I. H. Weiss. Vienna: Schlossberg Yaacov Hacohen, 1862. Photocopy New York: Om, 1947.

Sifra (Hebrew). Edited by M. Friedmann (Ish-Shalom). Breslau: M. and H. Marcus, 1915. Photocopy Jerusalem: Gvil, 1967.

Sifra, halachischer Midrasch zu Levitikus (Hebrew). Edited by J. Winter. Breslau: S. Munz, 1938.

Sifra (Hebrew). Vols. 2–3. Edited by Louis Finkelstein. New York: JTS, 1983.

Sifrei-Numbers, Sifrei Zuta, Sifrei Deuteronomy

Sifrei [Numbers and Deuteronomy] (Hebrew). Edited by J. Travis. Venice: Bombergui, 1545. Photocopy Berlin: Sefarim, 1925; Jerusalem: Makor, 1971.

Sifrei [Numbers and Deuteronomy] (Hebrew). Edited by M. Friedman (Ish-Shalom). Vienna: Halzwarta, 1864.

Sifre zu Deuteronomium. Translated by Gerhard Kittel. Stuttgart: W. Kohlhammer, 1922.

Midrash Sifre on Numbers: Selections from Early Rabbinic Scriptural Interpretations. Translated by Paul P. Levertoff. London: Society for Promoting Christian Knowledge, 1926.

Siphre ad Deuteronomium (Hebrew). Edited by Louis Finkelstein. Notes by H. S. Horowitz. Berlin: Various publishers, 1932–39. Photocopy New York: JTS, 1969.

Siphre ad Numeros adjecto Siphre Zutta (Hebrew with introduction in German). Edited by H. S. Horowitz. Leipzig: G. Fock, 1917. Photocopy Jerusalem: Wahrmann Books, 1966.

Der tannaïtische Midrasch Sifré zu Numeri. Translated by K. G. Kuhn. Stuttgart: W. Kohlhammer, 1959.

Sifre: A Tannaitic Commentary on the Book of Deuteronomy. Translated by Reuven Hammer. New Haven: Yale University Press, 1986.

Babylonian Talmud

Babylonian Talmud (Hebrew). Venice: Bombergui, 1520–22. Photocopy Jerusalem: Makor, 1968.

Babylonian Talmud (Hebrew). Vilna: Romm, 1880–86. *Most extant editions of the Babylonian Talmud are photocopies of this edition.*

Der babylonische Talmud. Translated by A. Goldschmidt. Leipzig: Otto Harrassowitz, 1906–35.

The Babylonian Talmud. Edited by I. Epstein. Various translators. London: Soncino, 1935–52.

Jerusalem Talmud

Jerusalem Talmud (Hebrew). Venice: Bombergui, 1523. Photocopy Berlin: Sefarim, 1925.

Jerusalem Talmud (Hebrew). Cracow, 1609.

Jerusalem Talmud (Hebrew). Vilna: Romm, 1922.

The Talmud of the Land of Israel. Vols. 26–35. Translated by Jacob Neusner. Chicago: University of Chicago Press, 1982.

Torah Shelemah

Torah Shelemah: Talmudic Midrashic Encyclopedia On the Pentateuch (Hebrew). 38 vols. [Gen. 1:1—Num. 12:15]. Edited by Menahem M. Kasher. Vols. 1–7: Jerusalem: Privately published. Vols. 8–29; New York and Jerusalem: American Biblical Encyclopedia Society. Vols. 30–38: Beth Torah Shelemah, 1927–83.

Tosefta

Tosephta (Hebrew). Edited by M. S. Zuckermandel. Pazwalleck: Yisachar
    bar Yitzhak Meir. Photocopy Jerusalem: Bamberger and Wahrmann
    Books, 1937, with a supplement by S. Lieberman. Photocopy Jerusalem:
    Wahrmann Books, 1970.
Die Tosefta (Hebrew & German). 6 vols. Edited by Ab. Marmorstein,
    G. Kittel, K. H. Regensdorf. Stuttgart: W. Kohlhammer, 1933–76.
The Tosefta (Hebrew). 4 vols. Tosefta Kiphshuta: Zeraim-Nashim. 8 vols.
    Commentary. Edited by S. Lieberman. New York: JTS, 1955–73. Order
    Nezikin, forthcoming.
The Tosefta. 5 vols. Translated by Jacob Neusner. New York: Ktav Publish-
    ing House, 1977–81.

Yalkut Shimoni

Yalkut Shimoni al HaTorah (Hebrew). 5 vols. Salonika: Soncino, 1521–27.
    Photocopy Jerusalem: Sifriat Mekorot, 1968.
Yalkut Shimoni (Hebrew). New York: Pardes, 1844.
Yalkut Shimoni al HaTorah (Hebrew). 6 vols. Edited by Dov Heyman and
    Yitzhak Shiloni. Jerusalem: Mossad Harav Kook, 1973–84. [Genesis–
    Exodus–Leviticus]

Tana de Bei Eliyahu (Seder Eliyahu)

Pseudo-Seder Eliyahu Zuta (Derech Ereç and Pirke R. Eliezer) (Hebrew).
    Edited by M. Friedmann. Vienna: Achiassaf, 1904. Photocopy Jerusalem:
    Bamberger and Wahrmann, 1960.
Seder Eliyahu Rabbah and Seder Eliyahu Zuta [Tanna d'be Eliyahu] (He-
    brew). Edited by M. Friedmann. Vienna: Achiassaf, 1902. Photocopy Je-
    rusalem: Bamberger and Wahrmann, 1960.

Others

Townsend, John T. "Minor Midrashim." In *Bibliographical Essays in Medieval
    Jewish Studies.* Contributors: Lawrence V. Berman, et al. New York: Bnai
    Brith, 1976, pp. 333–92.

STUDIES ON *AGGADAH AND TALMUDIC MIDRASHIM*

Aptowitzer, Viktor. *Kain und Abel in der Aggada der Apokryphen, der hellenistischen,
    christlichen und mohammedanischen Literatur.* Vienna: R. Löwit, 1922.
Bacher, Wilhelm. *Die Agada der babylonischen Amoräer: Ein Beitrag zur Geschichte
    der Agada und zur Einleitung in den babylonischen Talmud.* Strassburg, 1878; 2d
    ed., 1913. Photocopy of 2d ed., Hildesheim: G. Olms, 1967.

————. *Die Agada der palästinensischen Amoräer.* 3 vols. Strassburg: K. J. Truebner, 1892–99.

————. *Die Agada der Tannaiten.* 3 vols. Strassburg: K. J. Truebner, 1884–90;
2d rev. ed. (1 vol.), 1903.

————. *Die exegetische Terminologie der jüdischen Traditionsliteratur.* 2 vols. Leipzig:
1899–1905. Reprint Darmstadt: Wissenschaftliche Buchgesellschaft, 1965.

————. *Die Proömien der alten jüdischen Homilien, Beitrag zur Geschichte der Jüdischen
Schriftauslegung und Homiletik.* Leipzig: J. C. Hinrichssche Buchhandlung,
1913.

————. *Rabbanan: Die Gelehrten der Tradition: Beitrag zur Geschichte der anonymen
Agada.* Budapest, 1914.

Barth, Lewis. "Recent Studies in Aggadah." *Prooftexts*, 4, 2 (1984), 204–13.

Barton, John. *Reading the Old Testament: Method in Biblical Study.* London: Dort-
man, Longman and Todd, 1984.

Basser, Herbert W. *Midrashic Interpretations of the Song of Moses.* American University Studies. New York, Frankfurt am Main, Berne: Peter Lang, 1984.

Ben-Amos, Dan. "Generic Distinctions in the Aggadah." *SJF* 1 (1980), 45–
71.

Bialik, Chaim Nahman. *Halachah and Aggadah.* Translated by Leon Simon.
London: Education Department of the Zionist Federation of Great Britain and Ireland, 1944.

————. *Sefer HaAggadah: A Selection of Aggadot from the Talmud and the Midrashim*
(Hebrew). Tel Aviv: Dvir, 1948.

Bin Gorion, Emanuel. *The Paths of Legend: An Introduction to Folklore* (Hebrew).
Jerusalem: Mossad Bialik, 1970.

Bloch, Renée. "Ecriture et tradition dans le judaïsme: aperçus sur l'origine
du Midrash." *CaSi* 1 (1954), 9–34. Reprint Paris: Cahiers Sioniens, 1954.

————. "Midrash." *Dictionnaire de la Bible, Supplément 5.* 1950 ed. Translated
by M. H. Callaway. Reprinted in *Theory and Practice.* Vol. 1 of *Approaches to
Ancient Judaism.* Edited by William Scott Green. Missoula: Scholars Press,
1978, pp. 29–50.

————. "Note méthodologique pour l'étude de la littérature rabbinique."
RScR 43 (1955), 194–227. Translated by William Scott Green. Reprinted
in *Theory and Practice*, vol. 1 of *Approaches to Ancient Judaism.* Edited by William
Scott Green. Missoula: Scholars Press, 1978, pp. 51–75.

————. *Quelques aspects de la figure de Moïse dans la tradition rabbinique.* Paris:
Desclée, 1955.

Bowker, John. *The Targums and Rabbinic Literature: An Introduction to Jewish Interpretations of Scripture.* Cambridge: Cambridge University Press, 1969.

Braude, W. G. "Midrash as Deep Peshat." In *Studies in Judaica, Karaitica, and
Islamica: Presented to Leon Nemoy on his 80th Birthday.* Edited by Sheldon R.
Brunswick et al. Ramat Gan: Bar Ilan University Press, 1982, pp. 31–38.

Bregman, Marc. "Circular Petiḥtaot and Petiḥtaot of the Genre 'thus it is
said by Divine Inspiration' " (Hebrew). In *Heinemann*, pp. 34–51.

————. "The Darshan: Preacher and Teacher of Talmudic Times." *MelJ*
(Spring 1982), 3–19.

———. "Joseph Heinemann's Studies on the Aggadah." *Immanuel* 9 (1979), 58–62.

———. "Past and Present in Midrashic Literature." *HAR* 2 (1978), 45–59.

———. "The Triennial Haftarot and the Perorations of the Midrashic Homilies." *JJS* 32 (1981), 74–84.

Brown, Ronald Nathaniel. "The Enjoyment of Midrash: The Use of the Pun in Genesis Rabba." Dissertation, Hebrew Union College, 1980.

———. "Midrashim as Oral Traditions." *HUCA* 47 (1976), 181–89.

Buber, Martin. *On the Bible: Eighteen Studies.* Edited by Nahum N. Glatzer. Introduction by Harold Bloom. New York: Schocken Books, 1982.

Cohen, Norman J. "Structural Analysis of a Talmudic Story: Joseph-Who-Honors-the-Sabbath." *JQR* 72 (1982), 162–77.

Copperman, Hillel, ed. and comp. *B'Netivot HaMidrash: A Comprehensive and Exhaustive Lexicon of All Subjects Dealt with in Midrash Rabbah on the Chumash and the Five Megillot* (Hebrew). Jerusalem: Privately printed, 1985.

Ehrlich, A. B. *Mikra Kifshuto; The Bible According to Its Literal Meaning* (Hebrew). 3 vols. Berlin, 1899–1901. Reprint New York: Ktav Publishing House, 1969, with an introduction (English) by Harry Orlinsky.

Eliner, A. "Derasha." *Hebrew Encyclopaedia* (Hebrew). 1969 ed.

Finkelstein, Louis. *Introduction to the Treatises Abot and Abot of Rabbi Nathan.* New York: JTS, 1950.

———. *The Mekilta and Its Text.* New York: JTS, 1934.

———. *The Oldest Midrash: Pre-Rabbinic Ideals and Teachings in the Passover Haggadah.* HTR 31 (1938). Reprint Cambridge, Mass., 1938.

———. *Prolegomena to an Edition of the Sifre on Deuteronomy.* Philadelphia: American Academy for Jewish Research, 1931–32.

———. *The Sources of Tannaitic Midrashim.* Philadelphia: Dropsie College for Hebrew and Cognate Learning, 1941.

Fishbane, Michael. "Torah and Tradition." In *Tradition and Theology in the Old Testament.* Edited by Douglas A. Knight. London: SPCK; Philadelphia: Fortress Press, 1977, pp. 275–300.

———. *Biblical Interpretation of Ancient Israel.* Oxford: Clarendon Press, 1985.

Fleisher, Ezra and Jacob Petuchowski, eds. *Research in Aggadah, Targum and Jewish Liturgy in Memory of Joseph Heinemann* (Hebrew). Jerusalem: Magnes Press, 1981.

Fraenkel, Jonas. "Bible Verses Quoted in Tales of the Sages." *SH* 22 (1971), 80–99.

———. *Exploration of the Spiritual World of the Aggadic Story* (Hebrew). Tel Aviv: Kibbutz HaMeuchad, 1981.

———. "Time and Its Shape in the Aggadic Story" (Hebrew). In *Heinemann,* pp. 133–62.

Frankel, Israel. *Peshat in Talmudic and Midrashic Literature.* Toronto: La Salle Press, 1956.

Gaster, Moses. *The Ancient Collections of Aggadoth: The Sefer HaMaasiyoth and Two Facsimiles.* In Judith Montefiore College (Ramsgate) Report, 1894–96.

————. *Eliezer Crescas and His Bet Zebul: The Bible References in Talmud and Midrash.* Cincinnati: Hebrew Union College, 1929.

Ginzberg, Louis. "Some Observations on the Attitude of the Synagogue towards the Apocalyptic Eschatological Writings." *JBL* 41 (1922), 115–36.

————. *A Commentary on the Palestinian Talmud: A Study of the Development of the Halacha and Haggadah in Palestine and Babylonia.* 3 vols. New York: JTS, 1941.

————. *Die Haggadah bei den Kirchenvätern.* Amsterdam, 1899.

————. *On Halacha and Aggadah: Studies and Lectures* (Hebrew). Edited by A. Judah Naditch. Tel Aviv: Dvir, 1960.

————. *The Legends of the Jews.* 7 vols. Philadelphia: Jewish Publication Society of America, 1909–38. Abridged ed. *Legends of the Bible.* New York: Jewish Publication Society of America, 1968.

————. *Midrash and Haggadah.* Vol. 1 of *Genizah Studies in Memory of Doctor Solomon Schechter.* New York: JTS, 1928.

Glatzer, Nahum Norbert. "A Study of the Talmudic-Midrashic Interpretation of Prophecy." In his *Essays in Jewish Thought* (English, 1 essay in Hebrew). Alabama: University of Alabama Press, 1978, pp. 16–35.

Goldberg, Arnold. "Versuch über die hermeneutische Präsupposition und Struktur der Petihta." *FJB* 8 (1980), 1–59.

Goldin, Judah. *The Song at the Sea.* New Haven: Yale University Press, 1971.

————. "From Text to Interpretation and from Experience to the Interpreted Text." *Prooftexts* 3, 2 (1983), 157–68.

Goldschmidt, Daniel. *The Passover Haggadah: Its Sources and History* (Hebrew). Jerusalem: Bialik, 1977.

Gordis, Robert. "Quotations as a Literary Usage in Biblical, Oriental and Rabbinic Literature." *HUCA* 22 (1949), 157–219.

Halivni, David Weiss. *Midrash, Mishnah and Gemara: The Jewish Predilection for Justified Law.* Cambridge: Harvard University Press, 1986.

————. *Sources and Traditions* (Hebrew). Vols. 1–2 Tel Aviv: Dvir, 1968; vols. 3–4 New York: JTS, 1982.

Heinemann, I. "On the Development of the Technical Terms for Biblical Explication" (Hebrew). *Leshonen* 14–16 (1945–49), 182–89, 108–15, 20–28.

————. *The Methods of the Aggadah* (Hebrew). 3d ed. Jerusalem: Magnes Press, 1970.

Heinemann, J. *Aggadah and its Development: Studies in the Continuity of a Tradition* (Hebrew). Jerusalem: Keter, 1974.

————. "The Art of Composition in the Midrash Leviticus Rabbah" (Hebrew). *Ha-Sifrut* 2 (1971), 808–34.

————. "Homily on Jeremiah and the Fall of Jerusalem." In *The Biblical Mosaic.* Edited by Robert M. Polzin and Eugene Rothman. Philadelphia: Fortress Press, 1982, pp. 27–41.

————. "On Life and Death: Anatomy of a Rabbinic Sermon." *SH* 27 (1978), 52–65.

————. "The Proem in the Aggadic Midrashim: A Form-Critical Study." *SH* 22 (1971), 100–22. Reprinted (Hebrew) in *Proceedings of the Fourth World Congress for Jewish Studies,* vol. 2. Jerusalem, 1969, pp. 42–47.

―――. "Profile of a Midrash." *JAAR* 39 (1971), 141–50.

Heinemann, J. and D. Noy, eds. *Studies in Aggadah and Folk Literature.* (SH 22) Jerusalem: Magnes Press, 1971.

Heinemann, J. and S. Werses, eds. *Studies in Hebrew Narrative Art through the Ages.* (SH 27) Jerusalem: Magnes Press, 1978.

Hendel, Russell Jay. "Peshat and Derash: A New Intuitive and Analytic Approach." *Tradition* 18, 4 (1980), 327–40.

Herr, Moshe David. "The Essence of Aggadah." (Hebrew) Maḥanayyim 100, 1 (1966), 63–69.

―――. "Midrash." *Encyclopaedia Judaica.* 1971 ed.

Holtz, Barry, ed. *Back to the Sources: Reading the Classic Jewish Texts.* New York: Summit Books, 1984.

Kadushin, Max. "Aspects of the Rabbinic Concept of Israel in the Mekhilta." *HUCA* 19 (1945–46), 57–96.

―――. *Organic Thinking: A Study in Rabbinic Thought.* New York: JTS, 1938.

―――. *The Rabbinic Mind.* New York: JTS, 1952.

Kagan, Z. "Divergent Tendencies and Their Literary Moulding in the Aggadah." *SH* 22 (1971), 151–70.

Kasher, M. S. and J. I. Blechnovitz, eds. *The Interpretations of the Maharal from Prague on the Talmudic Aggadoth* (Hebrew). 3 vols. Jerusalem: Ginzei Rishonim, 1958.

Kugel, James L. *The Idea of Biblical Poetry: Parallelism and Its History.* New Haven: Yale University Press, 1981.

Le Deaut, R. "A propos d'une définition du midrash." *Biblica* 50 (1969), 395–413. Reprinted in *Interpretation* 25 (1971), 259–82.

Loewe, Raphael. "The 'Plain' Meaning of Scripture in Early Jewish Exegesis." *Papers of the Institute of Jewish Studies London* 1 (1964), 140–85.

Mann, J. *The Bible as Read and Preached in the Old Synagogue: A Study in the Cycles of the Readings from Torah and Prophets, as well as from Psalms, and in the Structure of the Midrashic Homilies.* 2 vols. Vol. 1 Cincinnati: Privately published, 1940. Photocopy Israel, 1970. Vol. 2, edited by Mann and Sonne. Cincinnati: Hebrew Union College, 1966. Reprint Ktav.

Maybaum, S. *Die ältesten Phasen in der Entwicklung der jüdischen Predigt.* Berlin, 1901.

Meir, Ofra. "The Acting Characters in the Stories of the Talmud and Midrash" (Hebrew). Dissertation, Hebrew University, 1977.

Meozi, I. "The Influence of the Midrash on the Choice of Words of the Targum on the Pentateuch" (Hebrew). *Tarbiẓ* 46, 3–4 (1977), 212–30.

Mintz, Alan. "Midrash and the Destruction." In his *Ḥurban: Responses to Catastrophe in Jewish Literature.* New York: Columbia University Press, 1984, pp. 49–83.

―――. "The Song at the Sea and the Question of Doubling in Midrash." *Prooftexts* 1, 2 (1981), 185–92.

Mirsky, Aharon. *The Structure of the Genres of Piyyut: The Growth and Development of Forms in Early Palestinian Poetry* (Hebrew). Jerusalem and Tel Aviv: Schocken Books, 1968.

Moore, George F. *Judaism in the First Centuries of the Christian Era*. 3 vols. Cambridge: Harvard University Press, 1927–30.

Neusner, Jacob. *Midrash in Context: Exegesis in Formative Judaism*. Philadelphia: Fortress Press, 1983.

———, ed. *The Palestinian and Babylonian Talmuds*. Vol. 2 of *The Study of Ancient Judaism*. New York: Ktav, 1981.

———. "Types and Forms in Ancient Jewish Literature: Some Comparisons." *HR* 11 (1972), 354–90.

Noy, Dov. *Folktale in the Talmud and Midrash* (Hebrew). Edited by Joseph Tubi. Jerusalem: Akademon, 1968.

———. "The Jewish Versions of the 'Animal Languages' Folktale (AT 670)—A Typological-Structural Study." *SH* 22 (1971), 171–208.

Petuchowski, J. J. "The Vast Variety of Aggadah: [On] J. Heinemann, 'Aggadah and its Development,' 1974." *Judaism* 26 (1977), 248–49.

Rabinowitz, Z. M. "Lost Midrashim in the Liturgical Poems of Yannai." *Proceedings of the Third World Congress of Jewish Studies*, vol. 8, Jerusalem, 1971. Hebrew Literature sec. 8, pp. 1–3.

Rathaus, Ariel. "Reading the Bible in the Midrashic Tradition." *SIDIC* 9, 2 (1976), 12–18.

Rawidowicz, Simon. "On Interpretation." In his *Studies in Jewish Thought*. Edited by Nahum N. Glatzer. Philadelphia: Jewish Publication Society of America, 1974, pp. 45–80.

Sandmel, Samuel. "The Haggadah within Scripture." *JBL* 80 (1961), 105–22.

Sarason, R. S. "Toward a New Agendum for the Study of Rabbinic Midrashic Literature." In *Heinemann*, pp. 55–73.

Scholem, Gershom. "Revelation and Tradition as Religious Categories in Judaism." In *The Messianic Idea in Judaism*. New York: Schoken, 1971, pp 282–303.

———. "The Name of God and the Linguistic Theory of the Kabbalah." *Diogenes* 79–80 (1972), 59–80, 164–94.

Schwartz, Howard. "The Aggadic Tradition." In his *Gates to the New City*. New York: Avon Books, 1983, pp. 3–10.

———. "Reimagining the Bible." In his *Gates to the New City*. New York: Avon Books, 1983, pp. 11–34.

Segal, E. L. " 'The Same from Beginning to End': On the Development of the Midrashic Homily." *JJS* 32 (1981), 158–63.

Shinan, Avigdor. *The Aggadah in the Aramaic Targums to the Pentateuch* (Hebrew). Jerusalem: Makor, 1979.

———. "Aggadic Literature: From Oral Narrative to Written Tradition" (Hebrew). *RFol* 1 (1981), 44–60.

———. "The Petiḥta to Midrash Rabbah on Exodus" (Hebrew). In *Heinemann*, pp. 175–83.

———, ed. *A Reader in Aggadic Literature: Studies and Sources* (Hebrew). Jerusalem: Magnes Press, 1983.

Silberman, Lou H. "A Theological Treatise on Forgiveness; Chapter 23 of Pesikta de-Rav Kahana" (Hebrew). In *Heinemann*, pp. 95–107.

————. "Toward a Rhetoric of Midrash: A Preliminary Account." In *The Biblical Mosaic*. Edited by Robert M. Polzin and Eugene Rothman. Philadelphia: Fortress Press, 1982, pp. 15–26.

Slonimsky, Henry. "The Philosophy Implicit in the Midrash." *HUCA* 27 (1956), 235–90. Reprint New York: Ktav, 1968.

Smid, M. "The Language of Clarity in the Aggadic Midrash" (Hebrew). *Leshonnenu* 13 (1944–45), 139–62.

Sperber, Daniel. "[On] J. Heinemann, 'Agadot VeToldotan'—Aggadah and Its Development, 1974." *BO* 33 (1976), 356–57.

Spiegel, Shalom. *The Last Trial: On the Legends and Lore of the Command to Abraham to Offer Isaac as a Sacrifice*. Translated by Judah Goldin. New York: Pantheon, 1967.

Stein, Edmund. "Die homiletische Peroratio im Midrasch." *HUCA* 8–9 (1931–32), 353–71.

Steinsaltz, Adin. *The Essential Talmud*. Translated by Chaya Gadai. New York: Bantam, 1970.

Stern, David. "Interpreting in Parables: The Mashal in Midrash, with Special Reference to *Lamentations Rabbah*." Dissertation, Harvard University, 1980.

————. "Rhetoric and Midrash: The Case of the Mashal." *Prooftexts* 1, 3 (1981), 261–91.

Strack, Hermann Leberecht. *Introduction to the Talmud and Midrash*. Philadelphia, 1931. Reprint New York: Atheneum, 1969.

Tigay, J. "An Early Technique of Aggadic Exegesis." In *History, Historiography and Interpretation: Studies in Biblical and Cuneiform Literatures*. Edited by H. Tadmor and M. Weinfeld. Jerusalem: Magnes Press, 1983, pp. 169–89.

Towner, Wayne Sibley. "Hermeneutical Systems of Hillel and the Tannaim: A Fresh Look." *HUCA* 53 (1982), 101–35.

————. *The Rabbinic "Enumeration of Scriptural Examples": A Study of a Rabbinic Pattern of Discourse with Special Reference to Mekhilta D'R Ishmael*. Leiden: E. J. Brill, 1973.

Urbach, Efraim Elimelech. "Review of I. Heinemann's *Darkhei Ha-Aggadah*" (Hebrew). *Kirjath Sefer* 26 (1950), 223–28.

————. *The Sages: Their Concepts and Beliefs*. 2 vols. Translated by Israel Abrahams. Jerusalem: Magnes Press, 1975.

Vermes, Geza. "Bible and Midrash: Early Old Testament Exegesis." In *From the Beginnings to Jerome*. Vol. 1 of *The Cambridge History of the Bible*. Edited by P. R. Ackroyd and C. F. Evans. Cambridge: Cambridge University Press, 1970, pp. 199–231.

————. *Post-Biblical Jewish Studies*. Leiden: E. J. Brill, 1975.

————. *Scripture and Tradition in Judaism: Haggadic Studies*. Leiden: E. J. Brill, 1961; 2d rev. ed. 1973.

Wartski, I. *The Language of the Midrashim* (Hebrew). Jerusalem: Mossad Harav Kook, 1970.

Weingreen, J. "Exposition in the Old Testament and in Rabbinic Literature." In *Promise and Fulfilment*. Edited by F. F. Bruce. Edinburgh: T. & T. Clark, 1963, pp. 187–201.

———. "Rabbinic Type Glosses in the Old Testament." *JSS* 2 (1957), 149–62.

———. "The Torah Speaks in the Language of Man" (title and quotations in Hebrew). In *Interpreting the Hebrew Bible: Essays in Honor of E. I. J. Rosenthal*. Edited by J. A. Emerton and Stephan C. Reif. Cambridge: Cambridge University Press, 1982, pp. 267–75.

Winfeld, Samuel Judah Halevi. *The Cantillation Notes of Scripture* (Hebrew). Jerusalem: Eshkol, 1972.

Witman, Ze'ev. "On the Relationship of the Midrash and the Peshat" (Hebrew). *HaMa'ayan* 18 (1978), 26–50.

Wright, Addison G. *The Literary Genre Midrash*. Staten Island, N.Y.: Alba House, 1967.

Zunz, Y. L. *Die gottesdienstlichen Vorträge der Juden, historisch entwickelt: Ein Beitrag zur Alterthumskunde und biblischen Kritik, zur Literatur- und Religiongeschichte.* Berlin, 1832. rev. ed., 1892.

———. *The Drashot in Israel and Their Historical Development* (Hebrew). Translated by M. E. Zack and rev. Ch. Albeck. Jerusalem: Mossad Bialik, 1947.

STUDIES IN MIDRASH AND NEW TESTAMENT

Bonnet, Jacques. *Le "Midrash" de l'Evangile de Saint-Jean.* Introduction by Armand Abécassis. St. Etienne: Le Hénaff, 1982.

Borgen, Peder. *Bread from Heaven: An Exegetical Study of the Concept of Manna in the Gospel of John and the Writings of Philo.* Leiden: E. J. Brill, 1965.

Bowker, J. W. "Speeches in Acts: A Study in Proem and Yelamedenu Form." *NTS* 14 (1968), 96–111.

Brown, Raymond E. *The Birth of the Messiah: A Commentary on the Infancy Narratives in Matthew and Luke.* Garden City, N.Y.: Doubleday; London: G. Chapman, 1977.

Crockett, I. "The Old Testament in Luke with Emphasis on the Interpretations of Isaiah 61:1–2." Dissertation, Brown University, 1966.

Daniélou, Jean. *Études d'exégèse judéo-chrétienne.* Paris: Beauchesne et ses fils, 1966.

Daube, David. "The Earliest Structures of the Gospels." *NTS* 5 (1958–59), 174–87.

———. *The New Testament and Rabbinic Judaism.* London: University of London Press, 1956.

Davies, William David. *Paul and Rabbinic Judaism: Some Rabbinic Elements in Pauline Theology.* 3d ed. London: SPCK, 1970.

Derrett, J. D. M. "Law in the New Testament: Fresh Light on the Parable of the Good Samaritan." *NTS* 11 (1964), 22–37.

Doeve, J. W. *Jewish Hermeneutics in the Synoptic Gospels and Acts.* Assen, Netherlands: Van Gorcum, 1954.

Drury, John. *Tradition and Design in Luke's Gospel: A Study in Early Christian Historiography.* Atlanta: John Knox Press; London: Darton, Longman and Todd, 1976.

Ellis, E. E. "Midrash, Targum and New Testament Quotations." In *Neotestamentica et Semitica: Studies in Honor of Matthew Black*. Edited by E. E. Ellis and Max Wilcox. Edinburgh: T. & T. Clark, 1969, pp. 61–69.

Finkel, Asher. "Midrash and the Synoptic Gospels: An Introductory Abstract." *SBL* 11 (1977), 251–56.

Flusser, David. "The Parables of Jesus and Parables in Rabbinic Literature" (Hebrew). In his *Jewish Sources in Early Christianity*. Tel Aviv: Sifriat Hapoalim, 1979, pp. 150–209.

Ford, J. Massingbird. "The Parable of the Foolish Scholars." *NT* 9 (1967), 107–23.

Gerhardsson, Birger. *The Good Samaritan—The Good Shepherd?* Upssala, Lund: G. W. K. Gleerup, 1958.

————. *Memory and Manuscript: Oral Tradition and Written Transmission in Rabbinic Judaism and Early Christianity*. Translated by Eric Sharpe. Upssala, Lund: G. W. K. Gleerup, 1961.

————. "The Parable of the Sower and Its Interpretation." *NTS* 14 (1967–68), 165–93.

————. *The Testing of God's Son. Matt. 4:1–11 and par. An Analysis of an Early Christian Midrash*. Translated by John Toy. Upssala, Lund: G. W. K. Gleerup, 1966.

Gertner, M. "Midrashim in the New Testament." *JSS* 7 (1962), 267–92.

Goldsmith, D. "Acts 13:33–37: A Pesher on 2 Samuel 7?" *JBL* 87 (1968), 321–24.

Goulder, Michael Douglas. *Midrash and Lection in Matthew*. London: SPCK, 1974.

Johnson, Marshall D. *The Purpose of the Biblical Genealogies: With Special Reference to the Genealogies of Jesus*. Cambridge: Cambridge University Press, 1969.

Kister, M. "The Sayings of Jesus and the Midrash." *Immanuel* 15 (1982–83), 39–50.

Klijn, Albertus Frederik Johannes. *Seth in Jewish, Christian and Gnostic Literature*. Supplement to *NTS* 46. Leiden: E. J. Brill, 1977.

Malina, B. "Matthew 2 and Isaiah 41:2–3: A Possible Relationship?" *SBF* 17 (1967), 291–303.

Marmorstein, A. "Judaism and Christianity in the Middle of the Third Century." *HUCA* 10 (1935), 223–63.

Miller, Merrill P. "Targum, Midrash and the Use of the Old Testament in the New Testament." *JSJ* 1–2 (1970–71), 29–82.

Montefiore, Claude Joseph Golsmid. *Rabbinic Literature and Gospel Teachings*. 1930. Reprint New York: Ktav, 1970.

Perrot, C. "Les Récits d'enfance dans la Haggadah." *RScR* 55 (1967), 481–518.

Sanders, Ed Parish. *Paul and Palestinian Judaism: A Comparison of Patterns of Religion*. London: SCM Press; Philadelphia: Fortress Press, 1977.

Sandmel, Samuel. *Judaism and Christian Beginnings*. New York: Oxford University Press, 1978.

Winter, P. "Jewish Folklore in the Matthewan Birth Story." *HibJ* 53 (1954–55), 34–42.

STUDIES IN MIDRASH AND HELLENISM

Bergmann, I. *Die stoïsche Philosophie und die jüdische Frömmigkeit, Judaica, Festschrift zu Hermann Cohens siebzigsten Geburtstage.* Berlin: Cassirer, 1912, pp. 145–66.

Boman, Thorleif. *Das hebräische Denken im Vergleich mit dem griechischen.* Göttingen: Vandenhoeck & Ruprecht, 1954. Translated by Jules L. Moreau. *Hebrew Thought Compared with Greek.* New York: Norton, 1970.

Daube, David. "Rabbinic Methods of Interpretation and Hellenistic Rhetoric." *HUCA* 22 (1949), 239–64.

Edelman, R. "Some Remarks on the Literary Aspect of the Talmud and Midrash in Their Relation to Hellenistic Civilization." In *Proceedings of the Third World Congress of Jewish Studies, Talmud and Rabbinics.* Jerusalem, 1961, sec. 4, pp. 1–7.

Fischel, Henry A., ed. *Essays in Greco-Roman and Related Talmudic Literature.* New York: Ktav, 1977.

———. *Rabbinic Literature and Greco-Roman Philosophy.* Leiden: E. J. Brill, 1973.

Halevi, Elimelech Epstein (A. A.). *Aggadoth of the Amoraim: The Biographical Aggadah of the Amoraim of the Land of Israel and Babylon, in View of Greek and Latin Sources* (Hebrew). Tel Aviv: Dvir, 1977.

———. *The Gates of Aggadah: On the Essence of Aggada, Its Types, Methods, Teleology and Its Relation to Its Historical Environment* (Hebrew). Tel Aviv: Dvir, 1972.

———. *The Historico-Biogaphical Aggadah in View of Greek and Latin Sources* (Hebrew). Tel Aviv: Tel Aviv University Press, 1975.

———. "Homilies from the Bible and Homer." In *Proceedings of the Third World Congress of Jewish Studies,* Jerusalem, 1961, sec. 5, pp. 1–2.

———. *Subjects in Aggadah in View of Greek Sources* (Hebrew). Haifa: University of Haifa Press, 1973.

———. *Values in Aggadah and Halakha in View of Greek and Latin Sources* (Hebrew). 4 vols. Tel Aviv: Dvir, 1979–82.

———. *The World of Aggadah: The Aggadah in View of Greek Sources* (Hebrew). Tel Aviv: Dvir, 1972.

Kaminka, A. "Les Rapports entre le rabbinisme et la philosophie stoicienne." *REJ* 82 (1926), 232–52.

Lieberman, Saul. *Hellenism in Jewish Palestine: Studies in the Literary Transmission, Beliefs and Manners of Palestine in the I Century B.C.E.–IV Century C.E.* New York: JTS, 1950.

Marmorstein, Arthur. "The Background of the Haggadah." *HUCA* 6 (1929), 141–204.

———. *Studies in Jewish Theology.* London: Oxford University Press, 1950.

Porton, Gary. "Midrash: Palestinian Jews and the Hebrew Bible in the Greco-Roman Period." *ANRW,* vol. 11, pt. 9, sec. 2 (1979), 103–38.

STUDIES IN MIDRASH, THE CHURCH FATHERS, AND MEDIEVAL LITERATURE

Aptowitzer, Viktor. "Rabbinische Parallelen und Aufschlüsse zur Septuaginta und Vulgata." *ZAW* 29 (1900), 241–52.

Bacher, Wilhelm. "Eine angebliche Lücke im hebräischen Wissen des Hieronymus." *ZAW* 22 (1902), 114–16.

Bardy, G. "Aux origines de l'école d'Alexandrie." *RScR* 27 (1937), 65–90.

———. "St. Jérome et ses maîtres hèbreux." *RBen* 46 (1934), 145–64.

———. "Les Traditions juives dans l'oeuvre d'Origéne." *RB* 34 (1925), 217–52.

Berger, Samuel. *Histoire de la Vulgata: pendant les premiers siècles du moyen âge.* Paris, Nancy, Strasbourg: Berger-Levrault, 1893.

Blumenkrantz, Bernhard. *Les Auteurs Chrétiens Latins du moyen âge sur les juifs et le judaïsme.* Paris, The Hague: Mouton, 1963.

Condamin, Albert. "L'Influence de la tradition juive dans la version de St. Jérome." *RScR* 5 (1914), 1–21.

Daube, David. "Origen and the Punishment of Adultery in Jewish Law." *StPatrist* 2 (1957), 109–13.

de Lange, Nicholas Robert Michael. *Origen and the Jews;: Studies in Jewish-Christian Relations in Third-Century Palestine.* Cambridge: Cambridge University Press, 1976.

Derrett, J. Duncan M. "The Parable of the Prodigal Son: Patristic Allegories and Jewish Midrashim." *StPatrist* 2 (1957), 219–24.

Eliott, C. J. "Hebrew Learning among the Fathers." In *Dictionary of Christian Biography.* Vol. 2. Edited by William Smith and Henry Wace. London: John Murray, 1880.

Figueras, P. "A Midrashic Interpretation of the Cross as a Symbol." *LA* 30 (1980), 159–66.

Friedländer, Moritz. *Patristische und talmudische Studien.* Vienna, 1878. Reprint Farnborough: Gregg International Publishers, 1972.

Funk, Salomon. *Die haggadischen Elemente in den Homilien des Aphraates, des persischen Weisen.* Vienna: M. Knöpflmacher, 1891.

Ginzberg, Louis. *Die Haggada bei den Kirchenvätern und in der apokryphischen Literatur.* Berlin: S. Calvary, 1900.

Golfahn, A. H. *Die Kirchenvätern und die Agada-Justinus Martyr und die Agada.* Breslau, 1873.

Goodenough, Erwin R. "The Judaism of the Dura Synagogue." In *Proceedings of the Third World Congress of Jewish Studies, Archaeology.* Jerusalem, 1961, sec. 7, pp. 1–3.

———. *Symbolism in the Dura Synagogue.* Vol. 10 of *Jewish Symbols of the Greco-Roman Period.* Bollingen ser. New York: Pantheon, 1964.

Graetz, H. "Hagadische Elemente bei den Kirchenvätern." *MGWJ* 3–4 (1854–55).

Güdemann, Moritz. *Religionsgeschichtliche Studien.* 2 vols. Leipzig: O. Leiner, 1876.

Halperin, Herman. *Rashi and the Christian Scholars*. Pittsburgh: University of Pittsburgh Press, 1963.

Hanson, Richard Patrick Crosland. *Allegory and Event: A Study of the Sources and Significance of Origen's Interpretation of Scripture*. Richmond: John Knox Press; London: SCM Press, 1959.

Krauss, S. "The Jews in the Works of the Church Fathers." *JQA* 5–6 (1892–94). Reprinted in *Judaism and Christianity: Selected Accounts 1892–1962*. Edited Jacob B. Agus. New York: Arno Press, 1973.

Jaeger, H. "The Patristic Conception of Wisdom in the Light of Biblical and Rabbinic Research." *StPatrist* 4 (1961), 90–106.

Lamirande, E. "Étude bibliographique sur les Pères de l'Église et l'Aggadah." *VC* 21 (1967), 1–11.

Lewis, Jack Pearl. *A Study of the Interpretation of Noah and the Flood in Jewish and Christian Literature*. Leiden: E. J. Brill, 1968.

Lieberman, S. *Shkiin: Some Remarks on the Aggadot, Customs and Literary Sources of the Jews* (Hebrew). Jerusalem: Wahrmann, 1970.

Loewe, R. J. "Herbert of Bosham's Commentary on Jerome's Hebrew Psalter." *Biblica* 34 (1953).

———. "The Medieval Christian Hebraists of England: Herbert of Bosham and Earlier Scholars." *TJHSE* 17 (1953), 225–50.

———. "Midrashim and Patristic Exegesis of the Bible." *StPatrist* 1 (1957), 492–514.

Marmorstein, Arthur. "Agada und Kirchenväter." *Encyclopaedia Judaica* 1934 ed.

———. *Die Bezeichnungen für Christen und Gnostiken im Talmud und Midrash*. Vol. 1 of *Religionsgeschichte Studien*. Skotschau, 1910.

Montaiglon, Anatole de. *Recueil général et complet des fabliaux des XIIIe et XIVe siècles: Imprimés où inédites*. 5 vols. Paris: Librairie des Bibliophiles, 1872–83.

Murmelstein, Benjamin. "Agadische Methode in den Pentateuchhomilien des Origines." In *Zum vierzigjährigen Bestehen der israelitisch-theologischen Lehrenstalt*. Vienna: Israelitisch-theologischen Lehrenstalt, 1933, pp. 93–122.

Nequam, B. "Berachiah (Mishley Shualim) and Chaucer's 'Squire's Tale.'" *MeH* 1 (1970), 57–65.

Parkes, James Williams. *The Conflict of the Church and Synagogue: A Study in the Origins of Antisemitism*. London, 1934. Reprint New York; Atheneum, 1969.

Pépin, Jean. *Mythe et allégorie: Les Origines grecques et les contestations judéo-chrétiennes*. Paris: Editions Montaigne, 1958.

Preus, James S. *From Shadow to Promise: Old Testament Interpretation from Augustine to the Young Luther*. Cambridge: Belknap Press, 1969.

Rahmer, Moritz. *Die hebräischen Traditionen in den Werken des Hieronymus*. Breslau: H. Skutsch, 1861.

Rosenthal, Erwin I. J. "Edward Lively: Cambridge Hebraist." In *Essays and Studies Presented to Stanley Arthur Cook in Celebration of His Seventy-fifth Birthday, 12 April 1948*. Edited by D. Winton Thomas. London: Taylor's Foreign Press, 1950, pp. 95–112.

———. "Sebastian Münster's Knowledge and Use of Jewish Exegesis." In

Essays in Honor of the Very Reverend Dr. J. H. Hertz. Edited by I. Epstein, E. Levine, and C. Roth. London: Edward Goldston, 1943, pp. 351–69.

———. "The Study of the Bible in Medieval Judaism." In *The Cambridge History of the Bible.* Vol. 2. Edited by G. W. Lampe. Cambridge: Cambridge University Press, 1969, pp. 252–79.

Saperstein, Marc. *Decoding the Rabbis: A Thirteenth-Century Commentary on the Aggadah.* Cambridge: Harvard University Press, 1974.

Secret, François. *Le Zôhar chez les kabbalistes Chrétiens de la renaissance.* Paris, The Hague: Mouton, 1964.

Shinan, Avigdor. "The Chronicle of Moses: The Genre, Time, Sources and Literary Nature of a Medieval Hebrew Story" (Hebrew). *HaSifrut* 24 (1977), 100–16.

Smalley, Beryl. "Andrew of St. Victor, Abbot of Wigmere: A Twelfth-Century Hebraist." *RTAM* (1938), 358–73.

———. *The Study of the Bible in the Middle Ages.* Oxford: Clarendon Press, 1941.

Urbach, E. E. "The Homiletical Interpretations of the Sages and the Exposition of Origen on Canticles, and the Jewish-Christian Disputation" (Hebrew). *Tarbiz* 30 (1960–61), 148–70.

Wilken, Robert L. *Judaism and the Early Christian Mind.* New Haven: Yale University Press, 1971.

Wolfson, Harry Austryn. *Faith, Trinity, Incarnation.* Vol. 1 of *The Philosophy of the Church Fathers.* Cambridge: Harvard University Press, 1956; 3d rev. ed., 1976.

———. *Studies in the History of Philosophy and Religion.* Edited by Isadore Twersky and George H. Williams. Cambridge: Harvard University Press, 1973.

MIDRASH IN ISLAMIC STUDIES

Baumstark, Anton. "Jüdischer und christlicher Gebetstypus im Koran." *Isl* 16 (1927), 229–48.

Cohen, Boaz. "Une légende juive de Mohammet." *REJ* 88 (1929), 1–17.

Finkel, Joshua. "Jewish, Christian and Samaritan Influences on Arabia." In *The MacDonald Presentation Volume: A Tribute to Dunkan Black MacDonald consisting of Articles by Former Students, Presented to Him on His Seventieth Birthday, April 9, 1933.* Edited by William G. Shellabear et al. Princeton: Princeton University Press; London: Oxford University Press, 1933, pp. 145–66.

Gastfreund, I. *Mohammed nach Talmud und Midrasch.* Berlin: L. Gerschel, 1875.

Geiger, Abraham. *Judaism and Islam* (1898). Translated by F. M. Young. New York: Ktav, 1970.

Goitein, S. D. "Israelitat: The Circle of Malach ben Dinar" (Hebrew). *Tarbiz* 6 (1934–35), 510–22.

———. "Israelitat: Malach ben Dinar" (Hebrew). *Tarbiz* 6 (1934–35), 89–101.

———. "Jewish Subject Matter in 'Ansab al-Asraf' of Al Baladhori" (Hebrew). *Zion* 1 (1935–36), 75–81.

———. *Jews and Arabs: Their Contact through the Ages.* New York: Schocken Books, 1955; 3d rev. ed. 1974.

Grünbaum, Max. *Neue Beiträge zur semitischen Sagenkunde*. Leiden: E. J. Brill, 1893.

Guillaume, Alfred. "The Influence of Judaism on Islam" In *The Legacy of Israel*. Edited by Edwyn R. Bevan and Charles Singer. Oxford: Clarendon Press, 1927, pp. 129–71.

Hayek, M. *Le Mystère d'Ismaël*. Tours: Mame, 1964.

Heller, B. "La Légende biblique dans l'Islam. Récents travaux et nouvelles méthodes de recherches." *REJ* 98 (1934), 1–18.

———. "Muhammedanisches und Antimuhammedanisches in den Pirke Rabbi Eliezer," *MGWJ* 69 (1925), 47–54.

———. "Récits et personnages bibliques dans la légende mahométane." *REJ* 85 (1928), 113–36.

Jomier, Jacques. *The Bible and the Koran*. Translated by Edward P. Arbez. New York: Desclée, 1964.

Katsh, Abraham Isaac. *Judaism and the Koran*. New York: A. J. Barnes, 1954.

Lazarus-Yafeh, H. "Judaism and Islam: Some Aspects of Mutual Cultural Influences." In her *Some Religious Aspects of Islam: A Collection of Articles*. Leiden: E. J. Brill, 1981, pp. 72–89.

Leveen, J. "Mohammed and His Jewish Companions." *JQR* 16 (1903–04), 399–406.

Masson, D. *Le Coran et la révélation Judéo-Chrétienne: Études comparées*. 2 vols. Paris: Librairie d'Amérique et d'Orient-Adrien-Maissonneuve, 1958.

Moubarac, Y. *Abraham dans le Coran*. Paris: J. Vrin, 1958.

Obermann, Julian. "Islamic Origins: A Study in Background and Foundation." In *The Arab Heritage*. Edited by N. A. Faris. Princeton: Princeton University Press, 1944, pp. 58–119.

———. "Koran and Agada." *AJSLL* 58 (1941), 23–48.

———. "Ein Werk agadisch-islamischen Synkretismus." *ZS* 5 (1927), 43–69.

Rosenthal, E. I. J. *Judaism and Islam*. London: Thomas L. Yoseloff, 1961.

Schapiro, Israel. *Die haggadischen Elemente im erzählenden Teil des Korans*. Leipzig: G. Fock, 1907.

Schussman, A. *Stories of the Prophets in Muslim Tradition* (Hebrew). Jerusalem: The Hebrew University. The Institute for African-Asian Studies, 1981.

Schützinger, H. *Ursprung und Entwicklung der arabischen Abraham-Nimrod Legende*. Bonn: Selbstverlag des orientalischen Seminars der Universität Bonn, 1961.

Sidersky, D. *Les Origines des légendes Musulmanes dans le Coran et dans les vies des prophètes*. Paris: P. Geuthner, 1933.

Speyer, Heinrich. *Die biblischen Erzählungen im Qoran*. Berlin: Akademie Verlag, 1913. Photocopy Hildesheim: G. Olms, 1961.

Taylor, W. R. "Al-Buhkari and the Aggada." *MW* 33 (1943), 191–202.

Torrey, Charles Cutler. *The Jewish Foundation of Islam*. Introduction by Franz Rosenthal. New York: Ktav, 1967.

Weil, G. *The Bible, the Koran and the Talmud*. London: Longman, Brown, Green and Longman, 1846.

————. *Biblische Legenden der Muselmänner*. Frankfurt am Main: Literarische Anstalt, 1845.

MIDRASH IN THE REFORMATION

Ages, Arnold. "Luther and the Rabbis." *JQR* 63, 1 (1967), 63–68.

Box, G. H. "Hebrew Studies in the Reformation Period and After: Their Place and Influence." In *The Legacy of Israel*. Edited by Edwyn R. Bevan and Charles Singer. Oxford: Clarendon Press, 1948, pp. 315–75.

Geiger, L. *Die deutsche Literatur und die Juden*. Berlin: G. Reimer, 1910.

————. *Johann Reuchlin: Sein Leben und seine Werke*. Leipzig: Duncker, 1871.

Ginsburg, C. D. *Jacob ben Chajim Ibn Adonijah's Introduction to the Rabbinic Bible* (Hebrew & English). London: Longman, Green, Reader and Dyer, 1867. Reprint Ktav, 1968.

Holmio, Armas. *The Lutheran Reformation and the Jews: The Birth of the Protestant Jewish Missions*. Hancock, Mich.: Finnish Lutheran Book Concern, 1949.

Kraeling, Emil Gottlieb Heinrich. *The Old Testament since the Reformation*. New York: Schocken Books, 1955.

Maurer, Wilhelm. *Kirche und Synagogue: Motive und Formen der Auseinandersetzung der Kirche mit dem Judentum im Laufe der Geschichte*. Stuttgart: Kohlhammer, 1953.

Moore, George Foote. "Christian Writers on Judaism." *HTR* 14, 3 (1921), 197–259. Reprinted in *Judaism and Christianity: Selected Accounts 1892–1962*. Edited by Jacob B. Agus. New York: Arno Press, 1973.

Newman, Louis Israel. *Jewish Influence on Christian Reform Movements*. New York: Columbia University Press, 1925.

Schwartz, R. *Esther im deutschen und neu lateinischen Drama des Reformationszeitalters; eine literarhistorische Untersuchung*. 2d ed. Oldenburg: Schulzesche Hof Buchhandlung und Hof Buchdruckerei, 1898.

Siirala, Aarne. "Luther and the Jews." *LW* 11, 3 (1964), 337–58.

MIDRASH IN THE RENAISSANCE AND SEVENTEENTH CENTURY

Allen, Don Cameron. "Milton and Rabbi Eliezer." *MLN* 63 (1948), 262–63.

Baroway, I. "The Bible in the Renaissance." *JEGP* 32 (1933), 447–80.

Blau, J. L. *The Christian Interpretation of the Kabbalah in the Renaissance*. New York: Columbia University Press, 1944.

Butterworth, C. C. *The Literary Lineage of the King James Bible, 1340–1611*. Philadelphia: University of Pennsylvania Press, 1941.

Cohen, Joseph W. "The Jewish Role in Western Culture." In *Jews in a Gentile World: The Problem of Antisemitism*. Edited by I. Graeber and S. H. Britt. New York: Macmillan, 1942, pp. 329–59.

Daiches, David. *The King James Version of the English Bible*. Chicago: Chicago University Press, 1941.

Deutsch, G. N. "Légends Midrashiques dans la peinture de Nicholas Poussin." *JJewA* 9 (1982), 47–53.

Erwin, I. J. "Rashi and the English Bible." BJRL 24 (1940), 138–67.

Evans, J. M. *Paradise Lost and the Genesis Tradition.* Oxford: Clarendon Press, 1968.

Farbridge, Maurice Harry. *English Literature and the Hebrew Renaissance.* London: Luzac, 1953.

Fisch, Harold. *Jerusalem and Albion: The Hebraic Factor in 17th Century Literature.* New York: Schocken Books, 1964.

Fishlock, A. D. H. "The Rabbinic Material in the 'Esther' of Pinto Delgado (marrane à Rouen, 1697)." JJS 2 (1950), 37–50.

Fletcher, Harris Francis. *Milton's Rabbinical Readings.* Urbana: University of Illinois Press, 1930.

Gaster, Moses. "Jewish Sources of, and Parallels to, the Early English Metrical Romance of King Arthur and Merlin." In *Papers Read at the Anglo-Jewish Historical Exhibition, Royal Albert Hall, London 1887.* London: Office of the Jewish Chronicle, 1888, pp. 231–52.

McColley, Grant. "The Book of Enoch and *Paradise Lost.*" HTR 31 (1938), 21–39.

Mendelsohn, L. R. "Milton and the Rabbis: A Later Inquiry." SEL 18 (1978), 125–35.

Mirsky, Aaron. "Rabbinical Exposition in English Biblical Poetry." In *Hayyim Schirmann Jubilee Volume* (Hebrew). Jerusalem: Schocken Institute for Jewish Research, 1970, pp. 179–94.

Nicholson, Marjorie Hope. "Milton and the *Conjectura Cabbalistica.*" PQ 6 (1927), 1–18.

Robins, Harry F. *If This Be Heresy: A Study of Milton and Origen.* Urbana: University of Illinois Press, 1963.

Rosenblatt, Jason. "A Reevaluation of Milton's Indebtedness to Hebraica in *Paradise Lost.*" Dissertation, Brown University, 1969.

Roston, Murray. *Biblical Drama in England: From the Middle Ages to the Present Day.* London: Faber & Faber, 1968.

Roth, Cecil. "In the Steps of Dante." In his *The Jews in the Renaissance.* Philadelphia: Jewish Publication Society of America, 1959, pp. 86–110.

Roth, Leon. "Hebraists and non-Hebraists of the Seventeenth Century." JSS 6 (1961), 204–21.

Stollman, S. S. "Milton's Rabbinical Readings and Fletcher." MiS 4 (1972), 195–215.

Teicher, J. L. "Maimonides and England." TJHSE 16 (1952), 98–100.

Wallerstein, Ruth. "Schooling and Approaches to Theory." In her *Studies in Seventeenth-Century Poetic.* Madison: University of Wisconsin Press, 1950, pp. 11–58.

Werblowsky, R. J. Zwi. "Milton and the *Conjectura Kabbalistica.*" JWCI 18 (1955), 90–113.

Werman, Golda Spiera. "Midrash in *Paradise Lost: Capitula Rabbi Eliezer.*" MiS 18 (1983), 145–71.

———. "Paradise Lost and Midrash." Dissertation, University of Indiana, 1982.

Williams, A. *The Common Expositor: An Account of the Commentaries on Genesis, 1527–1633.* Chapel Hill: University of North Carolina Press, 1948.

MIDRASH IN THE EIGHTEENTH AND NINETEENTH CENTURIES

Ages, Arnold. *French Enlightenment and the Rabbinic Tradition.* Frankfort am Main: V. Klosterman, 1970.
———. "Montesquieu and the Jews." RF 81, 1–2 (1969), 214–19.
———. "Voltaire, and the Old Testament." StudVoltaire 62, 1 (1968), 43–63.
Altmann, A. "William Wollaston, English Deist and Rabbinic Scholar." TJSHE 16 (1952), 185–211.
Bédarride, I. *Les Juifs en France et en Italie.* Paris: M. Levy, 1859.
DeLaura, David. *Hebrew and Hellene in Victorian England: Newman, Arnold and Pater.* Austin: University of Texas Press, 1969.
Dussaud, René. *L'Oeuvre scientifique d'Ernest Renan.* Paris: P. Geuthner, 1951.
Herr, Mireille (Dorès). "La Tragèdie biblique au dix-huitième siècle." Dissertation, University of Paris, 1982.
Jonas, Hans. "Judaism, Christianity, and the Western Tradition." *Commentary* 44 (November 1967), 61–68.
Labrousse, Elisabeth. *Pierre Bayle et l'instrument critique.* Paris: Editions Seghers, 1965.
Levi, D. *Voltaire et son exégèse du Pentateuque.* StudVoltaire 30 (1975).
Liebermann, Judith Berlin. *Robert Browning and Hebraism: A Study of the Poems of Browning Which Are Based on Rabbinical Interest and Other Sources in Jewish Literature.* Jerusalem: Azriel, 1934.
Roston, Murray. *Prophet and Poet: The Bible and the Growth of Romanticism.* Evanston: Northwestern University Press, 1965.
Wade, Ira. *The Clandestine Organization and Diffusion of Philosophic Ideas, 1700–1750.* Princeton: Princeton University Press, 1938.
———. *Voltaire and Madame du Châtelet: An Essay on the Intellectual Activity at Cirey.* Princeton: Princeton University Press, 1951, pp. 108–26.
Weil, J. "Un texte de Montesquieu sur le judäisme." REJ 49 (1904), 150–53.

MIDRASH AND SOME PARALLELS IN CONTEMPORARY THEORY

Atkins, G. Douglas. "Dehellenizing Literary Criticism." CE 41 (1980), 769–79.
Barthes, Roland. *The Pleasure of the Text.* Translated by Richard Miller. New York: Hill and Wang, 1975.
———. "The Struggle with the Angel." *Image Music Text.* Translated by Stephen Heath. London: Fontana Collins; New York: Hill and Wang, 1977, pp. 125–41.
Bloom, Harold. *Agon: Towards a Theory of Revisionism.* New York: Oxford University Press, 1982.
———. *The Breaking of the Vessels.* Chicago: University of Chicago Press, 1982.

———. *Kabbalah and Criticism.* New York: Seabury Press, 1975.

Bruns, Gerald L. *Inventions: Writing, Textuality, and Understanding in Literary Theory.* New Haven: Yale University Press, 1982.

———. "Midrash and Allegory: The Beginnings of Scriptural Interpretation." In *Harvard Guide to the Bible,* ed. Frank Kermode and Robert Alter. Cambridge: Harvard University Press, forthcoming.

Derrida, Jacques. *Dissemination.* Translated by Barbara Johnson. Chicago: University of Chicago Press, 1981.

———. "Edmond Jabès and the Question of the Book." *Writing and Difference.* Translated by Alan Bass. London: Routledge & Kegan Paul, 1978, pp. 64–78.

———. *Glas.* Paris: Editions Galilée, 1974.

———. *Of Grammatology.* Translated by Gayatri Chakravorty Spivak. Baltimore and London: Johns Hopkins University Press, 1974.

———. "The White Mythology: Metaphor in the Text of Philosophy." *NLH* 6, 1 (1974), 7–74.

Frye, Northrop. *Creation and Recreation.* Toronto: University of Toronto Press, 1980.

———. *The Great Code: The Bible and Literature.* London: Routledge & Kegan Paul, 1982.

Handelman, Susan A. "Fragments of the Rock: Contemporary Literary Theory and the Study of Rabbinic Texts—A Response to David Stern." *Prooftexts* 5, 1 (1985), 75–95.

———. *The Slayers of Moses: The Emergence of Rabbinic Interpretation in Modern Literary Theory.* Albany: State University of New York Press, 1982.

Hartman, Geoffrey H. *Beyond Formalism: Literary Essays, 1958–1970.* New Haven: Yale University Press, 1970.

———. *Criticism in the Wilderness: The Study of Literature Today.* New Haven: Yale University Press, 1980.

———. *The Fate of Reading and Other Essays.* Chicago: University of Chicago Press, 1975.

———. *Saving the Text: Literature/Derrida/Philosophy.* Baltimore: Johns Hopkins University Press, 1981.

Hartman, Geoffrey H. and Michael Fishbane. " 'An Interpretation of Jeremiah 20:7–12' and 'Jeremiah 20:7–12: A Literary Response.' " In *The Biblical Mosaic.* Edited by Robert M. Polzin and Eugene Rothman. Philadelphia: Fortress Press, 1982, pp. 169–95.

Kermode, Frank. *The Genesis of Secrecy: The Interpretation of Narrative.* Cambridge: Harvard University Press, 1979.

———. *The Sense of an Ending: Studies in the Theory of Fiction.* New York: Oxford University Press, 1967.

Krupnick, Mark, ed. *Displacements: Derrida and After.* Bloomington: Indiana University Press, 1983.

Levinas, Emmanuel. *Difficile Liberté: Essais sur le judaïsme.* Paris: Editions Albin Michel, 1963.

——. "To Love the Torah More than God." Translated by Helen A. Stephenson and Richard Sugarman. *Judaism* 28 (1979), 216–23.

——. *Quatre Léctures Talmudiques.* Paris: Editions de Minuit, 1968.

Mehlman, Jeffrey. "The 'floating signifier': From Lévi-Strauss to Lacan." YFrS 48 (1972), 10–37.

Needler, Howard I. "Sacred Books and Sacral Criticism." NLH 13, 3 (1981), 393–409.

Neher, André. *The Exile of the Word: From the Silence of the Bible to the Silence of Auschwitz.* Translated by David Maisel. Philadelphia: Jewish Publication Society of America, 1981.

Ricoeur, Paul. *The Conflict of Interpretations: Essays in Hermeneutics.* Evanston: Northwestern University Press, 1974.

——. *Essays on Biblical Interpretation.* Philadelphia: Fortress Press, 1980.

Shneidau, Herbert N. *Sacred Discontent: The Bible and Western Tradition.* Berkeley: University of California Press, 1976.

Stern, David. "Literary Criticism or Literary Homilies? Susan Handelman and the Contemporary Study of Midrash." *Prooftexts* 5, 1 (1985), 96–103.

——. "Moses-cide: Midrash and Contemporary Literary Criticism." *Prooftexts* 4, 2 (1984), 193–204.

Wolosky, Shira. "Derrida, Jabès, Levinas: Sign-Theory as Ethical Discourse." *Prooftexts* 2, 3 (1982), 283–302.

SUPPLEMENT, 1988

Barth, Louis M. "Literary Imagination and the Rabbinic Sermon." In *Proceedings of the Seventh World Congress of Jewish Studies* (Studies in the Talmud, Halacha, and Midrash), pp. 29–36. Jerusalem: World Union for Jewish Studies, 1981.

Baskin, Judith R. *Pharaoh's Counsellors: Job, Jethro, and Balaam in Rabbinic and Patristic Tradition.* Brown Judaic Studies, no. 47. Chico, Calif.: Scholars Press, 1983.

Basser, Herbert W. *Midrashic Interpretations of the Song of Moses.* American University Studies, ser. 7 (Theology and Religion), vol. 2. New York, Frankfurt am Main, Berne: Peter Lang, 1984.

Boyarin, Daniel. "Analogy vs. Anomaly in Midrashic Hermeneutic: Tractates Wayyassa and Amaleq in the Mekilta." *Journal of the American Oriental Society* 106 (1986): 659–66.

——. "Voices in the Text: Midrash and the Inner Tension of Biblical Narrative." *Revue biblique* 93 (1986): 581–97.

Boyarin, Daniel, and David Stern. "An Exchange on the Mashal: Rhetoric and Interpretation: The Case of the Nimshal." *Prooftexts* 5 (1985): 269–80.

Braude, William G. "The Relevance of Midrash." *Central Conference of American Rabbis Yearbook* 65 (1955): 133–42.

Cohen, Norman J. "Analysis of an Exegetic Tradition in the Mekilta de-Rabbi Ishmael: The Meaning of *Amanah* in the Second and Third Centuries." *AJS Review* 9 (1984): 1–25.

————. "Leviticus Rabbah, Parashah 3: An Example of a Classic Rabbinic Homily." *Jewish Quarterly Review* 72 (1981): 18–31.

Daube, David. "The Form Is the Message." In *Ancient Jewish Law: Three Inaugural Lectures*. Leiden: E. J. Brill, 1981.

Eilberg-Schwartz, Howard. "When the Reader Is in the Write" (Review of Faur, *Golden Doves with Silver Dots*). *Prooftexts* 7 (1987): 194–208.

Elbaum, Yaakov. "From Sermon to Story: The Transformation of the Akedah." *Prooftexts* 6 (1986): 97–116.

Faur, José. *Golden Doves with Silver Dots: Semiotics and Textuality in Rabbinic Tradition*. Bloomington: Indiana University Press, 1986.

Finkelstein, Louis. "Midrash, Halakhah and Aggadot." In *F. Baer Jubilee Volume*, ed. S. W. Baron et al., pp. 28–47. Jerusalem, 1960.

Fishbane, Michael. "Jewish Biblical Exegesis: Presuppositions and Principles." In *Scripture in the Jewish and Christian Traditions: Authority, Interpretation, Relevance*, ed. Frederick E. Greenspahn, pp. 92–110. Nashville: Abingdon, 1982.

Fox, Harry. "The Circular Proem Composition: Terminology and Antecedents." *Proceedings of the American Academy for Jewish Research* 49 (1982): 1–33.

Fraade, Steven. *Enosh and His Generation: Pre-Israelite Hero and History in Post-Biblical Interpretation*. Society of Biblical Literature Monograph Series, 30. Chico, Calif.: Scholars Press, 1984.

————. "Interpreting Midrash 1: Midrash and the History of Judaism." *Prooftexts* 7 (1987): 179–94.

————. "Interpreting Midrash 2: Midrash and Its Literary Contexts." *Prooftexts* 7 (1987): 284–300.

————. "Sifre Deuteronomy 26 (ad Deut. 3:23): How Conscious the Composition?" *Hebrew Union College Annual* 54 (1983): 245–301.

Gertner, M. "Terms of Scriptural Interpretation: A Study in Hebrew Semantics." *Bulletin of the School of Oriental and African Studies, University of London* 25 (1962): 4–14.

Goldberg, Arnold. "Form-Analysis of Midrashic Literature as a Method of Description." *Journal of Jewish Studies* 36 (1985): 159–74.

————. "Die funktionale Form Midrasch." *Frankfurter judaistische Beiträge* 10 (1982): 1–45.

————. "Die Peroratio (Hatima) als Kompositionsform der rabbinischen Homilie." *Frankfurter judaistische Beiträge* 6 (1978): 1–22.

————. "Der verschriftete Sprechakt als rabbinische Literatur." In *Schrift und Gedächtnis*, eds. J. Assmann and Chr. Hardmeyer. Munich, 1983.

————. "Versuch über die hermeneutische Präsupposition und Struktur der Petiha." *Frankfurter judaistische Beiträge* 8 (1980): 1–60.

(For further publications by this author and his work group, see the above journal and *Frankfurter judaistische Studien*.)

Goldin, Judah. "Midrash and Aggadah." *Encyclopedia of Religion* 9 (1987): 509–15.

Grozinger, K. E. *Musik und Gesang in der Theologie der frühen jüdischen Literatur*. Tübingen: J. C. Brill, 1983.

Halperin, David. *The Merkabah in Rabbinic Literature.* American Oriental Series, vol. 62. New Haven: American Oriental Society, 1980.

Hartman, Geoffrey. "Meaning, Error, Text." In *Yale French Studies*, no. 69, *The Lesson of Paul de Man*, pp. 145–49. New Haven: Yale University Press, 1985.

Himmelfarb, Martha. "R. Moses the Preacher and the Testaments of the Twelve Patriarchs." *AJS Review* 9 (1984): 55–78.

————. *Tours of Hell: An Apocalyptic Form in Jewish and Christian Literature.* Philadelphia: University of Pennsylvania Press, 1983.

Idel, Moshe. *Kabbalah: New Perspectives.* New Haven: Yale University Press, forthcoming.

Jaffee, Martin S. "The 'Midrashic' Proem: Towards the Description of Rabbinic Exegesis." In *Approaches to Ancient Judaism*, vol. 4, ed. W. S. Green, pp. 95–112. Chico, Calif.: Scholars Press, 1983.

Kadushin, Max. *A Conceptual Approach to the Mekhilta.* New York, 1969.

Kimmelman, Reuven. "Rabbi Yohanan and Origen on the Song of Songs: A Third-Century Jewish-Christian Disputation." *Harvard Theological Review* 73 (1980): 567–95.

Lauterbach, Jacob. "Midrash and Mishnah: A Study in the Early History of the Halakhah." *Jewish Quarterly Review*, n.s. 5 (1914): 503–27; n.s. 6 (1915): 23–95, 303–27. Reprinted in *Rabbinic Essays*, ed. Lou H. Silberman. Cincinnati: Hebrew Union College Press, 1951.

Lewis, Jack P. *A Study of the Interpretation of Noah and the Flood in Jewish and Christian Literature.* Leiden: E. J. Brill, 1968.

Meir, Ofra. "The Homiletical Story in Early and Late Midrash" (Hebrew). *Sinai* 86 (1980): 246–66.

Neusner, Jacob. *Comparative Midrash: The Plan and Program of Genesis Rabbah and Leviticus Rabbah.* Brown Judaic Studies. Atlanta: Scholars Press, 1986.

————. *Invitation to Midrash: The Working of Rabbinic Bible Interpretation: A Teaching Book.* San Francisco: Harper and Row, forthcoming.

————. *Midrash as Literature: The Primacy of Documentary Discourse.* Studies in Judaism. Lantham, Md.: University Press of America, 1987.

(For this author's further work, both translations and commentaries, see Brown Judaic Studies.)

Porton, Gary G. *Understanding Rabbinic Midrash: Text and Commentary.* New York: Ktav, 1985.

Roitman, Betty. *Feu noir sur feu blanc: Essai sur l'herméneutique juive.* Paris: Verdier, 1986.

Saperstein, Marc. *Decoding the Rabbis: A Thirteenth-Century Commentary on the Aggadah.* Cambridge: Harvard University Press, 1980.

Schafer, Peter. "Research into Rabbinic Literature: An Attempt to Define the Status Quaestionis." *Journal of Jewish Studies* 37 (1986): 139–52.

Shinan, Avigdor. "Aggadic Literature: Between Oral Recitation and Written Transmission" (Hebrew). *Jerusalem Studies in Jewish Folklore* 1 (1980–81): 44–60.

Shinan, Avigdor, and Y. Zakovitch. "Midrash on Scripture and Midrash within Scripture." *SH* 31 (1986): 257–77.

Slonimsky, Henry. "The Philosophy Implicit in the Midrash." *Hebrew Union College Annual* 27 (1963): 235–90.

Stern, David. "The Function of the Parable in Rabbinic Literature" (Hebrew). *Jerusalem Studies in Hebrew Literature* 7 (1985): 90–102.

———. "The Rabbinic Parable: From Rhetoric to Poetics." In *Society of Biblical Literature 1986 Seminar Papers*, ed. Kent Harold Richards, pp. 631–43. Society of Biblical Literature Seminar Papers Series, no. 25. Atlanta: Scholars Press, 1986.

Strack, H. L., and G. Stemberger. *Einleitung in Talmud und Midrasch*. Munich: C. H. Beck, 1982.

Talmage, Frank. "Apples of Gold: The Inner Meaning of Sacred Texts in Medieval Judaism." In *Jewish Spirituality: From the Bible through the Middle Ages*, ed. Arthur Green, pp. 313–55. Vol. 13 of *World Spirituality: An Encyclopedic History of the Religious Quest*. New York: Crossroad, 1986.

Towner, W. Sibley. "Hermeneutical Systems of Hillel and the Tannaim: A Fresh Look." *Hebrew Union College Annual* 53 (1982): 101–35.

Urbach, E. E. "The Homiletical Interpretations of Canticles." In *Studies in Aggadah and Folk-Literature*, Scripta Hierosolymitana, vol. 22, pp. 247–75. Jerusalem: Magnes Press, 1971.

Index of Biblical and Post-Biblical Citations

Refer to General Index for additional titles and works cited by author's name.

397

NEW TESTAMENT

General Index

R. Aba, 278
R. Abba bar Kahana, 64
R. Ab[b]ahu, 94
Abrams, M. H, 238–41, 244, 246–48
Absence of a letter, 77–78, 92, 132; and inspiration, 285
R. Abulafia, Abraham, 148–149, 151
Aggadah: and speech, 41; defined, 41–42, 58, 363; categories of, 43–44; and historical change, 45–46; and philosophy, 49–50; reciprocity with halakhah, 51; its institutional status, 53, 58–70. See also Midrash
Aginut, 294–302. See also Aporia, barred passage
Agnon, S. Y., 285–302 passim
R. Aha, 109
R. Ahi, 71n
Akavyah ben Mahalalel, 63
R. Akiba, 43, 45, 46, 62, 64, 116, 160, 174
Alazraki, Jaime, 259
Alexander the Great, 42
Alexandrian grammarians, 20
Alexandrian Judaism, 87
Alexandrian tradition, 184
Allegory, 171, 277, 343; Alexandrian, 87, 89, 209; and Song of Songs, 93–94; Antiochan, 184; kabbalistic, 187; in Defoe, 227; in Dante and Romantics, 242–44, 246, 251n
Allen, Woody, 278
R. Al-Nakawa, Israel, 60
Amadis de Gaul, 214
Ambiguity, 12
Amoraim, ix, 50, 52, 62, 363
Amos, 78–79, 92
Anagogic interpretation, 165, 167, 172
Andrew of St. Victor, 186

Anniversaries, 308, 313
Antioch, school of, 184, 187
Anti-text, 286
Anxiety of influence, 232
Aphasia, 216
Apocalypse, 86, 88, 90, 101n, 102n, 142
Apocrypha, 47, 53
Aporia, barred passage, 320, 323
Aquinas, Saint Thomas, 186
Architecture of kabbalistic universe, 166
Ari. See R. Isaac son of Solomon Luria
Aristotelianism, 143, 149, 229
Arnold, Matthew, ix–x
Arrian, 68
Ars combinatoria, 148
Ashkenazi, 363
Ashkenazi Hasidism, 130, 135
Asyndetic narrative, 14–15, 281n
Atomization, 101n, 110, 124n, 231
Auerbach, Erich, 3–4, 14–16, 121, 199, 204–06, 208, 272
Augustine, Saint, 121, 181, 184, 190, 283n
Austen, Jane, 222
R. Azzariah ben Oded, 32, 35

Ba'al Shem Tov, 364
Bacher, Wilhelm, 41
Baer, Yitzhak, 209
Bakhtin, Mikhail, 13
Bar Kokhbah, 45
Barr, James, 101n
Barrenechea, Ana María, 257
Barthes, Roland, 11, 14–15, 153n, 157n
Barton, John, 182
Bateson, F. W., 245
Batyah, 115–16. See also Name-changes
Bauer, Felice, 273, 276
Belkin, Samuel, 209

Contributors

Sanford Budick is Professor of English and Director of the Center for Literary Studies, The Hebrew University.

Joseph Dan is Gershom Scholem Professor of Kabbalah, The Hebrew University.

Jacques Derrida is Professor of Philosophy at the École des Hautes Études en Sciences Sociales, Paris.

Harold Fisch is Professor of English and Comparative Literature, Bar Ilan University.

Michael Fishbane is Samuel Lane Professor of Jewish Religious History and Social Ethics, Brandeis University.

Judah Goldin is Professor of Post-Biblical Hebrew Literature, University of Pennsylvania.

Geoffrey H. Hartman is Karl Young Professor of Comparative Literature, Yale University; and Director of the School of Criticism and Theory at Dartmouth College.

Joseph Heinemann was Professor of Hebrew Literature, The Hebrew University.

Moshe Idel is Associate Professor of Jewish Thought, The Hebrew University.

Edmond Jabès has written *Le livre des questions*, *Le livre des ressemblances*, and *Le petit livre de la subversion hors de soupçon*.

Frank Kermode is a Fellow of King's College Cambridge.

James L. Kugel is Professor of Near Eastern Languages and Civilizations, Harvard University.

Jill Robbins is Assistant Professor of English and Comparative Literature, State University of New York at Buffalo.

Betty Roitman is Associate Professor of French Literature, The Hebrew University.

Gershon Shaked is Professor of Hebrew Literature, The Hebrew University.

Myrna Solotorevsky is Associate Professor of Spanish and Latin American Studies, The Hebrew University.

David Stern is Assistant Professor of Medieval Hebrew Literature, University of Pennsylvania.

Joshua Wilner is Assistant Professor of English, City College, City University of New York.